VOID
Library of
Davidson College

McGill Hume Studies

STUDIES IN HUME AND SCOTTISH PHILOSOPHY

David Fate Norton, Editor

1

McGILL HUME STUDIES

EDITED BY
David Fate Norton
Nicholas Capaldi
Wade L. Robison

Austin Hill Press, Inc.
San Diego

Library of Congress Cataloging in Publication Data
McGill Bicentennial Hume Conference, McGill University, 1976.
McGill Hume studies

(Studies in Hume and Scottish philosophy ; 1)
Includes index.
1. Hume, David, 1711-1776—Congresses. 2. Philosophy, Scottish—Congresses. I. Norton, David Fate. II. Capaldi, Nicholas. III. Robison, Wade L. IV. Title. V. Series.
B1498.M27 1976 192 78-10398
ISBN 0-89690-000-2
ISBN 0-89690-001-0 pbk.

Copyright © 1979 by Austin Hill Press, Inc.
All rights reserved

First edition
Published by Austin Hill Press, Inc., 2955 Renault Place, San Diego, CA 92122
Printed in the United States of America

Acknowledgments

In preparing this volume the editors have benefited from the assistance of Terence Penelhum and J. C. A. Gaskin, as well as from the comments of other members of the Program Committee for the McGill Bicentennial Hume Congress, namely, Páll S. Árdal, Harry M. Bracken, Peter Jones, James King, Donald Livingston, James Noxon, and Ian S. Ross. For this assistance we are grateful indeed.

Thanks are also due the Canada Council, the Quebec Ministry of Education, and Vice-Principal Walter Hitschfeld of McGill University for their encouraging support of the Congress, and to the McGill Humanities Research Committee for a grant to assist in the publication of the volume.

Contents

Introduction: The Problem of Hume and Hume's Problem   3
NICHOLAS CAPALDI, *Queens College, CUNY*

The Social Background of Hume's Science of Human Nature   23
JAMES MOORE, *Concordia University*

Berkeley, Hume, and the Central Problem of Scottish Philosophy   43
GEORGE DAVIE, *University of Edinburgh*

A Prussian Hume and a Scottish Kant   63
LEWIS WHITE BECK, *University of Rochester*

Is Hume's Self Consistent?   79
JANE MCINTYRE, *Cleveland State University*

In Defense of Hume's *Appendix*   89
WADE ROBISON, *Kalamazoo College*

Hume's Theory of Mental Activity   101
FRED WILSON, *University of Toronto*

The Naturalism of Hume Revisited   121
ROBERT CONNON, *Dublin*

Hume, Atheism, and the "Interested Obligation" of Morality   147
J. C. A. GASKIN, *Trinity College, Dublin*

"Art" and "Moderation" in Hume's *Essays*   161
PETER JONES, *University of Edinburgh*

Time and Value in Hume's Social and Political Philosophy   181
DONALD LIVINGSTON, *Northern Illinois University*

The Nature of Hume's Skepticism   203
D. C. STOVE, *University of Sydney*

A Skeptic's Progress: Hume's Preference for *Enquiry I*   227
JOHN IMMERWAHR, *Villanova University*

The *Dialogues* as Original Imitation: Cicero and the Nature
of Hume's Skepticism 239
   CHRISTINE BATTERSBY, *University of Warwick*

Hume's Skepticism and the *Dialogues* 253
   TERENCE PENELHUM, *University of Calgary*

Philo Confounded 279
   PHEROZE WADIA, *Rutgers University*

Hume, Induction, and Natural Selection 291
   JOÃO-PAULO MONTEIRO, *University of São Paulo*

Hume and His Scottish Critics 309
   DAVID FATE NORTON, *McGill University*

Hume and the American Revolution: The Dying Thoughts
of a North Briton 325
   J. G. A. POCOCK, *The Johns Hopkins University*

Citation Index 345

General Index 347

McGILL HUME STUDIES

The Problem of Hume and Hume's Problem

Nicholas Capaldi

THE PRESENT COLLECTION OF ESSAYS ON DAVID HUME is a selection from papers presented at the McGill Hume Conference in the fall of 1976 to commemorate the two-hundreth anniversary of Hume's death. At the conclusion of the conference Antony Flew and Robert Fogelin were asked to present some summary remarks. Flew began by pointing out some remarkable differences between this 1976 conference and the 1939 Bicentennial of the publication of the *Treatise*. There was hardly anyone at this conference who would not like Hume as a man, and be, for example, eager to go to dinner with him. But just the reverse was the attitude of H. A. Prichard, A. E. Taylor, and other scholars of the 1930s. This is an important and happy change in Hume studies, a change made possible by scholarly work in the intervening period and originating perhaps with E. C. Mossner. Secondly, it is clear that the *Dialogues* have arrived in the sense that they are now viewed as an integral part of Hume's work. This is reflected in the present anthology in the essays by J. C. A. Gaskin, Christine Battersby, Terence Penelhum, and Pheroze Wadia. The same point can be made about Sections X and XI of the first *Enquiry*, which are no longer interpreted merely as appendixes. Finally, Flew stressed that there are so many strands in Hume relevant to pervasive philosophical questions that we run the risk of misperceiving him by concentrating on any one strand. In short, the very richness of Hume's philosophy leads to a bewildering variety of interpretations.

Both Flew and Fogelin remarked on the fascinating historical background to Hume's work, and both raised the issue of the relevance of background studies to philosophical issues. At the very least, we can all agree that too many alleged refutations of Hume have been refutations of straw men by writers not adequately familiar with Humean texts and with the intellectual context in which they were written. Fogelin went on to identify in even greater detail than Flew the key contrast in Hume between skepticism and naturalism. This contrast reflects a new direction in Hume studies. There was a time when it was taken for granted that Hume was a skeptic. This position is still held in a qualified way by some scholars, including D. C. Stove, whose highly articulate account still makes Hume a skeptic who has pulled the plugs on us about science, morals, and religion and is thereby the cause of "modern nervousness."

In an important sense, all of the other papers in this volume can be measured by how far they depart from Stove's interpretation. At the final session of the conference, Fred Wilson, Páll Árdal, Nicholas Capaldi, and Tom L. Beauchamp took great exception to Stove's views. Certainly, since the work of Norman Kemp Smith, it has become respectable to deny that Hume is a skeptic pure and simple and to search for the more positive doctrine in his works. That is why it is now so essential to define clearly what sort of skepticism one either attributes to Hume or does not attribute to him. John Immerwahr, Peter Jones, and Penelhum face this issue squarely. It is also crucial to work out the positive alternative in Hume, and the papers by Robert Connon, Wilson, and João-Paulo Monteiro concentrate on that issue.

Fogelin also remarked that people are now reading more than Book I of the *Treatise* and that we all have come to agree with Hume's own assessment of it as a young man's work. Yet it contains a great vision never to be recaptured; so perhaps we should not try to civilize it. Implicit in this remark is the recognition that Hume's thought underwent a profound development. This development, or change of heart, is an issue in both the Jane McIntyre and Wade Robison essays on Hume's comments on identity in the appendix, in the discussion of skepticism by Wadia, Immerwahr, and Penelhum, and in David Fate Norton's reflections on how Hume viewed his critics.

These last remarks will now allow us to answer more directly some of the questions about the rationale for this volume. In devoting an entire volume to the work of one philosopher, David Hume, we are not just engaging in an enterprise of historical justice. In an age when many professional philosophers claim to be working on the frontiers of knowledge and therefore have no time for the works of dead philosophers, one can reply in the spirit of gamesmanship that anything that gets into print — even the work of living philosophers — is already out of date. Too often those who think they are breaking new ground are merely returning to a field that has been left fallow. Not only have we not gotten the Humean argument right, but many of us feel that once we get it right something philosophically significant is to be found.

The development in Hume's thinking is of vital importance for a number of reasons. If Hume's thought did go through some sort of metamorphosis, then it is not possible to get his position or his arguments right by extracting passages from a number of diverse works, like picking flowers for a bouquet, without due regard for the order of composition. Second, if Hume rejected or revised some of his own early positions then it behooves those who claim him for their intellectual ancestry to consider whether they have perhaps followed the wrong path. Since it is fashionable even for professional philosophers recognized by the *New York Times* to cite Hume, this is all the more timely. Third, philosophers of science have now recognized as part of their legitimate task the study of conceptual development, the change and revision of ideas. Since it is in the works of key individuals that these revisions occur, the close scrutiny of some one philosopher such as Hume can serve as a microcosm for the comprehension of conceptual development. Fourth, Hume was directly aware of the process of conceptual development, both in general and in his own work. In his work as a historian he was concerned to trace the development of concepts and to account for them. This was not a sideline but an integral part of his intellectual endeavor. The essay by Donald Livingston makes this brilliantly clear. An even more fundamental ontological notion of conceptual variation and selection is traceable in Hume's work, as is emphasized in Monteiro's essay.

There is a final and most important reason for the prime focus on conceptual revision. If there is one thing for which Hume is well known it is his claim that we cannot give a purely formal account of our concepts. Some see in this a retreat to skepticism; others, as this anthology hopes to make clear, see in this a recognition of a new conception of rationality. This is Hume's new vision, a vision missed by those who are already committed to the philosophical ideal of a totally formal analysis of concepts. On the contrary, there is an explicit recognition in the essays by Connon, Wilson, and Monteiro that Hume is proposing a new and entirely different conception of rationality, and they have sought to stake out this new ground in Hume. Hume's Scottish contemporaries totally misunderstood what he was about, as Norton reminds us. Kant alone correctly suspected what Hume was up to, as Lewis White Beck makes clear, even though Kant did not completely share that conception.

Part of Hume's rejection of a purely formal account of concepts is the further recognition that there are nonformal criteria for the development, application, and revision of concepts. In the words of his critics, this is Hume's alleged confusion of philosophy and psychology. And it is precisely those critics who attribute a confusion to Hume who will see some of the articles in this anthology as purely historical (sociological or psychological) rather than philosophical. It is here that we come face to face with the problem that interpreting the history of philosophy is itself a philosophical activity. What we have are rival conceptions of philosophy. But it is precisely the commitment to a purely formal notion of conceptual analysis that blinds Hume's critics and the critics of some of his expositors to the existence of conceptual variation, conceptual selection—in short, conceptual development. The commitment to a purely formal analysis is a commitment to an antihistorical position, to an outright rejection of, if not myopic blindness to, what Hume proposed and did, and to the inability to appreciate what some Humean scholars are up to. "We suppose, it would seem, that concepts sprout in the individual mind like leaves on a tree, and we think to discover their nature by studying their birth: we seek to define them psychologically, in terms of the nature of the human mind. But this account makes everything subjective, and if we follow it through to the end, does away with truth. What is known as the history of concepts is really a history either of our knowledge of concepts or of the meanings of words."[1] If nonformal and perhaps causal factors play an inescapable role in our conceptual development, then not only is this what Hume himself was among the first to advocate, but it is equally impossible to comprehend what Hume advocated unless we are somewhat familiar with, among other things, the "Social Background of Hume's Science of Human Nature" (James Moore), the "Central Problem of Scottish Philosophy" (George Davie), the influence of Cicero (Battersby), and even Hume's political persuasions (J. G. A. Pocock) and religious goals (Gaskin).

Stuart Hampshire once made the remark that "it was the application of a true understanding of human nature, with a view to a sane management of human affairs, that finally interested Hume, rather than pure philosophy so called."[2] This insightful remark contains the germ of a point that will help us to understand the nonformal elements of Hume's philosophy. Recall that Hume says in his analysis of the passions and in his essays that man is a creature who seeks activity. Recall Hume's emphasis in Section I of the first *Enquiry* that man is an active being, not just an intellectual being. It is not only the case that Hume wants to make his philosophical reflections relevant to the great practical issues of the day (Pocock); he also does not think that any philosophical analysis of knowledge can be adequate if it does not recognize the practical roots (genesis) and nature of knowing. Davie has made this clear in his review

---

[1] Gotlobb Frege, *The Foundations of Arithmetic*, trans. J. L. Austin, 2nd rev. ed. (New York: Harper Torchbooks, 1960), p. xix.

[2] In D. F. Pears, ed. *David Hume: A Symposium* (London: MacMillan, 1963), p. 6.

of Hume's account of the rise of science. Jones has reinforced this point by quoting in his paper Hume's criticism of the aridity and sterility of philosophy in the academies.

It could be remarked that all of this historical background is interesting but that it does not make Hume's philosophy true. The genesis of an idea is irrelevant to the validity, or so the slogan goes. On the contrary, as Livington and Monteiro have argued, the Humean analysis is basically a historical analysis, for Hume contends that no other frame of reference can be a valid one. This just sharpens once more the contrast between formalists and nonformalists such as Hume. We might point out that since no formal analysis has succeeded to date, Hume's criticisms have not been rebutted. The formalist may complain that he or we will be successful at some future date. It is this eschatological contention, that the future will justify present formalist analyses, that is precisely what Hume criticized not only in his epistemology but, as Livington makes clear, in his social philosophy. Hume considered such views dangerous. The formalist fallacy is the assumption that any intellectual discipline must consist of a single, monolithic, coherent logical system. Its analogue in politics is the assumption that society forms such a single coherent and functional whole. What begins to emerge is not just a controversy over strategies, but an ontological controversy; for behind each alternate lies a world view.

Let us now turn to some of the more specific issues and begin by classifying them into five general categories: (1) skepticism, (2) religion, (3) the self, (4) Hume's naturalism, and (5) social philosophy.

With regard to skepticism, we must avoid getting lost in terminology. There are different kinds of skepticism and skeptics, and if one attributes it to Hume or denies it of him the assertions may be compatible if we are talking about different kinds of skepticism, momentous if something serious follows, or trivial. To sort out this issue we would have to do the following. First, review the meanings of the term "skepticism" in the history of philosophy before Hume. Second, note those occasions on which Hume explicitly addresses himself to this issue and compare the extent to which he fits the previous models of skepticism. Third, we would have to distinguish between epistemological skepticism, which is concerned with the issue of the justification of specific assertions, and ontological skepticism, which is concerned with our ability to gain access to the real world.

At first sight, this last distinction may seem specious, for surely, it will be argued, the epistomological issue depends upon the ontological issue. That is, if we cannot gain access to the real world, how can any assertion be justified? The answer to this objection is that the whole point of Hume's philosophy is to redefine what it means to make knowledge claims. Traditional rationalist philosophers from Plato to Locke all assume that knowledge claims must be justified by reference to the "real" world. As such, the philosophies interpreted the common and esoteric rules of reasoning in terms of veridicality. Hume's negative position is that the foregoing interpretation is inadequate, and he drove home this point with a persistance that is numbing. In its place, Hume substitutes an agency interpretation of reasoning. As agents seeking to comprehend and direct our actions we ask not whether our assertions are "true" to "reality" but whether we are justified in having acted the way we did in the given circumstances. This agency interpretation of reasoning is social and moral; it involves nonformal criteria; it is more like legal reasoning than like solving a geometrical puzzle. Thus Hume does not deny the use of categories such as reasonable and unreasonable, but he does reject the alternative rationalist interpretations, and he does substitute his own interpretation.

There are two obvious questions raised by this approach. What are Hume's views about the "real" world, and what is the status of Hume's own account of how we reason? In short, what is the world like in order to make possible the agency account of reasoning? With regard to the question of "reality," and why I have been using quotation marks, it can be said that Hume shares with most modern philosophers from Descartes to Kant the view that there is an external physical world, that there is a "mental" internal world, that there is an interaction between the two, and—the great unsolved mystery of science and philosophy—that nobody has yet satisfactorily explained the interaction. This inability had not prevented people from philosophizing, nor had it dampened anyone's enthusiasm for thinking that Newton was right about the physical world. Thus the agency view with its nonformal criteria is fundamental to philosophical reasoning itself and more fundamental than the methodology of science; hence the new science of man. Even if one goes on to reject the whole framework of modern dualistic philosophy, as has subsequently been done in a wide variety of ways, the agency interpretation of reasoning still survives intact. I know of no refutation of it; on the contrary, it has grown in sophistication. Even among those who still subscribe to the notion that we are seeking the real truth, there is a growing acceptance of informal factors as means to obtaining the truth.

Now it is not incumbent upon Hume to solve the physical problem of mind-body interaction (and he repeatedly admits that he cannot do so) in order for him to believe in an external physical world that causally influences his mind and the minds of others. Hume never pretended to refute the belief in the existence of such a world; rather, he rebutted the interpretations other philosophers gave of such a belief. Hume, in fact, gave his own interpretation. Since he believes in such a world, and since he has an agency interpretation of this belief, he is at liberty to speculate on how that world operates and how there can be both mechanical-physiological explanations of our *brain's* activity and natural-selection explanations of our *mind's* use of certain rules of reasoning. Hume can legitimately speak of secret causes both in the sense of those not yet discovered and in the sense of minute mechanisms we may never discover.

It is thus clear that Hume has a number of views about the "real" world and that he has an agency account to explain those views. But this still leaves us with the vital question of the status of his own account. This is Hume's central metaphysical problem. It seems that there are only two possible answers that Hume can offer. *Either* he thinks that his account is in some sense a true or real account, *or* he must argue that there can never be any such thing as a true account. That is, the second alternative must be that we can never have any but informal accounts.

Let us explore both alternatives. The first alternative assumes that Hume wants his account to be a real or true account. We may identify this as the neopositivist interpretation of Hume. Here it would be assumed that Hume's naturalistic science of man is a form of psychology in which he attempts to provide a totally empirical explanation of why human beings think, feel, and behave as they do. It should be clear that the psychological facts of human reasoning, on this interpretation, are at best a supplement to philosophy, not a substitute for it. But it should also be clear, on this interpretation, that psychological facts cannot be substitutes for philosophy and cannot solve philosophical puzzles. The puzzles remain. For, in order to claim that Hume's psychological facts really are facts one has to make use of principles about which Hume raises serious questions. This is not to say that Hume cannot use such principles, but only that he still fails to account for them. It postpones the issue to another level. There is nothing wrong per se in the psychology, but it is in one sense irrelevant, and it leads to seemingly unanswerable questions. This creates a space for a sort of skepticism; for if we claim that Hume's psychology is a true account but have no *independent* way of checking the account, then we are not sure what it means to say that the account is true or that it "really" is true.

The foregoing interpretation, even if correct, in no way discredits the more modest achievements of Hume's philosophy. His objections to alternative philosophical accounts still stand. Here we have the triumphant but negative Hume of the positivists. Moreover, it is still possible to agree with Hume that we do seem to employ certain rules (informal ones) in our reasoning, although their status is now unclear.

Let us try the second alternative. On this interpretation, which I suggest is the correct one, there can be only informal reasoning. Hence all accounts of even the informal rules are informal. There can be no empirical account (justifications, and so on) of the norms of empirical science. This is why Hume stressed at the very beginning of the *Treatise* that the best we can hope for is the statement of what we find to be the most general rules. Thus we cannot stand outside of the universe and watch man interact with the universe. Thus we witness the birth of transcendental arguments (common sense in Hume). On this interpretation Hume does not confuse psychology and philosophy but rather transcends both. Even at this point one may raise the spectre of skepticism, but the skepticism would be of the ontological variety, namely, that it makes no sense to ask whether the mind truly reflects the independent world. This, of course, is to turn the term "skepticism" into a pejorative rhetorical device to be used by people who reject Hume's ontology. We are now no longer dealing with counterargument but with counterassertion.

We are not completely out of the woods, however. If we are always left with informal accounts, what is to prevent one from demanding an informal account of informal accounts? Such a demand is consistent. If so, can there be alternative informal accounts of the informal rules of reasoning? Could it be possible to speculate on the "divine" origins of our informal rules? That is, how can Hume honestly *refute* his Scottish critics?

To begin with, Hume refuted only the formalist pretensions of his Scottish critics. They had claimed more for their account than they were entitled to (by the formal rules). For exposing their intellectual pretensions Hume earned their undying enmity. Second, by exposing their informal (religious hypothesis) account as a mere informal account, he undermined their claim to moral (social and political) authority. This they took, no doubt sincerely, to be a threat to social stability. It was in fact one of Hume's major contentions that alternative hypotheses about informal rules were not only possible but were morally neutral. That is, morality itself depended upon just such a set of informal rules.

Even here it is possible to pursue Hume. What if there are conflicts among people with alternative sets of informal moral rules? How can we rule out such conflicts? This is Kant's objection to Hume. At one point Hume seems simply to assume that there is uniformity. Kant could argue that such uniformity is only empirical and fragile. This explains why Kant took the self out of the world and made it absolutely impervious to alteration. Kant was, of course, rightly concerned with the problem of human freedom and the threat posed to it by the then current notion, as formulated in the Newtonian laws of mechanics, that the physical world was subject to a determinism.

Hume's more considered response was the following. First, physical determinism is at most constant conjunction. Second, morality demands human freedom. Third, human behavior is predictable not because our motives are determined but because we consciously choose to follow certain rules. Fourth, sympathy is the medium for the social spread of these rules. Fifth, our choice of rules is historically and analogically oriented but not determined. The first three points anticipate Kant. The last two deviate crucially. Hume admits the problem of reconciling a belief in freedom with the notion of a mechanical physical world, and this is just another dimension of the mind-body problem.

Does this help us shed any further light on the problem of the status of Hume's informal analysis? I think it does. Even if the potential of moral conflict were real, this would not of itself discredit Hume's informal analysis. But on further reflection such conflict is not ultimately real. If we are free, then none of us is determined to act according to any one set or interpretation of the informal rules. Conflict is not inevitable. If there are no absolute justifications for any one interpretation of the informal rules, then there is no justification for dogmatism or for imposing one's interpretation on another. Since all the contestants admit that the rules are informal, then each is bound by this admission to a form of mutual respect. In short, we seem to operate with the informal rules on how to act even when we do not have the same interpretation of specific informal rules. It should also be clear that, in a world where absolutes do not count, skepticism loses its meaning rather than poses a threat. As has been wisely remarked, the only way to handle skeptics is for each of us to become one. Finally, if Hume is really moving to a position that denies that there is a permanent and absolute external structure to the world, then determinism in physics is not a troublesome truth but a way of interpreting the world. This would reinforce our notion of our freedom to persuade instead of to coerce. Here we may note that although Hume never denied secret causes, he did deny that we would ever discover ultimate causes.

There are two indications of Hume's willingness to develop this radical line of thought. In denying the existence of a nature, Hume came increasingly to see reality as a developing relationship between human minds operating with informal rules and a natural world where neither the minds nor the world was invariant. Moreover, given the difficulty of making this convincing in the context of eighteenth-century mechanical science or of the persisting mind-body problem, it was much easier to apply this radical line of thought within human cultural affairs.

With the aid of the following outline of Hume's position we can begin to tally the insights contained in the essays in this volume.

HUME'S PROBLEM

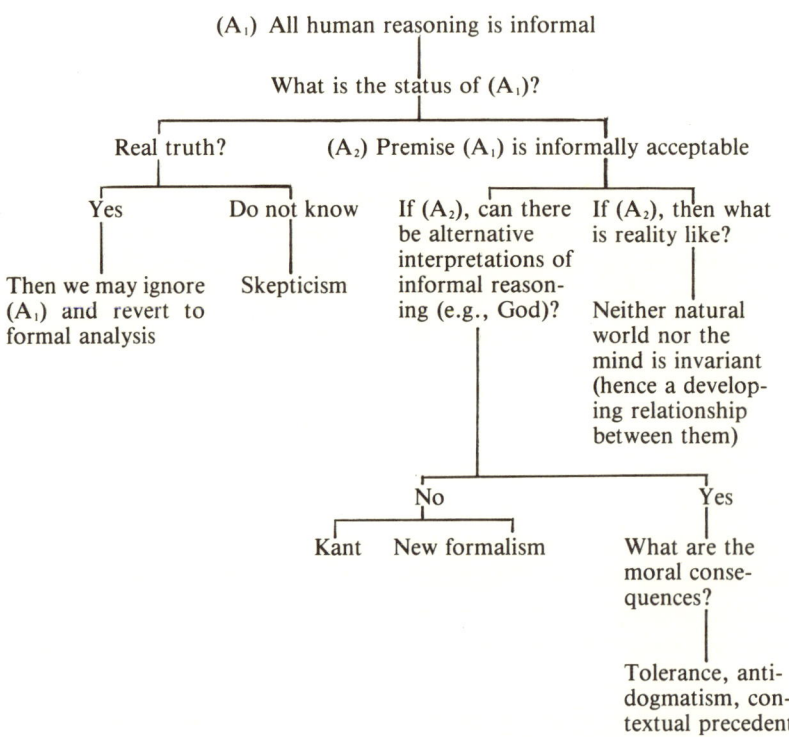

Both Immerwahr and Penelhum document a shift in Hume's handling of the problem of skepticism. Both note a difference between the *Treatise* and the first *Enquiry*. In the *Treatise* Hume seems to rely almost exclusively on the view that we are saved from skepticism only by psychological factors that condition our judgments and control our behavior despite the inability of reason, as understood by the rationalists, to perform this function. When Hume came to the first *Enquiry* he felt it necessary to change his tack. Here he seemed more concerned to emphasize the informal rules of reasoning and not just the psychological necessity to act and believe. How do we account for this shift? Immerwahr notes that the first *Enquiry* is a response to Hume's critics who had ignored his discussion of informal rules in the *Treatise* and who had misunderstood and misrepresented his position on skepticism. Furthermore, Immerwahr sees that the informal rules of reasoning still preclude any formal "proof" of God's existence. It might also be added that the informal rules, on Hume's account, prevent deriving any peculiar moral implications from the hypothetical existence of a first cause.

Here Penelhum's paper can shed much light. The problem with a purely psychological account of our beliefs is that it might be argued that we also have to believe in a God. It will not be sufficient simply to add that the informal rules cannot prove God's existence. The informal rules by Hume's own admission do not rule out that possibility. Besides, it is possible to maintain the hypothesis that God is responsible for the informal rules and "guarantees" their veridicality. Hume's Scottish critics, as Norton points out, held just such a thesis. Hume's point now can be only that the informal rules make the religious hypothesis morally irrelevant.

But when Hume comes to the *Dialogues* he seems, in Penelhum's view, to revert to the position of the *Treatise*. That is, he seems to make the concession through Philo that belief in design is an unavoidable belief, but he still maintains its practical moral irrelevance. That is, Hume conceded more to his opponents in order to emphasize the practical implications of the informal rules.

Penelhum objects to Hume's move on the grounds that Hume never really demonstrates how skeptical doubts can be removed. That is, Hume's argument is ultimately psychological and is unconvincing on those grounds. Penelhum also objects to transcendental arguments—a form of what I have been calling informal rules of reasoning—on the grounds that such arguments do not serve psychologically to remove our persistent question about what lies beyond our informal rules. Hume himself would agree: as agents we accept the common ground rules, but as philosophers we still want to know why or how. There is a way out for Hume that is consistent with what he says. Within the parameters of his own philosophy Hume could plausibly maintain that there is no fixed, permanent, and absolute reality. Hence there is no ultimate truth about which we can have the right interpretation. Rather, the informal rules are all we ever have, and it is always possible to offer alternative hypotheses about the rules, including the religious hypothesis. This route preserves us from the dangers of a fanatical moral code, and it makes extreme skepticism unintelligible. On the ontological level we have a world in flux that interacts with human beings with subsequent modifications of each. Our understanding of such a world would be necessarily historical and normative, and it would be compatible with, if not requiring, a belief in human freedom.

Let us now turn back to the question of Hume's positive views to see how far such a possibility can enlighten us about the text.

We begin with Hume's celebrated analysis of the self. This much is clear: as opposed to his predecessors, Hume denies that we can know or cognize a self as a permanent mental substance. On the other hand, we can think of such a self, that is, we can have an idea of it; and as a matter of fact we both need and acquire this idea from our position as agents. The idea of the self emerges among the passions, and when Hume explains the habits of the mind he presupposes a self as the entity that acquires and exercises such habits. So far so good. Yet when we come to the appendix of the *Treatise*, Hume seeks to discard his theory and expresses concern for its consistency.

In response to this problem, McIntyre comes to Hume's defense. First, she argues that there is no real inconsistency in Hume's views, however problematic they may be. Second, after a review of the vast literature on the problem of the identity of the self, she shows how it is possible to defend Hume's conception of identity by reference to the association of ideas. In short, despite his critics, Hume is well aware of the different ways in which we can ascribe identity.

In support of McIntyre's point I wish to call attenton to a passage overlooked by Hume's critics. At the very beginning of the *Treatise*, Hume specifically warns his readers that his account of personal identity will be not in terms of the strict sense of identity but in other terms:

Identity may be esteem'd a second species of relation. This relation I here consider as apply'd in its strictest sense to constant and unchangeable objects; without examining the nature and foundation of personal identity, which shall find its place afterwards. Of all relations the most universal is that of identity, being common to every being, whose existence has any duration.[3]

Nevertheless, we still are left with a problem. As Robison argues, even if McIntyre is right about the problem of identity, there is another problem of the self; perhaps this is what Hume had in mind when he wrote about his misgivings in the appendix. At some level or other, Hume's account presupposes the activity of a mind that associates ideas as it does. To say that the mind has a natural tendency to attribute loose identity to a collection solves the problem of identity but not the problem of how we are to account for this mind, a mind whose existence can be thought of but never observed or known.

I believe that Robison's well-argued demur can be amplified in terms of our previous reconstruction. Let us suppose that the informal rules—including, among other things, the loose sense of identity—do operate. How can Hume account for the influence of, let us say, the brain (a physical entity) on the mind (a mental or nonphysical entity or process), by means of which the informal rules come into play? If there is a "real" influence, then surely we cannot know it since *"the mind never perceives any real connexion among distinct existences"* (*Treatise*, app. p. 636).

On the other hand, to argue that even the explanation of the influence of the brain on the mind (physiology, psychology, sociology, history) is ultimately informal still leaves hanging the question of how to account for the informal rules$_2$ that account for the informal rules$_1$. This is exactly what Hume recognizes and admits: "All my hopes vanish, when I come to explain the principles[$_2$], that unite our successive perceptions in our thought or consciousness[$_1$]" (*Treatise*, app., pp. 635-36). The ultimate logic of a purely and persistent informal account is that there can be no permanent system in terms of which we explain. That is why Hume "cannot discover any theory, which gives (him) satisfaction on this head" (*Treatise*, app., p. 636). The Newtonian mechanical hypothesis (Connon), and all of the Humean insights about natural selection and how it operates on the mind (Monteiro), however helpful, are at best

---

[3] Ed. L. A. Selby-Bigge (Oxford, 1888), I, I, IV, p. 14 (hereafter cited as *Treatise*).

informal accounts and hence must be ultimately inadequate as "real" accounts.

As our previous reconstruction indicates, if all explanations are ultimately informal, then one possibility we face is that there may be alternative accounts given of informal rules. One such alternative account is the religious hypothesis about God. None of this undermines Hume's arguments that there are no formally rational grounds for the religious hypothesis. These arguments still stand. And they earned the undying enmity of intellectually pretentious eighteenth-century clergymen. Moreover, Hume can defuse the religious hypothesis by arguing that further informal rules make the hypothesis morally neutral or harmless.

There is nothing novel about the recognition on Hume's part of the possibility of alternative hypotheses. The modern origin of this problem lies in the Ptolemaic-Copernican controversy, and the earliest recognition of its crucial importance is found in Galileo's discussion of the two chief world systems. The problem is recognized as well by Francis Bacon: "Many hypotheses with regard to the heavens can be formed, differing in themselves, and yet sufficiently according with the phenomena."[4] Michel de Montaigne in his *Apologie de Raimond Sebond* had perhaps pushed this recognition in a new direction when he argued that the inability to choose "rationally" between alternative systems should lead us to confine our attention to moral matters. In an important sense, Hume pursues this same argument, but he subtly alters it to include a new analysis of what it means to be rational. What dampens Hume's enthusiasm is the further recognition that his own system is subject to the same liability: "I had entertain'd some hopes, that however deficient our theory of the intellectual world might be, it wou'd be free from those contradictions, and absurdities, which seem to attend every explication, that human reason can give of the material world" (*Treatise*, app., p. 633). This recognition explains the shifts noted by Immerwahr and Penelhum in Hume's attitude toward skepticism.

The shift raises as well some new questions about Hume's analysis of religion. The tradition going back to Kemp-Smith's interpretation has it that Hume refuted the argument from design in the guise of Philo in the *Dialogues*. This view has come increasingly under attack as the subtlety of Hume's position has become more widely recognized. Wadia has returned to the passage in the *Dialogues* in which Philo is seemingly

---

[4] Cited in Martin Gardner, *The Relativity Explosion* (New York: Random House, 1976), p. 191.

confounded by one of Cleanthes' challenges. I say "seemingly" because it is widely assumed that the incident is rhetorical and that Philo could have responded. But as Wadia persuasively argues, what Cleanthes offers is a kind of hypothesis that makes the design argument intelligible if not convincing. In short, Philo can argue, at best, only for a lack of present evidence and for the inability of formal argument to sustain the conclusion of the design argument. Philo has not and, more importantly, *cannot* rule out the design hypothesis. Hume must settle for the position that "reasonable men may be allowed to differ, where no one can reasonably be positive,"[5] for that is the all-important moral neutrality of the existence of competing hypotheses. Gaskin reinforces this conclusion in his examination of the eighteenth-century context. What Hume contributed to that debate was a carefully calculated presentation of morality as religiously neutral and, in fact, as wholly secular. Thus the existence of alternative world hypotheses does not influence the informal rules of moral practice. In fact, we may go further, as Battersby suggests, by laying out Hume's claim that where we cannot be certain we must entertain "that hesitation or balance that the dogmatist so much dislikes." The formal possibility of alternative hypotheses requires the informal practical rule that we tolerate divergent viewpoints. In short, Hume derives moral conclusions from the epistemological standoff.

It is well to remember that the shifts in Hume's philosophy that we have noted so far do not invalidate his critiques of alternative philosophical positions or his own contentions about how the mind operates in terms of informal rules influenced by external natural-selection factors. But these shifts can help to clarify Hume's relationship both to Kant and to his Scottish critics. Beck goes out of his way to avoid the tiresome and misleading claims about Kant's providing some sort of refutation or answer to Hume's challenge. On the contrary, as Beck's title indicates, Hume and Kant are really much closer than is usually thought. In addition, Hume is profitably interpreted not as a skeptic but as a naturalist. Objectively speaking, Kant adds a clarification to Hume's account. The concept of causation is not derived from experience but is something which we, or the mind, bring to experience. It is Beattie who misled Kant into thinking that Hume had derived the principle from experience. On the contrary, Kant makes the presupposition of the concept perfectly

---

[5] *Dialogues concerning Natural Religion*, ed. Norman Kemp Smith (Indianapolis: Bobbs-Merrill, 1947), p. 128 (hereafter cited as *Dialogues*).

clear. Only on its presupposition can we distinguish the objective from the subjective and apply the specific rules of causal reasoning.

Since Beck does mention what he calls the "great divide between naturalism and transcendentalism," it might be useful to spell this out a bit more. As opposed to *all* previous philosophers who vainly tried to establish objective truths about the world itself, either by a priori arguments (Platonists such as Descartes and Leibniz) or by deriving these truths from experience (Locke), Hume and Kant take the Copernican turn in philosophy. That is, they argue that *all* such attempts must inevitably fail and that we can hope to understand what there is to understand only by reference to the "role of normative structures" brought to experience. Where they differed was on the status of such normative structures. As Connon and Monteiro help us to see, Hume believed these structures to be part of the world and subject to potential change. We might add that Hume also asserted that morality is intelligible only if people are responsible and therefore free. This freedom he cannot reconcile with any assumption that the world is deterministic. "To reconcile the indifference and contingency of human actions with prescience; or to defend absolute decrees, and yet free the Deity from being the author of sin, has been found hitherto to exceed all the power of philosophy."[6] The way out for Hume would be, as I have repeatedly expressed it, to recognize that all explanations are ultimately informal; and this implies that even our morality is subject to revisions and reconsideration.

Kant, of course, will have none of this. As he himself so clearly expressed it:

> Some one might propose to adopt a middle way between the two, namely, that the categories are neither self-produced first principles a priori of our knowledge, nor derived from experience, but subjective dispositions of thought, implanted in us with our existence, and so arranged by our Creator that their employment should accurately agree with the laws of nature, which determine experience (a kind of system of preformation of pure reason). But, in that case, not only would there be no end of such an hypothesis, so that no one could know how far the supposition of predetermined dispositions of future judgements might be carried, but there is this decided objection against that middle course that, by adopting it, the categories would lose that necessity which is essential to them. Thus the concept of cause, which asserts, under a presupposed condition, the necessity of

---

[6] *An Enquiry concerning Human Understanding*, ed. L. A. Selby-Bigge, 2nd ed. (Oxford, 1902), VIII, II, p. 103.

an effect, would be false, if it rested only on some subjective necessity implanted in us of connecting certain empirical representations according to the rule of causal relations. I should not be able to say that the effect is connected with the cause in the object (that is, by necessity), but only, I am so constituted that I cannot think these representations as connected in any other way. This is exactly what the sceptic most desires, for in that case all our knowledge, resting on the supposed objective validity of our judgements, is nothing but mere illusion, nor would there be wanting people to say they know nothing of such subjective necessity (which can only be felt); and at all events we could not quarrel with anybody about what depends only on the manner in which his own subject is organised. . . . (*Critique of Pure Reason*, B 168, Müller trans.)

That is, without the guarantee of a fixed transcendental framework, we can never silence the skeptic, moral or epistemological.

As Hume would no doubt respond, it is not realistic to expect to silence the skeptic, that is, to refute him. But it is not necessary to do so. The informal rules of moral practice preserve us and the epistemological skeptic from taking such skepticism seriously. Hence we are better off confining ourselves to explicating, as Hume does, the informal rules of social practice. It is the pressure of real life that gives rise to genuine theoretical analysis, not the other way around.

No doubt some readers will feel uneasy with Hume's reply. These readers will fall into two main categories: those who wish to return to the pre-Copernican turn and who insist on asking ontological questions, and those who wish to pursue transcendental philosophy and to avoid what they consider the horrors of moral relativism. The first group will rightly insist that Hume has damaged their position but not refuted it. When pressed to explain what would constitute a refutation of their position they will explain that a refutation is either the exposure of a logical contradiction or a state of affairs in experience incompatible with their theory. To this, Humeans can respond only by saying that one cannot formally refute formalism without establishing the truth of formalism. What Hume's first class of opponents demand is that he play by their rules when he insists on challenging their rules; but they will hear only challenges according to their rules; and so it goes.

With regard to the second group, those who fear moral relativism, I presume to answer on Hume's behalf. Let us distinguish between moral relativism and moral relativity. Moral relativism is based on the denial that there can be any cross-contextual criticism. Moral relativity, on the other hand, allows for cross-contextual criticism precisely because the informal rules do not form a closed logical system. Hume's denial of moral absolutism is thus an embracement of moral relativity, and not of moral relativism. Moral relativity is a theoretical disappointment only to those who think that moral absolutism is possible. Second, as Gaskin has expressed it, moral absolutists frequently practice a form of hypocritical self-deception that is more dangerous than even most forms of skepticism. Third, I would add the bold assertion that the great crimes of human history have always been perpetrated not by relativists but by those who thought they absolutely knew. Finally, I believe that nondogmatic relativity does imply a set of rules for operating in a contest where we have not settled on a final list of rules. This is what Hume meant when he said that "reasonable men may be allowed to differ, where no one can reasonably be positive" (*Dialogues*, p. 128).

It is perhaps well to recall Hume's study of the law and his recognition of the peculiar form of rationality inherent in Anglo-Saxon jurisprudence:

> In general, it may safely be affirmed that jurisprudence is, in this respect, different from all the sciences; and that in many of its nicer questions, there cannot properly be said to be truth or falsehood on either side. If one pleader bring the case under any former law or precedent, by a refined analogy or comparison; the opposite pleader is not at a loss to find an opposite analogy or comparison: and the preference given by the judge is often founded more on taste and imagination than on any solid argument. Public utility is the general object of all courts of judicature; and this utility too requires a stable rule in all controversies: but where several rules, nearly equal and indifferent, present themselves, it is a very slight turn of thought which fixes the decision in favour of either party.[7]

It is here that we can begin to locate Hume's model of what constitutes rationality. Informal rules of the mind can be best explicated as analogous to legal precedent. When we confront problems, or when we arrive on the scene, we do so with precedents in mind. We do not justify our precedents; that is, they need not be a priori, empirically verifiable, or guaranteed by God. We may inquire at most into their historical origin by way of explaining them. Moreover, the application of precedents to new cases is not a form of entailment but an argument by analogy, an appeal to resemblance.

---

[7] *An Enquiry concerning the Principles of Morals*, ed. L. A. Selby-Bigge, 2nd ed. (Oxford, 1902), App. III, pp. 308-9.

We may now point to some other contexts in which the concept of informal rules helps us to understand Hume. Jones makes an enlightening case for the fact that Hume's essays (moral, political, and literary) involve the application of what I have called informal rules. To this end, the notion of moderation in the essays is the application of the very same doctrine of mitigated skepticism. Moore stresses the extent to which Hume sees man as a social animal guided by informal rules. Thus the imagination is regulated by judgment, and sympathy is the process by which we create social uniformities. Man has no nature apart from the informal and nonteleological rules of social interaction. Thus the social scientist studies the uniformities as neither innate nor discovered external to the human world; rather, they are "invented." Pocock makes clear the extent to which Hume applied the informal rules of social life to specific historical issues. Here the informal rules emerge not only as objects of intellectual scrutiny but as instruments of social problem-solving and change. Hume is thus "both analyst of his own moment in history, and in the same act a maker and changer of intellectual history." Finally, having mentioned that the only rationale of precedents is a historical account of their origin, it is convenient to conclude with Livingston's brilliant reminder that time and precedent are built into Hume's very epistemology. Thus Hume's historicist epistemology contains the basis for a critique of atemporal political schemes as well as of providentialist or teleological social philosophies. Here again we should recall Norton's point that this is why Hume could never be accepted by his Scottish critics.

I cannot resist the temptation to emphasize again that the problem of understanding Hume is a problem only for those who insist upon timeless analysis, for those whose own philosophical analyses display a studied disregard for the history of philosophy. Hume's own problem, on the other hand, was the gradual recognition that if informal rules are the beginning and end of all analysis, then we must understand man on his own terms. The great mistake of all previous philosophy was to have transcribed to man what, without qualification, we have learned from other nonhuman disciplines. It is all right, of course, to climb up on the scaffolding of such other disciplines, as Hume's Newtonian program in the *Treatise* did, but *only* if we seek to recover in the scaffolding the original workmanship on the scaffolding itself. But there can be no original atemporal scaffolding. Thus it is necessary at some point to kick away the scaffolding, and this is what Hume proceeded to do in his subsequent works.

The Social Background of Hume's Science of Human Nature

James Moore

IT IS A CURIOUS BUT NOT OFTEN REMARKED CHARACTERISTIC of the philosophy of Hume that it is society alone that distinguishes the human from the animal world. It is not reason that differentiates human beings from animals, for animals have reason, as Hume understood it: they make inferences from the constant conjunction of ideas in experience. And because animals share this capacity for reasoning with human beings, Hume could say that "the experimental reasoning itself, which we possess in common with beasts, and on which the whole conduct of life depends, is nothing but a species of instinct. . . ."[1] Nor are pride and humility specifically human passions or emotions, as Hobbes, for one, seems to have thought.[2] For animals take pride in those things peculiarly or singularly related to themselves. Thus "the vanity and emulation of nightingales in singing have been commonly remark'd; as likewise that of horses in swiftness, of hounds in sagacity and smell, of the bull and cock in strength, and of every other animal in his particular excellency."[3] And animals are prompted by love and hate in much the same way as human beings; and they are also prompted by sympathy: they feel the same emotions as their fellow creatures, and even take pains when playing to "avoid harming their companion."[4] In all, the same nature is shared by human beings and by animals alike, whether one considers that nature from the standpoint of reason, passion, or sympathy. But although animals and human beings share a common nature, there is a basic

---

[1] *An Enquiry concerning Human Understanding*, ed. L. A. Selby-Bigge, 2nd ed. (Oxford, 1902), IX, p. 108. See also *A Treatise of Human Nature*, ed. L. A. Selby-Bigge (Oxford, 1888), I, III, XVI, pp. 176-79 (hereafter cited as *Treatise*). Hume recognized, to be sure, that there was a wide difference between human reasoning and the reasoning of animals: see "Of the Dignity or Meanness of Human Nature," in *The Philosophical Works*, ed. T. H. Green and T. H. Grose, 4 vols. (London, 1886), 3:152-53 (hereafter cited as *Works*). But the difference remained one of degree, not of kind. Hannah Arendt noted "with what care Hume repeatedly insisted that neither thinking nor reasoning distinguishes man from animal and that the behavior of beasts demonstrates that they are capable of both" (*The Human Condition* [New York: Doubleday Anchor, 1959], p. 326). However, see n. 55 below.

[2] *Leviathan*, ed. Michael Oakeshott (Oxford: Basil Blackwell, 1945), p. 111.

[3] *Treatise*, II, I, XII, p. 326.

[4] Ibid., II, XII, p. 398.

[23]

difference in the circumstances in which they respectively live out their lives. For human beings, unlike animals, inhabit a natural environment uncongenial to human wants and needs. Men are weak in relation to the elements; they are poor in relation to their wants; and they are insecure in relation to each other. It is by society alone, Hume tells us, that men are able to overcome their natural deficiencies and raise themselves to a position of superiority over the animals.[5]

The importance Hume accorded the idea of society in his science of human nature has not been widely recognized by students of his philosophy. But in the introduction to *A Treatise of Human Nature* Hume clearly indicated that his science of man would be based upon the experience of human conduct in society. Unlike the natural scientist, the scientist of human nature could not contrive experiments "purposely, with premeditation" without so disturbing the phenomena under investigation as to "render it impossible to form any just conclusion." The human scientist must "glean up" his experiments from observation of the conduct of men as they appear "in the common course of the world, by men's behaviour in company, in affairs, and in their pleasures."[6] The subject of the science of human nature was human experience in its normal and peculiarly human setting, the experience of men in society.

Perhaps the best indication of the context in which Hume thought his science of human nature should be located may be found in his allusion to "some late philosophers in *England*, who have begun to put the science of man on a new footing."[7] "He mentions, on this occasion," said Hume in The Abstract, "*Mr. Locke, my lord Shaftesbury, Dr. Mandeville, Mr. Hutchison, Dr. Butler*, who, tho' they differ in many points among themselves, seem all to agree in founding their accurate disquisitions of human nature entirely upon experience."[8] Now it has sometimes been wondered, given their different philosophical orientations, what sort of experience Hume presumed these thinkers might agree upon as the foundation for their studies of human nature. From the context it might appear that he regarded them as incipient Newtonians or experimentalists;[9] but this would be misleading: not one of them attempted in

---

[5] Ibid., III, II, II, pp. 484-85.

[6] Ibid., Intro., p. xxiii.

[7] Ibid., p. xxi.

[8] *An Abstract of A Treatise of Human Nature*, intro. J. M. Keynes and P. Sraffa (Hamden, Conn.: Archon Books, 1965), p. 7.

[9] John Laird, *Hume's Philosophy of Human Nature* (London: Methuen, 1932), p. 22.

any explicit or consistent manner to apply the experimental method of reasoning to moral subjects. A more plausible interpretation of the unifying element in this group of thinkers is that they advocated a form of naturalism: they agreed in assigning priority to the role of feeling or sentiment in human conduct, in opposition to those moral philosophers who upheld the primacy of reason.[10] But the difficulty with this interpretation is that Locke must be excluded, or his presence explained on other grounds; and Mandeville (although he endorsed the idea that reason was controlled by passion) must also be regarded as a special case. Recently, Duncan Forbes has found it curious that Hume should have mentioned these five thinkers to the exclusion of the modern natural lawyers, Descartes, Malebranche, and others. It must be assumed, Forbes advises, that "at this time Hume's thinking was dominated by the importance of the science of man in its narrower, exclusively psychological sense; the writers he mentions — a mixed bag otherwise, and why for that matter does he not mention Hobbes? — could all be regarded as having 'begun' a rather more intensive study of the human mind. . . ."[11] In the following discussion I would like to suggest that the common focus of this group of thinkers may have been that all of them were engaged in an extended debate about the qualities of human nature that enable men to live in society. Hume's reference to these particular philosophers may be interpreted as a signal to the reader of the context in which his study of human nature should be located. All of these philosophers, Hume included, assumed that society was the normal or the typical condition of human experience: their differences may be attributed to their different answers to the question, Is it natural for men to live in society? And if social life is natural, what meaning should be ascribed to the idea of nature? Hume's contribution to this debate was to have introduced to it the best method available to him for an understanding of nature, the method of Sir Isaac Newton. With the experimental method of Newton, and the understanding of human nature achieved by an application of that method to human experience, Hume proposed a resolution of the social question.

The debate had been launched by Shaftesbury in his extended and often incisive criticism of the social philosophy and epistemology of Locke. Shaftesbury had been a pupil of Locke's; and he was disposed to

---

[10] Norman Kemp Smith, *The Philosophy of David Hume* (London: Macmillan, 1941), pp. 18-19.

[11] *Hume's Philosophical Politics* (Cambridge: Cambridge University Press, 1975), p. 8.

regard Locke's influence on moral philosophy as almost entirely disastrous: "'Twas Mr. Locke that struck at all fundamentals, threw all order and virtue out of the world and made the very ideas of these (which are the same as those of God) unnatural and without foundation in our minds."[12] There were two interrelated problems: one was Locke's formulation of the law of nature in *Two Treatises of Government*; the other was the diffidence Locke expressed concerning any form of the law of nature in *An Essay concerning Human Understanding*. The problem with the law of nature as Locke had presented it in *Two Treatises*, and the problem, by implication, with the model of society that followed from it, was the assumption that men are naturally independent and must rely upon their own powers to preserve themselves. That assumption of natural independence on which so much of Locke's argument in *Two Treatises* was based seemed to Shaftesbury an egregious misunderstanding of human nature. If the powers men exert to preserve themselves are natural, then the affections and instincts conducive to the preservation of human beings must also be considered natural. Familial affection, parental love, the sexual instinct, must all be considered natural. And from these instincts and affections the congregation of human beings in society could be explained in a simpler and more satisfactory manner than the contractual explanation offered by Locke.[13] In brief, the first and most important principle of human nature was not the natural independence of men but rather the natural sociability of men, the love of company and of other persons.

Now the merit of the assumption that men tend to form associations — that they have an "associating inclination," as Shaftesbury sometimes put it — was that such an assumption pertained to an instinct, and as such it could not be compromised by Locke's critique of innate ideas. The associative principle was not an idea or even a sensation; it was a "presensation" and therefore a tendency that could be presumed to be operative among human beings at any time or place.[14] It was, in short, a principle that could replace the traditional precepts of natural law undermined by Locke's critique of innate ideas and thus provide a moral

---

[12] Shaftesbury to Ainsworth, January 1709, in *The Life, Unpublished Letters and Philosophical Regimen of Anthony, Earl of Shaftesbury*, ed. Benjamin Rand (London, 1900), p. 403.

[13] Shaftesbury, "Sensus Communis," in *Characteristics of Men, Manners, Opinions, Times*, ed. J. M. Robertson, 2 vols. in 1 (Indianapolis: Bobbs-Merrill, 1964), 1:74 (hereafter cited as *Characteristics*).

[14] "The Moralists, A Philosphical Rhapsody," *Characteristics*, 2:76, 136ff.

foundation for social life. Everything depended, however, on the meaning Shaftesbury assigned to nature in his conception of natural instincts and natural affections; for clearly not all associations could be thought to have a moral foundation, and some must be considered inconsistent with society itself. The instinctive and affective life of an individual was natural, in Shaftesbury's view, when his conduct reflected a balanced or harmonious disposition or temperament. A "natural temper" was one which conformed with the harmony and design to be discovered in nature, aesthetically appreciated or understood.[15] And to form such an appreciation, and to apply it to the cultivation of a balanced temper and harmonious relations with others, was the proper business of philosophy. "To philosophise, in a just signification, is but to carry good-breeding a step higher. For the accomplishment of breeding is, to learn whatever is decent in company or beautiful in arts; and the sum of philosophy is, to learn what is just in society and beautiful in Nature and the order of the world."[16]

Shaftesbury's emphasis on the role of natural instincts and natural affections in moral conduct has been recognized as the beginning of a new era in moral philosophy.[17] But the gravamen of his response to Locke makes it clear that the natural instincts and affections he found in human nature are those affections that relate human beings to each other as members of society. As Hume subsequently observed, Shaftesbury's defense of "the social passions" was the truly persuasive feature of his work.[18] The model of society that emerged from the work of Shaftesbury and from his conception of philosophy as an extension of politeness or good breeding was a distinctive kind of society, one that may be typified

---

[15] "Soliloquy, or Advice to an Author," *Characteristics,* 1:136, 214ff. See also Ernst Cassirer, *The Platonic Renaissance in England* (Edinburgh: Thomas Nelson and Sons, 1953), pp. 166, 193.

[16] "Miscellaneous Reflections," *Characteristics,* 2:255.

[17] For example, by Henry Sidgwick, *Outlines of the History of Ethics,* 6th ed. (London: Macmillan, 1931), p. 190.

[18] "Of the Dignity or Meanness of Human Nature," *Works,* 3:154n., where Hume wrote that it "has been prov'd beyond Question by several great Moralists of the Present Age, that the social Passions are by far the most powerful of any, and that even all the other Passions receive from them their chief Force and Influence. Whoever desires to see this Question treated at large, with the greatest Force of Argument and Eloquence, may consult my Lord SHAFTESBURY's Enquiry concerning Virtue." The role of the social affections in Shaftesbury's work has been explored by Stanley Grean, *Shaftesbury's Philosophy of Religion and Ethics* (Athens, Ohio: Ohio University Press, 1967), chap. 9. Shaftesbury's response to Hobbes and Locke has been discussed by David Fate Norton, "Shaftesbury and Two Scepticisms," *Filosofia* 46 (1968):1-12.

in the idiom of the period as polite society. But there was a tension in Shaftesbury's conception of polite society: "All politeness," he observed, "is owing to liberty. We polish one another, and rub off our corners and rough sides by a sort of amicable collision."[19] The achievement of politeness and good breeding required liberty, or the social conditions afforded only in free or republican governments such as those of ancient Greece and ancient Rome and the mixed government of Great Britain. The artificial politeness of the French was regarded by Shaftesbury as inferior to the natural politeness of English manners,[20] a preference directly contrary, it may be noted, to the preference shown by Hume. For Hume rejected the argument that politeness flourishes best in republican governments. The best conditions for the rise of politeness were provided by the artificial manners of civilized monarchies, where the subject could depend on those superior to him in rank to conduct themselves according to standards of polite, or civilized, behavior.[21] An adequate model of polite society required more than the natural affections as Shaftesbury had described them: polite society depended upon artificial restraints on human conduct, a dimension of polite society rejected by Shaftesbury but forcefully presented by his most capable critic, Bernard de Mandeville.

Mandeville once remarked that "two systems cannot be more opposite than his lordship's and mine."[22] Mandeville's opposition to Shaftesbury's view of human nature in society was not an attempt to revert to the Lockean model of society or to rehabilitate the postulates of natural independence and natural rights: his frame of reference, like Shaftesbury's, was polite society. But whereas Shaftesbury regarded politeness as due entirely to natural affection or an agreeable disposition, Mandeville attributed politeness entirely to artificial restraints on human nature. His approach to the study of human nature was, as he liked to say, the approach of an anatomist, not that of an artist or virtuoso.[23] And to

---

[19] "Sensus Communis," *Characteristics*, 1:46.

[20] "Soliloquy, or Advice to an Author," *Characteristics*, 1:142ff.

[21] "Of the Rise and Progress of the Arts and Sciences," *Works*, 3:186ff.; and "Of Civil Liberty," ibid., 158-59. I have developed this argument of Hume's more fully in "Hume's Political Science and the Classical Republican Tradition," *Canadian Journal of Political Science* 10 (1977):809-39.

[22] Bernard de Mandeville, "A Search into the Nature of Society," *The Fable of the Bees*, ed. F. B. Kaye, 2 vols. (Oxford: Clarendon Press, 1924), 1:324 (hereafter cited as *Fable*).

[23] *Fable*, Preface, 1:3ff. See also Leslie Stephen, *History of English Thought in the Eighteenth Century*, 2 vols. (London, 1876), 2:39-41.

study human nature in a clinical manner was to expose the passions lying beneath the surface of society. The most important quality, or passion, of human nature considered in this view was pride, or honor, or, as Mandeville later preferred to call it, self-liking.[24] It was this passion and the multitude of vices related to it that caused the demand for the proliferation of goods and services that formed so conspicuous a part of the benefits derived from life in society. If sociability were as natural or as instinctive as Shaftesbury had supposed it to be, then the forms of politeness would be the same in every polished or refined society. And men, like other sociable creatures such as bees or sheep, would congregate in hives or herds of indistinguishable structure or shape.[25] But if it were assumed instead that pride, not love of company, was the basic passion of human nature in society, then there was no difficulty in accounting for the various forms of polite behavior and address: they were the products of a divison of labor, of the efforts of innumerable legislators and leaders of fashion, or the *beau monde*.[26] The intent of these leaders was invariably the same—to make men more sociable or easier to govern. And the means by which this end was achieved were equally uniform—by persuading men that those who could best conceal or contain their pride and self-liking were entitled to feel (but not to seem) the proudest of all.[27] Thus politeness was ultimately no less a product of human artifice or contrivance than any other useful device in society. It merely seemed more natural because it was more necessary for the maintenance of society itself.

The artificial model of society that Mandeville presented provoked a great diversity of responses. But the ablest defenses of the naturalistic model were offered in the work of Francis Hutcheson and Joseph Butler. Their work called attention to the distinctively moral qualities required of man in society; and Hutcheson, in particular, elaborated new ideas of what might be meant by "natural," in the claim that it was natural for men to live in society. Hutcheson conceived his earliest work in moral

---

[24] *An Enquiry into the Origin of Honour and the Usefulness of Christianity in War* (1732), ed. M. M. Goldsmith (London: Frank Cass, 1971), p. 12.

[25] *Fable*, 2:187: "What changes have ever been made in their furniture or architecture? Have they ever made cells that were not sexangular, or added any tools to those which nature furnished them with at the beginning?"

[26] Ibid., 142ff., 287ff.

[27] "An Enquiry into the Origin of Moral Virtue," *Fable*, 1:42ff.

philosophy as a defense of Shaftesbury's principles against the author of *The Fable of the Bees*.[28] It will suffice to mention only two of his arguments against Mandeville's model of human nature in society. He argued that Mandeville would have been more consistent in his use of moral terms had he called a virtue any act or quality that contributed to the good of society and abandoned a usage in which virtue continued to be linked to self-denial or self-control. Secondly, he argued that unless men were moved by an instinctive concern for the good of society it would never have been possible to inculcate such a concern by whatever artifices or means of persuasion legislators and social leaders might employ.[29] Hutcheson's criticisms of Mandeville rested, then, on the presumption that all men have a concern for the good of society. This was more than natural affection or love of company as Shaftesbury had conceived it; it was a distinctive moral sense or capacity for benevolence. It was a quality of human nature not confined to extraordinary individuals or to persons in authority who might simulate such a concern to engender it in the minds of subjects. It was a propensity of human nature that everyone was presumed to have: "we are so far from imagining all men to be acted only by self-love, that we universally expect in others a regard for the public; and do not look upon the want of this, as barely the absence of moral good or virtue, but even as positively evil and hateful."[30]

Hutcheson's principal difficulty in sustaining his theory that benevolence was the quality enabling men to live in society was a lack of correspondence between the theory and the observed behavior of men of his own time. He alluded to this difficulty as "the corruption of manners so justly complained of everywhere."[31] But his remedy for the problem was not to propose alterations in the model of society; it was rather to discover a stronger foundation in human nature for the sense of benevolence. In his second formulation of the theory he added two new senses: a sense of honor and a public sense to complement and reinforce the moral

---

[28] Francis Hutcheson, *An Inquiry into the Original of our Ideas of Beauty and Virtue; in which the Principles of the late Earl of Shaftesbury are Explained and Defended against the Author of the Fable of the Bees, etc.* (London, 1725); hereafter cited as *Inquiry*.

[29] These criticisms of Mandeville were set out most succinctly by Hutcheson in letters written to the *Dublin Journal*, Feb. 4, 11, and 18, 1726, and reprinted in *Reflections upon Laughter and Remarks upon the Fable of the Bees* (Glasgow, 1750).

[30] *Inquiry*, p. 156.

[31] Ibid., p. 221.

sense he had described in the *Inquiry*.³² The problem, then, was to ensure that all of these senses were controlled by benevolence in the way that conscience was thought to superintend the other qualities of human nature in the moral philosophy of Bishop Butler. The particular manner in which other qualities were supposed by Butler to obey the promptings of conscience—specifically Butler's suggestion of an analogy between the obedience of other faculties to conscience and the duty of passive obedience of subjects to civil authority³³—did not afford a model Hutcheson could accept, on political grounds, among others. The problem was to avoid the mechanistic idea of submission to a central governing agency while maintaining the idea of a defining role for benevolence. In pursuit of this aim, Hutcheson was moved to adopt a teleological idea of nature in which man was conceived to fulfill his nature by actualizing his capacity for benevolence.³⁴ And this meaning of nature was succeeded by still another, in which benevolence was thought to be natural in the Stoic sense that it was, in the last resort, its own reward.³⁵

Hutcheson's quest for an idea of nature that would permit him to conclude that men are social beings by nature had led him through four distinguishable ideas of nature. It was his third idea of nature, in particular, that seems to have informed his critical remarks on Hume's *Treatise*. In replying to Hutcheson's remarks Hume rejected the teleological idea of nature unequivocally: "I cannot agree to your Sense of *Natural*. Tis founded on final Causes; which is a Consideration, that appears to me pretty uncertain & unphilosophical."³⁶ The approach to nature and to human nature that Hume thought more promising was the method of the

---

³² *An Essay on the Nature and Conduct of the Passions and Affections with Illustrations upon the Moral Sense* (London, 1728).

³³ Joseph Butler, *Fifteen Sermons Preached at the Rolls Chapel* (London, 1726), Sermon 3, pp. 44ff.

³⁴ Hutcheson's inaugural lecture, *De Naturali Hominum Socialitate*, delivered on 30 November 1730, exhibits a teleological approach to the study of human nature; it also reflects, as the title suggests, his continuing preoccupation with the qualities that permit men to live in society. The teleological phase of Hutcheson's thought found its fullest expression in *A System of Moral Philosophy* (London, 1755). This book was written, it would seem, between 1734 and 1737 (see W. R. Scott, *Francis Hutcheson: His Life, Teaching and Position in the History of Philosophy* [Cambridge, 1900], pp. 113, 210ff.).

³⁵ *Philosophiae Moralis Institutio Compendiaria* (Glasgow, 1742), subsequently translated as *A Short Introduction to Moral Philosophy* (Glasgow, 1747).

³⁶ Hume to Hutcheson, 17 September 1739, *The Letters of David Hume*, ed. J. Y. T. Greig, 2 vols. (Oxford: Clarendon Press, 1932), 1:33 (hereafter cited as *Letters*). See also

anatomist, not that of the moralist or the virtuoso. The proper approach in the study of the mind, as in the study of the body, was "to discover its most secret springs and principles," not "to describe the grace and beauty of its actions." It was possible that "an Anatomist, however, can give very good Advice to a Painter or Statuary: And in like manner, I am perswaded, that a Metaphysician may be very helpful to a Moralist; tho' I cannot easily conceive these two Characters united in the same Work."[37] The contrast Hume perceived between his and Hutcheson's approach to the study of human nature recalls the idiom employed by Mandeville to express the difference between his perspective and Shaftesbury's. And the parallel between the two exchanges is underlined by the directly related and crucial difference between Hutcheson and Hume concerning the nature of society, with Hume's insistence on the artificial origin of the basic institutions of social life, justice, and property. Hume's persistent adherence to the idea that justice and property were artificial in origin was considered by Hutcheson, Kames, and other thinkers of the Scottish enlightenment to be highly idiosyncratic. Kames explained Hume's position on this matter as being the result of an early conviction he was reluctant to relinquish: "that justice is an artificial virtue was a favourite principle of his, early adopted, so as to become in him a sort of natural principle."[38] Because of his long-standing friendship with Hume, Kames was in a position to know just how early his friend's adoption of the artificial perspective on social life may have been. From the record of Hume's correspondence and literary interests it would seem that his tendency to emphasize the artificial dimension of life in society began very early indeed.

The idea of politeness appears to have had an early and abiding fascination for the group of younger men associated with Kames in the 1730s, a group that included David Hume, Michael Ramsay, and James Forrester.[39] In 1734 James Forrester published a tract entitled *The Polite Philosopher* in which he proposed certain rules for men to observe in their conduct if they wished to be sociable and agreeable in their relations

---

David Fate Norton's essay in this volume, "Hume and His Scottish Critics," where the teleological assumptions of Hutcheson and other Scottish philosophers are contrasted with Hume's critical assessment of final causes.

[37] *Letters*, p. 33. See also *Treatise*, III, III, VI, pp. 620-21.

[38] Henry Home, *Essays on the Principles of Morality and Natural Religion* (1751), 3rd ed. (Edinburgh, 1779), p. 149. The observation was added in this edition.

[39] Ian Simpson Ross, *Lord Kames and the Scotland of his Day* (Oxford: Clarendon Press, 1972), p. 76; and A. F. Tytler, *Memoirs of the Life and Writings of the Honourable Henry Home of Kames*, 2 vols. (Edinburgh: 1807), 1:58.

with others. Such rules, he observed, were intended not "to amend people's hearts" so much "as to regulate their conduct." The rules of politeness and good breeding were artificial; but natural politeness, he went on to remark, "can be no other way attained than through an intimate acquaintance with the other sex."[40] This suggestion that politeness depended on both artificial and natural qualities or virtues was no more than intimated in Forrester's pamphlet, but the idea was developed more fully in a letter Hume wrote in the same year to Michael Ramsay, recording his first impression of France. It was the "real politeness" of French society that most impressed him:

> By real Politeness I mean Softness of Temper, & a sincere Inclination to oblige & be serviceable; which is very conspicuous in this Nation, not only among the high but low, insomuch that the Porters & Coachmen here are civil, & that not only to Gentlemen but likewise among themselves, so that I have not yet seen one Quarrel in France, tho' they are every where to be met with in England.[41]

The real politeness of French society was, however, an artificial phenomenon, for the forms in which it was expressed were invariably exaggerated. The English manner of expressing politeness was unquestionably more natural:

> An English fine Gentleman distinguishes himself from the rest of the World, by the whole Tenour of his Conversation, more than by any particular part of it; so that tho' you are sensible he excells, you are at a loss to tell in what, & have no remarkable Civilities & Complements to pitch on as a proof of his Politeness.[42]

But however natural and agreeable the manners of an English gentleman might be, compared with the elaborate ceremonies employed at every level of society in France, the latter was more useful and effective in achieving a polite society. "After all it must be confest, that the little Niceties of the French Behaviour, tho' troublesome & impertinent, yet serve to polish the ordinary Kind of People & prevent Rudeness &

---

[40] *The Polite Philosopher: or an Essay on that Art which makes a man happy to himself and agreeable to Others* (Dublin: 1734), pp. 22, 49.
[41] 12 September 1734, *Letters*, 1:20.
[42] Ibid.

Brutality."[43] The repetition of certain forms of address had an educational role analogous to the repetition of phrases and movements in devotional rituals and to the forms of training designed for recruits to military service. Repetition, as Hume subsequently observed in the *Treatise*, always influenced the imagination; the problem was to ensure that the imagination was also regulated by judgment and experience.

Now Hume had ample opportunity to observe social conduct in France. In another letter, written at the same time from Rheims, he reported of the local people that "every Day in some of their Houses, they make Parties of Diversion to show me more Company...."[44] Even in La Flèche, he remarked, the people were "generally so sociable and complaisant to strangers" that a new arrival might spend all of his time in company; he added that he preferred to "spend always more of my time in study."[45] But Hume consistently maintained that philosophy had suffered in earlier times "by being shut up in Colleges and Cells, and secluded from the World and good Company." The philosopher must consult experience if he would avoid the chimerical conclusions and unintelligible style of presentation of the monastic philosophers and the schoolmen; he must consult "Experience, where alone it is to be found, in common Life and Conversation."[46] In this light it would appear that Hume's decision to recast his philosophy in the form of essays marks no radical break with the orientation of his earliest philosophical reflections. His concern throughout was to understand human nature in the condition that seemed to him the usual or typical condition of human experience, the experience of men in society.

French society seemed always to Hume to be the model of a truly polite society. There were other societies, however, in which the rules and conventions of social behavior assumed the most extravagant forms the imagination and fancy of human beings could contrive. In what may be the earliest of his essays, "An Historical Essay on Chivalry and modern Honour," Hume attempted to explain the curious forms of social conduct that prevailed among the barbarian peoples following the collapse of the Roman empire in the West. The barbarians could not have failed to be impressed, Hume thought, by the refined manners of the Romans; but

---

[43] Ibid., p. 21.

[44] Hume to James Birch, 12 September 1734, *Letters*, 1:22.

[45] E. C. Mossner, "Hume at La Flèche, 1735: An Unpublished letter," *Texas Studies in English* 38 (1958):32.

[46] "Of Essay Writing," *Works*, 4:368.

having no experience in the polite and social arts, the barbarians were unable to form a judicious conception of social behavior. Their minds, prompted by an impression of a "degree of virtue and politeness beyond what they had ever before been acquainted with . . . would necessarily stretch themselves into some vast conception of things which not being corrected by sufficient judgment and experience must be empty and unsolid. . . . 'Twas thus that that monster of romantic chivalry or knight errantry was brought into the world."[47] The conventions of barbarian and feudal society were the result of unregulated imagination, or imagination unchecked by judgment and general rules based upon experience. There was, moreover, a parallel between the unregulated imagination of the barbarians and the imaginary or hypothetical systems of mystics and theologians where the mind "buries itself in its own whimsies and chimeras and raises up to itself a new set of passions, affections, desires, objects, in short a perfectly new world of its own. . . ."[48] This fanciful approach to the study of human nature was not confined to the world of the barbarians and theologians; it was typical, as Hume observed in his letter to a physician, of the moral philosophy "transmitted to us by Antiquity," which "labor'd under the same Inconvenience that has been found in their natural Philosophy, of being entirely Hypothetical, & depending more upon Invention than Experience."[49]

The remedy for this neglect of experience in moral philosophy was the introduction of the Newtonian, or the experimental, method of reasoning into moral subjects. Hume's use of the Newtonian method has been scrutinized with care in recent studies of Hume's philosophy,[50] but it is worth remarking that Hume's conception of the experimental method did not rest upon any extensive knowledge of or interest in natural philosophy. His early memoranda contain only 9 notations under natural philosophy, as contrasted with 40 entries under "philosophy" (really natural religion) and 269 entries under "general" that in fact relate specifically to politics. All but four of the entries under politics pertain incidentally to material that was to appear only in the *Political Discourses* of 1752, a circumstance that would seem to point to a later dating

---

[47] Reprinted with an introduction by Mossner, in "David Hume's 'An Historical Essay on Chivalry and modern Honour'," *Modern Philology* 45 (1947):57.
[48] Ibid.
[49] Letter to a physician, 1734, *Letters*, 1:16.
[50] James Noxon, *Hume's Philosophical Development* (Oxford: Oxford University Press, 1973) and Nicholas Capaldi, *David Hume: The Newtonian Philospher* (Boston: Twayne, 1975).

for the memoranda than Ernest Mossner has ascribed to them.[51] But however this may be, there is very scanty evidence indeed of any preoccupation on Hume's part with the natural sciences in the period prior to the publication of the *Treatise* or, for that matter, in his later writings. The focus of his concern, as we have seen from his early correspondence and literary endeavors, was human nature in society, the concern that informed the debate among the philosophers he recognized as his predecessors in the science of human nature.

When Hume's science of human nature is located in its social context it is possible to recognize the basis of his preference for general rules based upon judgment over rules based upon the imagination alone. Hume's most extended use of this distinction may be found in his discussion of the rules that determine property, the institution he regarded as fundamental to the existence of society. Now there can be no doubt that Hume's point of departure in his discussion of the rules that determine property was the Roman law of property as expounded in the prescribed textbooks in civil law that he had studied at the College of Edinburgh. And it has been suggested that the modern natural- or civil-law tradition provides the best example of what Hume came to call the experimental method of reasoning in morals.[52] But the little evidence available in Hume's writings and memoirs of this very early period in his life reveals a particular repugnance for the civil law: while his parents fancied he was "poring over Voet and Vinnius, Cicero and Virgil were the Authors which [he] was secretly devouring."[53] Johannes Voet and Arnoldus Vinnius were Dutch jurists of the seventeenth century, the authors of the authoritative commentaries for this period on *The Pandects* and *The Institutes* of Justinian. Hume's disenchantment with these authors was prompted, as his memoir recalls, by the superior attractions of philosophy and poetry afforded by the work of Cicero and Virgil. The attraction of poetry is especially manifest in Hume's discussion of property. For his concern throughout his discussion of the rules of property was to emphasize the merely fanciful or imaginary nature of the rules. In contrast to that of the natural lawyers, who endeavored to show that the rules of property could be discovered by reason in the nature of things, Hume's

---

[51] E. C. Mossner, "Hume's Early Memoranda, 1729-1740: The Complete Text," *Journal of the History of Ideas* 9 (1948):492-518.

[52] Forbes, chap. 1.

[53] Hume, "My Own Life," in E. C. Mossner, *The Life of David Hume* (Edinburgh: Thomas Nelson and Sons, 1954), p. 611.

concern was to show that those rules have no other foundation in the understanding than the imagination or fancy. The rules of ownership were fictions, were products of the legal imagination; but their utility depended upon the uniform manner of their application by judges or magistrates. It was a consistent and judicious application of the rules of civil law that Hume sought, one that would provide a regular or uniform structure for social life. And in order to achieve that end he thought it appropriate to argue that the natural law assumption of a foundation for property in reason and the nature of things was to claim for distinctions of ownership a foundation that human nature could not sustain and that justice, property, and the institution of society did not require.[54]

It was imagination regulated by judgment that supplied such permanence or structure as society might afford. In the absence of the corrective role of judgment, the imagination might feign a belief in the necessary connection of persons and their property that judgment and experience could not substantiate. This had occurred most conspicuously in the related theories of property and power found in the philosophy of Locke. Hume represented Locke's theory of the natural right of the proprietor and his difference with it in the following manner:

> Some philosophers . . . [say] that every one has a property in his labour; and when he joins that labour to any thing, it gives him the property of the whole: But . . . we cannot be said to join our labour in any thing but in a figurative sense. Properly speaking, we only make an alteration on it by our labour. This forms a relation betwixt us and the object; and thence arises the property, according to the preceding principles.[55]

The idea that a man might mix his labor in an object and thereby make it his own was perceived by Hume as a confusion of two entities that must

---

[54] Hume's response to the natural law tradition is discussed in more detail in my article "Hume's Theory of Justice and Property," *Political Studies* 24 (1976):103-19.

[55] *Treatise*, III, II, III, p. 505, n. 1. It is curious to find in perhaps the most profound analysis of the activity of laboring in the literature of political thought the assertion that "Hume, and not Marx, was the first to insist that labour distinguishes man from animal" (Arendt, p. 326). While this remark is no more than an aside in Arendt's work, it calls attention to a central theme in the social and political thought of Hume. Thus it may be relevant to emphasize that not only does society alone distinguish human from animal life in the philosophy of Hume, but that Hume's rejection of the labor theory of property would seem to have profound implications for his theory of causality, and therefore for his entire philosophy of human nature.

be conceived separately; namely, the individual and his external goods. For property was "a particular species of causation,"[56] and in any causal relationship the cause must be conceived separately from the effect. This is just the case in ownership of property. External goods are easily separated from their owners: the imagination prompts the owner to suppose that his goods are necessarily connected with him, but judgment secures that connection in the rules of justice and property ownership. And the confusion of personality and property presented in Locke's political theory was directly parallel to the difficulty presented by his idea of power or causality. Locke had argued that the idea of power was suggested to the understanding by the experience of production in human action. For in observing that human beings can act or refrain from acting, and in observing also the effects natural bodies are able to produce upon each other, the understanding forms the idea of power.[57] The confusion in Locke's idea of power could be resolved, Hume thought, if it is understood, first, that the assumption that everything must be produced by something begs the question—for to conceive of something, it is not necessary to conceive of its having been produced[58]—and, secondly, that in the experience of human agency men often imagine they have a power even though that power has never been exercised.[59] The imagination of the actor must be corrected by the judgment of the spectator, who concludes from his experience of the conduct and character of the actor how he is likely to behave.[60]

Hume's response to Locke's theory of property and power thus complemented Shaftesbury's critique of the Lockean assumption of the natural independence of individuals and their power to preserve themselves. Hume concurred with Shaftesbury's view that Locke had ignored the fundamental importance of the natural and social affections with their profound implications for life in society. But Hume rejected the implication drawn by Shaftesbury, and still more explicitly by Hutcheson, that an ever-widening circle of affection must spread from family to society, and perhaps beyond to humanity at large. It was not natural affection

---

[56] *Treatise*, II, I, X, p. 310; III, II, III, p. 506. See also the note appended in 1760 to "A Dissertation on the Passions" (*Works*, 4:151) in which Hume reiterated his view that property provides the best illustration of his idea of causation.

[57] *An Essay concerning Human Understanding*, ed. Peter H. Nidditch (Oxford: Oxford University Press, 1975), II, vii, 8, p. 131.

[58] *Treatise*, I, III, III, p. 81; XIV, p. 157.

[59] Ibid., II, I, X, p. 313.

[60] Ibid., III, II, pp. 408–9.

or benevolence that provided the connecting link of individuals in society; the quality of human nature that made life in society irresistible was sympathy: "We can form no wish, which has not a reference to society.... Whatever other passions we may be actuated by; pride, ambition, avarice, curiosity, revenge or lust; the soul or animating principle of them all is sympathy; nor wou'd they have any force, were we to abstract entirely from the thought and sentiments of others."[61] It is sympathy that enables men to feel as others feel; it enlivens our ideas of the passions of others, giving those ideas the force or vivacity of impressions or immediate experience. In this respect the role of sympathy in Hume's theory of the passions was analogous to the role of the imagination in his theory of the understanding, and it was prompted by the same associations of ideas and individuals: the resemblance of individuals with each other, their contiguity, and constant conjunction, all prompt the passion of sympathy.

The natural relations or associations of men in society were fixed, Hume believed, by the influence of sympathy. For it was through sympathy that the individual discovered himself in the responses of others to his character and conduct: "Ourself, independent of the perception of every other object, is in reality nothing: For which reason we must turn our view to external objects; and 'tis natural for us to consider with most attention such as lie contiguous to us, or resemble us."[62] In this respect sympathy reinforced that concern for the self, which Hume took to be the foundation of pride. But the passion of sympathy encountered a formidable obstacle in the natural relation of resemblance of proud men with each other. The difficulty had been identified by Mandeville, who had observed that none are so much offended by the pride of their fellow men as the proudest of all.[63] The problem, Hume agreed, could not be resolved by sympathy or within the society formed by the natural relations of individuals with each other. For although the natural relation of resemblance might afford a basis for sympathy, the same natural relation prompts the imagination to make comparisons, which in turn provoke hostility. Thus sympathy and the imagination must be checked by judgment and general rules; and such was the origin of the artificial rules of politeness and good breeding.[64]

---

[61] Ibid., II, V, p. 363.
[62] Ibid., II, pp. 340–41.
[63] *Fable*, 1:124.
[64] *Treatise*, III, III, II, pp. 596–97.

Hume attached great importance to artificial rules in his understanding of social relationships. The natural relations of individuals in society invariably prompted the imagination to form associations of ideas that, if left unchecked, would be destructive of social order. The natural relation of resemblance on which sympathy ultimately depended would prompt hostility if that relation were not checked by the rules of politeness and good breeding. The natural relation of causation, or constant conjunction, between individuals and their external goods would generate erroneous relations of proprietorship but for the uniform application of the rules of property by magistrates and judges. And the contiguity of the external goods of others would prompt the imagination to prefer the abandonment of the rules of justice and property if those rules were not enforced by rules of allegiance and the constitutional rules and conventions of government. In his attachment to artificial rules of social conduct Hume was emphasizing the dimension of social life that had been explored by Mandeville. But Hume's artificial rules were not artifices or tricks played by politicians and men of fashion, as Mandeville had claimed;[65] their artificiality derived from their origin in judgment and their role in regulating the natural relations formed by sympathy and the imagination. Such agreements of judgment or conventions are reached in an experimental or empirical manner, over long periods of time, and after repeated experiences of the inconveniences of behaving otherwise. In this respect, the artificial rules or conventions of society are like experimental rules, which are "very easy in their invention, but extremely difficult in their application."[66] The difficulty of arriving at an appropriate set of arrangements for life in society "will easily appear, if we consider, that in order to establish a general rule, and extend it beyond its proper bounds, there is requir'd a certain uniformity in our experience, and a great superiority of those instances, which are conformable to the rule, above the contrary."[67] Thus societies become polished or refined as the "uniformity in our experience" that life in society affords is extended by modification and amendment of the conventions of social life.

Hume's conception of the experimental method of reasoning thus stands intimately related to the problem of providing the general rules and artificial restraints that make life in society possible. And the experimental nature of the rules and conventions of society was to become

---

[65] Ibid., II, III, p. 500; III, I, p. 578.
[66] Ibid., I, III, XV, p. 175.
[67] Ibid., II, II, V, p. 362.

Hume's point of departure for a science of politics in which forms of government and policies were themselves regarded as experiments, as uncertain trials of judgment by which politicians have attempted to contrive a world consistent with the uniform interests and passions, the needs and wants of human beings. But any adequate discussion of the manner in which experimental reasoning is employed by politicians must lead beyond the context of the present discussion to some consideration of the very different traditions to which Hume was responding in the *Essays, Moral and Political*, the *Political Discourses*, and *The History of England*. For Hume was perhaps unusual among philosophers in having been a scholar as well as a philosopher. And it would be folly to suggest that there is a single context in which his work may be located. But among the many contexts and traditions that may illuminate Hume's philosophy, one of the earliest and not least significant must be allowed to have been the debate on the qualities enabling men to live in society that was conducted by the philosophers he regarded as his predecessors in the science of human nature.

Berkeley, Hume, and the Central Problem of Scottish Philosophy

George Davie

I

How much the development of Scottish philosophy owes to an earlier Irish Enlightenment is often overlooked. Berkeley, of course, is recognized as providing an Irish dimension to eighteenth-century British thought, but so too does Francis Hutcheson, and central ideas of each come together in the former's *Alciphron* (1732). *Alciphron* is Berkeley's critical and systematic challenge to the radical reductivist empiricism produced in an effort to make Locke consistent with himself, to the aestheticism of Shaftesbury's moral philosophy, and to the cynical economism of Mandeville's "private vices, public virtues" view of social philosophy. Hutcheson, from northern Irish Presbyterian roots, was gradually led by his own concerns with these same elements to shift from the monographic approaches of his early works (*Inquiry concerning Beauty and Virtue*, 1725; *Essay on the Passions and Affections, With Illustrations on the Moral Sense*, 1728) to provide a systematic response to them in his *Compendium* of 1742.

In the last analysis, the creative element in this Irish Enlightenment, the element responsible for preparing the way for the classical period of Scottish philosophy, consisted not only in the parallel pioneering by both Berkeley and Hutcheson, with system-building as the proper way to answer the free thinkers, but also, and more importantly, in the very sharp and stimulating tension between the syntheses constructed or outlined by the two Irish philosophers as the proper way out of the difficulty. Agreeing with one another about the excesses of the new economics, Berkeley and Hutcheson differed radically on the respective values of Shaftesburian ethics and radical empiricism as components in the system that was to check the errors of the *Fable of the Bees* while at the same time preserving its more valuable insights. Berkeley had no sympathy whatever for Shaftesbury's aestheticist brand of ethics or for the common-sense intuitionism it implied, but he saw much promise in the atomistic reductionism and the egoistic utilitarianism of the free-thinking empiricism, provided that it was accompanied and offset, in a dualistic way, by a revival of a metaphysically-minded rationalism modeled on

Cartesianism. Hutcheson, on the other hand, had the strongest objection to the utilitarianism-reductivism of the free thinkers, as well as to the Cartesian rationalism added to the mixture by Berkeley as a corrective; but by contrast he saw great promise, epistemological as well as ethical, in Shaftesbury's appeal to the intuitions of common sense, provided that they could be broadened in such a way as to free them from their aestheticist exclusiveness. Already, in the Dublin of the late twenties, the opposition had thus begun to emerge between the contrasting positions that in their tension provided Scottish philosophy with its central problem: the Berkeleian system, according to which, in the interests of reconciling progress with traditional standards, we are to set aside the instincts of the farmer in favor of the sophistication of the philosopher and to think with the learned while we talk with the vulgar; and the Hutchesonian system, according to which, with the same aim of reconciling material advance with the intellectual principle, we are to respect the instincts of the farmer as against the sophistication of the philosopher and initiate a sort of dialogue between the vulgar and the learned, instead of talking down to the farmer from the standpoint of the philosopher.

Understood in these terms, the intellectual divergence between the principal protagonists of the Irish Enlightenment already contains implicitly the central problem of the classical Scottish philosophy; and in this matter I am inclined to think that Sir James Mackintosh was perfectly right when he claimed that the two great Irish philosophers may be said "to have co-operated in calling forth the metaphysical genius of Scotland," in the sense that "though Hutcheson spread the taste and formed the principles" of what was to be called the Scottish philosophy of common sense, Berkeley, by his attacks on common sense and intuitionism, "undoubtedly produced the scepticism of Hume which stimulated the intuitive school into activity."[1] As Hume makes clear, Berkeley's function in regard to Scottish philosophy was the purely negative one of shaking to its foundations, by means of his deadly arguments, the common-sense philosophy put over by Hutcheson in Glasgow and eagerly seized on by the Scots as the answer to the great problem of reconciling the old ethics with the new economics. Carried on against a Scottish background, the conflict of principle between these two philosophers

---

[1] *Dissertation . . . Exhibiting a General View of the Progress of Ethical Philosophy, chiefly during the seventeenth and eighteenth centuries*, prefixed to the 7th ed. of the *Encyclopedia Britannica* (Edinburgh, 1830), s.v. "Hutcheson," pp. 348-49.

"stimulates a series of major systems in which the problem of the relation of ethics to economics is approached through the fundamentally epistemological issue of the relation between vulgar common sense and philosophical reason.

II

In *Alciphron*, Dialogue 1, Berkeley asserts that the fundamental direction of the free-thinking movement, despite its claims to be deistic and to that extent spiritual, is toward putting modern society on a secularistic basis. Consistently carried out, the experimental or Lockeian approach to knowledge, though it has made possible great advances in physical science, leaves no room for such transcendental and metaphysical entities as God. "Atheism," Berkeley has his free thinker say, "that bugbear of women and fools, is the very type and perfection of free thinking."[2] In Dialogue 2 he takes up Mandeville's view that austerity, self-sacrifice, or thrift, whatever value they may have had in the stagnant society of a simpler age, are irrelevant in the new age of plenty. To Berkeley, the major weakness in this view is not the implicit hedonism—he does not quarrel with the claim that self-love is an active principle of man's nature—but rather the unenlightened nature of this hedonism. Mandeville's one-sided valuation of excessive consumption overlooks the fact that moderate consumption will do more for the growth of trade than will excessive consumption; the drink trade is cited as an example.

In Dialogue 3 Berkeley reveals that he is largely in agreement with the Shaftesburian view that a consumer society of the Mandevillian type can at best give only a very partial and unstable satisfaction of human needs. But although Berkeley agrees with Shaftesbury that "the mind of man attaineth to the highest nature of beauty, excellence and perfection, by contemplating the fitness and order of the parts of the moral system, knit together by mutual sympathies," he finds Shaftesbury's conception of the moral sense to be far too elitist to turn sensual and worldly-minded men to virtue.[3] Lacking, suggests Berkeley, are the "hope of reward and fear of punishment" which are "highly expedient to cast the balance of pleasant and profitable on the side of virtue and [are] thereby conducive

---

[2] *The Works of George Berkeley Bishop of Cloyne*, ed. A. A. Luce and T. E. Jessop, 9 vols. (London, Thomas Nelson and Sons, 1948-57), 3:44 (hereafter cited as *Works*).
[3] Ibid., p. 117.

to the benefit of human society."[4] In short, in Berkeley's opinion, the competing elements of Mandeville's economism and Shaftesbury's aestheticism cannot be reconciled in a social ideal flexible enough to combine comeliness of lifestyle with improved standards of living *unless* the experimentalist-scientific approach presupposed by these rival ethics can be shown to have transcendental-religious implications that have escaped the notice of both proponents. At this point, in Dialogue 4, Berkeley introduces another important theme in the Irish-Scottish debate on free thinking, namely, his own philosophy of the divine visible language. Empiricism, properly refined and reformulated, far from undercutting belief in God, becomes the foundation of a new, perceptually-based proof of Divine existence sufficiently cogent to satisfy Alciphron himself.

The key to the issue is to be found, we are told, in the *New Theory of Vision*, where Berkeley had revealed the phenomenological difference between an object of touch and an object of sight. Locke and traditional philosophy had considered sight and touch as different ways of presenting the same body; for Berkeley they are separate and quite independent modes of experience that nevertheless function together in a kind of organic unity, with visual experiences, strictly analyzed, constituting a form of language by which nature speaks to us about what lies ahead. Berkeley then concludes by claiming that this doctrine of "divine visible language" implicit in the *New Theory of Vision* constitutes a perceptually-based proof of the existence of God, analogous to our perceptually-based proof, via social experience, of the existence of other minds.

III

In Dublin Francis Hutcheson had made similar criticisms of Mandeville and had in fact anticipated Berkeley's charge of the elitism of the moral sense by "democratizing," as W. R. Scott puts it, Shaftesbury's ethics.[5] The all-important insights into the beauty of virtue, he insists, are possible for all men, are at least as possible for the honest farmer as for the virtuoso, and are best established, perhaps, by an appeal to a consensus of the farmer as a representative of the vulgar, and the virtuoso as representative of the learned. And not only did Hutcheson anticipate

---

[4] Ibid., p. 119.

[5] *Francis Hutcheson: His Life, Teaching and Position in the History of Philosophy* (Cambridge, Cambridge University Press, 1900), p. 186, passim.

Berkeley's challenge to Shaftesbury, he anticipated and found wanting Berkeley's solution to the foundation of morals. Hutcheson was not the man to be impressed by the fantastic exclusiveness of a metaphysical ethic that cuts off visual perception from its natural connection with tactual perception in order to constitute it the vehicle of some sort of public communing with the provident spirit of God. Instead of making a mystification of the visual sense that would represent the moral consciousness as a sort of Malebranchian listening-in to God, Hutcheson, in direct opposition to Berkeley, demystifies the latter's theory of vision as a first step in evolving a moderately common-sense view of mind. This brings the moral consciousness down from heaven to earth without returning to the heresy of the free thinkers, reducing the theoretical to the practical, or merging the spiritual and the material. In a letter of 1727 Hutcheson (as also Leibniz and Husserl) maintained that the Berkeleian denial of the common-sense connection between the visual and tactual experience of bodily shapes holds good only if we incongruously compare a "groping" experience of moving the feeling hand over an object with a static, fixed-eye experience in which the shapes under observation, cubes or spheres, are looked at through one constant angle of vision.[6] But, Hutcheson insists, the paradox of the *New Theory of Vision* is instantly dissolved as soon as we compare the experience of feeling around the contours of an object—in a series of progressive explorations—with the *activity* of a visual observation. In short, by keeping the eye on the move we are able to discover that the variety of successive visual perceptions is similar to the variety of successive tactual perceptions. Thus, confronted with the Berkeleian claim that a so-called visual sphere has, empirically speaking, as little in common with a tangible sphere as it has with a tangible cube, Hutcheson answers by drawing attention to the distinction that, whereas a single glance at a visible sphere may reveal no respect in which it is more like a tangible sphere than a tangible cube, a succession of views of the visible sphere, from different perspectives, will reveal that it corresponds closely to the sphere revealed by successive tactual explorations.

In attacking in this way the *New Theory of Vision*, which was so important to Berkeley as the foundation of his theological ethic, Hutcheson anticipated in outline the insight that was to prove so fundamental and fruitful for the entire Scottish school down to its final creative period in

---

[6] David Berman, "Francis Hutcheson on Berkeley and the Molyneux Problem," *Proceedings of the Royal Irish Academy*, 74:259-65.

the 1840s: Berkeley's arbitrary separation of the sense fields of sight and touch inevitably makes nonsense of our natural common-sense beliefs of perception, whereas, by contrast, a modern restatement of the traditional view of the two external senses as connected in the sense of being parallel or complementary not only brings us back to common sense in the current acceptation but, more importantly, enables us to restore and deepen the original meaning of the phrase "common sense" as it occurs in the Aristoteleian philosophy. Thus Hutcheson, in his argument with Berkeley in Ireland hits upon the vein of intersensorial speculation that was to be one of the chief inspirations of the Scottish philosophy of common sense. His analysis does not approach the profundity of later Scottish philosophers such as Smith, Reid, and Ferrier;[7] nevertheless, he is already, right at the beginning, fully master of the central insight at the basis of all these later insights, namely, that Berkeley's idealist paradoxes are the result of his excessive severance of touch from sight, and that the common sense of perception calls for a more enhanced role for the instinctive affinity of the two senses than Berkeley gives and for a correspondingly diminished role for the effect of mere external association as the thing holding them together. Stimulated by the brilliant originality of what the world considered Berkeley's metaphysical perversity, this northern Irishman, whose intellect had been formed in the renaissance of classical standards then under way in the Scottish universities — and not the least by the mathematical and philosophical lessons of his Glasgow teachers Robert Simpson and Gershom Carmichael, both of European eminence — thus opened in Dublin the line of inquiry that the Scottish philosophy of common sense was to follow with such distinguished results.

IV.

If we are to assess aright Hume's response to the criticism made of the *Fable of the Bees* by both Berkeley and Hutcheson, it is essential to bear in mind that appropriately enough to the privileged position of organized learning and of systematic argument in the Scottish way of life of the time, Hume's grasp of Mandeville's thesis considerably surpassed that of the Irish masters who were making such an impression on him. Appreciating the deeper side of what Mandeville said about the division of labor

---

[7] Each of whom presents a critique of Berkeley's *New Theory of Vision*.

and its advantages, Hume went beyond Hutcheson and Berkeley in understanding that the value of the exchange economy became palpable to the producers engaged in it only gradually, when the slow course of experience made them aware that the overall long-term economic benefit to society as a whole was the unintended consequence of the extension of a specialization that had arisen and developed in a haphazard manner prompted by local short-term arrangements. Furthermore, Hume is noteworthy for seeing even more clearly than did Mandeville himself that the system of equality before the law, necessary to the smooth working of the exchange and specialization system, does not require, as Hutcheson had thought, a concerted effort of warmhearted public-spiritedness, kept alive from pulpits and professorial chairs, to maintain its efficaciousness and even to bring it into being as a system of justice. Like the division-of-labor system with which it is so closely connected, equality before the law emerges as an accepted public institution only as the unintended consequence of a slow growth of the habit of piecemeal accommodation between individual participants in exchanges having nothing more in view than the narrow aim of mutual convenience. Stressing the thesis that the system of justice "comprehending the interests of each individual," though "of course advantageous to the public, . . . [was] not intended for that purpose by its inventors," Hume goes on in the sequel to denounce Hutcheson's idea that competitive individualism will not work in the interests of society as a whole unless a warmhearted morality of benevolence intervenes to check the inherent tendency to social divisiveness by ensuring due enforcement of the principles of justice appropriate to a commercial society.[8] Properly understood, the provocative slogan of "private vices, public benefits" contains the great truth, misunderstood by Hutcheson, that the principles of justice insuring the kind of equitable distribution appropriate to the productive system are brought into being and maintained, without any need for the preaching of public morality, by an analogous operation of the principle of unintended consequences that is also responsible for the spontaneous slow development of the division-of-labor system into the accepted principle of public economy. Without denying outright the reality of moral standards, Hume goes on to argue that the concerted efforts to generate enthusiasm for public

---

[8] *A Treatise of Human Nature*, ed. L. A. Selby-Bigge (Oxford, 1888), III, II, VI, p. 529 (hereafter cited as *Treatise*). Hume's position can be properly understood only if due weight is given to the discussion of the division of labor, found at the beginning of III, II, II.

morality are not, as Hutcheson seems to think, essential to the reconciliation of economic growth with the standards of civilization. Replying to Hutcheson's criticism of the point, Hume indicated that it would not be proper to introduce passages in praise of the beauty of virtue—passages meant to encourage the cultivation of public-spiritedness—in a book such as *A Treatise of Human Nature*, the aim of which is to try to bring to notice the sense in which the all-round social development of the standards of justice is, in the last analysis, less the result of planning and of moralistic intervention than of a sort of *laissez faire*.[9] Hutcheson no doubt thinks otherwise, but this is a topic which, as Hume jokingly points out in his letter of 1743, they will always be divided about.

At this point, however, there occurs one of these turnabouts in Hume's philosophy that have been so little understood.[10] After having explained at length the sense in which Mandeville is right and Hutcheson wrong, he abruptly proceeds to make clear the sense in which Hutcheson is right and Mandeville is wrong. Hutcheson, Hume says, was not wrong in upholding against Mandeville the fact of a moral sense—so far as it is constituted by my judgment as an impartial spectator, made possible by sympathy, upon the conduct of others and by my detached judgment upon myself—as coming about indirectly by my sympathetic identification with the sympathetic reaction of the spectators to myself. Where Hutcheson erred was in failing to see that the social role to be attributed to conscience is not moralistic, as an inspirer of public-spiritedness, but primarily and essentially logical or intellectual, as making possible the metaphysical self-transcendence essential to the impartiality of mind, required by science as well as by justice. As understood by Hume, Hutcheson's and Berkeley's problem of how to prevent a clash between Mandeville's program of economic growth and the standard of civilization is, so far as it is real, less a problem of morals and of moralizing, let alone theology, than a problem of knowledge—a problem even of producing systematic textbooks of scientific method that could be used as a vehicle of enlightenment.

Putting together the two points of view that Hutcheson had set against one another, Hume thus sees society's development as an interconnected operation at two levels. What he means is that the intellectual traffic in

---

[9] *The Letters of David Hume*, ed. J. Y. T. Greig, 2 vols. (Oxford: Clarendon Press, 1932), 1:35, esp. p. 47 (hereafter cited as *Letters*).
[10] *Treatise*, III, II, II, pp. 498-501.

ideas and theory that criticizes and modifies specialized production grows up side by side with the traffic in wares, being made possible by this latter. Originally not an object of distinct consciousness on its own account, the intellectual element in the social process, according to Hume, emerges to the view of the participants as a separate department, only when, with the growth of the community in size and complexity, the developments in the sciences and the arts and law cannot be carried through without a sufficient element of the free criticism of inherited taboos.[11] In a series of stimulating essays outlining his views on the sociology of knowledge,[12] Hume argues that in this conscious emergence of the intellectual side of the process as a relatively independent department, "according to the necessary progress of things,"[13] law must precede science. First, the growth of the division of labor, at least so far as concerns the rise of the "vulgar arts . . . of commerce and manufacture,"[14] creates the conditions for the rise of justice and law as a public institution. Subsequently, the mutual criticism and argument about the nature and application of laws that occurs in free societies[15] prepares the way for the higher branches of science such as philosophy and ethics, as well as for the exact sciences, which, beginning on an informal, trial and error basis, become established and institutionalized forms only when experience has enabled society to appreciate their relevance. Still building on Mandeville's foundations, but reconciling them with Hutcheson's ideas about the fundamental role of impartiality and detachment in civilization, Hume elaborates his vision of the development of the economy, law, and the sciences as interconnected elements in the spontaneous "ferment" that constitutes civilization.[16]

---

[11] Ibid., p. 499.

[12] See especially the connected trio from Part 1 of the essays, "Of Civil Liberty," "Of Eloquence," and "Of the Rise and Progress of the Arts and Sciences," and "Of Refinement in the Arts" in Part 2 (*The Philosophical Works*, ed. T. H. Green and T. H. Grose, 4 vols. [London, 1886], vol. 3 [hereafter cited as *Philosophical Works*]).

[13] Ibid., p. 180. On the previous page Hume notes that poetry and eloquence may in their turn precede law.

[14] Ibid., p. 303.

[15] For the relationship between free and unfree societies see "The Rise and Progress of the Arts and Sciences." According to Hume, it is the free societies that, through their liberty of opinion, make possible the inventiveness requisite to the rise of the arts and the sciences. The unfree societies, stifling inventiveness, develop chiefly by taking over techniques pioneered in the free societies; but, in compensation, they succeed in contributing to the movement of civilization certain qualities that are deficient in the free societies; for example, social discipline and polite deference.

[16] *Philosophical Works*, 3:301.

On the view I am taking it seems probable that the new "scene of thought," which Hume himself (as he reports in the Letter to a Physician) had found so overwhelming, arose from his sudden glimpse of the possibility that Mandeville's modern world of individualism, far from being incompatible with Hutcheson's social-minded doctrine, could not fulfill itself in the process of economic growth unless the individuals in question, in addition to their involvement with one another in the process of specialized production for exchange and profit, were also united with one another in a web of mutual sympathy or communication. By enabling each to enter into the other's point of view, this union made it possible for them to "see themselves as others see them," and thereby to acquire the sense of objectivity indispensable to the science and the justice required by an advanced economy. Without in the least denying Mandeville's *laissez faire* thesis that "through the joint labour of many ages" institutions "grow up in an unplanned way" that reconciles men's divergent interests, Hume goes on to challenge the implication that "the creation of even laws" that are to function as the rule for a given market society are brought about solely through the interplay of selfish interests and altogether apart from social feelings. On the other hand it would be impossible for the laws regulating commercial transactions and for the scientific standards required by a commercial society to become socially realized if the sympathetic identification with one's competitors — and also with disinterested third-party spectators — did not make it possible for the participants in the social process to become aware of their social blind spots and moral biases (in much the same way as one is able in sense perception to detect the illusions of a given sense by comparing its point of view with that of the other senses relevant to the situation). In this way Hume brings together Hutcheson's point about the analogy between the intersensorial and the interpersonal.[17]

But just at the very point where Hume seems to have brought to its full maturity the Hutchesonian project of a common-sense philosophy of progress by reconciling it with the Mandeville theory of free development that Hutcheson had found ethically unacceptable, there suddenly occurs a second and even more surprising turnabout. In responding to the strange and almost unearthly insights of Bishop Berkeley, Hume begins to subject the enlightenment philosophy, to which he has himself given a classic formulation, to a skeptical critique of an equally classic character

---

[17] See *Treatise*, pp. 581-82.

that, down to the present day, has perhaps never been adequately answered. Introducing the crisis of science he sees lurking beneath the surface of the movement of Western civilization as thus sketched, Hume starts from the point that the verification process, inseparable from the growth of science and law that guarantees continued progress, involves as a necessary component a social dimension (unnoticed by Cartesian individualism) constituted by the "sympathetic" communication of viewpoints between one leading section of the community and another. This makes possible the element of critical self-detachment essential to the maintenance of standards in the master science of philosophy and in the special sciences. At first sight, Hume goes on, this new sense of the social foundations of science bears a promising aspect for the present venture of civilization. As he points out in the piece written originally to introduce his essays as a whole,[18] the eighteenth century is witnessing a developing dialogue between the learned and the conversable—between the experts and the liberal-minded part of the laity—that is raising the intellectual standard of both parties and thus of society as a whole. This alters entirely the situation pertaining hitherto when, as the result of the intellectual barrier between the sections, the learned lost touch with practical life and wandered in merely speculative generalities, while the liberal laity could not rise above the particular and the inessential. Instead of taking an interest in history, poetry, politics, and even philosophy (at least, the easier parts) the laity occupied themselves with gossip and chitchat. Overcoming the atomizing sectionalization that had for centuries restrained progress, the ferment of public discussion characteristic of Western society in modern times not only enables the march of progress to reattain the classic heights it had reached in the best days of the Greeks and the Romans, but it seems to hold out the hope of building an even more durable civilization, in proportion as the guiding idea of philosophy since the Renaissance has a promise of surpassing in depth and solidity the philosophy by which ancient civilization steered itself.[19]

At the same time, in spite of these favorable prognostications, Hume was concerned to point out in his sociology of knowledge that there could be difficulties ahead for the progress of civilization. Formulating a principle of the inequality or peculiarity of cultural developments among the

---

[18] This suppressed essay on essay writing is found in *Philosophical Works*, 4:367-71.
[19] *An Enquiry concerning Human Understanding*, ed. L. A. Selby-Bigge, 2nd ed. (Oxford, 1902), I, p. 10.

various peoples constituting the spearhead of Western enlightenment, he argues that, owing to the unfathomably complicated conditions involved in the rise of cultures, they all suffer in one way or another from different intellectual weaknesses, either blind spots in their cultures or shallowness of their social bases. Thus, while there is no doubt a close connection between the rise of the vulgar arts of commerce and manufacture, on the one hand, and that of a properly constituted system of justice and equality before the law, on the other, there does not by any means seem to be so close a connection between a country's achievement of this combination of economics with justice and its subsequent appearance before the world as a hotbed of higher culture and science. Free societies such as Holland, despite the advanced state of their economy and their law, are nevertheless backward in literature and philosophy; and the English, too, notwithstanding their high achievements in trade and civil liberty, have certain noteworthy gaps—especially in the field of eloquence—to be set against their impressive list of achievements in philosophy and science. By contrast with the English and Dutch, the French can boast of a remarkable, many-sided intellectual achievement; yet the culture of France is somewhat of a fragile hothouse affair laboring under the obstacle that the society supporting it lacks civil liberty and is commercially backward. By bringing to light the relative independence of the cultural and intellectual side of society from its socio-economic side, Hume's sociology of knowledge also points to the existence of certain dangers to civilization that the next generation of Scottish philosophers were to highlight: the great advances in wealth and civil liberty, far from insuring a corresponding advance in higher science and culture, could hinder it; consequently the material progress of the West does not automatically guarantee the maintenance of a level of philosophy and invention adequate to insure the intellectual and scientific progress without which society is likely to stagnate or founder.[20]

But these reservations about the possibility of progress constitute only the beginning of Hume's warning to contemporary society. Deploying a skeptical detachment toward established dogma, which rivals in its boldness that of Berkeley, Hume proceeded to bring out the limitations of the Hutchesonian doctrine of social optimism by a highly original critique of

---

[20] Laurence Bongie's study of the reception of Hume's *History of England* in France is illuminating on this point (*David Hume: Prophet of the Counter-revolution* [Oxford: Clarendon Press, 1965]).

the social role of religion in which he presented it as a far more equivocal, not to say sinister, force in civilization than either the freethinkers or the Hutchesonian moralists could conceive. A recurrent factor in social life, religion, for Hume, constitutes the unpredictable, questionable element that, by its sudden upsurges, can reduce material progress to nothing by stultifying the critical debate essential to the advance of civilization. At the same time, however, religion occasionally leaves some unpredictable good in its wake — as happened in England when the enthusiastic subjectivism of the Puritans, which had done so much to foment the civil wars, mellowed into a principle of civil and religious liberty. Thus, although the freethinkers might be right in seeing religion as an unverifiable or even a nonsensical metaphysic responsible for much harm, they are quite wrong in their idea that otherworldly beliefs are due to die out in the new age of scientific enlightenment. On the other hand, establishment writers like Hutcheson, although they estimate better the likelihood of the continuing importance of religion in the life of modern society, are equally wrong in their estimate that religious belief, if critically and rationally presented, can provide a stable basis for the ethics of a civilized society. On the contrary, religion is likely to remain a principle of perverse irrationalism: "'Tis an observation suggested by all history that the religious spirit . . . contains in it something of the supernatural and unaccountable and that, in its operations upon society effects correspond less to their known causes than in any other circumstance of government."[21]

In such writings as the *Natural History of Religion* and the essay on miracles, Hume went on to give the reason why in his opinion religious phenomena were likely, for the foreseeable future, to defeat the calculations of the economists and the culture planners from which so much was hoped for. The fact of the matter was that, on the subject of religion, discussion between the learned and the vulgar does not lead to the same sort of common-sense consensus about standards that, in other fields of knowledge, were to serve as the support of civilization. Instead, it gives rise to irreconcilable disagreements of principle. Thus, in regard to the experimental sciences there can be some sort of *rapprochement* between the learned and the laity (not just the literate laity, but the masses). In the field of religion, on the other hand, concerned as it is with the transcendent, the teleological view of the experts is that the Divine is the imperceptible source of order and unity, whereas the vulgar (especially the

---

[21] *The History of England*, chap. 47, wherein James's visit to Scotland (1617) is described.

masses) regard it as the imperceptible source of whatever is capricious, accidental, and irrational. In a series of essays[22] as entertaining as they are penetrating, Hume boldly expounds views of the disturbing divisive role of religion that seem to have been considerably substantiated during the last 300 years in the area most familiar to him, namely, the Presbyterian belt, which stretches from the Lowlands of Scotland up into the Highlands and across the Celtic Sea into the North of Ireland.

The third and deepest phase of Humean skepticism—the one where the unearthliness, as I have called it, of the Berkeleian influence asserts itself against the earthiness of Hutcheson—commenced as soon as the question arose for Hume as to whether it would not be possible for him to sketch a philosophy of progress that, reconciling the Hutchesonian common sense with the scientific reductiveness and shortcuts proposed by the free thinkers, would serve as a guide to what mankind would be capable of if freed from the irrational spirit that religion keeps alive. After all, Hume allowed the religious spirit, in spite of its firm hold on society, to be probably a contingent, intrusive, "unnatural" element in mankind's equipment that it is possible to conceive as uprooted and abolished, at least in the distant future.[23] Why, then, should not Hume himself elaborate a blueprint for a complete system of enlightenment philosophy in the Baconian tradition? Gathering into one the valuable but fragmentary contributions found in the essays of English and Irish thinkers, this plan would bring together the learned and the vulgar in a fruitful program organized around the idea of experiment and observation, altogether freed from the irrationality of the suprasensible and supranatural. Indeed, so far as social philosophy was concerned, this common-sense goal had already been achieved by Hume himself, as the result of his criticizing Mandeville and Hutcheson in the light of one another. Why, then, should it not be possible to complete the system by extending it to cover the problem of our knowledge of nature, inherited from Descartes by way of Malebranche, Bayle, and Berkeley, not to mention Locke?

Hume was brought up in the education-minded polity of a Scotland in which, from 1690 to almost the end of the nineteenth century, the writing of academic textbooks of high quality was ranked among the greatest feats of literature. He was introduced to philosophy, moreover, by the works of living regents, the lectures of John Law of Edinburgh, and the

---

[22] That is, *The Natural History of Religion*.
[23] *Letters*, 1:150–51.

fine edition of Pufendorf by Gershom Carmichael of Glasgow. These scholars had played a prominent part in the controversial ambitions of preunion governments to restore the reputation of the country as a learned nation by sponsoring philosophical texts that might, at least so far as an academic introduction to the subject was concerned, be in some respects more satisfactory than those produced in other countries. Finally, Hume took as his mentor the professor of Ethics in Glasgow who, also brought up in the textbook tradition of Scotland, sought to write a compend capable of capturing the market from that of de Vries. Thus, Hume was ready on his own account, as he made clear in the essay on civil liberty, to admit the desirability of producing "a standard book which we can transmit to posterity." This would be a much better vehicle than those piecemeal monographs for making generally accessible as an instrument of enlightenment the first principles of the no-nonsense philosophy of experiment and observation that was England's great contribution to the modern world. In the event, however, the metaphysical difficulties Hume encountered in his prolonged struggle to produce such a book had the effect of convincing him that, however practicable the Baconian program might be from the standpoint of social philosophy, things stood quite differently in the even more fundamental field of intellectual philosophy—the philosophy of science. In the former it seemed to be plainly possible—at least if one kept out, by an abstraction, the irrationalities of religion—to evolve an experience-based philosophy that might serve both the vulgar and the learned, and through them the entire society, as a guide to social practice. By contrast, it was impossible in the latter complementary sphere—even if one kept out the religious element—to develop systematically a theory of sense perception calculated to do justice both to the learned and the vulgar standpoints without at the same time finding oneself involved not merely in the metaphysical nonsense one meant to avoid but, more seriously, in metaphysical nonsense so directly implicated in the experience under analysis as to be incapable of being in any way eliminated. Examining the implications of English empiricism in the light of the developments it had undergone when it came under the sharp scrutiny of the two sages of Dublin, Hume had found, in reference to the problem of the relation of knowledge to its sensory basis, that Hutcheson had been remarkably successful in reestablishing common sense about the intersensorial problem of sight and of touch against the fashionable reductivism that had formed the starting point for these strange Berkeleian speculations about the Divine visible language. But Hume also found that the Hutchesonian philosophy of common sense had proved powerless to shake Berkeley's even more unworldly speculations about our knowledge of the external world in which, by consistently pushing the simplifying positivist tendency to an extreme, which embarrassed its free-thinking proponents, he went on to demonstrate irrefutably the meaninglessness of our natural belief in body.

In the *Enquiry concerning Human Understanding* Hume speaks of the internal incoherence in the experimental philosophy that puts difficulties in the way of using it as an instrument of systematic enlightenment; namely, that the thesis about our knowledge of the external world expounded by Berkeley proves to be rationally founded to the point of irrefutability and yet incapable of carrying conviction, owing to its going against the "authority," as Kemp Smith acutely pointed out, of the Hutchesonian intuitionism. It is essential, I think, not only in the interests of Hume studies but even of the study of the classical Scottish philosophy in general, to understand that the contradiction spoken of by Hume is not between a rationally founded reduction of the *esse* of the body to its *percipi*, on the one hand, and a merely instinctive, nonrational refusal of this reduction on the other. Instead, the difficulty Hume brings to light is of a much subtler and deeper sort; *viz*, that in certain respects reason properly used is able to explain the grounding in experience of *some* of the paradoxical and seemingly transcendental aspects of the belief in body in accordance with the principles of classic common sense—the pooling of the sense fields of sight and of touch—revived by Hutcheson. There is no need to have recourse to the reductions that led Berkeley to his doctrine of the Divine visible language. But beyond that point, in reference to more fundamental aspects of belief in body (those involved in its existence as independent of perception), reason deserts Hutchesonian common sense and supports or seems to support the reductive paradoxes of Berkeley. Illustrated by reference to the point put forward in the *Dublin Post-boy* in 1732,[24] which irritated Berkeley so much,[25] the basis of the opposition between Berkeley and Hutcheson that was to reveal to Hume the impasse at the heart of the experimentalist program was as follows. The interpersonal as well as the intersensorial comparisons make

---

[24] "Had we but one sense, we might be apt to conclude there were no objects at all without us . . . but since the same object is the cause of ideas by different senses, thence we infer its existence" (Sept. 9 ed., in *Works*, 1:277).

[25] *Works*, 1:251.

it possible for me to have ideas of the relative independence of body that would not have been available to me if I had but one sense or lacked the possibility of sympathetic communion with another person. However, the same principle of sympathetic comparison cannot, as Berkeley pointed out, clarify and justify the natural belief of bodies existing unobserved by any human being except by introducing the idea—totally without foundation in our ordinary experience as understood by Hutcheson —of the bodies' continued existence, when unperceived by us, as objects of experience to some superhuman being who is in a position to communicate to us about them.[26] What Hume learned from Berkeley was thus that the problem of belief in the independent existence of body is the obstacle that utterly baffles Hutcheson's otherwise remarkably promising program of converting the English experimental philosophy into a kind of a social philosophy of classical common sense.

But it was not only in reference to the question of the empirical basis of our belief in the external world's transcendence that Berkeley's intervention established, so far as Hume was concerned, the impossibility of the *rapprochement* that the revival of the ancient principles of common sense might hope to bring about between the contrasting sides of natural consciousness that were being highlighted in the struggle between the rationalists and the empiricists—on the one hand, the transcendental perspectives it seems to give rise to; on the other, the earthbound empirical foundations in which it is rooted and to which in a sense it always seems to be confined. Thus it seems clear, with respect to the problem of mathematical foundations, that in the eyes of Hume the impact on the learned world of Berkeley's *Analyst* played a great and probably decisive role in exposing the futility of the chief rival views of geometry. There was the simplifying modernist view that, drawing its inspiration from the Cartesian device of reducing continuous or geometric quantity to discreet or arithmetical quantity, starts with the technical notion of a point as a *minimum visibile* or *tangibile* (an element capable of being empirically isolated in principle by sophisticated procedures) and then goes on to give a definition, incomprehensible to the vulgar, of a geometrical line as composed of a finite number of juxtaposed points and of a plane as composed of a finite number of lines. On the other side was the ancient holistic view of geometry taken by Hutcheson's mathematics teachers at Glasgow (anti-Cartesian and pro-Greek in their mathematics), according

---

[26] Ibid., 3:147.

to which a progressive series of comparisons, starting with ordinary three-dimensional bodies, elicits technical notions beyond the plain man's experience. By sensible abstraction this method discovers the germ of the Euclidean notion of lines and points in the familiar experience of the corners and the edges of things and then, by a revival of the method of exhaustion used by Archimedes and ancient geometers, ascends to the supersensible notion of a geometer's absolutely straight line or absolutely located point as entities capable of being approximated to without ever being reached. To the indignation of Scottish scientists Hume carried still further the skeptical critique of mathematics thus begun by Berkeley. He attacked with considerable severity the classical idea of the middle way in mathematics that, in a manner comparable to Hutcheson's work on the philosophy of society and of the sciences, Colin Maclaurin was contemporaneously engaged in developing as a counterblast to the *Analyst*. For Hume, the ancient method of starting with ordinary bodies in their concreteness and descending to their abstract aspects by "a distinction of reason," although it might work well enough at the level of sensible abstraction, entirely failed in its purpose at the subsequent stage of "mathematical abstraction." By appropriate comparisons of familiar objects such as roads it was possible to make sense, in a rough and ready way, of lines as possessing length without breadth; but the technical comparisons of the method of exhaustion, because they centered on the idea of approximating without ever reaching, were incapable of generating the quality of absoluteness required for mathematical accuracy. The modern method, however, based on the clear idea of the whole as nothing but the sum of separable parts—instead of the questionable idea of the whole as more than or different from the parts making it up—was up to a point more satisfactory logically. Properly understood, there was nothing absurd in principle about the idea of a line composed of a finite number of extensionless points, or *minima sensibilia*; yet, as Hume went on to point out, in the last analysis this reductivism was of no practical use in illuminating the basic ideas of Euclid since, as a matter of fact, *minima sensibilia* are incapable, either visibly or palpably, of being given in concrete isolation. Arguing in this way, that the Greek method, though perhaps practically useful in instruction and textbooks, is illogical, while the modern method, though logical, is unilluminating in practice, Hume is thus able to confront would-be revivers of the ancient philosophy of common sense with an embarrassing demonstration. However effective its comparative methods of the middle way are in clearing up some of the modern problems (in particular those concerned with the interpersonal and the intersensorial), it nevertheless has nothing comparable to offer in reference to the most important problem thrown up in post-Renaissance time, namely, the elucidation of the very thing that had made the running in all the social and material advances—the method of uniting mathematics with experiment in the investigation of nature.

Viewed as a somewhat uneasy compromise between the Berkeleian paradoxes about the material world as the object of the exact sciences, on the one hand, and Hutcheson's social philosophy of common sense, on the other, the *Treatise of Human Nature*, despite Hume's attempts to give it a rounded appearance, hardly achieves the systematic character essential to the sort of "standard-book" envisaged by him that could organize the piecemeal insights of his empiricist predecessors for "transmission to posterity." Moreover, Hume's difficulties in holding the two sides together were not resolved by the publication of the *Treatise*, and the more he pondered the problem the harder it seems to have become for him to uphold the claims of the vulgar consciousness against the philosophical doubts. Especially with the emergence of the contradictions about personal identity discussed in the appendix to *Treatise* III, Hume began to feel that the skeptical element was poised for a new thrust that would undermine the ordinary notions of conscience and self-valuation fundamental to the proper development of the Hutchesonian line in social philosophy and thus invade still more deeply whatever remained of systematism. Making the best of what was for him a bad situation, Hume suddenly set aside intellectual crisis by giving up the project of systematization in a grand manner, and by going back to the method of piecemeal exposition through essays, from which he had once hoped to escape. The result is the production of a sort of second philosophy, in which, without either concealing the skeptical element or pushing it to extremes, he sought to cover the entire field of human nature from theology and theory of knowledge to economics and aesthetics in a markedly serial manner that does not emphasize the difficulties of finding interconnections.

However, Hume's repudiation of system did not prevent the other Scottish philosophers from taking up the problem where he left it. In course after course of lectures, professor after professor—Reid, Stewart, Brown, Hamilton, Ferrier, and Adam Smith, in some ways the greatest of them all — sought to overcome the tension between the common sense of Hutcheson and the paradoxes of Berkeley by producing a system that would harmonize the standpont of the vulgar with the standpoint of the learned in a moderate philosophy of modern progress. Understood against the background of this century-long chain of thinkers, Sir James Mackintosh is surely quite right in presenting the two Irish philosophers, the opposition between whom is still visible in Ferrier's lectures in 1850, as having, by their co-operation, awakened and kept alive the metaphysical genius of Scotland.[27]

---

[27] For example, see the problem posed in *Treatise*, I, II, IV.

A Prussian Hume and a Scottish Kant

Lewis White Beck

I

IN A LETTER TO HERDER WRITTEN IN 1781, Hamann said of Kant, "He certainly deserves the title 'a Prussian Hume'."[1] No one, so far as I know, has had the temerity to state explicitly that Hume deserves the title "a Scottish Kant." However, one trend in contemporary Hume-interpretation may finally lead someone to make this claim, or accusation. H. H. Price refers to "a Scottish version of Kant's Copernican Revolution."[2] Robert Paul Wolff finds that Hume's propensities "play a role quite similar to that of the categories in the *Critique of Pure Reason*."[3] W. H. Walsh says of the Humean imagination that it is "simply the Kantian understanding in disguise."[4]

The traditional notion that Kant and Hume are diametrically opposed, and that whatever merit Kant's philosophy has depends upon his having given a cogent "answer to Hume," does not seem as obvious as it used to. Although no one would deny that the great divide between naturalism and transcendentalism[5] in the theory of knowledge separates these two thinkers, even that divide is not as clear-cut as it once appeared, and it is now rendered somewhat obscure by emphasis upon a pragmatism[6] believed to be pervasive in their constructions of a common world out of private experiences. With growing attention to the role of normative structures in Hume's analysis of experience, and to the possibility of

---

Reprinted by kind permission of the publisher from Lewis White Beck, *Essays on Kant and Hume* (New Haven: Yale University Press, 1978).

[1] *Hamann Briefwechsel,* ed. W. Ziesemer and A. Henkel, 8 vols. (Wiesbaden: Insel-Verlag, 1955), 4:293.

[2] *Hume's Theory of the External World* (Oxford: Oxford University Press, 1940), p. 9. See also F. W. Dauer, "Towards a Copernican Reading of Hume," *Nous* 9 (1975): 269-95.

[3] "Hume's Theory of Mental Activity," in *Hume,* ed. V. C. Chappell (Garden City, N.Y.: Anchor Books, 1966), p. 127.

[4] "Hume's Concept of Truth," in *Reason and Reality* (Royal Institute of Philosophy Lectures 1970-71), pp. 99-116, at end.

[5] R. A. Mall, "Humes Prinzipien- und Kants Kategoriensystem," *Kant-Studien* 62 (1971):319-34; idem, "Naturalismus und Kritizismus: Hume und Kant," *Akten des IV. internationalen Kant-Kongresses* (1974), Part 2, pp. 30-41.

[6] G. B. Mathur, "Hume, Kant, and Pragmatism," *Journal of the History of Ideas* 16 (1955):198-208. But see, to the contrary, W. L. Robison, "On the Consequential Claim that Hume is a Pragmatist," *Journal of Critical Analysis* 4 (1974):141-53.

relativizing the hard, fixed categorial lines found in Kant's analysis, it becomes possible to see Kant and Hume as engaged in a common project.[7] I do not wish to go too far and talk as if the differences were less important than the similarities between these two men. But I do wish to make it appear meet, fitting, and seemly to talk about Kant in a volume assessing Hume's thought—something that would, I think, have appeared thirty or forty years ago to be in bad taste.

The problem of causation has traditionally been seen as the bone of contention between Hume and Kant. I shall argue that, on the contrary, it is precisely here that a surprising degree of accommodation between them is possible. To this end, I shall first recount Kant's stand on the conception of causality both before and after Hume awoke him from his dogmatic slumber.[8] I shall then show that Kant misunderstood Hume's views in the *Treatise* but that this misunderstanding was a fruitful one. Finally, I shall try to show that something in fact needed by Hume but not supplied in the *Treatise* is given by Kant in his attempt to refute the point he erroneously believed to have been argued for by Hume.

II

Kant's treatment of the problem of causation goes through three distinct phases, which I shall call the pre-Humean, the quasi-Humean, and the post-Humean.[9]

---

[7] The most comprehensive treatment of the relations between Hume and Kant is to be found in Henri Lauener's *Hume und Kant: Systematische Gegenüberstellung einiger Hauptpunkte ihrer Lehren* (Bern und Munich: Francke, 1969); but this well-balanced book does not, in my opinion, break any new ground. See also, Hansgeorg Hoppe, "Kants Antwort auf Hume," *Kant-Studien* 62 (1971):335-50.

[8] The theory of affinity will have to be omitted from this discussion both because of lack of space and because of its perplexing obscurity. Its bearing upon Hume's "pre-established harmony between the course of nature and the succession of our ideas" repays careful study. See Henry E. Allison, "Transcendental Affinity—Kant's Answer to Hume," *Proceedings of the Third International Kant Congress* (1970), pp. 303-11.

[9] It seems hardly possible to formulate an account of Kant's gradually increasing knowledge of Hume that fits *all* the apparent facts. For a long time there has been extensive controversy concerning it. The account given here is a summary of my narrative in *Early German Philosophy* (Cambridge, Mass.: Harvard University Press, 1969), pp. 424-25, 451-53, 465-67, which, in turn, is in general agreement with Vaihinger, *Kommentar zu Kants Kritik der reinen Vernunft*, 2 vols. (Leipzig, 1881-92), 1:344-47. Vaihinger surveys all the polemical literature before his time, and most of his conclusions seem to me not to have been rendered less plausible by significant work done since his time. See L. Robinson, "Contributions à l'histoire de l'évolution philosophique de Kant," *Revue de metaphysique et de morale* 31 (1924):269-353, esp. 303ff. See also below, n. 20.

1. In 1755, the year Sulzer translated Hume's *Enquiry concerning Human Understanding*, Kant was busy criticizing Wolff's derivations of the causal principle from that of sufficient reason and of the latter from the principle of contradiction. But in the work he wrote that year, the *Nova dilucidatio*, he attempted to give a rationalistic proof of the principle of efficient causality. This proof is vulnerable to Hume's refutation of all such arguments, which is to be found in the *Treatise*, I, III, III, but Kant was at that time, and perhaps always, ignorant of Hume's refutation.

2. In 1763, in the essay *Versuch, den Begriff der negativen Grössen in die Weltweisheit einzuführen*, Kant gave up his rationalistic arguments to demonstrate the logical necessity of causal judgments. Logical necessity, he says, depends upon identity and contradiction, but any causal judgment may be denied without contradiction, and no statement of identity entails a causal connection between things not identical: "The rain never follows the wind because of the law of identity"[10] Now, admittedly, this does sound like Hume, and by this time Kant had certainly read Sulzer's translation. But one cannot be sure that these new ideas are to be attributed to his reading of Hume, for there was another philosopher nearer home who had definitely influenced Kant and whose thoughts moved in the same direction. This was Christian August Crusius, an anti-Wolffian who had taught (if I may use later Kantian terminology) that the principle of causation, like every specific causal judgment, is synthetic and not analytic; and that the principle of causation, unlike any specific causal judgment, is a priori and not known as a result of induction. Although Crusius had given an account of the proclivity of the mind to think causally—not wholly unlike that given later by Thomas Reid—Kant then and always rejected Crusius's explanation because it required, he thought, a belief in a pre-established harmony and permitted a subjective necessity to masquerade as an objective necessity.[11] In 1763, however, Kant had little to say about his own theory of causation, and what he says is obscure and tentative.

Three years later, in the *Träume eines Geistersehers*, Kant writes in an ironic, semiskeptical manner strongly reminiscent of Hume. He insists

---

[10] *Kants gesammelte Schriften*, ed. the Prussian Academy of Sciences (Berlin, 1902–), 2:204 (hereafter cited as Ak).

[11] Kant to K. L. Reinhold, 19 May 1789, in *Kant's Philosophical Correspondence*, trans. Arnulf Zweig (Chicago: University of Chicago Press, 1967), p. 144; Reflexionen 4375, 4446 (Ak. 17:492, 554).

that causal connections are not intelligible, that is, not founded on reason, but appear to us to be intelligible simply because they are made familiar to us through repetitive experience. "That my will is capable of moving my arm is no more comprehensible to me than if someone told me he could stop the moon in its orbit."[12] "The grounds of reason, whether used as an argument for or against the possibility or impossibility of a thing, are absolutely irrelevant. The right of decision must be left to experience [*Erfahrungen*] alone."[13] The ultimate and irreducible causes of things, the *Grundkräfte*, are either unknown or unintelligible to us, and the a posteriori contingency of every causal judgment demands that the way be left open for continual revision of our putative causal knowledge. Kant, in good Humean idiom though citing only Voltaire, appeals to mankind to remain within the limits of experience, since specific causal knowledge is founded on and extends only as far as experience.

Although the sentiments in the ironical work resemble those we would expect Hume to express in the face of the fantastic stories of Swedenborg, once again there is no decisive reason to ascribe this essay to Hume's influence on Kant. Such ideas as those I have mentioned were widely accepted in Germany at this time, among natural scientists such as Maupertuis and anti-Wolffian philosophers such as Crusius and his extensive school, and Berlin enlighteners.[14] The skeptical conclusions that are so prominent a feature of Hume's *Enquiry* are here hardly more than obiter dicta; there is no argument that causal inferences depend upon irrational propensities in the mind and are instinctive. Most of the Humean ideas in this essay were very much in the air in Germany, and it would be difficult or impossible to trace them to one source.[15]

3. The post-Humean phase of Kant's treatment of causation is well

---

[12] Ak. 2:370 (trans. John Manolesco [New York: Vantage Press, 1969], p. 95). Almost the same example, used for the same purpose, is to be found in Hume's *Enquiry concerning Human Understanding,* ed. L. A. Selby-Bigge, 2nd ed. (Oxford, 1902), VII, I, p. 65: "planets in their orbits" (hereafter cited as first *Enquiry*).

[13] Ak. 2:371 (Manolesco, 96).

[14] Moses Mendelssohn, *Gedanken über die Wahrscheinlichkeit, Gesammelte Schriften,* ed. D. Elbogen, J. Guttmann, and E. Mittwoch (Berlin: Akademie-Verlag, 1929–), 1:156, says that Sulzer's translation of the *Enquiry* "is in everyone's hands."

[15] This is the conclusion reached by Giorgio Tonelli, "Die Anfänge von Kants Kritik der Kausalbeziehungen und ihre Voraussetzungen im 18. Jahrhundert," *Kant-Studien* 57 (1966):417–60. (I am indebted to Professor Tonelli also for a personal communication on how widespread was the knowledge of Hume's works in Germany.)

known. As I shall repeatedly have to refer to it in later parts of this paper, a brief historical account will suffice at this time. We must consider three events of the years 1770 and 1772.

(a) In 1770 Kant published his Inaugural Dissertation, which sharply separated the sensible from the rational faculties in man, distinguished between the sensible, or phenomenal, world and the intelligible, or noumenal, world, and formulated the a priori forms of both. The proper method of metaphysics, which is now seen as the systematic knowledge of the intelligible world, requires preventing the ascription of the forms of sensible knowledge (space and time) to the objects of pure reason; space and time are the subjective ways things look to human beings, but metaphysics is to deal with things as they are, and most errors in metaphysics arise from the surreptitious application of spatial and temporal predicates to purely intelligible things. Though Kant is copious in his elaboration of the forms of sensibility—so much so that his treatment passes over almost without change into the Transcendental Aesthetic of the *Critique of Pure Reason*—he finds comparatively little to say about pure intelligible forms. What he does say is hardly more than a warmed-over version of some parts of Wolff's ontology, and this little is jettisoned when he comes to write the Dialectic of the *Critique of Pure Reason*; for by then he has realized that there is no synthetic knowledge of what is not spatial and temporal. But this was not his belief in 1770, and he confidently expected to proceed immediately with his metaphysical writings that would expound the principles of pure reason in their application to a purely intelligible world.

Toward the end of the Dissertation, however, he introduces a strangely hybrid form of principle, principles that have a *purely subjective though purely intellectual origin*: "They are commended to us only by the special nature of the intellect, owing to their convenience for its free and extended employment . . . upon conditions under which the intellect seems to itself to make easy and ready use of its insight." They are "principles of convenience," or "rules of judgment, to which we willingly submit and to which we cling as if they were axioms [which they are not], solely for the reason that if we gave them up, scarcely any judgment about a given object would be possible to our intellect."[16] The first of these rules of convenience is the principle of causality according to the law of nature.

---

[16] *Forms and Principles of the Sensible and Intelligible Worlds*, sec. 30.

(b) In his famous letter of 21 February 1772 to Marcus Herz, Kant refers to an objection raised by Lambert[17] to the Inaugural Dissertation's application of theoretical concepts (presumably including the concept of causation) to purely intelligible objects. He confesses that in writing what he is now engaged upon, the *Critique of Pure Reason*, he noticed that "something essential was lacking" in his account of how purely intelligible concepts, which originate a priori in the mind, can refer to objects: "If such intellectual conceptions depend on our inner activity, whence comes the agreement that they are supposed to have with objects?"[18] He rejects the answers given by Plato, Malebranche, and Crusius but does not give his own answer; rather, he claims to have found a rule or rules for the discovery of such concepts. To use the later terminology of the *Critique*, he has discovered the root of the Metaphysical Deduction of the Categories and presumably thinks that it can do the work later assigned to the Transcendental Deduction of the Categories,[19] for he expresses confidence that the book will be finished in three months.

(c) What led to the extension of the three months to nine years? The third event is more conjectural, but I believe there is sufficient evidence to substantiate it. At Easter time, 1772, there was published a German translation of Beattie's *Essay on the Nature and Immutability of Truth*.[20] Suddenly, through copious quotations, there was opened to Kant many of the riches of Hume's *Treatise of Human Nature*. Kant now realized

---

[17] See my *Essays on Kant and Hume* (New Haven: Yale Univeristy Press, 1978), pp. 107-9.

[18] In Zweig, p. 72.

[19] See H. J. de Vleeschauwer, *La Déduction transcendentale dans l'oeuvre de Kant*, 3 vols. (1934-37; reprint ed., New York: Garland Publishing Co., 1976), 1:171, 217ff, for a different interpretation of the order of discovery.

[20] Vaihinger (*Kommentar*, 1:347) seems to have been the originator of this hypothesis. It is defended most fully by Robert Paul Wolff, "Kant's Debt to Hume via Beattie," *Journal of the History of Ideas* 21 (1960):117-23. It is possible that Kant had not hitherto known even of the existence of Hume's *Treatise*; Tetens, whose knowledge of things English (and of the English language) was better than Kant's, referred to Hume and to "the heroic skeptic, the author of the *Treatise of Human Nature*" as if they were two different men (*Ueber die allgemeine spekulativische Philosophie* (1775), ed. Wilhelm Uebele [Berlin: Reuther & Reichard, 1913], p. 12). Karl Groos, "Hat Kant Humes Treatise gelesen?" *Kant-Studien* 5 (1901): 177-81, points to some striking resemblances, partly verbal and partly substantive (dealing with existence as a predicate), between the *Treatise* and Kant's *Einzig möglicher Beweisgrund zu einer Demonstration des Daseins Gottes* (1763), and proffers them as evidence (against Benno Erdmann's "Kant und Hume um 1762," *Archiv für Geschichte der Philosophie* 1 [1887]:62-77, 216-30) that Kant had been influenced by the *Treatise*; but Wolff (p. 122) has located possible common sources for both Hume and Kant.

that Hume had not confined his skeptical attacks to the putative necessity and intelligibility of specific causal judgments—attacks he himself had participated in—but had raised a serious problem about the causal principle itself. In Beattie's words, "Our opinion of the necessity of a cause to the production of everything which hath a beginning, is by Mr. Hume supposed to arise from observation and experience."[21]

It was this suggestion (*Erinnerung*)[22] of Hume's that awoke Kant from his "dogmatic slumber."[23] He was "far from following [Hume] in the conclusions he arrived at by regarding, not the whole of his problem, but

---

Upon reading Beattie in 1772, Kant was oddly selective in what he learned, saying that Hume had examined only part of his problem, that concerned with cause and effect (*Prolegomena*, Ak., 4:260). Yet from Beattie he could have learned of the following topics in the *Treatise* absent from the *Enquiry*: the status of material objects, and the identity of the self. He might have learned, too, from a cryptic note in Beattie (*Essay on the Nature and Immutability of Truth* [Edinburgh, 1770], p. 162; German trans. [Copenhagen and Leipzig, 1772], p. 125n.), that Hume was a skeptic about geometry, but he continued to ascribe to Hume only the mathematical teaching of the *Enquiry* (see *Kritik der praktischen Vernunft*, Ak., 5:14). In spite of this, there is so striking a resemblance between Kant's explanation of why "A straight line is the shortest distance between two points" is not analytic (*Critique of Pure Reason*, B 16) and Hume's explanation of why it is not a definition (*A Treatise of Human Nature*, ed. L. A. Selby-Bigge [Oxford, 1888], I, II, IV, pp. 49-50 [hereafter cited as *Treatise*]) that one can hardly believe that Kant did not know of Hume's argument; yet the passage in question is not in Beattie.

[21] *Essay*, p. 108; German trans., p. 85. I do not wish to challenge Beattie's statement that this was Hume's opinion, though so far as I can see, it is not ever explicitly argued for in the *Treatise* or elsewhere. A reader properly primed by an earlier reading of the *Treatise* might perhaps discern the view in the first *Enquiry* (IV, II, p. 35, 5 lines from foot of page), but the *Enquiry* so conflates the two questions formally separated in the *Treatise* that it is never clear (even in the passage just alluded to) that Hume is discussing the causal maxim and not some specific causal generalization. In the letter to John Stewart in 1754 (*The Letters of David Hume*, ed. J. Y. T. Greig, 2 vols. [Oxford: Clarendon Press, 1932], 1:187; hereafter cited as *Letters*), he asserts that the certainty of the falsity of the proposition that anything might arise without a cause proceeds "neither from Intuition nor Demonstration; but from another Source"—presumably experience. But this remains a presumption based solely on the exclusion of the two alternatives Hume does discuss and is never supported by any positive argument.

[22] In my edition of the *Prolegomena* (Indianapolis: Bobbs-Merrill, 1950) I translated *Erinnerung* as if it referred to Kant's recollection of what Hume had said, not to Hume's suggestion or hint, and explained my choice in a footnote. In *Early German Philosophy*, p. 465, n. 104, I wavered; now I wish to renounce that translation not merely on grammatical grounds (the 1950 reading was strained) but on the grounds that Kant could not, in 1772, have "recollected" what Hume had said.

[23] Kant used the metaphor "dogmatic slumber" several times. In *Prolegomena*, §50, he says that the antinomy is "a very powerful agent to arouse philosophy from its dogmatic slumber." Robinson has concluded that the allusion to Hume in the introduction is not meant to be historically accurate, but is an "exposé d'un caractère préconçue et plutôt

a part"; he "generalized" Hume's problem and found that "the connection of cause and effect was by no means the only concept by which the understanding thinks the connections of things a priori."[24] Thus was born the fundamental question, How are synthetic judgments possible a priori? Kant finds Hume to be correct in rejecting the possibility of necessary synthetic judgments that go beyond experience, but he thinks Hume was in error in failing to see the difference between a priori in the sense of "going beyond possible experience" and a priori in the sense of "underlying possible experience."[25] As heretofore, he accepts Hume's conclusion that all specific causal judgments are contingent, but under the tutelage of Beattie he states, "Hume was in error in inferring from the contingency of our determinations in accordance with the law [of causality] the contingency of the law itself."[26]

Had Beattie not said that Hume treated the causal principle in the same way that he had dealt with specific causal laws, and with the same skeptical conclusions,[27] there would have been no interruption of Kant's dogmatic slumber. But I shall now attempt to show that Beattie, though he could have documented his statement (he did not) with at most two or three quotations from the *Treatise*, may have misled Kant into thinking that there was an argument to which he needed to reply, not just an "opinion." There is no such argument, and Hume's implicit account of the causal principle is much more like Kant's own than Kant had any reason to suspect. This suggests that we owe the inception of the *Critique of Pure Reason* to a fortunate historical error.

---

systématique du rapport de sa doctrine avec celle de Hume" (p. 305). This I find hardly credible, especially since the tone of the introduction passage, unlike that of §50, is autobiographical. Benno Erdmann, in his edition of *Prolegomena* ([Leipzig, 1878], pp. lxxxv-vi) argues that the passage in §50 refers to 1769, the year that "brought great light" and prepared the way for the Inaugural Dissertation, which showed that intelligible objects are not spatial (the first consequence of the antinomy); that the allusion to Hume in the introduction refers to the very different problem that arose after the Dissertation; and that the two passages were allowed to stand in the *Doppelredaktion* that the *Prolegomena* underwent as a result of the Garve-Feder review. According to Erdmann's stratification of the text, §50 was in the original manuscript, and the Hume passage was added in the revision.

But in a letter to Garve (21 September 1798, in Zweig, p. 252) the autobiographical claim, missing from §50, is supplied when Kant says that the antinomy "is what first aroused me from my dogmatic slumber." This is indeed puzzling. Can it be due to a lapse of memory? The letter is filled with complaints about Kant's declining health and mental abilities.

[24] *Prolegomena*, Ak., 4:260.
[25] *Critique of Pure Reason*, A 765 = B 793.
[26] Ibid., A 766 = B 794.
[27] Beattie, of course, believed that the principle was known intuitively.

III

Hume distinguishes two questions concerning necessary connection: (a) "For what reason we pronounce it *necessary*, that every thing whose existence has a beginning, shou'd also have a cause?" and (b) "Why we conclude, that such particular causes must *necessarily* have such particular effects."[28] I shall simplify and restate these by referring to them respectively as the questions of (a) why every event necessarily has some cause, and (b) why the same cause necessarily has the same effect. Still more briefly, I shall refer to the two principles Hume is investigating as (a) every-event-some-cause and (b) same-cause-same-effect.

Hume concludes that the principle every-event-some-cause is not known by intuition or reason and hence that "that opinion must necessarily arise from observation and experience," but I look in vain for an answer to the question Hume now formulates concerning "*how experience gives rise to such a principle.*" Having asked this question, he not only never answers it, he does not even discuss it again.

He finds that it will be "more convenient" to answer the question *why same-cause-same-effect* and then to "sink" the question *why every-event-some-cause* in it, in the expectation that "'twill, perhaps, be found in the end, that the same answer will serve for both questions."[29] This conjecture leads us to expect a Mill-like argument that the former principle is an induction from cases falling under the latter, an induction from successful inductions, for that is the only way in which the principle every-event-some-cause could possibly arise from observation and experience. But, as we shall see, Hume does not anticipate Mill's argument and, in fact, never answers the first question at all. Though he says "it is universally allowed that nothing exists without a cause of its existence,"[30] he also grants that it is easy to conceive "that there is no absolute nor metaphysical necessity, that every beginning of existence shou'd be attended with [a cause]."[31] Question (a), having once been sunk in question (b), never re-emerges.

Rather, I shall try to show that the principle every-event-some-cause remains on dry land, ready to rescue the principle same-cause-same-effect when the latter is threatened by recalcitrant experience. Hume availed

---

[28] *Treatise*, I, III, II, p. 78.
[29] Ibid., III, p. 82.
[30] First *Enquiry*, VIII, I, p. 95. See Hume to Stewart, February 1754, *Letters*, 1:187.
[31] *Treatise*, I, III, XIV, p. 172.

himself of the principle every-event-some-cause precisely in those cases where the intimate connection he had discovered among regular sequence, contiguity, association, belief, and causation can get no purchase on experience because regular sequence is lacking.

Had the application of the two principles always had the same occasion and outcome, naturally Hume would have preferred to use the second, which he does fully account for. But where they do not, he uses the first to permit the extrapolation of the second beyond and even against the teachings of experience, and he gives much the same kind of practical justification for so using it that he had already given for using the principle same-cause-same-effect. Usually Hume warns against giving causal explanations where there is no association of ideas and induction to back them up, thinking that that is the operation of fancy. But there is at least one instance of the proper use of causal explanation that is both counter-associational and practically justified.

I refer to Hume's account of the porter's coming into his room. Hume is sitting in his chamber when suddenly he hears a noise as of a door opening and a little after sees a porter advance upon him with a letter. "This gives occasion to many new reflexions and reasonings," as follows:

> To consider these phaenomena of the porter and the letter in a certain light, they are contradictions to common experience [in which the sound of a door opening is commonly associated with the sight of its opening], and may be regarded as objections to those maxims, which we form concerning the connexions of causes and effects. I am accustom'd to hear such a sound, and see such an object in motion at the same time. I have not receiv'd in this particular instance both these perceptions. These observations are contrary. . . .[32]

The conclusion is that "as all reasoning concerning matters of fact arises only from custom, and custom can only be the effect of repeated perceptions, the extending of custom and reasoning beyond the perceptions can never be the direct and natural effect of the constant repetition and connexion, but must arise from the co-operation of some other principles."[33]

Before considering what these other principles are, we must say something about the role of principles and general rules in Hume's philosophy.[34] Hume often writes, and is usually read, as if belief and causal belief

---

[32] Ibid., IV, II, pp. 196–97.
[33] Ibid., p. 198.
[34] See Walsh, *Reason and Reality*; Thomas K. Hearn, Jr. "'General Rules' in Hume's

are created in us passively by the mechanism of association. Yet Hume is not content to explain why we believe as we do; he wants to give rules for the correction of our beliefs. These rules, of course, do not have a transcendental origin or sanction, though they function normatively as if they were a priori regulative. What they are is revealed in Hume's study of the functions of the imagination whereby we may believe mere coincidences to be causally connected, and in his study of "the general and more establish'd properties of the imagination," which is understanding,[35] whereby the brute-custom origin of causal beliefs is refined by more cautious inquiry, and superstition is made to give way to science. The human mind is in constant battle with itself:[36] there is a struggle between its instinctive inference to causation from mere association that may be accidental, on the one hand, and its reflective weighing of evidence to achieve a conception of the world less affected by the vagaries of accidental experience, on the other. Hume remarks that "reflexion on *general rules* keeps us from augmenting our belief upon every increase of the force and vivacity of our ideas."[37]

What is needed in the case of the porter is the inverse of this consideration: a reflection on the general rule every-event-some-cause keeps us from *reducing* our belief in same-cause-same-effect upon every diminution of force and vivacity of our ideas that occurs when the impression generally associated with an idea is lacking. Regrettably, Hume does not cite this general rule, which cannot have originated in the same way as did the generalization that is contradicted by the case of the porter. Rather, he cites explicitly only the general rule that objects intermittently perceived should be ascribed continued existence when thought governed by this rule will increase the coherence of experience. Presumably, he cited only this rule because of his predominant concern in that chapter with the status of unobserved objects.[38] The general rule arises from the

---

Treatise," *Journal of the History of Philosophy* 8 (1970):405-22; P. V. Vanterpool, "Hume's Account of General Rules," *Southern Journal of Philosophy* 12 (1974):481-92.

[35] *Treatise*, I, IV, VII, 267; II, III, IX, 440.

[36] Ibid., I, III, XIII, p. 147. Similarly, in moral judgment there is a conflict between immediate sympathy and "general establish'd maxims" (ibid., II, I, VI, pp. 293-94).

[37] Ibid., App. p. 632.

[38] Price (p. 8) complains about the order in which Hume discusses necessary connection and the existence of objects, which misleads the reader into failing to notice that the discussion of the former requires formulation in the light of the latter. Price says that it is as confusing as if Kant had put the Analogies before the Transcendental Deduction; I would say rather, the Second Analogy before the First (see below, third paragraph from the end).

following consideration: "Objects have a certain coherence even as they appear to our senses; but this coherence is much greater and more uniform, if we suppose the objects to have continu'd existence; and as the mind is once in the train of observing an uniformity among objects, it naturally continues, till it renders the uniformity as compleat as possible."[39]

This gives rise to the theory of double existence, which he says has the backing neither of reason nor of imagination.[40] It does not follow from the standard Humean analysis of causation; it follows rather from Hume's (and the common man's) conviction that if the cause of an event is not found within experience, it must be feigned to lie outside it. That is why I said that the first principle, instead of being sunk in the second, is used to rescue the second when experience "contradicts" it.

The description Hume gives of the objects perceived is, in Locke's terminology, in terms of coexistence, not of causation. "Objects have a certain coherence," he says; but the constancy of conjunction of simultaneous properties is not essentially different from the constancy of conjunction of serial properties. In both there is association and consequent belief.

In Hume's observation of the porter entering his room, there is a manifest absence of coherence. He knows that an opening door (as seen) is associated with a particular sound. But here one is present to his senses and the other absent. If coherence and causation were based exclusively on association of impressions, this would be a negative instance. It would lead the pure inductivist to say that the association between the sight and the sound is weaker than it had been; and the probability of the causal judgment, less than it had been. He might even deny that the noise had a cause. Neither Hume nor the common man will draw such a conclusion. Both claim that had they been looking, they would have seen the door open. Why? Because we believe that every event has some cause, even if the preceding impression is not the same. "There is nothing existent, either externally or internally, which is not to be consider'd either as a cause or an effect."[41]

The counterfactual claim is supported by *two* principles: every-event-some-cause and same-cause-same-effect. It would be of little use to assert

---

[39] *Treatise*, I, IV, II, p. 198.
[40] Ibid., p. 212.
[41] Ibid., III, II, p. 75.

the former without the latter, for to get any practical benefit we must use the latter. But while the first is independent of the second, we cannot maintain the second without the first, since the case before us is a counterexample to the second taken alone.

Thus Hume did not "sink" the first question in the second so successfully that the first question need not be raised again. Hume's principle same-cause-same-effect is an induction from his answer to simpler questions about what causes what. But he has no answer to the question about every-event-some-cause, since that is not an induction from the second; rather, it comes into its own where the second breaks down. The principle every-event-some-cause permits us to reinstate the principle same-cause-same-effect in the face of negative instances. We reinstate it for the sake of our need to make our experiential coherence "much greater and more uniform" than the intermittent perceptions we actually have; but it cannot itself be the result of associations of perceptions, because it functions precisely where our perceptions are *not* regular enough to support associations, causal beliefs, and the principle same-cause-same-effect.

IV

This reading of Hume takes at least a small step toward justifying the epithet "the Scottish Kant." It shows that Hume distinguished the a posteriori causal laws induced from the experience of regular sequences from a quite different causal law, which is not based on mere association and is thus not vulnerable to disconfirmation when the sequence of impressions is not uniform. It is a principle of a higher order that regulates our ascription of causality in the absence of association and even where association and expectation are flouted by the actual course of our impressions. Naturally, Hume does not have a theory that one of the conceptions of causation is a priori and the other is a posteriori; but a priori is as a priori does, and when a principle is called upon to correct experience, it is functioning in an a priori manner regardless of its origin. It is at least debatable whether Kant's a priori principles have any higher function in spite of their nobler ancestry.

This reading of Hume also throws interesting light on Kant's theory of causation and on the true nature of his "answer to Hume." It has often been objected that Kant's Second Analogy does nothing to support the principle same-cause-same-effect.[42] This is true, but it was not Kant's purpose there to support *that* principle; he was concerned only with the principle every-event-some-cause and did not "sink" this principle in same-cause-same-effect. He says, "The accepted view is that only through the perception and comparison of events repeatedly following in a uniform manner upon preceding appearances are we enabled to discover a rule according to which certain events always follow upon certain appearances, and that this is the way in which we are first led to construct for ourselves the concept of cause."[43]

Kant accepts the first of these tenets. The discovery of what is the cause of what is exactly the same for Kant as for Hume. Kant makes no claim that we can discover by reason, or know a priori, the connection of any specific cause with a specific effect and understand its necessity.[44] Even the principle same-cause-same-effect is not known a priori to be true. For Kant, it is a regulative principle[45] functioning like the principle Hume postulates that unobserved causes must be like observed ones.[46] So far there is little dispute between Kant and Hume. But a significant difference lies in the second clause of the "accepted belief," namely, that the concept of cause arises in the same manner as the knowledge of what is the cause of some event. Kant insists that the first principle cannot arise in the way the second principle does according to Beattie's reading of Hume but is rather an a priori condition for the discovery and use of the second.

I shall try to show why Hume did not agree with this, and how Kant supported it. Every reader of Hume is baffled by his repeatedly and

---

[42] For example, A. O. Lovejoy, "On Kant's Reply to Hume," *Archiv für Geschichte der Philosophie* 20 (1906), reprinted in M. S. Gram, *Kant: Disputed Questions* (Chicago: Quadrangle Books, 1967), pp. 300-301.

[43] *Critique of Pure Reason*, A 195 = B 240-41. What is puzzling about this passage is that Kant calls what he now thinks is Hume's view "the accepted view." *This* view can hardly have been widely accepted in Germany where the Wolffian theory was still strong even against the Crusian.

[44] Kant repeatedly asserts that empirical laws cannot be derived from a priori principles of the understanding; yet he believed some of them to be necessary. Those are the ones involved in an over-all theory whose principles are derived from the a priori principles of "rational science" or "pure physics" (see *Critique of Pure Reason*, A 127-28; A 270 = B 252; B 165; A 216 = B 263). Where the over-all theory is lacking (as in chemistry), the principles are only empirical and the laws are only "laws of experience" without any "consciousness of necessity" attaching to them. The body of knowledge containing them should be called "a systematic art" and not a "science" (*Metaphysical Foundations of Natural Science*, Ak. 4:468).

[45] *Critique of Pure Reason*, A 657 = B 686.

[46] *Treatise*, I, III, VIII, p. 104.

arbitrarily shifting back and forth between talking about objects and events and talking about impressions.[47] Sometimes he tries to justify this,[48] and sometimes he anticipates Kant in distinguishing between them in a phenomenalistic way.[49] But usually, I think, he is just careless and profits from this carelessness. Because he does not clearly maintain the distinction, in setting up his problem he fails to distinguish between his awareness of a sequence of states in a perceived object and a sequence of mere impressions of a perceived object. He believes he can see objective events, distinguish them from mental events, feel a "gentle force" among the latter that is absent from the former, and by repeated observation of ordered pairs of objective events come to read the gentle force into them.

But if Hume had rigorously employed the phenomenalistic language to which he alone is entitled, he would not have been able to draw his prima facie distinction between a sequence of impressions and a sequence of perceived objective events, as if the latter were as directly given as the former. He would have seen that the sequence of impressions of a house and the sequence of impressions of a moving ship require rules for interpreting one sequence of impressions as the perception of a stationary permanent object and the other sequence as the perception of a sequence of states or positions of a changing object. Until these rules are made and justified, Hume has no right to use the concept of objective event in classifying some impressions as impressions of events that are observed to occur in ordered pairs so that same-cause-same-effect could appear to be an empirical generalization from these observations. But Hume does not see that he must justify the use of the concept of objective event before he can establish, even in his own way, the principle same-cause-same-effect. Objective events are not "just given"; as much goes into their construction as Hume properly saw goes into the construction of an identical object intermittently perceived.

Kant's Second Analogy is meant to provide precisely this justification for talk about objective events, and he sees the connection of the two problems by coupling it with the First Analogy, which deals with continued existence. He shows that the concepts of objective event and cause-and-effect are related to each other necessarily, and not by mere association. Only much later, in an essentially Humean kind of

---

[47] I cannot say that Kant is entirely innocent of the same fault, but in the Second Analogy, where it counts here, he is careful not to commit the error.

[48] *Treatise*, I, II, VI, p. 67; III, X, p. 118; IV, II, p. 218.

[49] Ibid., III, IX, p. 108, IV, V, p. 242.

argument, does he deal with the question of the justification of the principle same-cause-same-effect. He is explicitly following a line of argument that I have suggested Hume actually followed, in contradistinction to the one that Beattie said and Kant believed that Hume had followed.

Looked at in this way, the charge that "Kant begged Hume's question" and ended up in the same boat with Reid, Oswald, and Beattie is easily answered. Kant's argument in the Second Analogy does not simply dignify as a priori a principle that Hume, according to Beattie, believed to be a posteriori and therefore uncertain. Rather, it begins with an assumption that Hume never thought of doubting, namely, that we can distinguish between a sequence of impressions of an enduring object and a sequence of impressions indicating that an objective change is occurring. Hume's answer to how we know same-cause-same-effect could never have been given without this assumption. But Kant raises a question that neither Hume nor any other philosopher before him had raised: How do we distinguish between the two kinds of sequences?

Kant's answer is that any sequence taken to represent an objective change of states of affairs, or an event, must be taken as a necessary sequence, and that the concept of a necessary sequence is the concept of causation. Without possessing the concept of causation we could not distinguish between objective events and subjective sequences, and therefore the concept of a causal connection between objective events cannot arise from observation of them, but rather must be presupposed in recognizing them. Given the first principle, every-event-some-cause, which fixes our realm of discourse, we can then, in good Humean fashion, go about finding uniform ordered pairs of events by straightforward observation and induction. Kant does not challenge this; he argues only that his principle (the Second Analogy of Experience) like Hume's principle (every-event-some-cause) is a necessary condition for Hume's second principle, which we know by repeated observation.[50] I have argued that, once we modify or reject Beattie's interpretation, we can see that such an argument is not wholly unlike Hume's procedure when faced with the example of the porter, however little Hume would be inclined to use the language of a priori judgments and transcendental principles.

---

[50] The argument given all too dogmatically in this paragraph is based on a fuller treatment in my book *Essays on Kant and Hume*, pp. 130-53.

Is Hume's Self Consistent?

Jane L. McIntyre

ATTRIBUTIONS OF INCONSISTENCY are a philosopher's stock-in-trade. It is rare, however, to find a philosopher who brings this charge against himself. The infrequency of the phenomenon may explain why such self-accusations, when they occur, are not subjected to critical scrutiny. But an examination of Hume's treatment of personal identity in the *Treatise* makes it apparent that such attempts at self-analysis *should* be well scrutinized. For, I will argue, critics have been perhaps too quick to join Hume in the condemnation of his original view.[1]

1. HUME'S VIEW OF THE SELF IN BOOK I OF THE *Treatise*

The basic outlines of Hume's account of personal identity in the *Treatise* (I, IV, VI) are clear enough. We cannot, according to Hume, discover any simple impression remaining the same through all of our experiences, and hence we have no intelligible idea of the self as a substance that remains the same throughout our lives. The mind, therefore, is nothing over and above a collection of individual perceptions. "There is properly no *simplicity* in it at one time, nor *identity* in different."[2] Our *belief* in a self that remains identical is based on the relations of similarity and causation holding between those perceptions, making it possible for the imagination to feign the existence of an unchanging self when actually presented with a succession of related selves.

It should be noted that Hume recognized that the idea of the self that philosophers and others take themselves to have is the idea of a subject of various experiences. He was aware that when we refer to ourselves we mean not simply "these thoughts, these feelings, these sensory impressions" but "the thing which has these thoughts, feelings and impressions." But if we ask ourselves which thing that is, the only way it can be identified is by referring to the thoughts, feelings, impressions, and so on,

---

[1] Hume has not been entirely without defenders. Recently Lawrence Ashley and Michael Stack have argued in "Hume's Theory of the Self and its Identity" (*Dialogue* 13 [1974]: 239-54) that Hume's account of personal identity is more acceptable than most critics have claimed. However, they are more concerned with refuting other criticisms of Hume, particularly those of Penelhum, than in addressing the issue of inconsistency.

[2] *A Treatise of Human Nature,* ed. L. A. Selby-Bigge (Oxford, 1888), I, IV, VI, p. 253 (hereafter cited as *Treatise*).

that it has. The phrase "the subject of my experiences" will therefore never do more than refer to the collection of experiences of which it is supposed to be the subject. For we have no *independent* way of discovering the subject of experience: we have only our experiences. We have a tendency to look for a subject of experience to *explain* the connectedness or unity we feel in experience. But any appeal to such a notion will always be fruitless, for the only possible understanding we could ever have of "the subject of experience" would be in terms of the perceptions whose unity it is invoked to explain. An appeal to a concept of the self as the subject of experience would give us only the appearance of an explanation of personal identity. Any meaningful (in Hume's empiricist sense) idea of the self must therefore be limited to the idea of a collection of perceptions.

In the appendix to the *Treatise* Hume rejects his analysis of personal identity, retreating to the skeptic's privileged stance of noting paradoxes and withholding judgment. These passages in the appendix shed a good deal of light on Hume's theory of mind and his corresponding theory of personal identity. The question to be addressed in this paper is whether Hume's objections to his initial account of personal identity are well founded.

2. Hume's Attack on his Account of the Self in the Appendix: Problems of Interpretation

In the appendix Hume states:

> Thought alone finds personal identity, when reflecting on the train of past perceptions, that compose a mind, the ideas of them are felt to be connected together, and naturally introduce each other. . . . But all my hopes vanish, when I come to explain the principles, that unite our successive perceptions in our thought or consciousness. I cannot discover any theory, which gives me satisfaction on this head.
>
> In short, there are two principles, which I cannot render consistent; nor is it in my power to renounce either of them, viz. *that all our distinct perceptions are distinct existences*, and *that the mind never perceives any real connexion among distinct existences*. Did our perceptions either inhere in something simple and individual, or did the mind perceive some real connexion among them, there wou'd be no difficulty in the case.[3]

---

[3] Ibid., pp. 635-36.

This brief statement, which summarizes Hume's dissatisfactions with his theory of personal identity, is problematic from several points of view. First, the principles to which Hume attributes inconsistency are not inconsistent: as a matter of fact, as Kemp Smith has noted, the second is derived from the first![4] It is fairly clear that Hume is asserting in this passage that these two principles are inconsistent with any acount of the unity or identity of the self. This, however, introduces a second difficulty. By the standard invoked in the last sentence of the passage above, not only should the account of the identity of the self through time fail, the account of our idea of continually existing material substances should fail, too. For the distinctness of the perceptions and the principles relating them are the same in both cases. If, as Hume suggests, in order to explain our ideas of persisting things, either perceptions must inhere in some substance or the mind must grasp real connections among perceptions, then the account in the *Treatise* of the belief in physical objects is obviously defective. Since Hume is *not* criticizing that account there must be some other reason why the belief in the persistence of the self through time presents a problem for Hume.

There is a further problem concerning Hume's despair at finding any real connections between the distinct existences that constitute the mind. It would seem that, given his own account of necessary connection, the only kind of connection he could consistently hope to find would have to be interpreted as feelings resulting from association. If the dissatisfaction that Hume is expressing in the appendix is that connections so interpreted fail to give us any basic or essential insight into "the nature of the self" or any knowledge of the reasons why impressions present themselves to us in certain orderly ways, then it is his account of necessary connection, not of personal identity, that must be taken to be unsatisfactory. On his view, no more basic understanding of the connections between things is possible. It may be that Hume's problem with respect to personal identity is merely that he is appealing to a standard of adequacy that is inconsistent with the account of connections he gives in the *Treatise*. But if Hume's problem is not merely this, what is it?

3. Hume's Fundamental Problem with the Idea of the Self

In this section I will try to offer a plausible account of the unique problem Hume faces in explaining *personal* identity. This explanation of

---

[4] Norman Kemp Smith, *The Philosophy of David Hume* (London: Macmillan, 1960), p. 558.

Hume's difficulty is suggested by an analysis of the role of the self in Book I, taken in conjunction with his comments in the appendix. In point of fact, this account is now gaining currency among Hume's critics (in particular, Robison, Penelhum, and Nathanson), for the problem that it locates in Hume's theory seems to be a devastating one.[5] I should perhaps point out here that I agree with Hume's recent critics *only* in the identification of the source of Hume's problem. Contrary to their view, I hold that the problem can be solved and the inconsistency in Hume's theory eliminated.

Hume's accounts of our belief in material substance and the idea of necessary connection are similar in the following respect: custom or habit plays a significant role in each. In the former case, regular recurrences of resembling impressions lead the imagination to feign the existence of a substance connecting those perceptions. In the latter case, constant conjunction of sets of events in the past leads to the expectation that the events will continue to be conjoined in the future. It is the reliance on custom in both of these accounts that creates critical difficulties for Hume's theory of the self, over and above those faced by his account of material substance. In order for the repetition of perceptions either to have an impact on the imagination or to result in the creation of expectations about future experiences, it would seem that the past perceptions would all have to be the perceptions of *one individual* perceiver. In order for past experience to condition belief, something must be continually there to be conditioned. Here, then, is the basis of Hume's special problem about the nature of the self and personal identity: the concept of the self that is essential to his account of the belief in a material world and the idea of a necessary connection—that is, the concept of a self that is *affected by experience* and therefore must *persist through experience*—is precisely the concept of the self that *cannot* be accounted for in the context of the theory of ideas presented in the *Treatise*.

In light of this we can explain why the account of personal identity comes up for special criticism in the appendix. Hume's account of personal identity attempts to explain the idea of the self in the same way that the idea of material substance is explained. But it would seem that unless the self is more than a fiction, more than a product of the imagination, no

---

[5] See Wade L. Robison, "Hume on Personal Identity," *Journal of the History of Philosophy* 12 (1974): 181-93; Terence Penelhum, "Hume's Theory of the Self Revisited," *Dialogue* 14 (1975): 389-409; Stephen Nathanson, "Hume's Second Thoughts on the Self," *Hume Studies* 2 (1976): 36-45.

account of any other phenomena in terms of custom will have any cogency. For Hume, if we cannot make good empiricist sense of the idea of *material* substances existing independently of ourselves, it is sufficient to explain why we *believe* in such substances. But we cannot so simply say that if we cannot make good empiricist sense of the idea of a continually existing self it will be sufficient to explain our belief in it. For the explanation of belief that Hume is committed to seems itself to *presuppose* a continually existing self. I take this to be the most plausible account of the inconsistency Hume was alluding to in the appendix. Furthermore, it is a much more serious difficulty for Hume than many of his critics may recognize, even though they agree that Hume's account of personal identity is defective. To admit the existence of a mind that was more than a collection of perceptions would, as most critics recognize, be tantamount to a rejection of Hume's theory of ideas. But *not* to admit a meaningful concept of mind-as-the-continuing-subject-of-experience seems equally damaging to the doctrines of Book I of the *Treatise*.

4. The Source of Hume's Problem: Conflicting Accounts of the Association of Ideas

One might note that in my description of Hume's dilemma I have referred to custom and habit in a manner that invites the type of difficulty I attribute to him. To speak of the imagination as something capable of noting resemblances among impressions and being affected by those resemblances is explicitly to attribute a continuing identity to that faculty. That is not, of course, any different from what Hume himself does when speaking of it. Many of Hume's most basic statements of the laws governing the association of ideas are couched in this sort ot terminology. In his discussion of necessary connection, for example, Hume states that

> Tho' the several resembling instances, which give rise to the idea of power, have no influence on each other, and can never produce any new quality *in the object*, which can be the model of that idea, yet the *observation* of this resemblance produces a new impression *in the mind*, which is its real model.[6]

This manner of speaking notwithstanding, there is a tension in Hume

---

[6] *Treatise*, I, III, XIV, pp. 164-65.

between *two* different implicit accounts of the association of ideas. On one account (as suggested by remarks like those above) ideas are associated *by a mind* according to certain principles. On the other, ideas are associated *directly*, rather than by their action on something else; they attract each other, much as physical objects attract each other by gravitation. This latter account is suggested when Hume first introduces the principles of association in Book I of the *Treatise*: "'Tis impossible the same simple ideas should fall regularly into complex ones (as they commonly do) without some bond of union among them, some associating quality, by which one idea naturally introduces another."[7] And, similarly, in Book II he states that "nature has bestow'd a kind of attraction on certain impressions and ideas, by which one of them, upon its appearance, naturally introduces its correlative."[8] Kemp Smith attributes these differing views on association to the conflicting influence of Hutcheson and Newton.[9] The tendencies toward the former account are strong enough to cause Robert Paul Wolff to argue that a full account of Hume's theory of mental activity might well be labeled a table of categories, as in Kant.[10] This Kantian (or, more accurately, Hutchesonian) view of association *is* inconsistent with Hume's account of the self in Book I; if ideas are associated by a self, the self cannot be explained as a fictional product of the association of ideas. If this were the only possible interpretation of the association of ideas, Hume would have good grounds for rejecting not merely his account of personal identity but all of Book I of the *Treatise*. However, Hume's explicit account of the nature of mind is more closely tied to the "Newtonian" (gravitational) model of association. At issue is the ability of *this* one account of association to play all the roles designed for human nature in the *Treatise*. And since the appeal to the force of *custom* in accounting for our beliefs and complex ideas seems to presuppose the continuing existence of a self underlying perceptions, the consistency of Hume's theory of the self turns on the possibility of making sense of custom's influence on belief without an appeal to the more "Kantian" account of association. I will argue that this is precisely what Hume's account of personal identity permits him to do, and for this reason his account of the self can be shown to be consistent.

---

[7] Ibid., I, IV, p. 10.
[8] Ibid., II, I, V, p. 289.
[9] Kemp Smith, pp. 73–76.
[10] "Hume's Theory of Mental Activity," *The Philosophical Review* 69 (1960), reprinted in V. C. Chappell, ed., *Hume* (Garden City, N.Y.: Anchor Books, 1966), pp. 99–128.

5. THE MIND AS A COLLECTION OF PERCEPTIONS: A RECONSTRUCTION OF HUME'S VIEW

For Hume, the mind is a collection of perceptions, but he takes it to be a collection in *two distinct* ways. As I noted earlier, Hume says that "there is properly no *simplicity* in it [the mind] at one time, nor *identity* in different." The self is not simply a collection in the sense of being a series of distinct perceptions through time. Even at any *one* time the mind is a collection of perceptions—sensory impressions, ideas, feelings, memories. The component perceptions are never entirely the same from moment to moment, and hence through time the mind is a series of distinct collections of perceptions—a collection of collections, as it were. The fact that even at any one time the mind is a collection of perceptions of different types can be easily overlooked when discussing Hume's account of the identity of the self through time. D. M. Armstrong, for example, argues that Hume cannot explain the collecting of perceptions into the experiences of one person by appealing to the supposed fact that the various perceptions resemble each other. For the perceptions of one picture by two individuals, for example, will more closely resemble one another than the successive perceptions of one individual as he, for example, looks around a room.[11] This argument ignores the important point that a person's sensory impressions are only a part of a very complex collection of perceptions that will include memories, feelings, and ideas derived from past experiences. Hume acknowledges this.

> Suppose we cou'd see clearly into the breast of another, and observe that succession of perceptions, which constitutes his mind or thinking principle, and suppose that he always preserves the memory of a considerable part of his past perceptions; 'tis evident that nothing cou'd more contribute to the bestowing a relation on this succession amidst all its variations.[12]

When all the components of the mind at any one time are taken into account the supposition of Armstrong's argument loses its plausibility; for the total collection of a person's perceptions in this inclusive sense will not be likely to resemble those of another person, even if their visual experiences are qualitatively identical.

---

[11] *A Materialist Theory of Mind* (New York: Humanities Press, 1968), pp. 16–18.
[12] *Treatise*, I, IV, VI, p. 260.

In general, the problem of personal identity is the problem of stating criteria for the reidentification of persons through time. Given Hume's view that at any one time persons are collections of perceptions, only the absolutely unchanging persistence of that collection would count as a person remaining identical. Persons, however, are constantly changing: we lose ideas through lapses of memory, we have new impressions, we form new fanciful ideas from old ones. According to Hume, therefore, what we think of as the persistence of a person through time is not to be understood in terms of the relation of identity. Our "identity" is analogous to the identity we (incorrectly) attribute to complex beings, like animals and plants, that develop through time. Relations of similarity and causation holding between what we can informally refer to as the temporally extended stages of a thing create in the mind a *feeling* of contemplating an unchanging object.

Once the complex character of the mind as a collection of perceptions at any *one* time is noted, the analogy of the identity of persons with that of animals and plants, with its connotations of growth and decay, is very suggestive. At any one time the collection of perceptions constituting a mind will include a set of current sensory impressions, a set of ideas derived from past impressions, and a set of feelings or impressions of reflection. Any addition of an impression or loss of an idea results in the destruction of the identity of the collection. However, even if no one component idea remains in the collection throughout its life history, some idea, or significant groups of ideas, particularly the record of past impressions in memory, may persist as strictly identical (that is unchanging) for some time. New collections of perceptions are not created *ex nihilo*; they are merely the result of additions to (or deletions from) old collections. When understood in this way the *similarity* of distinct collections from one moment to the next is the natural result of the *identity* of *parts* of the collections.

This model of the mind as a *series* of *collections* of perceptions related to each other by successive additions and deletions is, I believe, an accurate representation of Hume's theory of personal identity. It should be noted that on this account the relations holding among successive bundles are independent of their being identified as perceptions of one subject. More importantly, it is possible, on this model, for Hume to overcome the dilemma facing his account of personal identity.

6. THE RESOLUTION OF HUME'S PROBLEM

Hume's basic problem is that of reconciling two facts: first, a person is a series of distinct (i.e., nonidentical) collections of perceptions; but, second, a person is influenced by past experience. In a strict sense, the collections that constitute my past are as distinct from each other, and from me now, as my perceptions now are from those of anyone else at this moment. These various collections are not identical because they do not contain exactly the same constituent perceptions. But only *my* past perceptions are capable of influencing my current beliefs. Since the relationship between myself now and the collections of perceptions that constitute my past is *not* that of identity, it seems necessary to explain the fact that they have a special relevance to the formation of my beliefs, when those of others do not. This demand for an explanation of the force of custom, however, is easy to satisfy without giving up Hume's adherence to the strict nonidentity of the self through time—if Hume's account of *why* the self is not identical through time is taken seriously. Every additional impression that experience adds to a collection of perceptions destroys the self to which it is added. Continuing experience is one of the factors responsible for the nonidentity of the self through time. New impressions neither alter nor destroy other impressions or ideas. Rather, they alter and thus, in Hume's strict sense, destroy the *collection* to which those impressions and ideas belong. The destruction of the collection does not take place by the total destruction of its parts, but by *any* change in them. Yet, if past perceptions are not destroyed, the influence of perceptions from *collections* that no longer exist is in no way mysterious. I can be influenced by those past collections of perceptions some of whose constituent perceptions are constituents of me. The emphasis on the nonidentity of the *collection* of perceptions from moment to moment masks the underlying persistence of individual perceptions through time. Perceptions that persist through various collections can, of course, influence any of the collections in which they occur. Thus, properly understood, Hume's account of the self as a collection of perceptions *is* compatible with the role that self must play in the main arguments of Book I of the *Treatise*.

This analysis receives some indirect confirmation from its ability to solve another problem associated with Hume's account of personal identity. According to Passmore and MacNabb (and probably others), if one accepts the view that the mind is a collection of perceptions, then Hume's account of the generation of the idea of the self as a fiction is logically contradictory.[13] They question whether a single element in such a series (i.e., the self at a particular time) could be aware of itself as a member of a series, given that the members of the series are not identical. Although there is an air of paradox to this question, whether it reveals anything paradoxical in Hume's theory depends on the nature of the series in question. Given my model of Hume's account of personal identity, no mystery surrounds the answer to this question: the overlapping parts of the series provide the basis for an individual presently existing to be aware of its connection to past individuals not identical with it.

7. Conclusion

I have argued that conflicting tendencies in Hume's account of the association of ideas lead to the problem Hume encounters with respect to the nature of the self and personal identity. However, I have tried to show that the theory that the self is nothing more than a collection of perceptions — when properly interpreted — can be reconciled with the activities of the self required by Book I of the *Treatise*. If this is so, the charge that Hume's view is logically inconsistent, which first originated with Hume himself, can be refuted.

---

[13] John Passmore, *Hume's Intentions* (Cambridge: Cambridge University Press, 1952), p. 82; D. G. C. MacNabb, *David Hume* (London: Hutchinson's University Library, 1951), p. 152.

In Defense of Hume's Appendix

Wade L. Robison

ACCORDING TO A RECENT THEORY concerning Hume on personal identity, his *Appendix* is as expendable as the organ itself. It is a vestigial remnant of a view through which Hume's thought evolved and to which he returned only because he failed to realize his own development. The view left behind depends upon a standard of identity such that, for *a* to be identical with itself, *a* must remain invariable and uninterrupted in its existence from one time to another.[1] No person is thus the same from one moment to the next precisely because there is such variation in the perceptions that, Hume says, constitute a person: new perceptions occur, we forget, and so on. That Hume drew this skeptical consequence is so widely held that it may be called the standard view. Indeed, Hume is claimed to have subscribed to the view itself in the *Appendix* when he repeats the arguments he gave in the section "Of personal identity" and then throws up his hands over the fact that his premises have given birth to a view so at odds with the judgments we in fact make about personal identity.

By the recent theory, however, this is not all Hume did.[2] For it is claimed that in "Of personal identity," while explaining why we make judgments of personal identity anyway, he develops a new standard of identity that allows variable objects to be the same from one moment to the next.[3] Indeed, he ends the section by saying that a person can be the same from one moment to the next even with variation. That Hume lost

---

A rough draft of this paper was presented in the fall of 1975 at a Hume Conference at the University of Wisconsin-Madison. A very mangled version of the main argument was hardly amenable to criticism, but I thank the efforts of those who were present, especially Nathan Brett, my fellow symposiast.

[1] *A Treatise of Human Nature*, ed. L. A. Selby-Bigge (Oxford, 1888), I, IV, II, pp. 200–201 (hereafter cited as *Treatise*).

[2] Lawrence Ashley and Michael Stack, "Hume's Theory of the Self and its Identity," *Dialogue* 13 (1974), and James Noxon, "Sense of Identity in Hume's *Treatise*," *Dialogue* 8 (1969). The new theory is a theory in development, and what I give is a reconstruction of what I take to be its main claims. These are claims, I think, that any variant of the theory must maintain.

[3] I have not stated the new standard. I can find no definitive statement of it in those who claim it is there. This is not meant as a criticism. After all, it can be argued that since Hume is developing a new standard, it is too much to expect that it should be completely clear. Besides, since the details of the standard do not matter for what I shall argue, stating a version of it may misdirect critical comments.

track of his own development and reverted to his former view is unfortunate, it is claimed, because it has obscured the fact that he has a new standard of identity and, by it, is no skeptic about personal identity.

I intend to defend Hume's *Appendix*; but for a proper defense the new theory and the evidence for it must be set out more clearly than I think they have been so far. The theory is much more defensible than even its proponents have thought. For, first, it is structured in such a way that the usual defenses for the standard view are inappropriate, and, second, there is prima facie compelling evidence in its favor. Let me consider these points in turn.

The defense of the standard view consists, first, of an analysis of the section "Of personal identity." Hume uses the strict standard of identity in the first four paragraphs to show that "they are the successive perceptions only, that constitute the mind," there being "properly no *simplicity* in it at one time, nor *identity* in different." He then asks, in the lead sentence of paragraph five, " What then gives us so great a propension to ascribe an identity to these successive perceptions, and to suppose ourselves possest of an invariable and uninterrupted existence thro' the whole course of our lives?"[4] The rest of the section, it is claimed, answers that question, ending with a comparison of a person with a republic. The text thus divides into one part showing that persons are not the same from one moment to the next and another part showing why we make judgments of personal identity anyway. That is the first defensive move. The second is that this pattern of argumentation is the same one that Hume uses concerning our judgments about causation and about external objects.

When developed at length, these defenses provide a compelling presumption in favor of the standard view.[5] But they are irrelevant to the new theory. For the theory need claim only that, in working out the answer to the question of why we make judgments of personal identity anyway, Hume developed a standard on the basis of which such judgments are appropriate. That he worked out this new view within the framework of a set of questions tailored for a different view is no bar to the claim that he developed a new view. It rather explains why the new view has been missed by previous commentators and muddled and lost

---

[4] *Treatise*, I, IV, VI, p. 253.

[5] The best statements are those of Terence Penelhum. See his "Hume on Personal Identity," *The Philosophical Review* 54 (1955); "Hume's Theory of the Self Revisited," *Dialogue* 14 (1975); and *Hume* (London: Macmillan & Co., 1975), chap. 4.

by Hume himself. Indeed, without such an explanation for past failures, it would be difficult to explain the long-standing dominance of the standard view. For the evidence for the new theory is powerfully persuasive, once noticed. There are two main pieces of evidence.

(1) Hume typically explains our mistaken ascriptions by noting the existence of two entities that are closely similar and then by pointing out that the mental acts that occur when we perceive these similar entities are themselves similar and easily mistaken for each other.[6] He thus explains our propensity to make ascriptions of personal identity by pointing out that an invariable and uninterrupted object is similar to a succession of objects that vary slightly and that the mental acts occurring when we perceive such similar objects "are almost the same to the feeling," so that "in our common way of thinking they are generally confounded with each other." In giving this explanation Hume clearly contrasts "these two ideas of identity, and a succession of related objects," and were that all he had done, there would be no claim that any new standard of identity had been introduced.[7]

But Hume ends "Of personal identity" by saying that "the true idea of the human mind, is to consider it as a system of different perceptions or different existences, which are link'd together by the relation of cause and effect. . . ." He then compares those causal ties with "the reciprocal ties of government and subordination" in a republic and observes that "as the same individual republic may not only change its members, but also its laws and constitutions; in like manner the same person may vary his character and disposition, as well as his impressions and ideas, without losing his identity." How can that be? Hume immediately answers, "Whatever changes he endures, his several parts are still connected by the relation of causation."[8]

Hume thus seems to say that "a succession of related objects" — different perceptions and dispositions — can be a single identical object, a person in this case, if the relations between the objects are causal. If so, then he is making ascriptions of personal identity on the basis of some new standard of identity.

(2) Confirmation for this change seems to come when Hume summarizes what he calls "the whole of this doctrine" by declaring that "all the disputes concerning the identity of connected objects are merely verbal,

---

[6] See e.g., *Treatise*, I, IV, II, p. 203.
[7] Ibid., VI, pp. 253-254.
[8] Ibid., p. 261.

except so far as the relation of parts gives rise to some fiction or imaginary principle of union. . . ."[9] This is an odd passage, usually ignored, but it supports the new theory.

First, when Hume explains our mistaken ascriptions of personal identity, what he says is that we mistake a succession of related objects for an invariable and uninterrupted object *and* we "feign some new and unintelligible principle, that connects the objects together, and prevents their interruption or variation." What he clearly rejects is calling "a succession of related objects" the same *and* attempting to hold on to the old standard of identity by positing "a *soul*, and *self*, and *substance*, to disguise the variation."[10] Since there is no inconsistency in calling a succession of related objects the same object and *not* holding on to the old standard of identity, it is possible, at least, that Hume is rejecting the old standard to make way for the new.

Second, in order for matters of identity to be verbal matters for Hume, it must be the case that "we have no just standard, by which we can decide any dispute concerning the time, when they acquire or lose a title to the name of identity."[11] On the standard view, there is such a standard: Has the object varied or been interrupted in its existence from one time to another? But once one accepts that changes can occur without a loss of identity, then, as in the complete refitting of a boat over successive years, it may become a verbal matter whether one calls an object the same or not: there may seem no just standard that allows one to say that after so many changes it is a new object.

If, therefore, this is "the whole of this doctrine," Hume must have changed his standard of identity. If he did, then he could have meant what he seems to when he says, "the same person may vary. . . without losing his identity." So, the argument concludes, the new theory must be correct.

In assessing this theory I shall put to one side Hume's remarks about the issue's being verbal. Hume's use of critical terms is not as casual as it may sometimes appear, and any explanation of his calling the issue verbal must wander far afield to collect a general theory out of such obscure remarks as, for example, his discussion in the *Dialogues concerning Natural Religion* (Sect. XII) of why the question of God's attributes is a verbal issue. In any case, the crucial evidence is Hume's apparent claim

---

[9] Ibid., p. 262.
[10] Ibid., p. 254.
[11] Ibid., p. 262.

that a person can be the same despite variations. The question is thus, Are judgments of personal identity appropriate given the new standard of identity? I shall argue that they are not.

Let us look at what precedes the comparison of a person with a republic. After asking why we have "so great a propension to ascribe an identity to these successive perceptions," Hume examines identity in plants and animals. He then returns to personal identity and sums up the conclusions he drew at the beginning of the section with the statement that there is nothing "that really binds our several perceptions together." What is really at issue, he says, is what "associates ideas in the imagination." Of the three relations that associate, he rejects the natural relation of contiguity out of hand as having "little or no influence in the present case."[12]

In the following paragraph he talks briefly about how resemblance is important because memories resemble past perceptions so that "the whole (is made to) seem like the continuance of one object." And then, in the next paragraph, he turns to causation and begins the comparison of a person with a republic.[13]

The evidence is that he is considering in turn the *natural* relations of contiguity, resemblance, and causation. When he says that a person's "several parts are . . . connected by the relation of causation," he thus means that they are causally *associated*. But then, I shall argue, when he claims that the comparison of a person with a republic gives us "the true idea of the human mind," he means that that is the only idea we have, not that it is true that a person is the same from one moment to the next. But to see why this is so we must make a brief excursion into the much-disputed subject of the basis of Hume's distinction between philosophical and natural relations.

Hume introduces natural relations to account for the difference between those sequences of thoughts "without rule and method in their changes" and those that are orderly. It is simply a fact, he thinks, that once we see that Jupiter with its moons resembles a solar system, the thought of the one naturally leads us to "pass from (it) to what is resembling."[14] So this much seems undisputed about Hume's picture: natural relations sort out various sequences of perceptions, and they exist

---

[12] Ibid., pp. 259-60.
[13] Ibid., p. 261.
[14] Ibid., II, I, IV, p. 283. See also *An Abstract of a Treatise of Human Nature* (Hamden, Conn.: Archon Books, 1965), pp. 31-32.

because of our observation of other relations between what we perceive. What is unclear is whether natural relations are different in kind from philosophical relations, and if so, how.

The very formulaton of the picture seems to imply as a first step that, as Alan Hausman puts it, "*Philosophical* relations . . . connect ordinary objects; *natural* relations connect our thoughts about them."[15] In short, natural and philosophical relations are distinguished at least by their relata. But this will not do. A simple counterexample is succession. It is a philosophical relation, and yet perceptions can succeed one another. A more complex example turns on the natural and philosophical relations of causation. A natural relation holds if, when perceiving a billiard ball rolling toward another, one believes that it will strike the other. What are related here are an impression and an idea that is lively. But the empiricist principle also relates impressions and ideas, holding that *"all simple ideas in their first appearance are deriv'd from* (caused by) *simple impressions."*[16] The causal relation is philosophical; and so both a philosophical and a natural relation connect impressions with ideas. The two are thus not distinguished by their relata.

But Hume's picture naturally suggests another hypothesis. It says nothing about the nature of natural relations, and the suggestion is that natural relations are not a distinct kind of relation at all but simply the names of some philosophical relations—resemblance, contiguity, and causation—which, when observed, cause other philosophical relations to occur between perceptions.[17]

But this will not do as a general theory. Causation is the counterexample. For when Hume introduces the natural relation of causation, he is clear that phenomenologically it is different from the philosophical relation of causation. He says that "we . . . *feel* a determination of the mind," and he calls it "that propensity, which custom produces, to pass from an object to the idea of its usual attendant."[18] Whatever the problems of parsing Hume's conceptual confusion in identifying a feeling—what he calls an internal impression—with a mental propensity, it is clear enough that he thinks there is something more to the natural

---

[15] "Hume's Theory of Relations," *Nous* 1 (1967):255.

[16] *Treatise*, I, I, I, p. 4.

[17] See J. A. Robinson, "Hume's Two Definitions of 'Cause'," *Philosophical Quarterly* 12 (1962); reprinted in V. C. Chappell, *Hume* (Garden City, N.Y.: Anchor Books, 1966). References hereafter are to the reprint.

[18] *Treatise*, I, III, XIV, p. 165; emphasis mine.

relation of causation than the contiguity, succession, and constant conjunction he claims make up the philosophical relation. It looks as though it is different in kind, providing a real connection that the philosophical relation does not.

In the course of explaining how the natural relation of causation comes about, Hume suggests another basis of distinction that makes sense of that. He says that the philosophical relations of contiguity, succession, and constant conjunction exist "independent of, and antecedent to the operations of the understanding," and he goes on to claim that our observation of these philosophical relations produces the natural relation of causation.[19] Generalized, the suggestion is that philosophical relations are those that exist "independent of, and antecedent to the operations of the understanding," whereas natural relations are those that exist because of those underlying operations. The difference between the philosophical relation of causation in the empiricist principle and the natural relation between an impression and a lively idea is thus as follows. Although both relate an impression with an idea, the natural relation has come into existence only because prior observation of relations among, for example, billiard balls has activated underlying "operations of the understanding" to produce a propensity that in turn is activated to produce a lively idea upon the perception of one ball moving toward another.

This suggestion needs an elaborate explication and defense if it is to be accepted.[20] But if true, it has a number of implications. One is that "objective" does not mean for Hume "having to do with physical objects," as some have thought.[21] Rather, it means "independent of, and antecedent to the operations of the understanding." Another implication, more obviously relevant to our present concerns, is that an appeal to natural relations acquires a commitment to entities other than perceptions, in particular, mental dispositions and propensities. Thus when Hume appeals to the natural relation of causation in his comparison of a person with a republic, he carries extra baggage: underlying dispositions are being presupposed.

The critical point of that baggage can best be brought out by considering briefly what Hume is usually thought to be doing in making that

---

[19] Ibid., p. 164.
[20] I have presented a partial defense in "Glue Is Something Too," read at the Canadian Philosophical Association Meetings in Quebec City, June 1976.
[21] Robinson, p. 134.

comparison. On the standard view he is following a model of explanation he uses elsewhere. The model has two features relevant here: we mistake one entity for another, and the mistake is made for a reason. For instance, we mistake the natural relation of causation for the philosophical relation (which is why we think there is a necessary connection between a cause and its effect), and we make this mistake when the constant conjunction of objects produces the natural relation. That is, we call not just any objects cause and effect but only those so related as to produce, when observed, the relevant natural relation. There is thus a basis for our mistake.

In judgments of personal identity we mistake successive sets of perceptions for a single enduring entity, and there must be some feature or features of the mistaken object that tempt us to make the mistake. Nothing about the sets themselves or their members accounts for our mistake, Hume is saying. They are not marked in any internal way "James Thurber" or "Wittgenstein." What misleads us, Hume claims, are the relations in "the succession of objects." Thus the importance of the natural relation of resemblance is that it makes "the whole *seem* like the continuance of one object."[22] The natural relations of resemblance and causation are sufficient, Hume is claiming, to create such a succession of objects that we can be misled into claiming that there is a single entity. In short, there is an appearance of unity among succeeding sets of perceptions.

This is at best only an *appearance* of unity. On the one hand, precisely the point of Hume's introduction of natural relations is to explain why "not every thought to every thought succeeds indifferently."[23] But some *do* succeed indifferently, and these are not associated—causally or otherwise. On the other hand, there is no reason why my thought of a troubling net game might not be associated with your succeeding thought of Wheaties. Mere association is neither sufficient nor necessary to single out different sets of successive sets.

But, of course, association need not be for Hume.[24] After all, he uses the associative mechanism to explain our mistaken judgments. It does not matter to that explanation if the mechanism lets in some foreign

---

[22] *Treatise*, I, IV, VI, p. 261; emphasis mine.

[23] Hobbes, *Leviathan*, ed. Michael Oakeshott (Oxford: Basil Blackwell, 1960), p. 13.

[24] In appealing to principles of association, Hume is trying to explain—not to justify—ascriptions of personal identity. So the usual objection that the principles fail to sort out native from foreign perceptions is beside the point.

perceptions and leaves out some natives. What matters is that there be *some* basis for the mistake: we do not just guess wildly when we make such judgments. The mechanism need only provide enough of an appearance of unity to trigger the mistaken judgments.

In fact, however, there is not even the appearance of unity. For there are (at least) two problems of personal identity. The first is: (a) How can successive sets be identical? When Hume discusses our "great propension . . . to ascribe an identity" to persons, he concerns himself with this problem. Resemblance, remember, makes "the whole seem like the *continuance* of one object." But this first problem hides another: (b) How are sets singled out to begin with? Hume never tries to explain how we mistake a set of distinct objects for a single object: he never considers (b). But to ask how we mistake a succession of sets for a single enduring set is to presuppose that the sets in the succession have already been individuated.

It is this point, I suggest, that Hume came to see in the *Appendix*.[25] He says that his philosophy has "a promising aspect" up to where it claims that the ideas in a mind "are *felt* to be connected together, and *naturally* introduce each other."[26] But his hopes vanish, he says, when he comes "to explain the principles, that unite our successive perceptions."[27] The phrase "explain the principles" is a curious one, too unsteady in its application to force any one reading. But I suggest that in probing beneath the appearance of unity created by the natural relations Hume came to see, first, that his explanation of how we mistake a succession of perceptions for a single enduring entity presupposes a prior individuation of contemporaneous sets and, second, that such individuation is impossible within his system.

The difficulty is that the mind is complex: there are a number of perceptions existing at any one time, and there are underlying operations of the understanding. Thus there are two kinds of entities and three different sets of relations: relations among the contemporaneous perceptions, among them and the underlying operations, and among the underlying operations themselves. The associative mechanism at best only

---

[25] See my "Hume on Personal Identity," *Journal of the History of Philosophy* 12 (April, 1974). I made the same point there as I make here; but whereas here I exploit that feature of Hume's explanatory model that requires there to be something about the object that tempts us to make a mistake, there I exploited that feature of the model that requires there to be some being to make a mistake.

[26] *Treatise*, App. p. 635, emphasis mine.

[27] Ibid., pp. 635-36.

appears to unite, and then only perceptions, and only successive, not contemporaneous, ones. One might be misled into considering the contemporaneous perceptions somehow connected if one thought them closely tied to the operations of the understanding and thought those operations bound together. But those operations are not associated and are distinct existences within Hume's system: each can exist without any other and without inhering in anything. But if so, there is nothing that can sort out persons to begin with. As Hume sums up his difficulties in the *Appendix*, "Did our perceptions either inhere in something simple and individual, or did the mind perceive some real connexion among them, there wou'd be no difficulty in the case."[28] But there is a difficulty: if every entity that exists is a distinct particular, no complex entity can be unified.

Changing standards of identity will not give one a handle on this problem. As Hume saw, the difficulty lies much deeper within his system. Whether one requires strict identity through time or allows a succession of objects to be identical, one still presupposes that the object being singled out as identical through time has been singled out as distinct from other objects. But if that object is a complex, as the mind is, and if the elements of that complex are as distinct from each other as from any other entity, then the complex cannot be singled out. But judgments of personal identity certainly imply, if nothing else, that the entity being singled out as a person is distinct from other entities. That is the implication Hume relied upon when he considered our "great propension" to judge a succession of sets a single enduring set. For he supposed the prior individuation into sets that makes such judgments possible. But if such individuation is impossible, then changing standards of identity, which are applicable after such individuation has occurred, are of no help. Judgments of personal identity will still be inappropriate.

All this leaves us still with Hume's having introduced the comparison of a person with a state by saying that it is "the true idea of the human mind" and with his going on to say that "the same person may vary . . . without losing his identity." How is one to explain these remarks?

An essential feature of the sort of explanation Hume gives for our mistaken judgments is this: the only idea we have of a particular thing is not the idea we think we have. We thus start with causal judgments that, in an untutored state, we think assert a necessary connection between a

---

[28] Ibid., p. 636.

cause and its effect; but we discover, through philosophical analysis, that we have no idea of such a connection and that the only idea we have containing any entity that could be mistaken for that connection is derived in part from a propensity of the mind. It is thus appropriate to say that the *true* idea of causation is one that refers to a mental propensity. Of course, it does not follow that judgments of causation are true when construed as asserting a connection between a cause and its effect. In the same way, when Hume says he is introducing "the true idea of the human mind," he is to be read as saying that the *only* idea we have of a person is of "a succession of related objects." It does not follow from its being the only idea we have, and thus the true idea, that ascriptions of personal identity to such successions are true.

It might seem puzzling that Hume uses such an idea in judgments such as "the same person may vary . . . without losing his identity." If the idea is objectively false, as it were, how can Hume countenance such judgments? He does the same elsewhere, however. For instance, in the process of what the proponents of the new theory would have to call the development of his new standard, Hume observes that "it may be said without breach of the propriety of language, that such a church, which was formerly of brick, fell to ruin, and that the parish rebuilt the same church of free-stone, and according to modern architecture." It would certainly seem that Hume is maintaining here that it is acceptable to say such a thing. If it is false, how can it be acceptable? But he adds that we make such judgments because "we are never presented in any one point of time with the idea of difference and multiplicity; and for that reason are less scrupulous in calling them the same."[29] That is, we are speaking carelessly—with the vulgar, and not with the philosophers.

But even philosophers, he is fond of telling us, cannot maintain their philosophical stance and must revert to vulgar ways: we must make judgments of personal identity. They are just not true.

---

[29] Ibid., I, IV, VI, p. 258.

Hume's Theory of Mental Activity

Fred Wilson

COLERIDGE[1] AND BLANSHARD[2] HAVE ARGUED that mental associations can be counteracted and their consequences avoided through the activity of the active powers of the mind, guided by such ideals as those of aesthetics, logic, and (presumably in the case of empirical causation at least) the ideal of attaining better knowledge of matter-of-fact regularities. In contrast, it is suggested, Hume's associationism—the attempt to account for all mental activity in terms of the laws of association, that is, passivity—prevents him from recognizing the true role activity plays in our mental life. This point has been developed in detail by Robert Paul Wolff in his well-known essay "Hume's Theory of Mental Activity."[3] The twist he gives the thesis is his claim that in spite of the assertion of associationism Hume still, unconsciously as it were, recognizes the role of activity, an insight that was to be explicitly recognized and developed by Kant. Wolff explains that

> Hume began the *Treatise* with the assumption that empirical knowledge could be explained by reference to the contents of the mind alone, and then made the profound discovery that it was the activity of the mind, rather than the nature of its contents, which accounted for all the puzzling features of empirical knowledge. This insight, which was so brilliantly exploited by Kant . . . was used by Hume to clarify the nature of causal inference and to explain the origin of our concepts of material objects.[4]

We see here the passivity alleged to be entailed by the associationism contrasted to the supposed originating spontaneity of the human mind. And, no doubt, if Hume and the other associationists were so to deny activity in affirming passivity and also to appeal to activity in their accounts of mental development, then they would, as Basil Willey says,[5]

---

[1] Samuel Coleridge, *Biographia Literaria*, ed. J. Shawcross, 2 vols. (London: Oxford University Press, 1907), 1:73, 86.

[2] Brand Blanshard, "The Case for Determinism," in *Determinism and Freedom*, ed. Sidney Hook (New York: Collier, 1961), pp. 26f.

[3] *Philosophical Review* 69 (1960); reprinted in *Hume*, ed. V. C. Chappell (Garden City, N.Y.: Anchor Books, 1966), pp. 99-128 (all page references are to the latter).

[4] Ibid., pp. 99-100.

[5] *The Eighteenth Century Background* (New York: Columbia University Press, 1940), pp. 152-54.

be caught in a paradox of sorts. Now the crucial point here is the idea that associationism entails passivity. Unless that stands, no paradox is even apparent. What I propose to argue is that this crucial point is mistaken: it is in fact possible for an associationist to recognize that the mind might well actively control its own activities, in the sense of being guided, as Blanshard and Coleridge suggest, by various ideals. In particular, I want to argue that, contrary to Harrison,[6] Hume holds that not all habits of causal inference are completely unavoidable, but that the mind, guided by the ideal of improving its causal knowledge, can in fact actively modify its inferential habits.

The idea that associationism entails passivity arises, I believe, from the foisting upon Hume of a set of categories the applicability of which it is one of his main aims to deny. Philosophers may be divided in several ways; but when it comes to their accounts of what constitute explanations of events, perhaps the most important division is between those who argue that explanation is by appeal to active unanalyzable dispositions and those who argue that dispositions do not explain, that explanation is by laws, and that activity is not a basic ontological category.[7] Briefly, it is the division between Aristotelians and Humeans. Hume is a Humean: for him, activity plays no basic role in explanation, which means that explanation in terms of the laws of association implies neither passivity nor activity. Nor would the appeal to dispositions or tendencies imply any appeal to activity, since upon the Humean account these dispositions would not be unanalyzable, and appeal to them would reduce to an appeal to laws.[8] On the other hand, for the Aristotelian, "mere association" does imply passivity, whereas dispositions are active tendencies.[9] This means that if Hume is read through Aristotelian spectacles, then one will naturally find him caught up in Willey's paradox. But, to read him through such spectacles is to ignore a priori the Humean account of explanation Hume defends—the account stating that the Aristotelian categories are never appropriate, in other words, that the Aristotelian spectacles are always distorting. Furthermore, these spectacles obscure

---

[6] *Hume's Moral Epistemology* (London: Oxford Univesity Press, 1976), p. 45.

[7] See Fred Wilson, " Explanation in Aristotle, Newton and Toulmin," *Philosophy of Science* 36 (1969):291-310, 400-428.

[8] See F. Wilson, "Dispositions: Defined or Reduced?" *Australasian Journal of Philosophy* 47 (1969):184-204.

[9] See Coleridge's discussion of Aristotle on associative memory, the passive part of the mind, and its contrast with the active part (*Biographia Literaria*, chap. 5).

the role mental activity does play in Hume. While the Humean denies that activity is *basic* to explanation, he does not deny there are, in the ordinary senses, actions and, among these, mental actions. And Hume makes full use of the fact that we can actively control our thoughts and mental processes. Once the Aristotelian spectacles are put on, all this is for the most part missed. What is troublesome about Wolff's often illuminating discussion is that he never takes seriously Hume's own account of explanation and of causation. Wolff is, it seems to me, in far too great a hurry to get to Kant. Nothing could be more disastrous for a reading of Hume, for, whatever else he does, Kant does move away from Hume and back to Aristotle. From the viewpoint of a Humean, Kant's appeal to mental activities is, contrary to Wolff, no insight, not progress but regress.

1. HUME'S "EMOTIVIST" THEORY OF CAUSATION

As for associationism in a scientific theory, there is nothing a priori absurd in it—in fact, it can easily be restated in behavioristic terms[10]—and for a long time it yielded a flourishing research program. For various reasons, it eventually became degenerate, and what was best in it and worth keeping was ultimately absorbed into the mainstream of behavioristic psychology as it exists today.[11] We need not go into this history. That it exists suffices. For it shows that the theory does in fact have some evidential plausibility. There are data that do support it. And the history further shows that the theory is capable of criticism and of growth.[12] Though associationist ideas can be found as early as Aristotle, in his account of memory, it was of course Hume who first argued systematically for the theory. And that is to say that he appealed to the theory to explain, among other things, the facts of mental life. In particular, it was this theory "by which we explain the operations of the understanding, [and] the origin and connexion of the passions in man" and by which he "endeavoured to account for all experimental reasonings."[13]

---

[10] See Gustav Bergmann, "The Problem of Relations in Classical Psychology," in his *Metaphysics of Logical Positivism* (New York: Longmans, 1954), pp. 277-99.

[11] It is detailed in E. G. Boring, *A History of Experimental Psychology*, 2nd ed. (New York: Appleton-Century-Crofts, 1957); see especially pp. 343-44.

[12] For its last stages, see G. Humprey, *Thinking* (New York: Wiley, Science Editions, 1953), esp. chaps. 1-4.

[13] *An Enquiry concerning Human Understanding*, ed. L. A. Selby-Bigge, 2nd ed. (Oxford, 1902), IX, pp. 104-5 (hereafter cited as first *Enquiry*).

The theory itself is a case of "experimental reasoning." Therefore, in a way it applies to itself. This is not paradoxical: there is, after all, a psychology of psychology, just as there is a sociology of science. But it is important, for it is just this mind knowing itself, so to speak, that enables mind intelligently to interfere in its own activities and to direct them more efficiently for the best. But this is to slide into language that is too close for comfort to that of the Aristotelian or the Kantian, so we had best go rather more slowly. Let us look more carefully, therefore, at the associationist account of causal reasoning that Hume gives.

Hume gives two definitions of "cause."[14] There has been some controversy about this: How can one give two different definitions of the same notion without contradiction?[15] J. A. Robinson has suggested that the first definition is the *real* definition and that the second is *not* really a definition but is a psychological comment on the relation so defined.[16] There is a point to this, since it *is* clear that the second definition introduces an element of psychology derived from and explained by the associationist theory. On the other hand, it does fly in the face of Hume's explicitly saying that he is giving two definitions. More seriously, however, if one construes Hume as giving only the first definition as *the* definition of "cause," then one is attributing to him what A. C. Ewing has called the "regularity" theory of causality, which holds that there is nothing more to causal assertions than assertions of *de facto* regular connection.[17] It attributes to Hume an analysis of causation "as nothing more than an instance of a general uniformity of concomitance between two classes of particular occurrences."[18] But this theory may be criticized, as it is by Ewing, as being unable to distinguish causal associations from those that occur by chance, in other words, for being unable to distinguish laws from accidental generalities. The difficulty is that Hume never held this "regularity" theory.[19] The *Treatise* fully recognizes the

---

[14] *A Treatise of Human Nature*, ed. L. A. Selby-Bigge (Oxford, 1888), I, III, XIV, p. 172 (hereafer cited as *Treatise*).

[15] J. A. Robinson, "Hume's Two Definitions of 'Cause'," in Chappell, pp. 129-47; Thomas J. Richards, "Hume's Two Definitions of 'Cause'," ibid., pp. 148-61; and J. A. Robinson, "Hume's Two Definitions of 'Cause' Reconsidered," ibid., pp. 162-68. The mentioned question has been raised by Robinson, *ibid*, pp. 123, 162.

[16] Chappell, pp. 138-39.

[17] *The Fundamental Questions of Philosophy* (London: Routledge and Kegal Paul, 1951), chap. 8, "Cause."

[18] Robinson, in Chappell, pp. 138-39.

[19] See Norman Kemp Smith, *The Philosophy of David Hume* (London: Macmillan, 1941), pp. 91-92.

distinction Ewing's "regularity" theory denies between *post hoc* and *propter hoc*.[20] As it points out, "an object may be contiguous and prior to another, without being consider'd as its cause. There is a NECESSARY CONNEXION to be taken into consideration; and that relation is of much greater imporance, than any of the other two above-mention'd."[21] And most of the rest of Book I, Part III is devoted in one way or another to an investigation of the nature of this necessary connection. Robinson thus commits Hume to a theory Hume explicitly denies. It is the point of Hume's second definition, I suggest, to introduce the element of necessary connection that a "mere regularity" theory fails to capture. What must be done is to make clear how the two definitions are related to each other.

Fundamental to understanding Hume's account of causation is the distinction that can be drawn with respect to our beliefs between the propositional attitude and the propositional content. If one person believes that Toronto is west of Hamilton and a second disbelieves it, the propositional content of both beliefs is the same, namely, the proposition that Toronto is west of Hamilton. But the propositional attitudes in the two beliefs are different. In one case the attitude is that of believing or asserting; in the other it is that of disbelieving or denying. The propositional content is true or false. Its truth-value depends only on the facts it is about. In particular it does not depend upon what propositional attitude one has with respect to that content. This independence is important since it is precisely this independence that enables truth and falsity to function as *standards* justifying the attitude one has. The attitude of believing or asserting with respect to a proposition is *objectively justified* if and only if that proposition is true. And the attitude of disbelieving or denying is objectively justified if and only if the proposition is false. Clearly, if truth-value depended on attitude, the former could not provide an objective standard for evaluating the latter.

The first definition of "cause" is this: "*an object precedent and contiguous to another, and where all objects resembling the former are plac'd in a like relation of priority and contiguity to those objects, that resemble the latter.*"[22] In other words, one event causes a second where the two are

---

[20] Harrison, p. 44, suggests, wrongly, that Hume fails to distinguish *post hoc* and *propter hoc*: "He [Hume] also fails to distinguish between believing that whenever there is smoke there is fire, and that smoke is caused by fire."
[21] *Treatise*, I, III, II, p. 77.
[22] Ibid., XIV, p. 172.

subsumable under a matter-of-fact generality. Particular instances of causation are to be understood in terms of *de facto* regularities. This means that any proposition stating a causal regularity has the logical form $(x)(fx \supset gx)$, where the descriptive predicates are logically independent of each other. This renders in the language of Russell the Humean point that cause and effect are logically independent of each other.[23]

It follows that so far as propositional content is concerned, the assertion of a causal regularity involves no difference in logical form from the assertion of an accidental generality. Both are of the form $(x)(fx \supset gx)$, from which it follows that *objectively there is no logical difference between causal regularities and accidental generalities*. Objectively, then, there is no difference of a logical sort between *post hoc* and *propter hoc*. Yet such a distinction is to be drawn, as Hume recognizes;[24] so he raises the question, "*What is our idea of necessity, when we say that two objects are necessarily connected together.*"[25] What he finds is that when two sorts are causally connected, upon the appearance of an object of the one sort "the mind is *determin'd* by custom to consider its usual attendant" and that it is this "*determination*, which affords [him] the idea of necessity."[26] This yields the second definition of "cause" as "*an object precedent and contiguous to another, and so united with it in the imagination, that the idea of the one determines the mind to form the idea of the other, and the impression of the one to form a more lively idea of the other.*"[27] If a propositional content of the form $(x)(fx \supset gx)$ is such that as *a matter of psychological fact* it is used to support assertions of subjunctive conditionals ("the idea of the one determines the mind to form the idea of the other") and to make predictions ("the impression of the one [determines the mind] to form a more lively idea of the other"), *then* the assertion of that proposition is the assertion of a causal generality. A generality is lawlike just in case it is in fact used to predict and to support subjunctive conditionals; otherwise it is a statement of "mere regularity." The connection between lawlike generalities and subjunctive

---

[23] Ibid., XII, p. 139. See Alan Hausman, "Hume's Theory of Relations," *Nous* 1 (1967): 255-82.

[24] *Treatise*, I, II, III, p. 77: "An object may be contiguous and prior to another, without being consider'd as its cause. There is a NECESSARY CONNEXION to be taken into consideration; and that relation is of much greater importance, than any of the other two above-mention'd."

[25] Ibid., III, XIV, p. 155.

[26] Ibid., p. 156.

[27] Ibid., p. 172.

conditionals has often been remarked upon.[28] What Hume does is use this connection to *define* lawlikeness. A generality is causal or not depending upon its psychological context. Lawlikeness is a matter of the propositional attitude that obtains with respect to the generality. The generality is lawlike if and only if it is not merely believed or asserted but is asserted in a certain more specific way, namely, with a preparedness to take risks with it, that is, to predict and to assert subjunctive conditionals. We may call this the law-assertion attitude.

Lawlikeness thus becomes a subjective matter. It is not objective, a feature of the logical form of causal propositions. The thesis in ethics that value is a matter not of propositional content but rather of the psychological attitude is often called "emotivism." Hume's account of causation may therefore perhaps not unreasonably be characterized as an emotivist account of causation. Indeed, I think it is possible to push this analogy with various ethical theories—Hume's in particular, of course—some good distance. But one should be careful not to call Hume's ethical views "emotivist" *simpliciter*.[29] In particular, one must account for our correcting and adjusting our moral judgments, a point he emphasizes many times.[30] It is a point he also emphasizes in aesthetics: in his essay "Of the Standard of Taste,"[31] Hume discussed how we correct aesthetic judgments, giving a very detailed analysis of the process. This is, of course, the basis of my objection to the thesis of Blanshard and Coleridge that, on associationist principles, the mind cannot be guided by certain ideals and regulate its own activities in terms of those standards. In particular, I want to argue that Hume similarly holds, in a way compatible with his associationism, that mind, guided by the ideal of truth, can actively correct its causal judgments.

But now let us return to the point where Hume's theory of causal judgments is similar to emotivism—that causality, like value, is a matter not of propositional content but psychological attitude. As we noted, given this similarity, Hume's account of causation might be called an emotivist account. Once this is noted, one also recognizes similar objections that can be raised against both the thesis about moral judgments

---

[28] See, e.g., R. M. Chisholm, "Law Statements and Counterfactual Inference," *Analysis* 15 (1955):97–105.

[29] For a more adequate placing of Hume's ethical views see Páll Árdal, *Passion and Value in Hume's Treatise* (Edinburgh: Univesity of Edinburgh Press, 1966), esp. chap. 9.

[30] E.g., *Treatise*, III, III, I, p. 582.

[31] In *The Philosophical Works*, ed. T. H. Green and T. H. Grose, 4 vols. (London, 1886), 3:266–84.

and the thesis about causal judgments. As with the emotivist theory in ethics, the immediate question about the emotivist theory of causation is this: Does not emotivism, when it denies the existence of an objective standard, entail that whether the attitude is adopted is not something that permits of justification? Or, in other words, does not Hume's account reduce causal reasoning to irrationalism?[32]

Now the reply to this, in Hume's case as in ethics, is to challenge the presupposition of the objector's question and ask what one might *reasonably* mean by "justification" in this context. In ethics, if the emotivist's arguments that objectivism is false are accepted, then it is no serious objection to his account that he leaves no room for an objective justification of value judgments. Of course he has left no room: he has just finished arguing that such justification is not possible. And if it is not possible, it is not reasonable to insist upon it. Whatever justification amounts to in ethics, the one thing that cannot *reasonably* be demanded is objective justification. And in the case of Hume's account of causation the same sort of response is called for. *Given* Hume's argument that, objectively considered, all causal assertions are assertions of constant conjunction,[33] *then* it is not reasonable to demand an *objective* justification for the adoption of the law-assertion attitude toward some generalities rather than others.[34]

However, from the fact that no objective justification is possible, it does not follow that all adoptions of the law-assertion attitude are equally justified. Though the demand for objective justification is unreasonable, not all law-assertive attitudes are equally justified. Though the demand for objective justification is unreasonable, not all law-assertive attitudes are therefore equally reasonable. Hume clearly recognizes this point and explicitly draws our attention to cases where the law-assertion attitude holds but where it is also not justified. His discussions of credulity,[35] of the often adverse effects of education,[36] of the role

---

[32] H. A. Prichard, *Knowledge and Perception* (London: Oxford University Press, 1950), p. 184, suggests that Hume thus reduces all causal inferences to irrationality.

[33] For a discussion of Hume's positive case against necessary connections, see F. Wilson, "Acquaintance, Ontology, and Knowledge," *New Scholasticism* 54 (1970):1-48; also Hausman, "Hume's Theory of Relations."

[34] First *Enquiry* XII, II, p. 160. See J. Lenz, "Hume's Defense of Causal Inference," in Chappell, pp. 169-86; also A. J. Ayer, *The Problem of Knowledge* (Harmondsworth: Penguin Books, 1956), p. 75.

[35] *Treatise*, I, III, IX, p. 112.

[36] Ibid., p. 116. This discussion of the role of education cannot be fully understood until

of imagination,[37] of unphilosophical probability (to which a whole chapter is devoted),[38] all make evident that the *Treatise* draws a distinction between these cases where the attitude is unjustifiably held and cases where it is justifiably held, where its adoption is in accordance with the "Rules by which to judge of causes and effects," which appear in their own chapter with that very title.[39]

An assertive attitude is objectively justified if and only if the proposition in question is true. But this holds equally for laws and for "mere regularities"; provided that the latter are true, they may justifiably be asserted. So truth, while *sufficient* to justify the attitude of assertion or mere assertion, is only *necessary* to justify the attitude of law-assertion. Thus, if a generality is false, one is objectively unjustified in holding toward it the law-assertion attitude. This will be so even if the other necessary conditions of justification (whatever they may be) are all fulfilled. And it will be so even if we have *all possible reason* to believe that that necessary condition of truth is fulfilled.

A generality is a statement about a total population. Normally all one ever observes is a sample. Between sample and population there is a logical gap. This gap is such that properties regularly associated or constantly conjoined in the observed sample may not be constantly conjoined in the population. Hume argues for the existence of this logical gap,[40] which he at one point[41] expresses as the principles *"there is nothing in any object, consider'd in itself, which can afford us a reason for drawing a conclusion beyond it"* and *"that even after the observation of the frequent or constant conjunction of objects, we have no reason to draw any inference concerning any object beyond those of which we have had experience"* (that is, reason drawn from those objects "consider'd in

---

Hume explains, in Book II, the role of the principle of sympathy in the understanding of Human nature. See in particular ibid., II, I, XI, pp. 316-17. See also Árdal, pp. 46ff. This illustrates, what is too often not realized, that Book I of the *Treatise* cannot be fully understood if it is read independently of Books II and III. The same point should be made with respect to Hume's views on causation; indeed, the present paper argues that point in detail. One could in fact suggest that one good reason for Wolff's failure to do justice to the real elements of mental activity in Hume's account of causal reasoning lies in his failure to examine either Hume's account of human action in Book II or his account of our evaluations of human actions (i.e., primarily, but not exclusively, moral judgments) in Book III.

[37] *Treatise*, I, III, X, p. 123.
[38] Ibid., XIII, pp. 132ff.
[39] Ibid., XV, pp. 173ff.
[40] Ibid., III.
[41] Ibid., XII, p. 139.

themselves" rather than "never any sort of reason," for, after all, Hume does go on to give us the "Rules by which to judge of causes" where he sketches the conditions under which one *can* reasonably infer from a sample to a population). That properties are constantly conjoined in a sample is a necessary condition for their being constantly conjoined in the population. A necessary condition for justifiably making a law-assertion is that the generality asserted be true. Given the *logical* gap between sample and population, it is *not possible* to know whether this necessary condition is fulfilled simply by observing that the regularity obtains in the sample. The *best* we can do is to know that a necessary part of this necessary condition obtains, namely, that the regularity holds in the sample. That is the *best* we can do, short of omniscience. And since it is the best we *can* have, we must make do with it. *If we observe that a regularity holds in a sample, we thereby have every objective reason it is (at that point)*[42] *possible to have to justify one in believing that the regularity holds in the population.*[43] Subjectively, the only and best objective evidence a regularity obtains overall is that we have observed it to obtain among the facts we already know. So, subjectively, we may be justified in asserting a generality when objectively the assertion is not justified.[44] Still, if we have done the best we can do, if we assert only when we are subjectively justified, then we cannot be blamed for not having done more, even where we are objectivley unjustified. Fallibility is not a vice.[45]

We have still not distinguished causal from "mere" regularities. The remarks just made, drawing attention to our fallibility, apply equally to both sorts of regularity. An observed constant conjunction is a necessary condition for our being subjectively justified in adopting the law-assertion attitude toward a generality, but it is not a sufficient subjective condition. It is sufficient only if the acquisition of this evidence has proceeded in accordance with the "rules by which to judge of causes."

---

[42] I.e., without gathering more evidence, or enlarging the sample.

[43] This is a bit too simple. Contrary generalities can be confirmed if we pick our samples correctly; clearly, we are presupposing a principle of total evidence. But the point remains, since even the total evidence is but a sample relative to total population — the population of the universe.

[44] Compare the discussion of subjective and objective justification in G. E. Moore, *Ethics* (London: Oxford University Press, 1912), pp. 118-21, where it arises in the context of a discussion of utilitarianism.

[45] See T. Beauchamp and T. A. Mappes, "Is Hume really a Sceptic about Induction?" *American Philosophical Quarterly* 12 (1975):119-34.

Hume notes carefully that there are many situations in which the mind is confronted with a set of contrary hypotheses, each of which initially fits the data, fulfills the necessary condition for being subjectively justified.[46] Since these are contraries, the law-assertive attitude toward any particular one cannot be justified initially. But now suppose more data is sought, in accordance with the "rules by which to judge of causes." Suppose further that these data ultimately eliminate all but one of the contraries. In that case the adoption of the law-assertive attitude toward that hypothesis will be (subjectively) justified, that is, justified to the extent that it is reasonable to seek such justification. On the other hand, other principles of selection are possible.

Hume cites the principle that we choose as worthy of law-assertion the hypotheses we want to be true, quoting Cardinal de Retz on the principle that the wish is the father of the belief, *"that there are many things, in which the world wishes to be deceiv'd."*[47] Where the world wishes to be deceived it can avoid trying to gather together the *evidence* relevant to reasonably deciding among the possible hypotheses.[48] In the chapter "Of unphilosophical probability"[49] a number of such unreasonable principles are mentioned. Those who desire a *reasonable decision* among contrary hypotheses must go out and *actively collect* additional observational evidence that will permit a decision to be made. The data that is given is often acquired only with great difficulty. As Hume puts it, directly after stating the "rules by which to judge of causes":

> There is no phaenomenon in nature, but what is compounded and modify'd by so many different circumstances, that in order to arrive at the decisive point, we must carefully separate whatever is superfluous, and enquire by new experiments, if every particular circumstance of the first experiment was essential to it. These new experiments are liable to a discussion of the same kind; so that the utmost constancy is requir'd to make us persevere in our enquiry, and the utmost sagacity to choose the right way among so many that present themselves.[50]

One makes a reasonable decision among alternative possible hypotheses when one has *actively* sought out such data as would permit one logically

---

[46] *Treatise*, I, III, XII, pp. 131-35; XIII, p. 154.
[47] Ibid., XIII, p. 153.
[48] Ibid., pp. 152-53.
[49] Ibid., XIII.
[50] Ibid., XV, p. 175.

to make such a decision, eliminating or falsifying hypotheses until exactly one is rendered subjectively worthy of law-assertion. *The choice among hypotheses may be made* EITHER *by collecting relevant observational evidence according to the "rules by which to judge of causes"* OR *by some other principle. If on some basis other than such observational evidence, then the resulting law-assertion is unjustified.*

2. Reason and the Active Mind

But why pick out the rules Hume does as providing *reasonable* justification rather than some other rules? What makes Hume's rules the *reasonable* ones to adopt? Partly, the answer is that the data alone should decide among hypotheses and that until sufficient data are available the law-assertive attitude ought not to be adopted. But this is not the whole story. In order to see what else is involved we must look more closely at the associationist ideas Hume makes use of in his definition and, in particular, in his second definition of "cause."

The association may be stated in stimulus-response terms. A certain kind of stimulus comes to evoke a certain kind of response. The response is an idea: its kind is that it is an idea of an impression of such and such a sort. The stimulus that evokes this response is either an impression of kind so and so, or an idea of an impression of that kind. Briefly, a stimulus — either impression or idea — of kind so and so elicits a response of kind such and such. *This is a regularity. An association is always a regularity*: whenever one kind of thing is presented then some other kind of thing is thought of.[51] But such regularities do not hold unconditionally. Among the things such a regularity depends upon is repeated experience of the kind of impressions the association is about: "After a frequent repetition, I find, that upon the appearance of one of the objects, the mind is *determin'd* by custom to consider its usual attendant."[52] Whether contiguity is a sufficient condition for the establishment of all associations was a matter the associationists investigated in detail.[53] This controversy in learning theory need not detain us: it parallels such more recent controversies in learning theory as that between classical conditioning and reinforcement. Certainly, Hume is aware of

---

[51] See Wolff, p. 107.
[52] *Treatise*, I, III, XIV, p. 156.
[53] See Boring, pp. 191, 224, 228-29, 239.

the relevance of factors other than mere contiguity in establishing associations: I have already cited him on the principle that there are many things about which the world wishes to be deceived.[54] For our purposes it suffices to note that upon the associationist account there are laws of learning, or regularities that describe the conditions under which associations are formed. Now any associaiton may reasonably be conceived as a settled disposition or tendency for one thing to be thought of when another is presented.[55] Wolff makes this point, but he fails to note that what underlies the disposition-talk is the fact of the regularity.[56] And explanation is by way of appeal to this regularity, the fact of association, not by appeal to the disposition. Just as the conditional regularities, or associations, may be thought of in dispositional terms, so also one may think in dispositional terms of the more general and unconditioned regularities, describing the conditions under which associations are formed. In this case we will have dispositions to acquire dispositions, or, as Wolff calls them, propensities.[57] But again, explanation appeals to the regularity underlying the propensity-talk, not to the propensity as such. It is only by missing this point that Wolff makes Hume seem to be what he clearly is not, namely, a Kantian. The fundamental laws of learning, the basic propensities if you wish, Hume does not purport to explain: these are simply basic, an original quality of human nature.[58]

There are different kinds of associations: those that give meaning to general terms,[59] and those involved in causal inferences. Only the latter involve "necessity." Indeed, it is the particular kind of "determination" by "custom" in the case of causal inference "which affords me the idea of necessity,"[60] that is, of causal necessity. The difference here is between meaning and inference, and the point is that in inferring, the mind is active in a way that it is not in the case of merely thinking of some general kind or class. In the case of inference there is an element of mental impulse or activity that carries the mind from the existence of the condition (stimulus) to the actualization of the disposition (response). The mental impulse is involved here, it seems to me, in the same way in which

---

[54] *Treatise*, I, III, XIII, p. 153.
[55] Cf. G. Bergmann, "Dispositional Properties and Dispositions," *Philosophical Studies* 6 (1955):77-80.
[56] "Hume's theory of Mental Acitivity," pp. 104-5.
[57] Ibid., p. 106.
[58] *Treatise*, I, I, IV, p. 13.
[59] Ibid., VII, p. 22.
[60] Ibid., III, XIV, p. 156.

such conative mental states are associated with certain settled bodily dispositions.[61] Thus, with respect to certain people, regularly when presented with cookies, they tend to eat. This is a certain power or tendency, and its presence can be inferred from its exercise.[62] It is, furthermore, quite clearly an acquired rather than an instinctive behavior pattern. But besides the factors that bring about the presence of the disposition there is another factor that must be taken into account, namely, the fact that the exercise of the power is the consequence of an act of will: when presented with cookies one has an *impulse* to eat them. It is the exertion of the will that converts the power into action.[63] The point is that such conative impulses are connected with mental as well as bodily events, for Hume defines the will as that *"impression we feel . . . when we knowingly give rise to any new motion of our body, or new perception of our mind."*[64] As Hume defines it, "will" implies a degree of self-consciousness[65] that is perhaps absent from the most primitive of our causal inferences. For these latter the relevant conative impulse is perhaps more like those direct passions such as "hunger, lust, and a few other bodily appetites" that "arise from a natural impulse or instinct"[66] (save, of course, that Hume would no doubt argue that although the instinctive tendencies called bodily appetites are not learned, even the most primitive of our causal-inference dispositions are probably not native). Causal inferences, then, are the exercise of certain settled mental dispositions. Involved in the exercise of this is a certain conative impulse. This conative impulse determines the mind to move from the stimulus impression or idea to the response idea. This conative impulse Hume calls an "impression of reflexion."[67] It is this impression that yields the idea of necessity:

> The idea of necessity arises from some impression. There is no impression convey'd by our senses, which can give rise to that idea. It must, therefore, be deriv'd from some internal impression, or

---

[61] F. Wilson, "Why I Do Not Experience Your Pains," in M. Gram and E. Klemke, eds., *The Ontological Turn* (Iowa City: University of Iowa Press, 1974), pp. 276-300.

[62] *Treatise*, II, I, X, p. 311.

[63] Ibid., I, I, IV, p. 12.

[64] Ibid., II, II, XII, p. 399.

[65] Cf. Joseph Butler's point, at the beginning of his "Dissertation II: Of the Nature of Virtue," in *Works*, ed. S. Halifax (London, 1874), 1:328-39. Butler begins with the point that will and design constitute the very nature of actions (p. 330).

[66] *Treatise*, II, III, IX, p. 439.

[67] Ibid., I, I, II, pp. 7-8; cf. II, I, I, p. 275.

impression of reflexion. There is no internal impression, which has any relation to the present business, but that propensity, which custom produces, to pass from an object to the idea of its usual attendant. This therefore is the essence of necessity.[68]

The idea of necessity, then, is the idea of an internal impulse that operates, in the first instance at least, outside our control. Elsewhere Hume brings out explicitly the connection between causal necessity and felt inexorability.[69]

We may conclude, then, that in his account of causal inference Hume *does* introduce mental propensities, activities, and faculties. "How can there be, according to Hume," asks Prichard, "such a thing as a faculty, and if there can, how can we be aware of it?"[70] The answer is, of course, that in Prichard's (Aristotle's) sense there is for Hume no such thing as a faculty. There is rather only settled dispositions or regularities. But Hume does not need Aristotelian faculties. The settled dispositions or regularities explain all that needs to be explained. As for how we become aware of them, it is evident that there is no problem. Their presence is made known through their exercise, which, according to any Humean, is at bottom[71] the only way their presence can become known, since a disposition just *is* its regular exercise:[72] "The distinction, which we sometimes make betwixt a *power* and the *exercise* of it, is entirely frivolous, and . . . neither man nor any other being ought ever to be thought possest of any ability, unless it be exerted and put into action."[73] But in addition, in the case of certain powers, conative impulses are involved in their exercise. So for these we are aware, too, of the conative impulses. In this double way, then, we become aware of the mental faculties involved in causal inference.

Wolff suggests that "the factors in cognition which Hume labeled

---

[68] Ibid., I, III, XIV, p. 165.

[69] Ibid., II, III, I, pp. 406-7.

[70] *Knowledge and Perception*, p. 177. See also the discussion of Prichard in Hausman, sec. II (A).

[71] It is also possible to infer its presence *given* its having been observed *in its exercise* in analogous cases. See *Treatise*, II, I, X, pp. 311-13; also Wilson, "Dispositions: Defined or Reduced?"

[72] See Wilson, "Dispositions: Defined or Reduced?"; R. Grossman, *Ontological Reduction* (Bloomington, Ind.: University of Indiana Press, 1973), sec. 10; G. Bergmann, "Comments on Professor Hempel's 'The Concept of Cognitive Significance'," in his *Metaphysics of Logical Positivism*, pp. 255-67.

[73] *Treatise*, II, I, X, p. 311.

impressions of reflection—such as the impression of necessary connection—are really dispositions, and the ideas of necessary connection, . . . and so forth, are not copies of impressions but ideas of mental dispositions."[74] And he argues that Hume cannot have it both that the impression of necessary connection, "like an impression of love or envy, [is] a directly observable mental content"[75] and that the impression is the "propensity . . . to pass from an object to the idea of its usual attendant,"[76] that is, "that the impression *is* the transition."[77] Wolff attributes this confusion to Hume's having Kant's insight about mental activities but trying to put it into the strait jacket of associationism. What I have just argued is that Hume can and does have it both ways, and that there is nothing confused in this. By ignoring the impression of reflection Wolff not only fails to do justice to Hume, but he also fails to see the real role of mental activity, or conative impulse, in Hume's account of the understanding. And in failing to see this last, Wolff also fails to see the much more important role mental activity plays in Hume's account of mind.

Hume's account of mind, his account in terms of dispositions and propensities, is an account in terms of laws. These *laws* are themselves subject to a Humean analysis, of course. As Hume remarks, "The same experienc'd union has the same effect on the mind,[78] whether the united objects be motives, volitions and actions; or figure and motion."[79] What these laws of learning describe are (among other things) the conditions under which law-assertive attitudes are acquired. There are a number of sufficient conditions for acquiring this attitude. Frequent repetition by itself is one.[80] So is frequent repetition under the further condition that the "rules by which to judge of causes" have been conformed to. So is the wish that is father to the belief.[81] Let us call the acquisition of a law-assertive attitude *successful* just in case the predictions it yields turn out

---

[74] "Hume's Theory of Mental Activity," p. 107.

[75] Ibid., p. 111.

[76] *Treatise*, I, III, XIV, p. 165.

[77] Wolff, p. 112.

[78] I.e., upon the mind of the observer, the one thinking about the process. See *Treatise*, II, III, II, p. 408: "The necessity of any action, whether of matter or of the mind, is not properly a quality in the agent, but in any thinking or intelligent being, who may consider the action, and consists in the determination of his thought to infer its existence from some preceding objects. . . ."

[79] Ibid., pp. 406-7.

[80] Ibid., I, III, XIV, p. 156.

[81] Ibid., XIII, p. 153.

to be true. *If we are guided by the aim of discovering the truth, so far as we can, then we shall be aiming to acquire successful law-assertive attitudes.* What we discover are regularities to the effect that certain conditions bringing about law-assertive attitudes are more likely than others to yield successful law-assertive attitudes. These regularities are inductions about making inductions. The infirmities attaching to all inductive inference thus attach to these, and doubly so, if you wish. Yet we can and have tested them. Thus, of the three conditions I have mentioned, the third is much more likely than not to yield *unsuccessful* law-assertive attitudes. The first, too, except in very special cases, is unreliable. Only the second is in general relatively efficient in producing successful law-assertive attitudes. *This is a lawful fact we discover about ourselves, the world, and our interactions with it.* We discover that if we are serious about the truth, then we should put aside the pieties of religion (it is a "blameable" method of reasoning to condemn a doctrine because it is dangerous to religion)[82] and the platitudes put into us by education ("an artificial and not a natural cause" of belief)[83] and rely instead upon the "rules by which to judge of causes," the norms of "experimental philosophy."[84]

Previously I asked why it is reasonable to adopt Hume's "rules by which to judge of causes" as the conditions of subjective justification for adopting the law-assertive attitude, rather than some other rules. We now have our answer to that question. *Given that our end is to come to believe general truths, then what we discover is that, as a matter of lawful fact, conformity to these rules is the best or most efficient means for achieving that end, so far as we are able.* What we must do, then, is so discipline ourselves that we adopt the law-assertive attitude under only these conditions, not the others. Such self-discipline is, of course, difficult: "The utmost constancy is requir'd to make us persevere in our enquiry, and the utmost sagacity to choose the right way among so many that present themselves."[85] But such discipline is possible. And if our end is that of truth, then it is a discipline we *ought* to practice. We earlier emphasized that causal inference involved an element of conative impulse, of mental activity. What we are now seeing is that, like all appetites and impulses, these, too, can be disciplined. As Butler indicated,

---
[82] Ibid., II, III, II, p. 409.
[83] Ibid., I, III, IX, p. 117.
[84] Ibid., XV, p. 175.
[85] Ibid.

particular impulses are not to be denied, are not to be reduced to self-love,[86] though they are to be disciplined by the principle of self-love[87] and also by other higher principles.[88] So, also, according to Hume, are our mental impulses to be disciplined to higher ends: "Who indeed does not feel an accession of alacrity in his pursuits of knowledge and ability of every kind, when he considers, that besides the advantage, which immediately result from these acquisitions, they also give him a new lustre in the eyes of mankind, and are universally attended with esteem and approbation?"[89]

According to some, Hume holds that we have a causal belief only if that belief is caused by the observation of a constant conjunction in a sample.[90] This creates a picture of a mind of utter passivity, in the ordinary sense of passivity: there is nothing in the mind but what is passively received. Hume, of course, holds nothing like this: the causes of causal belief are many and varied. Far from being passive, the mind is too active: "superstition is much more bold in its systems and hypotheses than philosophy."[91] If the aim is truth, then imagination must be curbed. The mind, at least sometimes aiming at truth, discovers the laws of its own operation, including the laws describing the process by which it arrives at beliefs, successful and unsuccessful. Using these, and monitoring its own activities, it can regulate itself by this feedback process so as more efficiently to attain the truth as far as it is able. This element of feedback and self-discipline is crucial to understanding why Hume's "rules by which to judge of causes" are those that *reasonably* render a law-belief subjectively justified. The existence of such feedback mechanisms are, of course, quite compatible with Hume's account of causation. There is nothing in his discussion of laws that prevents there being laws governing feedback. What Wolff completely misses is the vast extent to which Hume, in his account of why some but not all causal inferences are reasonable, relies upon the possibility of an active mind, one which can observe itself, monitor its own activities, and discipline itself better to attain the truth.

And this is also, of course, precisely the point that places Hume's

---

[86] Preface to *Sermons*, *Works*, 2:xxi–xxii.
[87] Ibid., pp. xxvi–xxvii.
[88] "Dissertation II," *Works*, 1:330.
[89] *Treatise*, III, III, VI, p. 620.
[90] See, e.g., C. J. Ducasse, *Nature, Mind and Death* (Lasalle, Ill.: Open Court, 1951), pp. 91–100. Also, F. Wilson, "Hume and Ducasse on Causal Inference from a Single Observation," *Philosophical Studies*, forthcoming.
[91] *Treatise*, I, IV, VII, p. 271.

position beyond criticisms such as those of Coleridge, Willey, and Blanshard: an associationist can very well introduce into his account of mind the idea that it can discipline its own habitual and impulsive responses so as to bring itself more into conformity with certain standards it has set for itself.

Why is this point so often missed? I think that perhaps at least part of the problem lies in the structure of the *Treatise*. At the end of his discussion on causation Hume unfortunately does not fully develop the idea of the mind actively adjusting, in accordance with deliberately adopted rules, our law-assertive attitudes to systematically sought-out data. Of course, he *mentions* this point. That, after all, is why he included the section "Rules by which to judge of causes and effects." But it is still true that he does not develop it in detail. But there is perfectly good reason for the gap at this point in Hume's discussion. The *Treatise* is throughout a discussion of man in terms of psychological theory. Book I, "Of the Understanding," deals with what we would now call the psychology of cognition and of thought; Book II, "Of the Passions," deals with motivation; Book III, "Of Morals," deals with personality. As a matter of fact this is a perfectly reasonable organization for a psychology text. But it means that the description of the motivation for knowledge, and the psychological types appropriate to the active search for knowledge, cannot be given when Hume discusses the "rules" such persons use. It is only in Book II, Part III, Section X, "Of curiosity, or the love of truth," that Hume discusses the motive that is "the first source of all our enquiries."[92] And only in Book III, Part III, Section V, "Of natural abilities," does he deal with the qualities characteristic of persons who are able most judiciously to arrive at correct law-assertions;[93] though, as we saw, both motive ("constancy") and ability ("sagacity") were mentioned by Hume when he discussed the use of his "rules."[94]

If one's sole end were knowledge, then the search for relevant data would continue until only one of the possible hypotheses had been made subjectively worthy of law-assertion. And even then, in the ideal case there would be a residual doubt that the law-assertion was objectively justified. Certainly, one would have to keep one's mind open to the

---

[92] Ibid., II, III, X, p. 448.
[93] Ibid., III, III, IV, p. 610.
[94] See the passage cited by n. 50, above.

possibility that further observations might establish the objective unjustifiability of what would at that point be a subjectively justified law-assertion. But we should note with Hume, who discusses the two in the same context,[95] that both sagacity and vigilance are qualities worthy of praise. On the other hand, knowledge alone is often not the only consideration. Many times one must act before all evidence can possibly be collected, or before one can afford to collect it. In these cases a law-assertion must be risked prior to when considerations of reason alone would deem it worthy of assertion. Prudence must dictate what is reasonable here. Not surprisingly, prudence is another quality that, like sagacity, is worthy of admiration.[96]

Now it does seem to me that Hume's account of causation, in its outlines at least, is perfectly adequate, as is his account of when causal beliefs are justified. But this adequacy becomes apparent only if one recognizes that Hume does rely upon the notion of an active mind. As I have argued, the Humean mind *is* active, in several important ways. But in one way it is not active: none of its activities is an Aristotelian activity. For an Aristotelian, then, the Humean mind is thoroughly passive. That is why anyone who interprets Hume through Aristotelian spectacles is bound to miss precisely what is important for Hume's account. What we must realize is that Hume's theory of mental activity is a *Humean* theory of mental activity. I have tried to show here how Hume's Humean theory of mental activity is of central importance in the understanding of his account of causation.

---

[95] *Treatise*, III, III, IV, p. 610.
[96] Ibid.

The Naturalism of Hume Revisited

R. W. Connon

FOR ME, ONE OF THE MOST STRIKING EXPERIENCES of the two 1976 Hume Conferences I attended[1] was making the discovery that there was already substantial agreement among very many Hume scholars concerning much of what I myself wanted to say about Hume. In this essay, therefore, I wish to claim no particular originality for the views expressed.[2] Fortunately, there is much that is original in *Hume*, and it is out of a concern that some of the more neglected but nonetheless philosophically important expressions of that originality should be better appreciated that I have chosen to return to some of the issues raised by Norman Kemp Smith's pioneering article "The Naturalism of Hume."[3] I shall maintain that the Kemp Smith reading of the *Treatise* is not only the best one available but that it also suggests the historical judgment—which I hope not everyone will find heretical—that the most significant continuity from the point of view of the history of philosophy is not between Hume and the modern empiricists (who failed to understand him) but between Hume and the modern phenomenological movement, whose project of a descriptive psychology is clearly anticipated in the *Treatise*.

I have always tended to favor the Kemp Smith interpretation of the first book of the *Treatise* not only because it seems to be rooted in a close and insightful reading of the text but also because it affords a perspective on the *Treatise* that is sufficiently generous to reveal both the philosophical depth and the intellectual breadth of the work. Historically, it arose in opposition to another traditional interpretation that still survives in certain quarters. Upholders of this view (which I shall call the "Oxford view"),[4] while not denying that Hume occasionally branches off into

---

[1] The Edinburgh Hume Conference, 1976 and the McGill Bicentennial Hume Congress, in Montréal, 1976.

[2] I am grateful to Dr. George E. Davie of the University of Edinburgh for the valuable advice he has given me concerning Hume and the interpretation of the *Treatise*. I should also like to record my indebtedness to Dr. Robert Finkelstein, sometime lecturer in philosophy at the University of Manitoba. I should also mention that I first composed this paper without the benefit of having read Nicholas Capaldi's insightful book on Hume.

[3] *Mind* 14 (1905): 149-73, 335-47 (esp. the former).

[4] In the introduction to his edition of Hume's *History of England*, Duncan Forbes refers to "that old 'Oxford' view of Hume, the Locke-Berkeley-epistemology-only Hume"

other "nonphilosophical" areas such as psychology and anthropology, maintain that such lapses are peripheral to his main concern with certain traditional epistemological questions such as the justification for induction (in Book I, Part III). Kemp Smith's article, which first appeared in 1905, challenged this traditional picture of Hume and offered in its place the radically different thesis that the most important feature of Hume's philosophy was his "naturalism,"[5] an important part of which consisted in a positive account of how the mind operates.

I believe that Kemp Smith's reading of Book I is substantially correct. Indeed, this appears to have become more or less the standard view among Hume specialists.[6] Yet I think it fair to say that, despite its general acceptance, many Hume scholars remain unwilling to accept one important implication of Kemp Smith's interpretation. If Kemp Smith is right, the Hume of the *Treatise* should be understood primarily as a kind of psychological theorist.[7] Moreover, since on Kemp Smith's reading of Hume belief is in an important theoretical sense *prior* to knowledge, we may expect that an understanding of the epistemological implications of Hume's account of knowledge can be achieved only after we have understood his positive theory about natural belief.

I should say here that I do not wish to be taken as denying that skepticism plays an important role in the *Treatise*. I would like only to insist on the exegetical point that the discovery of what that role is should

---

(Harmondsworth, Middlesex: Penguin Books, 1970, p. 9). Historically, the classical expression of this view (which has its ultimate source in the writings of Reid and Beattie) is Green's lengthy introduction to the *Treatise* in Hume's *Philosophical Works*, ed. T. H. Green and T. H. Grose, 4 vols. (London, 1874). Green is largely responsible for establishing the practice of reading Hume's *Treatise* as a series of footnotes to Locke's *Essay*. Green's interpretation was carried over into the twentieth century in the work of the Oxford philosopher H. H. Price in the form of what we might now call the "Bundle of Contradictions Theory" of the *Treatise*.

[5] Kemp Smith had argued for the conclusion that "the establishment of a purely naturalistic conception of human nature by the thorough subordination of reason to feeling and instinct is the determining factor in Hume's philosophy" ("Naturalism of Hume," p. 150).

[6] See, for example, Terence Penelhum's *Hume* (London: Macmillan, 1975), p. 18.

[7] The criticism might even be made of Kemp Smith himself that he does not go quite far enough in exploring Hume's psychological theory. For instance, in his important book *The Philosophy of David Hume* (London: MacMillan, 1941) he seems to me to be somewhat overhasty in dismissing Hume's attempts to characterize belief in terms of "force," "vivacity," "solidity," "firmness," and so forth, with the consequence that he seems to have failed to grasp the theoretical significance of what Hume is doing, viz., attempting to combine a kind of phenomenological account of probable reasoning with an associationist view of the imagination.

be the conclusion rather than the starting point of any interpretation of the *Treatise*.[8] Suffice it to say, the problem of determining the precise nature of Hume's skepticism—once we take such a problem seriously—is both complex and difficult.[9] My objection to the "Oxford view," one traditionally associated with the claim that Hume had essentially skeptical intentions, is that it now seems to be rather more of an impediment to exegesis than an aid.

Anglo-American philosophers in general have been slow to appreciate Hume's positive psychological account of causal inference partly because it has not always been clear precisely how such an explanation may be construed as *any* solution to the epistemological problems with which Hume is traditionally supposed to have been concerned.[10] Thus, for instance, in his valuable book *Hume's Intentions*, John Passmore seems almost to accuse Hume of evasion, because Hume resorts in the last analysis to "a psychological expedient" or "a trick of the mind."[11]

I should like to question one assumption upon which this kind of disappointment seems to me to rest and that I believe derives from the "Oxford view" of Hume—the assumption that *in Part III of Book I Hume is primarily interested in asking and answering a question principally concerned with the* justification *for our common-sense causal assertions*. Hume, it should be noted, does not *say* that this is what he is doing. His inquiry in Part III concerns, he tells us, "the manner, *in which we reason beyond our immediate impressions, and conclude that such particular causes must have such particular effects.*"[12] These are the words Hume uses to describe the subject of discussion that takes up the greater portion of Part III.

---

[8] It is imposible to refer to the problem of skepticism without acknowledging the enormous contribution that Richard H. Popkin has made to our understanding of the history of modern skepticism and the role of skepticism in Hume's thought. See, for example, his *History of Scepticism from Erasmus to Descartes* (Assen: Van Gorcum, 1960), and "David Hume: His Pyrrhonism and His Critique of Pyrrhonism," *The Philosophical Quarterly* 1 (1951), reprinted in *Hume*, ed. V. C. Chappell (London: Macmillan, 1968), pp. 53-98. For recent discussions on the subject of Hume's skepticism see Terence Penelhum and David Stove. See also T. E. Jessop, "Hume's Limited Skepticism," *Revue Internationale de Philolsophie*, no. 115 (1976), pp. 3-27.

[9] See the opening sentence of Penelhum's essay in this volume.

[10] See Gerd Buchdahl, *Metaphysics and the Philosophy of Science* (Oxford: Basil Blackwell, 1969), p. 340.

[11] (London: Duckworth, 1968), pp. 34, 62.

[12] *A Treatise of Human Nature*, ed. L. A. Selby-Bigge (Oxford, 1888), I, III, XIV, p. 155 (hereafter cited as *Treatise*).

Although there is nothing in this description that, strictly speaking, tells against the "Oxford view" — that Hume's *real* intention was to argue a negative thesis concerning the justification for our causal inferences — it certainly raises the question of how we could come to have such a precise knowledge of what Hume really wanted to do but for some reason did not.[13]

It is a twentieth-century refinement of this view to represent Hume as a practitioner of modern conceptual analysis[14] — a tendency we might call "Twentiethcentrism." Such attempts are often justified on the grounds that they "throw light" on the text;[15] but I must confess that for my own part I have not found it particularly helpful to understand Hume as, say, someone who is struggling (unsuccessfully) to express a thesis (incorrect, as it turns out)[16] about "what it is for an expression to have meaning."[17] Everyone no doubt would accept that some kind of conceptual elucidation is required in cases where we are liable to be led into serious error. But if we come to rely too much upon such approaches, we are far more likely to be led into error by the analysis itself than by anything Hume ever wrote. In practice such unhistorical approaches to Hume also have the effect of making him appear to be less intelligent than his commentators.

Fortunately, in the case of the *Treatise*, speculation about Hume's actual intentions is not altogether idle in view of the new light thrown on the *Treatise* by the discovery of the *Abstract*. What, then, does Hume tell us in the *Abstract*? First of all, he says that he wrote the *Treatise* with a specific purpose in mind, viz., to remedy what he termed a "defect" in "the common systems of logic."[18] In what is almost certainly an allusion to the *Essais de Théodicée*, Hume refers to Leibniz's criticism of Locke, Arnauld, and Malebranche for not having devoted sufficient attention to a treatment of "probabilities" (*vrai-semblances*).[19] He goes on to

---

[13] For example, H. H. Price informs us of what Hume is "trying to say" but does not get "quite clear" ("The Permanent Significance of Hume's Philosophy," in *Human Understanding: Studies in the Philosophy of David Hume*, ed. Alexander Sesonske and Noel Fleming [Belmont, Calif.: Wadsworth, 1965], p. 5). See also p. 12 where he tells us what Hume "should have asked."

[14] See ibid., p. 13.

[15] See, for example, Jonathan Bennett, *Locke, Berkeley, Hume* (Oxford: Clarendon Press, 1971), p. 232.

[16] Ibid., p. 230.

[17] Ibid.

[18] *An Abstract of a Treatise of Human Nature*, intro. J. M. Keynes and P. Sraffa (Hamden, Conn.: Archon Books, 1965), p. 7 (hereafter cited as *Abstract*).

[19] Leibniz, "Discours de la Conformité de la Foi avec la Raison," *Essais de Theodicée*

describe the *Treatise* as an attempt to supply such an account.[20] In what follows I shall try to indicate how this purpose is pursued in Part III of Book I.

Before proceeding to this, however, I should like to consider the historical question of why there might have been a need at the time Hume was writing for a fuller account of probability and, in particular, of probable reasoning. Like most of the philosophical problems that arose in the late seventeenth and early eighteenth century, questions concerning probable reasoning may profitably be examined in connection with what was taking place in the scientific world.[21] Although it is widely acknowledged, it is perhaps insufficiently appreciated that by the time of Hume's writing, the practice of modern science—the new physics—had clearly established itself among the more intellectually progressive thinkers of the eighteenth century as a kind of paradigm of rationality.[22] By all historical accounts there were few educated men of the period who were seriously prepared to doubt that Newton's methods of investigation were capable of yielding truths. There is, if we examine it closely, very little in the *Treatise* to suggest that Hume was an exception and much to suggest that he was not.

But although the practice of the new science had been vindicated, largely on the basis of its very impressive results, there remained the philosophical problem of revealing the practice to be a rational one. This was not so much a problem of trying to *justify* the methods or conclusions of science; for these were not in question. Yet there were nevertheless certain questions bearing on scientific practice that science itself was not equipped to answer. One was the problem of accounting for the kind of mental operation involved in the making of scientific inferences, an example being the kind of inference J. E. McGuire calls "transduction"[23]—a kind of inferential leap required by every concrete application of Newton's third "Rule of Reasoning in Philosophy."[24]

[sic], 2 vols. (1734), 1:27-28. For more information concerning this identification see Didier Deleule's excellent French language parallel text edition of the *Abstract*, *Abrégé du "Traité de la nature humaine,"* (Paris: Aubier Montaigne, 1971), p. 97.

[20] *Abstract*, p. 8.

[21] See Mary Shaw Kuypers, *Studies in the Eighteenth Century Background of Hume's Empiricism* (New York: Russell and Russell, 1966), p. 45.

[22] See R. G. Collingwood, *The Idea of Nature* (Oxford: Clarendon Press, 1945), p. 112.

[23] "Atoms and the 'Analogy of Nature': Newton's Third Rule of Philosophizing," *Studies in History and Philosophy of Science*, I, pp. 3-58. See esp. pp. 3-5.

[24] This is the rule stating that "the qualities of bodies, which admit neither intensification nor remission of degrees, and which are found to belong to all bodies within the reach of

It was thought to be by means of this rule that we are entitled to move from the "premise" that all bodies we have seen are extended to the "conclusion" that all bodies whatsoever are extended. The most important application of this rule in Newtonian physics was in affirming the universal validity of the laws of motion both for celestial bodies and for the fundamental particles of matter; for "all bodies whatsoever." Now as McGuire points out, any application of the rule would seem to involve our passing from what is observable to what is *in principle* unobservable.[25] And this, perhaps, is the point behind Hume's observation that "we suppose, but are never able to *prove*, that there must be a resemblance betwixt those objects, of which we have had experience, and those which lie beyond the reach of our discovery."[26]

Now of course to adopt a set of rules (such as Newton's "Rules of Reasoning") that purport to show us how we *ought* to reason is to presuppose certain things concerning how we do *in fact* reason, how, in other words, our minds operate. To accept that the move in question is a valid one is, minimally, to accept that our minds can and do somehow make the "leap" involved in the inference.

The difficulty (at least this will be my contention) was that the picture of the mind most widely accepted in the early part of the eighteenth century—the scholastic view of induction—could *not* provide an adequate account of how the mind makes the leap, how it is able to pass from what is present to it to the idea of something not present to it. Newton never himself explicitly entertained the question of the basis of his Rules. Hume, like Bacon, saw that the old scholastic logic was incapable of providing an adequate account of the "operation of the mind"[27] that the practice of experimental reasoning seemed to require. Even so enlightened a Cartesian as Malebranche had been led to deny, on purely a priori grounds, that the New Philosophy was capable of yielding genuine knowledge. Thus, for example, he condemns the experimental philosophers because in "the Method of their Experiments" they are not

---

our experiments, are to be esteemed the universal qualities of all bodies whatsoever" (Issac Newton, *Mathematical Principles of Natural Philosophy and his System of the World*, trans. Andrew Motte, revised edition by Florian Cajori [Berkeley: University of California Press, 1946], 2:203).

[25] Cf. Hume's observation that the rules to direct our judgment in experimental reasoning require "the utmost stretch of human judgement" (*Treatise*, I, III, XV, p. 175).

[26] Ibid., VI, pp. 91-92 (my italics). That Hume may have had Newton's Third Rule specifically in mind is further suggested by the paragraph immediately preceding this quotation.

[27] To use the phrase Hume tends to use most frequently throughout Part III of the *Treatise*.

conducted by "the Light of Reason."²⁸ Such objections began to have less and less force as the New Philosophy began to replace mathematics as the most suitable method for the investigation of the universe, but there did remain the theoretical problem of providing an alternative picture of the mind that would explain how it was capable of performing the specific mental operation required in Newtonian experimental philosophy. Hence the need for a "logic of probable reasoning."

The term "logic" of course denoted a somewhat broader subject in the eighteenth century than it does now.²⁹ Moreover, in the early part of the eighteenth century the subject was still undergoing transformation in the wake of the Port Royal attack upon Ramism.³⁰ Hume, who adopts the Port Royal view,³¹ describes logic as a study having as its end an explanation of the *"principles and Operations of our reasoning faculty, and the nature of our ideas."*³² Further, since logic was supposed by Hume and his contemporaries to be derived from our reflection upon certain "operations of the mind,"³³ it includes a psychological dimension no longer present in our twentieth-century notion of logic. A "logic" of probable reasoning would have comprised, among other things, a *psychology* of probable reasoning.

---

²⁸ *Treatise concerning the Search after Truth*, trans. T. Taylor (London: W. Bowyer, 1700), bk. II, pt. II, chap. IX, p. 83. See also Malebranche's remarks concerning the superiority of mathematics over other methods for the "Discovery of unknown Truths" (ibid, p. 70).

²⁹ According to Robert McRae, Hume used the term in a broad sense to include everything in the *Treatise* under the title "Of the Understanding" ("Hume as a Political Philosopher," *Journal of the History of Ideas* 12 [1951]: 285-290). See also Passmore, p. 41n. See also Hume's use of the term in the *Abstract*, p. 24.

³⁰ In the late sixteenth century the scholastic logic, based primarily upon the logical treatises of Aristotle, underwent a reform at the hands of Petrus Ramus. This reformed version, or "Ramism," became the established logic of the schools. Of great importance with respect to the problem of determining whether and in what sense Hume subscribed to skepticism is the question of his attitude toward the controversy concerning both logic and rhetoric that played a major role in the debates of the late seventeenth and early eighteenth centuries. To my knowledge Peter Jones of the University of Edinburgh is the first Hume scholar to have undertaken a serious examination of Hume's writings from the point of view of their connection with these contemporary debates. For more information concerning seventeenth-century logic and rhetoric see Wilbur Samuel Howell, *Logic and Rhetoric in England, 1500-1700* (Princeton: Princeton University Press, 1956), esp. chap. 6.

³¹ Antoine Arnauld's *L'Art de Penser* (otherwise known as the "Port Royal Logic"), first published in 1662, was the most important attack on Ramism following Descartes's *Discours de la Méthode*. For a discussion of some of the affinities between the *Treatise* and the Port Royal Logic see Charles W. Hendel's foreword to *The Art of Thinking*, trans. James Dickoff and Patricia James (Indianapolis: Bobbs-Merrill, 1964), pp. xiv-xxiv.

³² *Abstract*, p. 7. See also the introduction to the *Treatise*, p. xix.

³³ Chambers mentions four basic "operations of the mind" from which *"logic* is, or

It is not mere pedantry to insist on this psychological dimension within the eighteenth-century notion of logic. It is all too easy to overlook the fact that a word such as "inference," which plays a central role in Hume's discussion of causation, denoted for him something essentially psychological, a particular kind of mental transition from one thought to another, and not, as some commentators have assumed, an exclusively logical operation.[34]

At this point I ought to try to indicate more precisely how Hume's essentially psychological interest in probable reasoning may nevertheless be seen to have some connection with a more purely epistemological interest in the foundations of empirical science. For if Hume's main concern in Part III is neither with an explication of the concept of causation nor with supplying an answer to the question of whether or not our causal assertions are ever rationally justifiable, but, instead, is with providing a broadly descriptive account of the mental operation that underlies probable reasoning, we seem to be left with a very different picture of Hume from the traditional one. On the "Oxford view" Hume is depicted as continuing a program initiated by Locke.[35] Locke, we are told, was concerned with the question of what we can know and so attempted in his *Essay* to "define the limits of the human understanding."[36] Hume is seen as extending this program with a more rigorous and systematic application of the epistemological principles Locke had developed.

---

ought to be wholly drawn" (viz., apprehension, judgment, discourse, and method). See his *Cyclopaedia*, 2nd ed. (London, 1738).

[34] See *Treatise*, I, III, VI, p. 88; I, III, VIII, pp. 103–4; I, III, XVI, p. 178; II, III, I, p. 405. See also *Abstract*, p. 13. Kemp Smith describes Hume's notion of inference as "nothing but the custom-bred transition from an impression to an enlivened idea" ("Naturalism of Hume," p. 164). See also Gerd Buchdahl's remarks concerning Hume's use of "inference" (*Metaphysics*, p. 340). Hume's special use of the words "inference" and "inferr'd" is evident in the *Treatise*, I, III, XIV, p. 159, second paragraph). He tends to use the word "reasoning" and not the word "inference" to denote the act of inferring (modern sense) conclusions from premises (*Treatise* I, III, I, p. 70; I, III, III, p. 79; I, III, XIV, p. 171; III, I, I, pp. 468, 469; also the *Abstract*, p. 14).

[35] See, for example, Bertrand Russell, *A History of Western Philosophy* (New York: Simon and Schuster, 1945), p. 659. I do not wish to be taken as saying that Locke was *not* in some respects also a psychological theorist.

[36] According to A. J. Ayer, Locke attempted in the *Essay* to determine "what knowledge consists in" with a view to determining the extent of human knowledge (*British Empirical Philosophers: Locke, Berkeley, Hume, Reid and J. S. Mill*, ed. A. J. Ayer and Raymond Winch [London: Routledge and Kegan Paul, 1952], p. 10). In the introduction to *An Essay concerning Human Understanding* Locke informs us that his purpose is to "enquire into

There is, however, a quite different way of approaching the problem of knowledge, one that may be seen as the antithesis of the former approach. Here, instead of proceeding from a set of epistemic criteria to an inventory of possible objects of knowledge, we begin by assuming the possibility of knowledge, and, taking certain kinds of knowledge as given, we try to arrive at a description of what was involved in our coming to acquire it.[37] It seems to me that this latter approach to the problem of knowledge is nearer to the one Hume actually adopted in Part III of the *Treatise* than is the traditional epistemological approach.

Perhaps the initial objection likely to be raised against this interpretation will be that it is an obvious nonstarter. One might well be prepared to concede that there is *more* in the *Treatise* than epistemological skepticism; one might not, however, be prepared to give consideration to an interpretation that completely *overlooks* its skeptical side. For it may appear that this is what I am doing in attributing to Hume not only a commitment to the possibility of knowledge of matters of fact, but even what we might call a *dogmatic* commitment to the possibility of such knowledge.

Now while I agree that Hume does on occasion advance skeptical arguments in the *Treatise*, I would deny that his main project in Part III ("Of Knowledge and Probability") is ultimately skeptical, or, rather, I would maintain that Hume's skepticism is employed for a specific purpose—to reveal the limitations not of our knowledge of matters of fact but of the schools logic,[38] which purported to explain how we come to acquire such knowledge. It takes the specific form of an attack on what we might call "the philosophy of pure reason": the view that all knowledge that goes beyond immediate sensation must have its origin in an act

---

the Original, Certainty and Extent of humane Knowledge; together, with the Grounds and Degrees of Belief, Opinion, and Assent" (*Essay*, ed. with an intro., critical apparatus, and glossary by Peter Nidditch [Oxford: Clarendon Press, 1975], p. 43).

[37] This would seem to be the position taken by Francis Bacon with respect to the question of our knowledge about the world. According to Benjamin Farrington, "Bacon thought that to *begin* from the question of the validity of our knowledge was a mistake. That was, perhaps, where we might *end*" (*Francis Bacon: Philosopher of Industrial Science* [London: Lawrence and Wishart, 1951], p. 96).

[38] The name "schools" refers to the scholastic philosophy (see also n. 30 above). It was the principle object of attack by such thinkers as Bacon, Hobbes, Descartes, and Hume. The dogmas of the schools were still being attacked as late as the mid-eighteenth century. See, for example, the article "École" in *The Encyclopédie of Diderot and D'Alembert*, selected articles ed. with an intro. by John Lough (Cambridge: Cambridge University Press, 1954), pp. 40-41.

of the reasoning faculty. To take the example of Hume's so-called attack on induction, as we shall see, it is not the *justification* for the practice of induction that Hume questions, nor is it the Newtonian assumption of the uniformity of nature.[39] Rather, he attacks the particular thesis that when we come to expect some future event on the basis of our present observation of another that we have found previously to accompany it, we are making a deduction, a reasoning by means of the interposition of ideas (to use Hume's idiom).[40] Hume is concerned to attack the thesis "that the mind is convinc'd by *reasoning* of that principle, *that instances of which we have no experience, must necessarily resemble those, of which we have.*"[41] What convinces us, Hume goes on, is a particular kind of "presuming."[42] The "Oxford view" tends to overlook this claim, or, rather, tends to dismiss it as a purely rhetorical reiteration of Hume's "skepticism," a way of drawing attention to the inherent irrationality of causal inference. But the question we must consider is whether in denying that such inferences are based upon *reason* (in the very narrow sense in which he uses that term throughout Part III),[43] Hume is thereby denying that such inferences can ever be (in our modern sense) *reasonable*. It is by no means clear that Hume intended such phrases as "founded in reason," "founded on reasoning," "supported by any argument or process of the understanding," "engaged by argument," and so forth, to mean, simply, "rationally justifiable."

Let us examine more closely the passage containing Hume's "attack" on induction. What I take Hume to be questioning (in the argument

---

[39] See, for example, Hume's remarks concerning any "seeming uncertainty" in the connection between all causes and effects (*Treatise*, I, III, XII, p. 132).

[40] Ibid., VII, p. 97n. See also Hume's question, "Where is the medium, the interposing ideas, which join propositions so very wide of each other?" (*An Enquiry concerning Human Understanding*, ed. L. A. Selby-Bigge, 2nd ed. [Oxford, 1902], IV, II, p. 37 [hereafter cited as first *Enquiry*]).

[41] *Treatise*, I, III, VIII, p. 104 (my emphasis of "reasoning").

[42] Ibid., I, III, VI, p. 90.

[43] It is quite clear from the context that Hume is using the word "reason" in this passage to mean "deductive reason." Thus, for example, he uses "reason" in opposition to "associationism" (ibid., pp. 88-89), in opposition to "probability" (ibid., pp. 90-91), and in opposition to "experience" (ibid., XIV, p. 157). This narrow or restricted sense would seem to have been the ordinary sense of the word in the late seventeenth and early eighteenth centuries. Cf. *The Spectator*, no. 588: "But to descend from Reason to Matter of Fact" (Joseph Addison, Richard Steele, and others, *The Spectator*, ed. G. Gregory Smith, 8 vols. in 4 (London: J. M. Dent [c. 1906], 7:114. Cf. also Newton's use of the word: "That all bodies are impenetrable we gather not from reason, but from sensation" (quoted in *Newton's Philosophy of Nature*, ed. H. S. Thayer [New York, 1953], p. 4).

beginning with the words "If reason determin'd us") is the thesis that it is some kind of reasoning that determines us to make the transition from "an impression present to the memory or senses to the idea of an object, which we call cause or effect."[44] Hume observes that if it *were*, such reasoning would require for its validity a certain premise, a "middle proposition," which he supposes to be the following: *"that instances, of which we have had no experience, must resemble those, of which we have had experience, and that the course of nature continues always uniformly the same."*[45] He then asks how we may arrive at such a premise and notices that the premise in question does not appear to have its origin in any of the ordinary reasoning operations. Its truth is plainly not revealed to us as a matter of logical necessity (*"demonstrative* argument"), since we can *conceive* of a change in the course of nature. Nor is it derived from some "probable argument." Since, as he has already shown, probability itself depends upon causal inference, we cannot without vicious circularity appeal to probability to explain the transition upon which causal inference itself depends. Since these are, moreover, the *only* sources upon which "such a proposition may be suppos'd to be founded," we are forced to conclude that no argument for induction is possible since it would require an apparently underivable premise. Hume concludes (by *modus tollens*) that it is *not* reason that determines us.

Now on the "Oxford view" Hume is taken to be drawing the more interesting conclusion that our inductions are *never justifiable*, that they are "fundamentally irrational."[46] Thus, for example, A. J. Ayer takes Hume to be seriously doubting whether we are ever justified in our reasonings concerning matters of fact. That such reasoning was both possible and reliable is a fundamental presupposition of scientific enquiry and, as such, would have been equally fundamental for Hume's "science of MAN."[47] Nonetheless, Ayer interprets Hume in this passage as calling into question the justification for the "uniformity" principle quoted above and then as drawing the skeptical conclusion that since all of our reasonings about matters of fact are based on it, these must be fundamentally irrational.[48]

---

[44] *Treatise*, I, III, VI, pp. 88–89.
[45] Ibid., p. 89.
[46] See, for example, Ayer and Winch, p. 26.
[47] *Treatise*, Introduction, p. xix.
[48] Ayer and Winch, p. 26. Ayer offers more or less the same interpretation of Hume in a more recent work: *The Central Questions of Philosophy* (London: Weidenfeld and Nicolson, 1973), pp. 138–40.

But it is important to notice that Ayer's reading of Hume is not so "rooted in the text" as his words might suggest. With respect to the first point he purports to be allowing Hume to speak for himself: "As Hume *puts it*, the question is whether we are *justified in believing* 'that instances of which we have had no experience, must resemble those of which we have had experience, and that the course of nature continues always uniformly the same'."⁴⁹ However, if we examine the passage of the text Ayer presumably has in mind, we find that Hume makes no mention whatsoever of such a "question."⁵⁰ Nor is it obvious from the text that Hume thought that all of our reasonings about matters of fact are indeed based upon the uniformity principle. Hume's point would seem to be rather the opposite of this: that they are based *not* upon any such principle but instead upon a psychological act of presuming, as indeed he tells us on the next page.⁵¹

The traditional skeptical interpretation of the *Treatise* has never been especially known for its close textual scholarship,⁵² and nowhere is this more conspicuous than in the way in which a skeptical view of causation has simply been read into Hume's doctrines concerning causal inference. A typical example is afforded by a passage in G. E. Moore's article

---

⁴⁹ Ayer and Winch, p. 26 (my italics). According to Price, Hume believed that it was somehow in our nature to make inductions, "but (*he says*) we have no justification for them whatever" ("Significance of Hume's Philosophy," p. 27, my italics). Price does not tell us exactly where in the text Hume makes this claim.

⁵⁰ Edmund Husserl regarded it as typical of empiricism to fail to distinguish questions about the psychological origin of certain general judgments from questions about their justification (*Logical Investigations*, trans. J. N. Findlay, 2 vols. [London: Routledge and Kegan Paul, 1970], 1:116-17).

⁵¹ *Treatise*, I, III, VI, p. 90.

⁵² One of the first proponents of the traditional skeptical view of Hume, James Beattie, simply ignores all of those passages in the *Treatise* containing Hume's positive doctrine of belief in favor of passages that, taken out of context, appear to support a radical and unmitigated form of skepticism. See, for example his *Essay on the Nature and Immutability of Truth*, 2nd ed. (1771), p. 174n. where he offers a maimed excerpt from p. 469 of the first edition of the *Treatise* (p. 270 in the Selby-Bigge ed.). On numerous occasions Beattie resorts to what can only be described as abusive parody: see the *Essay*, pp. 141, 159, 168, and esp. 172-76. Perhaps one historical consideration that might account for the absurdly skeptical interpretation placed upon Hume by Reid and Beattie is the fact that Hume was also supposed (by a few of his contemporaries at least) to be a skeptic with respect to the received arguments for the existence of God. Since such arguments were commonly thought to rest securely upon the discoveries of the new physics of Newton (via the argument from the order of the universe), someone who nevertheless persisted in questioning the rational basis for a belief in God would no doubt have struck many of his contemporaries as being not only perverse but also highly irrational.

"Hume's Philosophy,"[53] a classic statement of the traditional epistemological reading of Hume. Moore, after noting Hume's claim that all of our causal inferences are founded on custom, continues:

> And can we be said really to *know* any fact, for which we have no better foundation than this? Hume himself, it must be observed, never says that we can't. But he has been constantly interpreted as if the conclusion that we can't really know any one fact to be causally connected with any other, did follow from this doctrine of his. And there is, I think, certainly much excuse for this interpretation in the tone in which he speaks.[54]

Moore then goes on to expend considerable energy refuting what he terms "Hume's most sceptical argument (the argument which he merely suggests)."[55] It is interesting to notice that Moore did not feel called upon to consider the merits of the rival interpretation that had been advanced by Norman Kemp Smith four years earlier.

There is perhaps a qualified sense in which Hume may be said to have attacked the justification for certain sorts of induction. For in questioning what had been wrongly supposed to have been the psychological foundation for induction, Hume was *in effect* challenging the justification for inductions. In fact, the issue he raises is less, Why are we entitled? and more, Why do we *think* we are entitled?[56] to draw inductive conclusions. My point is simply that we have no reason for continuing to interpret Hume as if he were actually providing an argument for the stronger thesis that there is *no* rational justification for the practice of inductive inference.

Hume's real target in the "induction"[57] argument is, I believe, one of the dogmas of the schools amounting to the thesis that we think (as well as construct arguments) in terms of syllogisms. In a lengthy footnote in

---

[53] This article first appeared in the *New Quarterly* (1909). I quote from the version reprinted in G. E. Moore, *Philosophical Studies* (London: Kegan, Paul, Trench, Trubner and Co., 1922), pp. 147-67.

[54] Ibid., p. 155. A quite similar example of the apparent invulnerability to counter-evidence of this reading of the *Treatise* appears in a note to E. B. McGilvary's article "Altruism in Hume's *Treatise*," *The Philosophical Review* 12 (1903):274n.

[55] "Hume's Philosophy," p. 160.

[56] According to Buchdahl, examples may be found of writers in the mid-eighteenth century who maintained that Newton's laws of motion could be arrived at "by the path of reason alone" (*Metaphysics*, pp. 24-25, and esp. 326).

[57] Hume does not actually use the word "induction" in the passage we have been considering (i.e., *Treatise*, I, III, VI, pp. 88-90).

the section that follows ("Of the nature of the idea, or belief," I, III, VII), Hume draws attention to "a very remarkable error . . . frequently inculcated in the schools" and "universally received by all logicians."[58] This error, he tells us, had led them to accept a quite mistaken view of causal inference. Since (contrary to what the schoolsmen assert) it is possible to form a proposition "which contains only one idea" (he gives the example of an existential proposition),

> so we may exert our reason without employing more than two ideas, and without having recourse to a third to serve as a medium betwixt them. We infer a cause immediately from its effect; and this inference is not only a true species of reasoning, but the strongest of all others, and more convincing than when we interpose another idea to connect the two extremes.[59]

At the end of the note Hume insists that what really requires explanation is the particular manner of conceiving we call "belief," an "act of the mind" that "has never yet been explain'd by any philosopher." Here, then, we have a compendious statement both of the general position Hume is attacking and of the nature of the positive contribution he sought to provide — what Kemp Smith described in 1905 as a naturalistic theory of belief.

Hume's critical examination of the basis of induction is intended to reveal that on any retrospective reconstruction of an ordinary act of causal inference we are left with a logical hiatus. Admittedly, this raises problems for anyone seeking a "logical foundation for induction," but I do not think that this was ever Hume's problem. In company with Bacon,[60] Hobbes,[61] and (in this century) Wittgenstein,[62] Hume subscribed to the

---

[58] Ibid., VII, p. 96n. The error, Hume tells us, consists in their mistaken classification of the different acts of the understanding into three: conception, judgment, and reasoning. According to Hume, all three may be reduced to the first.

[59] Ibid., p. 97n.

[60] Bacon comments on the subject of induction in opposition to the scholastic doctrine: "For he that shall attentively observe how the mind doth gather this excellent dew of knowledge . . . shall find that the mind of herself by nature doth manage and act an induction much better than they describe it. For to conclude upon an enumeration of particulars, without instance contradictory, is *no conclusion, but a conjecture*. . ." (*The Advancement of Learning*, ed. William Aldis Wright, 3rd ed. [Oxford, 1885], bk. II, XIII, 3, p. 152, my italics). See also ibid., 1-2, pp. 149-152; XIV, 1-3, pp. 157-159.

[61] See, for example, *Leviathan*, ed. C. B. MacPherson (Harmondsworth, Middlesex: Penguin Books, 1968), pt. I, chap. 3, p. 97.

[62] See the *Tractatus*, 6.3631.

view that there can be *no logical* justification for induction, but only a psychological one.

But of course the most compelling reason for objecting to the traditional view that Hume intended to question and so to cast doubt upon the justification for our beliefs concerning matters of fact arises not from the negative consideration that he does not actually do so, but, rather, from the positive one that he makes his own epistemological commitments reasonably explicit.

The first indication in the *Treatise* that Hume himself had no practical scruples about probable reasoning is suggested by the full title: *A Treatise of Human Nature: Being An Attempt to introduce the experimental Method of Reasoning into Moral Subjects.*[63] It is hard to suppose that a writer would describe his work as an application of a particular method of investigation that he did not as a matter of fact believe to be reliable. As I mentioned before, by the time of Hume's writing the methods of modern science for investigating the natural world were regarded as perhaps the proudest achievement of the age and a striking vindication of the experimental method of Bacon. In fact, so fashionable were the procedures of the new natural philosophy that they were being widely recommended for the investigation of other areas of human experience as well.[64] Hume himself confidently asserts in the *Abstract* that the same reasoning that can account for the motions and operations of matter "extends to the operations of the mind."[65]

---

[63] See also Nicholas Capaldi, *David Hume: The Newtonian Philosopher* (Boston: Twayne, 1975), p. 38.

[64] See Newton's famous remark at the close of the *Opticks* (New York: Dover, 1952). See also the remarks made by John Clarke, Dean of Salisbury: "Whoever has a mind to proceed further, and to explain the more difficult and complicated Cases in the System of the World, may go upon the same Principles, and he will find that if they are rightly applied, there is no Phaenomenon, how irregular or minute soever it may seem to be, but the Propositions here demonstrated are sufficient to give the Reader a Relish for true Philosophy. . ." (*A Demonstration of some of the Principal Selectons of Sir Issac Newtons* [sic] *Principles of Natural Philosophy etc*. . . [London, 1730], p. vii).

[65] *Abstract*, p. 21. In her very interesting paper "Newtonian Method and Empirical Laws of Anthropology in *Treatise* II," read at the 1976 Edinburgh Hume conference, Mme. Nelly G. Demé provided a "Newtonian" reading of the section in the *Treatise* entitled "Experiments to confirm this system." In the course of her discussion Mme. Demé revealed many parallels with Newtonian method and mechanics. For example, she showed in detail how Hume's four cardinal passions (pride, humility, love, hatred) constitute a "mechanical" system and went on to reveal the way in which Hume employed such Newtonian concepts as the "composition of forces" and the "resolution of forces." See Madame Demé's paper in G. P. Morice, ed., *David Hume: Bicentenary Papers* (Edinburgh: Edinburgh University Press, 1977), pp. 139-45.

Hume's epistemological assumptions, insofar as these are revealed incidentally in the *Treatise*, also seem to be Newtonian, corresponding very closely to "the known rules, by which we judge of cause and effect in anatomy, natural philosophy, and other sciences."[66] Hume's reference was of course to the "Rules of Reasoning in Philosophy" that Newton had laid down in the *Principia*.[67] Although Hume makes tacit appeal to each of the four rules,[68] the rule most frequently applied in the *Treatise* and that he himself describes as "an inviolable maxim in philosophy,"[69] is Newton's second ("to the same natural effects we must, as far as possible, assign the same causes"), or, as Hume on another occasion states it, "a common effect supposes always a common cause."[70] That Hume should have availed himself so freely of the methodology of experimental philosophy is indeed difficult to reconcile with the view that he wanted to *question* the very possibility of such knowledge.[71] At the risk of being accused of employing the "infallibility assumption,"[72] I must say that I do not think that Hume was that incompetent. For it would be the crudest sort of circularity to take up the question of the epistemological justification for the practice of probable reasoning, while

---

[66] *Treatise*, II, I, VIII, p. 301.

[67] Buchdahl has suggested that Newton's third and fourth "Rules of Reasoning" play a central role in the fashioning of Hume's thinking (*Metaphysics*, p. 338).

[68] Hume's familiarity with and acceptance of Newton's "Rules" is suggested by his remark at *Treatise*, II, I, III, p. 282. See also II, I, XII, p. 328. For an instance of reasoning according to Rule 1, see III, II, VI, p. 526, where Hume refuses to posit theoretically unnecessary original principles. See also I, II, V, p. 64. With respect to Rule 3, see Hume's "Rule 4" of his "Rules by which to judge of causes and effects," I, III, XV, pp. 173-74. See also in this respect Hume's own conclusion concerning the resemblance between ideas and impressions, I, I, I, p. 5 (also I, III, VIII, pp. 104-05). For tacit references to Rule 4 see I, III, XVI, p. 178. In relation to Newton's "Analogy of Nature" see Hume's mode of argument in I, III, XVI, pp. 176; II, I, VI, p. 290; and II, I, XII, p. 327. See also Buchdahl, esp. pp. 338-39, and Passmore, pp. 43-44.

[69] Ibid., III, III, I, p. 578.

[70] Ibid., II, I, VIII, p. 300. See also Hume's statement: "from like effects, we presume like causes" (I, IV, IV, p. 227). Other instances of the application of this rule of reasoning may be found in I, III, X, pp. 119; I, III, XVI, p. 179; II, I, X, p. 311; II, I, XII, pp. 325, 328. See also Hume's index entry "Newton, Sir Isaac, his Rule of philosophizing, 419" (*Essays and Treastises*, 2 vols. [London, 1758], 2:536). The index reference corresponds to *An Enquiry concerning the Principles of Morals*, ed. L. A. Selby-Bigge, 2nd ed. (Oxford, 1902), III, II, pp. 203-4, where Hume concludes that utility is a common cause of our moral approbation of justice, veracity, integrity, and so on.

[71] See Collingwood, p. 112.

[72] Sometimes known as the "To error is not Humean" theory.

at the same time reserving the right to invoke the very epistemological presuppositions that were known to underlie probable reasoning.[73]

As some of Hume's remarks in the *Abstract* suggest, he believed the entire mental operation involved in causal inference, and thus in any a posteriori reasoning, to be a process not as yet fully explained. His main concern in Part III, therefore, is to explain the complex mechanism underlying any of our ordinary acts of causal inference. Since the mental transition that characterizes causal inference (and that we experience as a "presumption" or "feeling of determination") operates "before we have had time for reflection,"[74] we are unable to observe the process directly. We may, however, come to some knowledge of it through its effects. The problem, at least as Hume poses it, is very similar to the contemporary debate in natural philosophy concerning our knowledge of gravitation.

In order to understand more fully how Hume attempted to account for causal inference, we must begin with his fundamental principle governing mental operations—the association of ideas. In the *Abstract* Hume implies that his imaginative application of this principle to explain various features of human nature is his most important original contribution to philosophy.[75] I have argued elsewhere that Hume derived his version of the doctrine of associationism and, in all likelihood as well, the essence of his doctrine of causation from Thomas Hobbes.[76] We have also noted that Hume's critique of induction may be seen as a development of Bacon's attack on the scholastic view of induction via "middle propositions."[77] I am therefore inclined to take Hume seriously when he emphasizes that it is his *use* of the doctrine of the association of ideas that is his original contribution to philosophy.[78] Indeed, when we turn to the

---

[73] Probably the clearest indication of Hume's epistemological position is to be found in the section entitled "Of Miracles" in the first *Enquiry*, X, pp. 109-31.

[74] *Treatise*, I, III, VIII, p. 104.

[75] It is interesting to recall C. S. Peirce's estimation of the importance of the association of ideas. Peirce called it "the finest piece of philosophical work of the prescientific ages" (*The Philosophical Writings of Peirce*, selected and ed. Justus Buchler [New York: Dover, 1955], p. 2).

[76] See my D. Phil thesis, "An Examination of Some of the Central Doctrines of Hume's *Treatise of Human Nature* in the Light of Other Hume Material which Bears upon the Interpretation of that Work" (Oxford University, 1976), esp. chaps. 4 and 8.

[77] See *The Advancement of Learning*, bk. II, XIII, 3, p. 153.

[78] See also, in this connection, Richard H. Popkin's interesting note on Joseph Glanvill, another precursor of Hume ("Joseph Glanvill: A Precursor of David Hume," *Journal of the History of Ideas* 14 [1953]: 292-303).

Treatise we find that the principle is employed in some form or another in the development of virtually all of the positions he adopts.[79] It would be beyond the scope of this essay to offer anything more than a very brief account of the way in which the association of ideas was used by Hume to create a science of the mind, but I shall try to show how the principle is related to his "Newtonianism."[80]

It is clear from several of Hume's remarks in the *Treatise* that he thought he had found in the doctrine of the association of ideas a principle analogous in theoretical importance and generality to that of universal gravitation in natural philosophy, a principle that he tells us in the *Abstract* will be of "vast consequence" in the "science of human nature."[81] Whereas with Locke the association of ideas seems to have been something of an afterthought, it is abundantly clear that Hume regarded it as nothing less than the means of creating a systematic science of the mind.[82] Mental association or connection was taken by Hume to be a

---

[79] See Capaldi, p. 67. In the *Treatise* the principle is used to explain, among other things, abstract ideas, I, I, VII, p. 22; approbation of things useful (by means of sympathy; see "sympathy"), III, III, I, p. 588; artificial virtues (by means of sympathy), III, III, I, p. 577; belief in general, I, III, VI, p. 93, and IX, p. 112; belief in a connection between objects, I, IV, III, p. 223; belief in the idea of a "continu'd existence", I, IV, II, pp. 199, 204, 208, and III, p. 220; the belief that secondary qualities are in the objects themselves, I, IV, V, p. 237; beauty (our sense of depends on sympathy), III, III, I, p. 576; causal inference, I, III, VI, p. 92, VII, p. 97, XIV, p. 169, and I, IV, VI, p. 260; conditioned reflex (the phenomenon of), II, I, XII, p. 327; complex ideas, I, I, IV, p. 13; credulity, I, III, IX, p. 113; causal relation, I, III, XIV, p. 170; dramatic illusion in tragedy, I, III, X, p. 122; esteem for the rich, II, II, V, p. 362; identity, I, IV, VII, p. 262; identity (confusion with respect to), I, IV, VI, p. 254; identity (error with regard to), I, IV, II, p. 202; mental deception, I, IV, III, p. 224; general rules, I, III, XIII, pp. 147-148; judgment, I, III, IX, p. 108; memory, I, III, IX, p. 108, and Appendix, 627-628; moral approbation of justice (by means of sympathy), III, II, II, pp. 499-500; pity, II, II, VII, p. 369; praise or blame, I, III, XIII, p. 151; pride and humility, II, I, IV, p. 283, and VI, p. 290; reason (Hume's new concept of), I, III, XVI, p. 179; substance (idea of), I, I, VI, p. 16; sympathy, II, I, XI, pp. 318, 320; and thinking, I, IV, I, p. 184.

[80] See my thesis, esp. chaps. 4 and 8.

[81] *Abstract*, p. 32.

[82] Hume leaves us with little doubt about the fundamental importance he gives to the general phenomenon of the association of ideas: "Here is a kind of ATTRACTION, which in the mental world will be found to have as extraordinary effects as in the natural, and to shew itself in as many and as various forms. Its effects are every where conspicuous; but as to its causes, they are mostly unknown, and must be resolv'd into *original* qualities of human nature, which I pretend not to explain. Nothing is more requisite for a true philosopher, than to restrain the intemperate desire of searching into causes, and having establish'd any doctrine upon a sufficient number of experiments, rest contented with that, when he sees a farther examination would lead him into obscure and uncertain speculations. In that case his enquiry wou'd be much better employ'd in examining the effects than

purely contingent feature of our mental experience.[83] The laws that govern the movement of ideas in the mind, like any laws of tendency, are revealed to us only in and through experience.[84] They are "matters of fact" and as such (as indeed Hume is concerned to show in Part III) are never revealed to us by reason alone. It was therefore not surprising that, in the wake of the recent achievements of Newton in physics, Hume should have assumed that a scientific investigation of the mind should proceed along the lines of an intelligent application of Bacon's experimental method.

To return to the Newtonian metaphor, all of our mental processes take place within what Hume calls, on one occasion, "the universe of the imagination,"[85] and it is mediately from this source that we receive all of our ideas.[86] Once we have had a particular impression, something of that impression is retained within what Hume calls the "imagination" or the "fancy."[87] What is retained, the idea, also resembles the original impression, although it is itself a fainter perception. These ideas, which have

---

the causes of his principle" (*Treatise*, I, I, IV, pp. 12-13). Hume repeats this explicit comparison of the association of ideas with attraction near the beginning of his second book (II, I, IV, p. 283, and II, I, V, p. 289). The comparison is also implied in the last paragraph of the *Abstract*, pp. 31-32.

[83] Hume describes it as a "gentle force, which *commonly* prevails" (*Treatise*, I, I, IV, p. 10, my italics).

[84] Hume's use of the word "experience" is related to his use of the word "experiment." Both seem to have been taken over from Hobbes, who asserted that to have experience was to have had many "experiments" (remembrance of what antecedents have been followed by what consequents) (see *Human Nature*, in *English Works of Thomas Hobbes*, ed. W. Molesworth, 11 vols. [London, 1839-45], 4:16).

[85] *Treatise*, I, II, VI, p. 68. See also his reference to "the ideal world," I, IV, VI, p. 260.

[86] This is not, of course, to deny Hume's other claim that our ideas are ultimately derived from impressions of sensation; it is only to describe the nature of the psychological process Hume supposed to underlie all of our thought. (Here I am using "thought" in the sense in which Hume introduces the distinction between impressions and ideas in the opening paragraph of the *Treatise*.) Hume clearly has in mind something akin to our ordinary, preanalytic notion of thinking as an activity that concerns ideas as opposed to feelings (see *Treatise*, I, I, I, pp. 1-2).

[87] The "fancy," a word used throughout the *Treatise*, is a fundamental psychological category for Hume. His emphasis on the fancy and the importance he gives to those principles of the imagination that are "permanent, irresistable, and universal" (*Treatise*, I, IV, IV, p. 225) strongly suggest that he was developing Bacon's views on the positive role of the imagination in the acquisition of knowledge. See *The Advancement of Learning*, bk. II, XII, I, pp. 147-48.

Shozo Ohmori finds in Hume's concept of the fancy a useful notion for explicating some of the phenomenological ambiguities of perception and conception ("Beyond Hume's 'Fancy'," *Revue internationale de philosophie* 28 (1974):105).

their existence in the fancy, may under certain circumstances become forcefully present to the conscious mind. The ultimate cause of this process is, like the ultimate "force and efficacy of nature,"[88] completely beyond our apprehension.[89] However, it is possible to infer that there are certain regularities within the operations of the imagination. We may infer this from their effects upon our minds. Although we can never discover the *ultimate* cause of these regularities, we may nevertheless frame certain general laws regarding the manner in which the mind is affected both by the transcendent world it encounters in experience[90] and by the perpetual movement of its own thoughts and ideas in the imagination.[91] The outcome of this process of observation and generalization is the principle of the association of ideas together with the three "Laws" of mental motion—the qualities of resemblance, contiguity in time and place, and causation. These alone, Hume tells us, are the three qualities "from which this association arises, and by which the mind is . . . convey'd from one idea to another."[92] Hume's "Newtonianism," then, consists first of all in an "analysis" (which comprises an attempt to identify the most general principles that will account for the observed effects) and a "synthesis" (which consists in an attempt to explain other observed effects by means of these general laws or principles).

Before going on to consider Hume's positive account of the mental act of presuming, I would like to summarize the main points of the discussion thus far.

There now seems to be something like a consensus among Hume specialists that the *Treatise* contains a good deal more than epistemological skepticism. But the positive theory Hume advances in Book I, Part III, which takes the form of a constructive psychological theory, poses its own unique problems for interpretation. It has been argued that the traditional "Oxford view" of Hume, which sees him as continuing an

---

[88] *Treatise*, I, III, XIV, p. 159.
[89] Ibid., I, I, IV, p. 13.
[90] See Hume's concluding remarks in the *Abstract*: "'Twill be easy to conceive of what vast consequence these principles must be in the science of human nature, if we consider, that so far as regards the mind, these are the only links that bind the parts of the universe together, or connect us with any person or object exterior to ourselves. For as it is by means of thought only that any thing operates upon our passions, and as these are the only ties of our thoughts, they are really *to us* the cement of the universe, and all the operations of the mind must, in a great measure, depend on them" (p. 32).
[91] What Hume calls in a general sense "perceptions."
[92] *Treatise*, I, I, IV, p. 11.

epistemological program inaugurated by Locke, has become an obstacle to further progress on this exegetical problem and ought, if possible, to be rejected in favor of an interpretation that better reflects Hume's declared aim of introducing "the experimental method of reasoning into moral subjects."

In the last section I tried to emphasize the self-conscious Newtonianism reflected in Hume's special use of the doctrine of the association of ideas, since I believe that it alone provides the crucial point of access to Hume's thought in the *Treatise*. After having established, by the end of Part III, what he takes to be the most general laws governing the workings of the mind, Hume uses the remainder of the work to show how various other phenomena may be exhibited as mere instances of their operation. His theory of natural belief and causal inference, his doctrine of sympathy as the foremost principle in his theory of morals, and indeed all of the other positions that constitute Hume's science of human nature may be seen as, in some sense, an expression of this basic project.

I turn now to Hume's important assertion in Part III that our causal inferences are the result of an act of presuming.[93] This claim deserves rather more consideration than it has been given in the literature on the *Treatise*, particularly in view of the fact that *most* of Part III is devoted to a description and explanation of this act of the mind. Hume, I would suggest, regarded this act of presuming as the distinctive mental operation involved in probable reasoning. Without it we should never be able to proceed upon a rule such as Newton's "Third Rule of Reasoning" and so go beyond immediate experience. Indeed, we should never be able to advance a single step beyond immediate sensation. In like manner, Newton's "Second Rule," which Hume on one occasion describes as Newton's "Rule of Philosophizing," rests ultimately upon a case of presuming. Hume's own reformulation of this rule makes this quite explicit: "from like effects we *presume* like causes."[94] The mind is

---

[93] *Treatise*, I, III, VI, p. 90. According to Buchdahl, Hume's position regarding induction and its relation to Newton's Third Rule of Reasoning is "not too unlike that implied by Newton: treating the inductive projection process (the 'inference') as something that is altogether 'natural'; where all that is needed is a survey of its genetic conditions, the human frame of mind when it thus operates on the results of experiment and observation" (*Metaphysics*, p. 340). Buchdahl places the term "inference" in scare-quotes in recognition of the fact that Hume denies "that there *is* any inference; or at least, a 'rational move', proceeding by virtue of a principle of sanction" (ibid.).

[94] *Treatise*, I, IV, IV, p. 227, my italics.

determined to perform this act of presuming simply by custom,[95] from a past repetition "without any new *reasoning* or conclusion."[96] In his own index to the *Enquiry concerning Human Understanding* Hume describes custom as "the Source of Experimental Reasoning."[97]

As to the questions of what Hume supposed this act of presuming to consist in and what evidence he produced for its existence, I am afraid that what I am able to say within the scope of this essay will be far too brief to be of much value. Hume's attempt in Part III to provide a description of and explanation for the mental experience underlying our ordinary causal and inductive inferences does not lend itself to easy and concise adumbration. Part of the problem is Hume's manner of exposition, which is to depict (rather too faithfully, perhaps) the tortuous progress of his own ideas on the subject of causal inference[98] rather than to present a clear and methodically developed argument.

Another problem that seems to be involved in any attempt to set out Hume's positive account of the mental act of presuming is that to accept the validity of such an inquiry is to call into question certain fundamental presuppositions, not only of traditional empiricism, but also of Western analytic philosophy (a thankless task).[99] For to remain within the

---

[95] Ibid., III, XIV, p. 156.

[96] Ibid., VIII, p. 102, my italics.

[97] See "Custom," *Essays and Treatises*, 2:533. Hume's own index to his philosophical works (comprising the two *Enquiries* and the *Dissertation on the Passions*) does not appear in any modern editions of the *Enquiry concerning Human Understanding*. The index was first compiled by Hume for the 1758 Quarto edition and thereafter appeared in several editions, including the posthumous edition of 1777. A. G. N. Flew's new edition of the *Enquiry* (New York: Collier Books, 1962), though said in the editor's note to be "a complete text based on the posthumous edition of 1777," is in fact a reprint of the Hendel edition (Indianapolis: Bobbs-Merrill, 1955). Flew unfortunately also follows Hendel in omitting Hume's index. For evidence of Hume's authorship of the index see my thesis, Appendix II. Here I should like to record my indebtedness to my former tutor in Oxford, Dr. John D. Kenyon, St. Peter's College, for lending me his own copy of the 1758 edition of Hume's *Essays and Treatises*.

[98] At the end of the second section Hume completely abandons any methodical way of proceeding and announces that he will "proceed like those, who being in search of any thing that lies conceal'd from them, and not finding it in the place they expected, beat about all the neighbouring fields..." (*Treatise*, I, III, II, pp. 77-78). In other words, Hume tells us that he will release his mind to follow its own *natural* path; he will allow it to "range" like a spaniel in search of his quarry (to use a simile Hobbes once used to describe the same phenomenon). Hume's conceit, which was to have its literary counterpart later in Sterne's *Tristram Shandy*, is to reveal the operation of the mind according to the principle of the association of ideas by documenting the progress of his own ideas.

[99] Indeed, Hume's *Treatise* may be read as a critique of the psychological presuppositions of analytic philosophy.

traditional framework of what we might call "Anglo-American philosophy" we seem obliged to regard Hume's "subjective" enquiry into the feeling of necessity either as an unfortunate and unaccountable lapse in his "philosophical" analysis[100] or else as his oblique way of denying the possibility of "objective" knowledge of matters of fact — in other words, as skepticism.

In Hume's psychological account of probable reasoning we may discern two different kinds of investigation. On the one hand, there is a kind of quasi-empirical examination of the objective conditions that must obtain before the mechanism of causal inference can be set in motion; on the other, there is what amounts to a phenomenological[101] treatment of the feeling of determination that underlies our idea of necessary connection. It is of course true that throughout much of Part III Hume appears to be concerned not with the mind as such but rather with causally related objects. But it was in order to make a statement about the *mind* that Hume found it necessary to talk about *objects*.[102] In order to describe what we see and feel when we are attending to two causally related objects Hume was obliged to make reference to the objects themselves. However, the fact that Hume uses the language of realism must not conceal from us the fact that his main concern is with the mental. Many of Hume's statements have an inherent ambiguity (such as his statement that we can conceive any effect to follow from any cause)[103] and can be taken either as observations about the world we experience or, alternatively, as observations concerning our experience of the world. He sometimes contributes to this ambiguity through his failure to make clear whether he is talking about *objects* or about our *ideas of objects*.[104] This

---

[100] Jonathan Bennett, for example, states that "the crucial trouble" with Hume is that his "meaning-empiricism" is "genetic rather than analytic." Hume, Bennett goes on to observe, "would have done better" to have turned his "meaning-empiricism" theory from a "genetic one into an analytic one" (*Locke, Berkeley, Hume*, pp. 230-31).

[101] Husserl himself had great praise for Hume's "richly brilliant psychological analyses," (*Logical Investigations*, 2:404).

[102] See Gilles Deleuze, *Empirisme et subjectivité*, 2nd ed. (Paris: Presses Universitaires de France, 1972), p. 2. It is also important in this connection to remember that Hume had no already existing theories of psychology to fall back upon.

[103] *Abstract*, pp. 13-14.

[104] Hume sometimes refers to the mind's passing from one *object* to another (e.g., *Treatise*, I, III, XIV, p. 163; see also p. 165). It is interesting to note that Hume himself warns us against the possibility of confusing our experience of necessity, which, being an impression of reflection, arises from some combination of *ideas*, with some real relation between objects (ibid., p. 167).

may explain the apparent nonequivalence in the two definitions of "cause" Hume offers toward the end of Section XIV.[105] They may be seen as definitions of two different things, the first being some relation between objects, the second being a relation between the ideas of the objects.[106]

I cannot forbear observing (to adopt Hume's way of introducing a last digression) that there seems to be some vague incompatibility in Hume's attempt to offer both a description of the mind in terms of its operations as subjectively experienced and a reductionist explanation of the "dynamics" of mental motion. The constructive part of his psychology is, I believe, vitiated by his failure to keep quite separate two tasks: providing an adequate *description* of consciousness, and providing a suitably "scientific" *reduction of the phenomena* of consciousness. For on occasion Hume tends to conflate his description of the feeling of determination with his explanation of the origin of the feeling in terms of the psychological laws of association.

Whereas Newton had demonstrated that to reduce the complex phenomena of the material universe was to offer a more profound description of those phenomena, when we turn our attention to the phenomena of the human mind, as Hume did, we enter a world in which to *reduce* is not always to *describe*. For, in the final analysis, Hume's Newtonianism of the mind does not and, more importantly, *cannot* yield an adequate synthesis. I therefore cannot agree with Kemp Smith's conclusion that most of the defects in Hume's system are the result of his failure to meet the requirements of his Newtonian method.[107] Many of the shortcomings in Hume's psychological theory testify to the inherent unsuitability of that method itself for the investigation of consciousness. The regular operations of the mind that Hume thought underlay all of our mental experience are merely inferred. They are not in any straightforward sense part of that experience. It is for this reason that we have difficulty in accepting Hume's description of the "essence of necessity" as no more than the "propensity, which custom produces, to pass from an object to the

---

[105] Ibid., p. 170.

[106] Strictly speaking, the second definition is stated in terms of a relation between objects and the impressions and ideas of some implied observer. It is (in a Husserlian sense) implicitly intentional. Another way of expressing the fact that the definitions are of different things would be to say that whereas the first depicts a relation between two entities (or kinds of entities) — the cause and the effect — the second defines a relation that is supposed to exist between three — the cause, the effect, and some observer.

[107] *Philosophy of Hume*, p. 547.

ideas of its usual attendant."[108] Nor can we accept, as a psychological description, his assertion that the idea of extension is composed of parts that are themselves ideas of smaller parts.[109] What Hume leaves out of account is something akin to what Brentano called the "intentionality of consciousness." It is precisely because Hume fails to identify that elusive quality marking the difference between the mental and the physical universe that he cannot in the end provide a just description of our mental experience.

I began this essay by paying homage to Kemp Smith's pioneering article, "The Naturalism of Hume" and this has led through various twists and turnings to a discussion of Hume's "phenomenology." In conclusion I should like to draw attention to a recent paper that has shown more clearly than I can how these two threads may be connected. In a plenary session of the Edinburgh Hume Conference George E. Davie drew attention to Edmund Husserl's tribute to "the as yet . . . unrecognised greatness of Hume."[110] Davie emphasized the important contribution to our understanding of Hume made by members of the phenomenological school, and he went on to point out that one expression of this influence outside the Continent was the work of Norman Kemp Smith, whose interpretation of Hume's *Treatise* was importantly influenced by his contact with phenomenology. For some time now there has been an apparently unbridgeable gap separating us from this valuable movement within Continental philosophy. Perhaps Hume, a common ancestor, may yet bring about a *rapprochement*.

---

[108] *Treatise*, I, III, XIV, p. 165. See also the *Abstract*, p. 23.
[109] *Treatise*, I, II, III, p. 38.
[110] "Edmund Husserl and 'the as yet, in its most important respect, unrecognized greatness of Hume'" (*Bicentenary Papers*, pp. 69–76). In the conclusion of her paper, Mme. Demé (see n.65 above) drew attention to Hume's inauguration in Book I of the *Treatise* of what might be called the method of phenomenology (*Bicentenary Papers*, p. 144).

Hume, Atheism, and the "Interested Obligation" of Morality

J. C. A. Gaskin

I

A DISTINCTION BETWEEN PRACTICAL AND SPECULATIVE ATHEISM was widely recognized in early eighteenth-century philosophical and theological writings. The distinction was employed in both polemic and serious intellectual discussion. The speculative atheist[1] was one who laid claim to having rational grounds for denying the existence of any god. But the very possibility of such an absurdly irrational creature was sometimes put to question (e.g., Locke, *Essay*, I, iv, 16), and in the first half of the eighteenth century no one, with the arguable exception of Anthony Collins,[2] was prepared to admit to being one. The practical atheist was one who denied the existence of God in his actions, that is, one whose immoral behavior showed that he did not believe in a god. But the view that *acts* of immorality can deny the *proposition* that God exists is peculiar. How, we may ask, can acts deny propositions, and why is immorality a sign of atheism?

The answer to the first question is given very clearly by William Wollaston: "*A true proposition may be denied,*" he writes, "*or things may be denied to be what they are, by deeds, as well as by express words or another proposition.*" Later he adds, "I lay this down then as a fundamental maxim, *That whoever acts as if things were so, or not so, doth by his acts declare, that they are so, or not so*; as plainly as he could by words, and with more reality."[3] The position is open to the difficulties posed by unintentional acts or acts that ambiguously affirm or deny more than one proposition or that affirm contrary propositions. But leaving these and other difficulties aside, the position that Wollaston states—a position to which many of his contemporaries would have subscribed—clearly allows anyone adopting it or anything like it to say that a man's

---

[1] For Hume's use of the term see *An Enquiry concerning Human Understanding*, ed. L. A. Selby-Bigge, 2nd ed. (Oxford: Clarendon Press, 1902), XII, I, p. 149 (hereafter cited as first *Enquiry*).

[2] See D. Berman "Anthony Collins and the Question of Atheism in the Early part of the Eighteenth Century," in *Proceedings of the Royal Irish Academy* (1975), pp. 85–102.

[3] *The Religion of Nature Delineated*, 5th ed. (London, 1731), pp. 8, 13.

immoral deeds (practical atheism) assert that no god exists (speculative atheism) "as plainly as words and with as much reality," *provided* that immorality is taken to be a sign of atheism. This assumption or its converse — that moral behavior and religion are so closely related that an atheist can be *expected* to be immoral — is a commonplace of early eighteenth-century thought. Thus Locke can speak without hesitation of religion being the only true foundation of morality,[4] and even the urbane Shaftesbury seriously debates "whether it be a true Saying, *That it is impossible for an Atheist to be virtuous.*"[5] Given the assumption that religion is the only foundation for morality, the conclusion is obvious: whatever damages religion also damages morality. The same thought was to be put more dramatically by Dostoevski in the next century: "If there is no god, then anything is permitted." Even today there are plenty of folk for whom religion is the ultimate ground of the moral life, either because religion is supposed to provide a guarantee of moral justice, or because it provides an omnipresent moral spectator of one's secret deeds, or because its god assures us that moral values are ultimate in the nature of things. My point is that although we are at present discussing an early eighteenth-century issue to which (as I shall show) Hume contributed by pointing out the *independence* of religion and morality, the issue is big enough to cast a shadow down the years that reaches even to us in the agnostic twilight of the late twentieth century.

But what precisely was it or is it that so unites religion and morality that the former is supposed to be the only true foundation of the latter? The union is not and never has been a well-grounded empirical generalization that religious believers are usually virtuous and atheists usually scoundrels. The systematic collection of data to establish such a generalization was never undertaken, nor is it easy to see how it could be undertaken, given the complexity and privacy of many moral acts and the distortion of behavior that would be introduced by the observational process itself. But even if a systematic observation of moral acts were possible, there is no a priori reason to expect that it would show a striking moral superiority among religious people. It might; but equally it might confirm, what is probably the common observation, that atheists

---

[4] See, for example, *An Essay concerning Human Understanding*, IV, x, 7; and his first letter to the Bishop of Worcester, in *The Works of John Locke*, 11th ed., 12 vols. (London, 1812), 4:53.

[5] *Characteristicks*, 2 vols. (London, 1732), 2:7. Shaftesbury's discussion is almost certainly influenced by Bayle's *Pensés diverses* (1682) and its continuations (see n. 17 below).

and believers are not readily distinguished by the quality of their moral life. Nevertheless, the principle that morality depends upon religion was so strong in the eighteenth century that in those conspicuous cases that appeared to be at variance with the principle an argument of the no-true-Briton type prevailed: the speculative atheist could not *really* be an atheist if he were a good and honorable man. Thus certain of Hume's friends, particularly toward the end of his life, knowing his moral excellence and noticing his calm acceptance of his own extinction in death, found it difficult to believe that he had as little religious faith as he appeared to have. Indeed, some of the criticism directed at Adam Smith, for publishing in 1777 his exceedingly generous and patently sincere account of Hume's character and death, derived from the harm Smith was supposed to have done both to religion and to morality by extolling the virtues of an irreligious man.

It is, then, not observation that establishes religion as the only true foundation for morality, but something else. This something else is the belief that religion provides a transcendent obligation (the phrase does not carry all the right overtones, but it is difficult to find a better) for morality that atheism can never properly replace. I say "transcendent *obligation*" because it appears to me that if religion provides a foundation for morality at all, it is in answer to the question, *Why* should I do what I recognize to be good? not in answer to the question, *What* is good? It seems perfectly possible that there could be two people, one an atheist and the other a Christian, who agreed in all cases which things were morally good and which evil but who disagreed about why, and possibly even whether, they should do the good. (Bentham with his atheistical utilitarianism and Paley with his theological utilitarianism could be such a pair). But this transcendent obligation for morality requires elucidation. It is provided by theistic religion in two ways.

The first derives from the theist's belief in a personal god who is concerned with the good for mankind. What precisely *the good* for mankind is, may be debated. But that God wills that men should do good and avoid evil is not seriously disputed by any theist (and is for Aquinas, for example, a primary precept of the natural law). Now since the theist lives in the sight of God — a god at least thought of as an ever present unobserved observer, and at best as him in whom we live and move and have our being — and since the theist lives with his god in a reciprocal relationship of love, he is strongly and personally obligated to do good and avoid evil. Or perhaps one should say that his total, personal commitment is to a way of life in which God is central, dominant, and morally concerned with what a man does, or even thinks about doing; and the values his god embodies are for him rendered ultimate in the nature of things by this embodiment.

The second part of the transcendent obligation to do good and avoid evil (but this time it might better be called prudential motivation) is provided for those theists who believe in an after-death existence whose quality is related to conduct in this life. To put it baldly: the Christian (and Mohammedan) believes that God will punish sinners and that the righteous will live forever in a situation of maximum felicity. (The religious concepts "sin" and "righteousness" are not defined in the same way as the moral concepts "evil" and "good," but in theistic religions their extensions are, as a matter of fact, largely identical.) As Locke prudently observes, "The rewards and punishments of another life, which the Almighty has established as the enforcements of his law, are of weight enough to determine the choice against whatever pleasure or pain this life can show, when the eternal state is considered but in its bare possibility."[6] Even Shaftesbury, who has some claim to be socially if not intellectually the leading free thinker, is obliged to admit that "the Principle of *Fear of future Punishment*, and *Hope of future Reward*, how mercenary or servile soever it may be accounted, is yet, in many Circumstances, a great Advantage, Security, and Support to Virtue,"[7] while Hobbes complains about the existence of such penalties and rewards because they can be expected to have more influence than the temporal rewards and punishments that govern civil society.[8]

From these two aspects of his obligation to do good and avoid evil the theist's argument now proceeds as follows: The atheist, as atheist, cannot have the obligational grounds that the theist has for acting morally. Therefore, either he has no grounds or, at the very best, his grounds cannot be as strong as the theist's. Now since the theist can see that those grounds of obligation to morality that are uniquely his are also to him uniquely important, he claims that *loss* of these grounds will destroy the foundations of *his* morality. I emphasize *his grounds* and *to him* because there may well be a difference in human nature between the moral effect of losing religious belief and the moral effect of never having had a religious belief in the first place. As Shaftesbury judiciously observes,

---

[6] *Essay concerning Human Understanding*, II, xxi, 70.

[7] *Characteristicks*, 2:60.

[8] *Leviathan*, chap. 38.

atheism as such is morally neutral. It simply has nothing to say about moral obligation. But loss of belief in a god may deprive a man of the moral influences of religion without making him recognize "the true obligations of virtue." What these "true obligations" are, distinct from the motivations and obligations provided by religion, is set out at length by Hume, particularly in the *Enquiry concerning the Principles of Morals*, to which I shall return later.

At the beginning of this paper I defined the speculative atheist as one who laid claim to having rational grounds for denying the existence of any god. But the word "any" overstates the matter. No one before about 1770 was eager to commit himself to such total atheism. The atheism of which people were accused in the first half of the eighteenth century was disbelief in the god of Christian theism. But even this atheism is enough to "subvert the foundations of morality" because the relation of morality and religion is destroyed by any position that denies the *moral* attributes of the deity. The agreement of Hume's characters at the beginning of the *Dialogues* that "the question is not concerning the *being* but the *nature of God*" is thus slightly disingenuous because, as Cleanthes subsequently points out, there is no point in establishing the existence and power of a divine intelligence if the moral attributes of the divine intelligence remain in doubt. There is no point because such a god provides no focus for the typically theistic belief in an immanent, compassionate, moral god and hence no focus for a foundation of morality. Thus, for the purposes of discussing the relation between morality and religion, the atheist will be anyone who denies the existence of any god *having moral attributes*. The point is important because in the second part of my paper I shall take it that Hume is an atheist in this restricted sense — which I shall call moral atheism — though not in the sense that he denies the existence of all gods whatsoever — total atheism.[9] In a somewhat similar way many of the English free thinkers classified by Sir Leslie Stephen as "critical deists" were moral atheists, but none of them — Collins possibly excepted — were total atheists.

The theist's assumption that religion is the only true foundation for morality provides him with a weapon of immense power in any society in which religious belief is dominant or even prevalent. A result of this

---

[9] I have already argued this in *Philosophy* 49 (1974): 281-94, in *Journal of the History of Philosophy* 14 (1976): 301-11, and in my book *Hume's Philosophy of Religion* (London: Macmillan, 1978).

assumption is that anyone who challenges theistic belief, however slightly, is open to the charge that he is subverting the foundations of morality: anything that tends to moral atheism tends also to promote immorality, and this is a nasty charge *ad hominem* as well as *ad argumentum*. It was made against Hume both during his life (for example in 1745 during his candidature for the chair of Moral Philosophy at Edinburgh) and after his death (by the first reviewer of the *Dialogues*, among others). I do not wish to argue that Hume is unique in answering the charge or even that he was the first to do so. But his answer is strikingly complete and modern (or ancient, if the similarity with the pre-Christian, nonreligious ethics of Aristotle is noted). It is, in brief, that the "interested obligation" (Hume's phrase) to morality has or need have nothing to do with religion, and that the "transcendent obligation" (my phrase) provided by religion either does not operate at all or operates in a mischievous or insignificant manner.

II

Writing in the *Monthly Review* for 1779, the first reviewer of the *Dialogues concerning Natural Religion* fastened upon what I have called Hume's moral atheism and put clearly and judiciously the charge that it subverts morality:

> But suppose Mr Hume's principles are let loose among mankind, and generally adopted, what will then be the consequence? Will those who think they are to die like brutes, ever act like men? Their language will be, *let us eat and drink, for tomorrow we die*. When men are once led to believe that death puts a final period to their existence, and are set free from the idea of their being accountable creatures, what is left to restrain them from the gratification of their passions but the authority of the laws? But the best system of laws that can be formed by human wisdom is far from being sufficient to prevent many of those evils which break in upon the peace, order and welfare of society. A man may be a cruel husband, a cruel father, a domestic tyrant; he may seduce his neighbour's wife or his daughter, without having any thing to fear from the law; and if he takes pleasure in the gratification of his irregular appetites, is it to be supposed that he will not gratify them? What, indeed, is to restrain him?[10]

---

[10] *The Monthly Review* 61 (July-December, 1779): 347.

It is clear that the reviewer has foremost in his mind the system of postmortem punishments and rewards that everyone took Hume to deny and that he did deny. But in the first *Enquiry*, Hume had already made the reviewer's point against himself:

> Men reason not in the same manner you do, but draw many consequences from the belief of a divine Existence, and suppose that the Deity will inflict punishments on vice, and bestow rewards on virtue, beyond what appear in the ordinary course of nature. Whether this reasoning of theirs be just or not, is no matter. Its influence on their life and conduct must still be the same. And, those, who attempt to disabuse them of such prejudices . . . free men from one restraint upon their passions, and make the infringement of the laws of society, in one respect, more easy and secure.[11]

There is no attempt to reply to this in the first *Enquiry*. But in the last part of the *Dialogues* Cleanthes raises the matter again:

> The doctrine of a future state is so strong and necessary a security to morals, that we never ought to abandon or neglect it. For if finite and temporary rewards and punishments have so great an effect, as we daily find: How much greater must be expected from such as are infinite and eternal?[12]

Philo's answer, which is left substantially uncontroverted when the *Dialogues* conclude, is fourfold.[13]

1. If religion is so salutary to society, why is it, asks Philo, that history abounds with accounts of its pernicious consequences in public affairs? (In the *History of England* Hume had found many occasions to instance the gratuitous misery introduced into the world by religion. In our own day it is unnecessary to advert to an inquisition when we have so readily at hand a religious injunction that would have families of ten, twelve, or even fourteen children born to parents who neither want nor can sustain them.)

2. There is, Philo asserts, a tendency in religion to set up "new and frivolous species of merit" that form a substitute for morality. Moreover, "the preposterous distribution which it [religion] makes of praise and

---

[11] First *Enquiry*, XI, p. 147.
[12] *Dialogues concerning Natural Religion*, ed. N. Kemp Smith (Indianapolis: Bobbs-Merrill, 1947), XII, p. 219.
[13] Ibid., pp. 220–22.

blame, must have the most pernicious consequences, and weaken extremely men's attachment to the natural motive of justice and humanity."

3. As a matter of experience, a natural inclination to humanity and benevolence has a more constant and reliable effect on men's conduct "than the most pompous views suggested by theological theories and systems."

4. As a matter of observation, says Philo, it is just not established that the temporary and finite rewards and punishments of this life have less influence than the possible eternal and infinite ones of the next.

These four points are in effect a summary of Hume's whole indictment of the moral consequences of religion—an indictment set out in general terms in the *Natural History of Religion* and particularized in his *History of England*. But the crucial point for present purposes is the last—the contention that infinite and eternal rewards and punishments do not have the here and now effect we might expect. There is, Hume is saying, always a tendency to minimize or ignore the long-term consequences of wrongdoing (as with smoking): very nasty, but not *now*, not *tomorrow*, and maybe not any time. Moreover, there is always—well, almost always—time to repent (give up smoking), and this will let me get away with my indulgence *now*. But in a well-ordered civil society, Hume would say, the punishment for misconduct (legal and social punishment) is not remote, problematic, and amenable to true repentance. It is quick, unpleasant, and difficult to avoid. Hume's teasing ridicule of the theologian's attempt to have it both ways is worth quoting:

> When divines are declaiming against the common behaviour and conduct of the world, they always represent [the attachment, which we have to present things] as the strongest imaginable (which indeed it is) and describe almost all human kind as lying under the influence of it, and sunk into the deepest lethargy and unconcern about their religious interests. Yet these same divines, when they refute their speculative antagonists, suppose the motives of religion to be so powerful, that, without them, it were impossible for civil society to subsist.[14]

But if the conclusion is that divine retribution does not have the practical influence that its awesome character might lead us to expect, why is Hobbes, for example, as a moral atheist, so anxious to show that there is

---

[14] Ibid., pp. 220-21.

no divine retribution? An answer I would suggest but cannot follow up within the limits of the present essay is this: there have been societies and there have been individuals to whom the fear and hope of divine retribution is unusually real. Hobbes's society was such a one. Hume's was not. Neither is ours.

But Hume's moral atheism goes much deeper than a denial of the practical efficacy of the threats and promises of divine retribution. His discussion of what we can know about God, though it explicitly does not amount to total atheism, does amount to moral atheism. The divine intelligence that might exist, and that might be found at the end of a series of questionings about why things are as they are, cannot, according to Hume, be known to have any *moral* qualities. The god, if such there be, "has no more regard to good above ill than to heat above cold";[15] and this conclusion absolves men from any realistic possibility of living in the love of God and doing his will. At this point it might be objected that in Hume we are getting nothing but a more judiciously argued and modestly expressed version of Hobbes's onslaught against religious morality. Differences there are between Hobbes and Hume, and these could be detailed at length. But the vital one for present purposes is Hume's own alternative account of how morality functions: alternative, that is to say, *both* to Hobbes's portrait of all realistic human actions as self seeking *and* to the theist's portrait of morality underpinned by belief in a personal, loving god who embodies ultimate moral values.

This is not the place to discuss in full Hume's account of what, in the *Enquiry concerning the Principles of Morals*, he calls the "interested obligation" to morality, but in very sketchy outline the relevant parts of his account are these: Our moral discriminations derive from the approval or disapproval we experience in contemplating certain actions. When an individual approves of an action he is inclined to call it good. When most people approve of it the action is called good in the society they form. But we may ask whether this approval is entirely contingent upon accepted conventions in a given society—however outrageous these conventions might seem to other societies—or whether there is some feature common to the various actions approved that elicits the approval. According to Hume there is such a feature. It is that in some way or other the approved actions are useful or are believed to be useful in contributing to the welfare and happiness of people. We perceive or are persuaded

---

[15] Ibid., XI, p. 212.

that an action is useful in this sense, and experience approval of it. The next question is, Why do we experience this approval? Hume's answer leads to an account of the psychological mechanism of sympathy. The account is mostly in the *Treatise* and need not concern us here. But the remaining question—Why should I do that which I perceive to contribute to the welfare and happiness of people?—is vital, because it is in answering this question that the theist claimed, and sometimes still claims, a monopolistic reply: that obedience to the will of God backed up with eternal rewards and punishments is the only reason why I should do what I know to be good. Hume's reply is that the "interested obligation" to do good and avoid evil arises from a variety of sources that either do not, or need not, include religion. Some of the secular sources for the interested obligation to morality Hume identifies as follows:

1. *Self-interest.* Hume is perfectly willing to admit that a man is sometimes—even frequently—activated by self-interest. But on the one hand, the self-interest may not be detrimental to anyone (as when self-interest prevents me from "the unlimited use of strong liquors"); on the other, it may regulate my actions by the do-as-you-would-be-done-by consideration. It is this latter that makes self-interest part of interested obligation.

2. *Benevolence.* But in addition to any calculation of advantage to myself, I am sometimes activated by an immediate desire for the good of others. The source of this is the aspect of human nature that operates as sympathy. We directly *feel* the misery or joy of other people known to us.

3. *The good regard of others.* As Hume puts it, "Would you have your company coveted, admired, followed; rather than hated, despised, avoided?" Under this heading can be comprehended all those family and social pressures that make one wish not to appear in a certain character—callous, insensitive or selfish, for example— to other people.

4. *The good regard of oneself.* Again, as Hume puts it, "Inward peace of mind, consciousness of integrity, a satisfactory review of our own conduct; these are circumstances, very requisite to happiness."[16] Furthermore, "the immediate feeling of benevolence and friendship, humanity, and kindness" is peaceful and agreeable in oneself.

Without following up these sources in detail, I would suggest that they add up to a formidable enumeration of the considerations that could— Hume would say do—lead men to behave in sociably acceptable ways

---

[16] Second *Enquiry*, IX, II, p. 283.

even in areas where the surveillance of the law is not possible. Furthermore, these considerations do not include the obligations or motivations of religion, nor need these be added.

Now my contention is this. Hume's disbelief in immortality and all that immortality implies, and his skepticism about the existence of a theistic god embodying moral values, has become the entirely typical position for those late twentiety-century secular societies that do *not* embody the quasi-religious authoritarian atheism of a Marx or, much less likely, a Nietzsche. What is more, his enumeration of the factors that make up the interested obligation to morality in post-Christian, non-Marxist man are precisely those factors that operate in modern social democracies and that can be and are nurtured by society through family, school, and other social units. In short, Hume's answer, and *our* answer, to his reviewer's question, What is to restrain men from the gratification of their passions? is: self interest, benevolence, regard for one's own character, and the pressures of friends, family, and society, *quite apart from legal penalties* that may also be thrown into the balance against certain grossly immoral conduct.[17]

But the theist will have at least two objections to all this. In the first place, he will say that the obligations of morality are weakened in secular morality, whatever Hume or anyone else says, since they are diminished by the absence of commitment to a personal god who guarantees the ultimate significance of moral values, quite apart from the possibility that the god protects the moral values with a system of penalties and rewards. To this it is possible that the Marxist may be able to reply that his system entirely replaces these personal religious obligations to an imaginary god with personal political obligations to a very real party, and the values that *it* embodies are guaranteed permanent force by the dialectic of

---

[17] Cf. Bayle: "As to Manners and Civil Life [a Commonwealth of Atheists] would exactly resemble a Commonwealth of Pagans; 'twill indeed require very severe Laws, and very well executed. But does not every State require the same?" (*Miscellaneous Reflections Occasion'd by the Comet* [London, 1708], p. 329). And again in his "Appeal to all the Universities of Europe" (ibid., p. 545): "So that if some Men are more virtuous than others, this proceeds either from Natural Constitution, or education, or from a Love for certain kinds of Praise, or from fear of Reproach etc." It is apparent from these and other sources in the *Pensées* and *Continuation des Pensées*, as well as from Hume's "Early Memoranda" (see E. C. Mossner's edition in *Journal of the History of Ideas* 9 [1948]) that, as Kemp Smith points out (*Dialogues*, p. 80), Hume—as well as Shaftesbury—owed much to Bayle. In the context of the present discussion Hume's advance on Bayle consists in a more careful, complete, constructive alternative to religious morality than is provided by the penetrating but slightly chaotic and very inaccessible insights of his French original.

history. But the social democrat can appeal only a posteriori, as Hume did: If religion is so salutory to society and to morality, why is it not more obviously the case that societies dominated by religion are morally better than those in which religion is dormant?

The theist's second objection is that a man's "interested obligation" to morality may be swept aside by an interested selfishness. Hume makes the point against himself at the end of the second *Enquiry*:

> According to the imperfect way in which human affairs are condducted, a sensible knave, in particular incidents, may think that an act of iniquity or infidelity will make a considerable addition to his fortune, without causing any considerable breach in the social union and confederacy. That *honesty is the best policy*, may be a good general rule, but is liable to many exceptions; and he, it may perhaps be thought, conducts himself with most wisdom, who observes the general rule, and takes advantage of all the exceptions.[18]

The reply Hume offers is that if interested obligations fail to provide an answer to such reasoning, "it will be a little difficult to find any which will to him appear satisfactory and convincing." He could also have retorted that nothing guarantees that the religious man will behave decently in every case in which his interest competes with his morality — especially when true repentance can put everything right later on. But these replies do not entirely measure up to the importance of the assumption that lies behind the theist's objection in the present instance. His hidden, and correct, assumption is that in the terms of his morality some values are absolute. They are not up for reappraisal in special situations. But, the assumption goes on, in the secular man's morality no value need ever be absolutely sacrosanct. In a particular case this might mean, for example, that the religious man refuses ever to take innocent life. But the secular man may well waive this general rule if the advantages (not necessarily to himself) to be gained from doing so are overwhelmingly great. Even if the religious man is willing to recognize the possible moral justification of what the secular man has done in a *particular* case, he may still be reluctant to admit the particular breach in his absolute values because it could open the way to a general breach. What is absolutely forbidden need never be considered. What is occasionally permitted may become a fashion. A whole society may develop that fails to embody

---

[18] IX, II, pp. 282-83.

regard for innocent life. The theist can and will deplore such a society. The secular man, thinking in the pattern suggested by Hume, is apparently left in the position to which (subject to qualifications) Basil Mitchell reduced Lord Devlin: "We are committed to the view that the positive morality of a given society is beyond criticism. Apartheid must be accepted in South Africa, genocide in Nazi Germany."[19] But there is more appearance than reality in this as a comment upon the deficiencies of nonreligious morality. Although there is an appearance of great moral strength in a position that says "*never*, whatever society thinks or demands, will I take or acquiesce in taking an innocent life," the reality is hedged by the word "innocent." Who is innocent? Is the man who willfully rejects my faith innocent? Is the heretic innocent? Indeed, the secular moralist might retort, the theist's account of what constitutes absolute value is just as subject to qualification according to time and place and person as the secular moralist's notion of happiness; and, once again, in the actual a posteriori outcome, the atheist and the theist are not readily distinguished according to the quality of their moral performances.

To offer Hume's conclusions in the terms with which I began the discussion: There is no necessary connection between religion and morality, between speculative atheism and practical atheism, between doing mischief and being or not being either a Christian or an atheist. Part of Hume's position had already been put by Shaftesbury when he concluded that "religion (according as the kind may prove) is capable of doing great Good or Harm; and Atheism nothing positive in either way."[20] To this Hume added two footnotes of abiding importance: (1) that all men in society have an interested obligation to morality irrespective of religion, and (2) that if we "treat of religion as it has commonly been found in the world," we find that it has done more harm than good.

---

[19] Basil Mitchell, *Law, Morality and Religion in a Secular Society* (Oxford: Clarendon Press, 1967), p. 42.
[20] *Characteristicks*, p. 51.

"Art" and "Moderation" in Hume's Essays

Peter Jones

IN THE ORIGINAL PREFACE to the 1741 edition of his *Essays*, Hume pointed out that "most of these ESSAYS were wrote with a View of being published as WEEKLY-PAPERS, and were intended to compehend the Designs both of the SPECTATORS & CRAFTSMEN." He also hoped that his reader would "approve of my Moderation and Impartiality in my Method of Handling POLITICAL SUBJECTS."[1] The dominant aspect of the essays is certainly political or, in a wide sense, moral, many of his discussions being focused on the nature of the public good and the methods of its attainment. Almost no attention is given to the strictly epistemological issues discussed in the first book of the *Treatise*. On the other hand, there is a good deal of comment, explicit and implicit, on the roles of philosophy in society. Many of Hume's observations may be viewed as part of a broad approach toward understanding human practices, against the background of the narrower conceptual investigations in the *Treatise*. In this paper I shall address myself to three questions: (1) Under what conditions did Hume think that art could grow and flourish? (2) What is the central notion in Hume's account of those conditions? (3) How does that notion influence Hume's view of philosophy?

I

In 1719 the Abbé Dubos published his influential *Reflections on Poetry, Painting and Music*. Hume refers to this work in his own early memoranda,[2] but its impact is discernible also in many of his later essays, especially when the topic is art. Dubos argues that both moral and physical causes "determine the fate of the arts and sciences," and among the physical influences he mentions climatic features that affect the quality of

---

[1] *The Philosophical Works*, ed. T. H. Green and T. H. Grose, 4 vols. (London, 1886), 3:41 (hereafter cited as *Works*). Sympathizers with Bolingbroke might thus expect to find their "moderate" political views expressed with suitable Addisonian "moderation."

[2] E. C. Mossner, "Hume's Early Memoranda, 1729-1740: The Complete Text," *Journal of the History of Ideas* 9 (1948). I discuss in detail the influence of Dubos on Hume in "Hume on Art, Criticism and Language: Debts and Premises," *Philosophical Studies* 33 (1978).

the air and, in turn, the quality of the blood. The genius of the fine arts consists, he tells us, "in a happy arrangement of the organs of the brain, in a just conformation of each of these organs, as also in the quality of blood which disposes it to ferment during exercise, so as to furnish a plenty of spirits to the springs employed in the functions of the imagination."[3] Dubos emphasizes that a proper contribution to the debate over the relative merits of the ancients and the moderns requires attention to the physical aspects of life as well as to its social aspects. Many of Hume's essays are contributions to the same debate, and it is therefore not surprising that he should keep in mind Dubos's methods and claims. In order to underline man's responsibility for his actions, Hume seeks to minimize reliance on and reference to physical factors,[4] but we shall see that not far beneath the surface of his discussion there lurk some imprecise physical assumptions.

The opening paragraph of a new essay inserted in the posthumous 1777 edition of his essays summarizes an argument he elaborated in both his 1742 and 1752 essays.

> Man, born in a family, is compelled to maintain society, from necessity, from natural inclination, and from habit. The same creature, in his farther progress, is engaged to establish political society, in order to administer justice; without which there can be no peace among them, nor safety, nor mutual intercourse.[5]

To determine Hume's views on the nature of art and on the conditions under which it can grow and flourish it is helpful to look at his political essays of 1752. Hume contends that the first "savage state" of man, in which all are hunters, is succeeded by a society consisting of those who manage the agriculture and those who "work up the materials furnished by the former, into all the commodities which are necessary or ornamental to human life."

In time "superfluous hands" become available, and if they "apply

---

[3] J-B. Dubos, *Réflexions critiques sur la poesie et sur la peinture*, 2 vols. (Paris, 1719), 2:xiv: "les causes morales ne décident pas seules de la destinée et des arts." And 2:ii: "le génie de leurs Arts consiste dans un arrangement heureux des organs du cerveau, dans la bonne conformation de chacun de ces organes, comme dans la qualité du sang, laquelle le dispose à fermenter durant le travail, de manière qu'il fournisse en abondance des esprits aux ressorts qui servent aux fonctions de l'imagination." I have followed the first English translation by T. Nugent (London, 1748).
[4] "Of National Characters," *Works*, 3:244.
[5] "Of the Origin of Government," *Works*, 3:113.

themselves to the finer arts, which are commonly denominated the arts of *luxury*, they add to the happiness of the state; since they afford to many the opportunity of receiving enjoyments, with which they would otherwise have been unacquainted." The ambitions of the state or its sovereign and the luxury of individuals act as mutually restraining forces — a claim that Hume says is based "on history and experience."[6] The liberal arts flourish in times of peace and successful foreign trade, and have effects "both on *private* and on *public* life."

> Human happiness, according to the most received notions, seems to consist in three ingredients; action, pleasure, and indolence: And though these ingredients ought to be mixed in different proportions, according to the particular disposition of the person; yet no one ingredient can be entirely wanting, without destroying, in some measure, the relish of the whole composition. Indolence or repose, indeed, seems not of itself to contribute much to our enjoyment; but, like sleep, is requisite as an indulgence to the weakness of human nature, which cannot support an uninterrupted course of business or pleasure. That quick march of the spirits, which takes a man from himself, and chiefly gives satisfaction, does in the end exhaust the mind, and requires some intervals of repose, which, though agreeable for a moment, yet, if prolonged, beget a languor and lethargy that destroys all enjoyment.[7] Education, custom, and example, have a mighty influence in turning the mind to any of these pursuits; and it must be owned, that, where they promote a relish for action and pleasure, they are so far favourable to human happiness. In times when industry and the arts flourish, men are kept in perpetual occupation, and enjoy, as their reward, the occupation itself, as well as those pleasures which are the fruit of their labour. The mind acquires new vigour; enlarges its powers and faculties; and by an assiduity in honest industry, both satisfies its natural appetites, and prevents the growth of unnatural ones, which commonly spring up, when nourished by ease and idleness. Banish those arts from society, you deprive men both of action and of pleasure; and leaving nothing but indolence in their place, you even destroy the relish of indolence, which never is agreeable, but when it succeeds to labour, and recruits the spirits, exhausted by too much application and fatigue.[8]

---

[6] "Of Commerce," *Works*, 3:289-90.

[7] Dubos's opening section I, i, entitled "De la nécessité d'être occupé pour fuir l'ennui," begins: "L'ennui qui fait bientôt l'inaction de l'ame, est un mal si douloureux pour l'homme, qu'il entreprend souvent les travaux les plus pénibles, afin de s'épargner la peine d'en être tourmenté."

[8] "Of Refinement in the Arts," *Works*, 3:300-301.

Hume claims that "the spirit of the age affects all the arts," and that "refinements in the mechanical arts . . . commonly produce refinements in the liberal"; furthermore, "the more these refined arts advance, the more sociable men become." Ultimately, "they must feel an encrease of humanity, from the very habit of conversing together, and contribute to each other's pleasure and entertainment. Thus *industry, knowledge,* and *humanity,* are linked together by an indissoluble chain, and are found, from experience, as well as reason, to be peculiar to the more polished, and, what are commonly denominated, the more luxurious ages.'"[9]

Hume draws a moral and a political conclusion from these reflections. First, "the more men refine upon pleasure, the less they indulge in excess of any kind; because nothing is more destructive to true pleasure than such excesses." Second, it is advantageous to society to "multiply those innocent gratifications to individuals" because they "are a kind of *storehouse* of labour, which, in the exigencies of state, may be turned to public service." The interconnection of Hume's tenets is important: "Knowledge in the arts of government naturally begets mildness and moderation, by instructing men in the advantages of humane maxims above rigour and severity, which drive subjects to rebellion. . . ." The arts enervate neither mind nor body, nor do they beget corruption; the Roman state declined because of bad government, not because of the arts. On the contrary, "a progress in the arts is rather favourable to liberty, and has a natural tendency to preserve, if not produce a free government." Only where luxury ceases to be innocent, that is, only when it engages a man's complete attention to the exclusion of his other duties, does it cease to be beneficial, and threaten political society.[10]

Hume has so far maintained that the provision of a moderate amount of pleasure is necessary to the physical well-being of the individual and to the political well-being of society. I shall return to this notion of moderation later, but we must first look at an earlier essay, published in 1742 and entitled "Of the Rise and Progress of the Arts and Sciences." There, Hume suggests that although it is probably pointless to ask why Homer, say, lived and flourished at the time and in the place he did, it is not pointless to ask why one nation "is more polite and learned, at a particular time, than any of its neighbours"; although poets constitute a minority in any society, they do not live and work in a complete cultural and

---

[9] "Of Refinement in the Arts," *Works,* 3:300-302.
[10] Ibid., 302-7.

social vacuum, and we should reflect on "the taste, genius, and spirit" of the people among whom they live.¹¹ Hume makes four main points. First, the arts and sciences can arise only among peoples who possess a free government;¹² second, "neighbouring and independent states, connected together by commerce and policy," because they check any ambitions toward expansion of power and at the same time constitute a source of emulation, help to foster learning; third, although "the only proper *nursery*" of the arts and sciences is a free state, they may be transplanted into any government, a republic being most favorable to the growth of science and a civilized monarchy to that of the polite arts; fourth, the perfection of any art or science is "naturally, or rather necessarily" followed by its decline. For Hume, "stability and order" are secured by "laws, and methods, and institutions," but "law, the source of all security and happiness, arises late in any government, and is the slow product of order and liberty." Law is a hardy plant, when it has taken root, but "arts of luxury, and much more the liberal arts, which depend on a refined taste or sentiment, are easily lost; because they are always relished by a few only, whose leisure, fortune, and genius fit them for such amusements." In contrast, the "coarser and more useful arts" more readily influence other nations and develop more quickly than the refined arts even if they originated after them. Hume contends that "there is a very great connection among all the arts, which contribute to pleasure; and the same delicacy of taste, which enables us to make improvements in one, will not allow the others to remain altogether rude and barbarous." Because monarchies have commonly received "their chief stability from a superstitious reverence to priests and princes," they "have commonly abridged the liberty of reasoning, with regard to religion, and politics, and consequently metaphysics and morals. All these form the most considerable branches of science. Mathematics and natural philosophy, which only remain, are not half so valuable." Consequently, the arts tend to succeed in monarchies, and sciences in republics. Hume suggests that an important factor in the rise and progress of the arts might be the

---

¹¹ "Of the Rise and Progress of the Arts and Sciences," *Works*, 3:177.

¹² Three of the four points are taken from Dubos. On the first point compare "Of the Origin of Government," *Works*, 3:116: "The government, which, in common appellation, receives the appellation of free, is that which admits of a partition of power among several members, whose united authority is no less, or is commonly greater than that of any monarch; but who, in the usual course of administration, must act by general and equal laws, that are previously known to all the members and to all their subjects."

possession "of patterns in every art, which may regulate the taste, and fix the objects of imitation." But he then wonders why classical Greek models did not benefit the Romans although they did inspire the Renaissance. Two considerations occur to Hume. A nation can be discouraged by the conspicuous success of its neighbors and fail to develop its own talents; similarly, artists can be overawed by their models. Above all, however, "the arts and sciences, like some plants, require a fresh soil."[13]

II

In 1742 Hume remarked that "it is allowed on all hands, that beauty, as well as virtue, always lies in a medium." Ten years later, in the second *Enquiry*, Hume quotes the Peripatetics with approval: "A due medium ... is the characteristic of virtue."[14] Such views as these, on a proper medium or on moderation, recur throughout Hume's work and are important for an understanding of his own attitude toward philosophy.

Hume took his inspiration in these matters from Aristotle, Cicero, and Shaftesbury. Indeed, in 1739 he wrote to Hutcheson: "I desire to take my Catalogue of Virtues from *Cicero's Offices*, not from the *Whole Duty of Man*. I had, indeed, the former Book in my Eye in all my Reasonings."[15] Hume is here referring to the completed but still unpublished third book of the *Treatise*, but the influence of Cicero extends far beyond that work. For example, Cicero's discussion of the similarities and differences between man and other animals clearly influenced Hume's essay "Of the Dignity or Meanness of Human Nature"[16] as well as closely parallel passages in the *Treatise* and first *Enquiry*.[17] The notion of moderation in

---

[13] "Of the Rise and Progress of the Arts and Sciences," *Works*, 3:181-97.

[14] *An Enquiry concerning the Principles of Morals*, ed. L. A. Selby-Bigge, 2nd ed. (Oxford, 1902), VI, I, p. 233 (hereafter cited as second *Enquiry*); *Works*, 3:242.

[15] *The Letters of David Hume*, ed. J. Y. T. Greig, 2 vols. (Oxford: Clarendon Press, 1932), 1:34 (hereafter cited as *Letters*).

[16] Cicero, *De Officiis* 1. 4; *De Finibus Bonorum et Malorum* 2. 14. C. E. Edmonds, editor of Bohn's edition (London, 1853), draws the reader's attention to many parallels between Cicero and Hume, but almost the only recent philosopher to take note of them is John Laird (*Hume's Philosophy of Human Nature* [London: Methuen, 1932]). Laird also noted Cicero's influence on Bayle. I discuss the influence of Cicero, Pufendorf, Malebranche, and others on Hume in my *Aspects of Hume*.

[17] *Works*, 3:150ff.; *A Treatise of Human Nature*, ed. L. A. Selby-Bigge (Oxford, 1888), I, III, XVI, pp. 176ff. (hereafter cited as *Treatise*); *An Enquiry concerning Human Understanding*, ed. L. A. Selby-Bigge, 2nd ed. (Oxford, 1902), IX, pp. 104ff. (hereafter cited as first *Enquiry*).

Cicero is denoted not only by *moderatio* and *modestia* but is also an integral element in *mediocritas, clementia, prudentia,* and *honestum*.[18] When referring to these terms in the second *Enquiry* Hume also refers to Aristotle, and at least three tenets from Book 2 of the *Nicomachean Ethics* seem to have been absorbed into Hume's own pronouncements on moderation: (a) the view that excess destroys virtue; (b) the warning that it is often difficult to discern which actions and passions admit of a mean, and where it is to be found; and (c) Aristotle's claim that "a master of any art avoids excess and defect, but seeks the intermediate and chooses this—the intermediate not in the object but relatively to us."[19] Finally, two observations from Shaftesbury may be quoted, from among many others (perhaps Hume expected his contemporaries to recognize the dependency of his own discussions), as relevant to our enquiry: Shaftesbury contends that we may "surely place it as a principle, 'That if anything be natural, in any creature, or any kind, 'tis that which is preservative of the kind itself, and conducing to its welfare and support'." A little later he remarks that "the true men of moderation . . . are secure of their temper, and possess themselves too well to be in danger of entering warmly into any cause, or engaging deeply with any side or faction."[20]

Hume's own views on moderation may be considered, conveniently but artificially, under four aspects. Behind most of his claims, however, there lies an assumption that the health of an organism and the efficiency of a machine both require the proper functioning of all their constituent elements. Thus, "When the affections are moved, there is no place for the imagination. The mind of man being naturally limited, it is impossible that all its faculties can operate at once: And the more any one predominates, the less room is there for the others to exert their vigour."[21] This

---

[18] Second *Enquiry*, app. 4, pp. 318, 319n. Characteristic passages on *honestum* may be found in *De Officiis* 1. 4. 14; 4. 3. 13; and *De Finibus* 2. 14. 45; 5. 23. 66.

[19] *Eth. Nic.* 2. 1106b9. In his earliest extant essay, possibly written in 1725, Hume refers approvingly to "the just mean." See Mossner, "David Hume's 'An Historical Essay on Chivalry and Modern Honour'," *Modern Philology* 45 (1947).

[20] *Characteristics of Men, Manners, Opinions, Times*, ed. J. M. Robertson, 2 vols. in 1 (Indianapolis: Bobbs-Merrill, 1964), pp. 74, 77. Later, Shaftesbury refers to the need to be "healthy, and uninjured by excess" (p. 325) and to the "good of moderation" (p. 327). Cicero himself had discussed self-preservation and propagation (*De Officiis* 1. 17; *De Finibus* 4. 10. 25) and the view that the supreme Good was "life according to Nature." In the *Abstract* Hume implies that allusions to Shaftesbury will be recognized by readers of the *Treatise*. "Of the Dignity or Meanness of Human Nature" (*Works*, 3:154n.) also refers to Shaftesbury by name.

[21] "Of Simplicity and Refinement in Writing," *Works*, 3:242.

particular quotation implies, of course, that man cannot achieve a perfect balance; it is consistent with the passage, however, to see man's duty as the restraint of the more powerful faculties with the aim of a democratic representation for them all.

First, an attitude of moderation is a condition of understanding. Philosophers sometimes overwork a favorite explanation, reducing the dissimilar to the similar, or conflating causes and collateral effects;[22] on other occasions they rely on a single source of evidence or fail to see that the evidence is incomplete or inconclusive.[23] "Impartiality" is the quality needed, parallel to disinterestedness in the moral realm; and the criteria, as we shall see later, are precisely those adumbrated for mitigated skepticism.[24]

Second, Hume consciously adopts an attitude of moderation as a rhetorical means to secure communication and conviction. Expressions such as "perhaps I have gone too far in saying"[25] indicate a move akin to artillery bracketing, where the proper range is determined by shots both beyond and short of the target. Rhetorically, this allows the audience the opportunity to think through its own position and prepare its defenses before encountering the full attack. In partial contrast to this device, however, is another whereby moderation is recommended as a means to elicit moderation in response.[26] Newtonian reasons clearly lie behind Hume's thinking here, with frequent allusions, if not explicit references, to equal and opposite forces and to inertia: thus "one extreme produces another,"[27] a claim that Hume is willing to treat as "necessary."[28] A state of equilibrium or balance, on the other hand—and Hume seems to consider this to be the proper or natural condition of most bodies—is displaceable only by some force. In an essay of 1758, significantly entitled "Of the Coalition of Parties," Hume writes that "moderation is of advantage to every establishment: Nothing but zeal can overturn a settled

---

[22] "The Sceptic," ibid., 3:214; "Of Money," ibid., 320; "Of Interest," ibid., 328.

[23] "The Sceptic," *Works*, 3:229n; "Of the Populousness of Ancient Nations," ibid., 400; "Of the Balance of Power," ibid., 351n.

[24] "Of the Populousness of Ancient Nations," *Works*, 3:414n. I have discussed other aspects of this issue, in connection with aesthetic judgments and interpretations, in "Cause, Reason, and Objectivity in Hume's Aesthetics," in D. W. Livingston and J. T. King, eds., *Hume: A Re-evaluation* (New York: Fordham University Press, 1976).

[25] "Of the Delicacy of Taste and Passion," *Works,* 3:93; cf. "Of Tragedy," ibid., 259n.

[26] "On the Independency of Parliament," *Works*, 3:117n.

[27] "Of the Populousness of Ancient Nations," *Works*, 3:409; cf. "Of Passive Obedience," ibid., 462.

[28] "Of the Balance of Power," *Works*, 3:355.

power: And an over-active zeal in friends is apt to beget a like spirit in antagonists."[29]

The same model of opposing forces lies behind his pendulum metaphors and the claim that "violent Things have not commonly so long a Duration as moderate";[30] although this sounds like a definitional truth, Hume apparently puts it forward as an empirical claim. As a result of his historical analyses, however, he came to see that what is judged, initially, as an excessive deviation from a given condition may acquire, merely because of duration, the status of a new condition with its own center of gravity and balance. Thus, "Time, by degrees . . . accustoms the nation to regard, as their lawful or native princes, that family, which, at first, they considered as usurpers or foreign conquerors."[31] One other important feature should be noted in connection with the rhetorical aspect of moderation. A moderate attitude enables one more easily to acknowledge mistakes and change one's mind, without causing discomfort to oneself or confusion to others.[32] The best way to secure peace between opponents is "to prevent all unreasonable insult and triumph of the one party over the other, to encourage moderate opinions, to find the proper medium in all disputes, to persuade each that its antagonist may possibly be sometimes in the right, and to keep a balance in the praise and blame, which we bestow on either side." Rhetorically, then, moderation requires careful assessment of a speaker's needs as well as of the audience's conditions and commitments, together with the skillful adaptation of available means toward the desired ends: "there is not a more effectual method of betraying a cause, than to lay the stress of the argument on a wrong place."[33]

The third and fourth aspects of moderation are the concern of morality and politics. Cicero had said that everything in the conduct of our life should "balance and harmonize, as in a finished speech," and that moderation was, above all, "the science of doing the right thing at the right time."[34] In Hume's view, moderation is an essential constituent of genuine humanity and reveals itself in balanced judgments.[35] Any "original

---

[29] "Of the Coalition of Parties," *Works*, 3:469.
[30] "Of the Parties of Great Britain," *Works*, 3:144n.
[31] "Of the Original Contract," *Works*, 3:451.
[32] "Of the Parties of Great Britain," *Works*, 3:141n.
[33] "Of the Coalition of Parties," *Works*, 3:464, 470.
[34] *De Officiis* 1. 40.
[35] "Of Civil Liberty," *Works*, 3:162; "Of National Characters," ibid., 247n; "Of the Populousness of Ancient Nations," ibid., 408.

inclination . . . or instinct" that a man has toward exclusive self-concern must be "checked and restrained by a subsequent judgment or observation. . . . it is reflection only, which engages us to sacrifice such strong passions to the interests of peace and public order."[36] It is as important, of course, to moderate the strength of our passions as it is to broaden their scope, but this does not mean that we should adopt an attitude of "provoking coolness and indifference."[37] Nowhere does Hume imply that it is a proper act of moderation to mediate between or compromise with both of two adversaries who are equally wrong or immoral; moderation, for Hume, involves neither taking the halfway position between any two views, whatever they are, nor seeking peace at any price.[38] We should distinguish between the procedures appropriate to enquiry and judgment and those appropriate to action based on such judgment. Sometimes, there is a special task for the philosopher

> who is of neither party, to put all the circumstances in the scale, and assign to each of them its proper poise and influence. Such a one will readily, at first, acknowledge that all political questions are infinitely complicated, and that there scarcely ever occurs, in any deliberation, a choice, which is either purely good, or purely ill. Consequences, mixed and varied, may be foreseen to flow from every measure: And many consequences, unforseen, do always, in fact, result from every one. Hesitation, and reserve, and suspense, are, therefore, the only sentiments he brings to this essay or trial."[39]

Readers of the *Treatise* recall that to achieve a balanced view, to arrive at a "*stable* judgment of things, we fix on some *steady* and *general* points of view," because "'tis impossible we cou'd ever converse together on any reasonable terms, were each of us to consider characters and persons, only as they appear from his peculiar point of view."[40] The common point of view, and the agreed descriptions dependent on it, will constitute the standard, norm, mean, measure, or *modus* against which deviations

---

[36] "Of the Original Contract," *Works*, 3:455.

[37] "The Stoic," *Works*, 3:206; "The Sceptic," ibid., 214, 222; "Of the Standard of Taste," ibid., 281; "Of the Populousness of Ancient Nations," ibid., 408.

[38] But see the conclusion to *The Natural History of Religion*: "In general, no course of life has such safety (for happiness is not to be dreamed of) as the temperate and moderate, which maintains, as far as possible, a mediocrity, and a kind of insensibility, in every thing" (*Works*, 4:361-62).

[39] "Of the Protestant Succession," *Works*, 3:475.

[40] *Treatise*, III, III, I, pp. 581-82.

will be measured (Cicero himself noted that one aspect of moderation was associated with *modus*).⁴¹ It is easy to see how a common point of reference acting as a condition of intelligibility and communication acquires a normative dimension, since the adoption of a shared viewpoint helps to secure social cohesion and stability. There is no equivocation in maintaining, although it is rarely spelled out in this way, that one ought to adopt a certain position in order to understand a certain situation, and that one ought to do certain things as a result of such understanding.

Politically, Hume maintains that moderation is integral to peace, stability, law and order, and, like Shaftesbury before him,⁴² is ready to inveigh against enthusiasm and superstition, faction, fanaticism and zeal, wherever they appear—in politics, morality, or religion.⁴³ Consistent with these views, "violent innovations no individual is entitled to make," even though the consequences be desirable and beneficial.⁴⁴ Hume contends that "factions subvert government, render laws impotent, and beget the fiercest animosities among men of the same nation, who ought to give mutual assistance and protection to each other."⁴⁵ Man is an essentially social being, and "the chief source of moral ideas is the reflection on the interests of human society"; chaos results from a total opposition between those engaged in such reflection, and that is why "the only dangerous parties are such as entertain opposite views with regard to the essentials of government."⁴⁶ Hume held that where customs had failed to establish moderation in a society, good laws could do so; such laws must be concerned with establishing or preserving liberty and serving the public good—ends worthy of the most strenuous pursuit.⁴⁷ Although his own ideal was a commonwealth, Hume believed it necessary to defend the "regular system of *mixed* government"⁴⁸ of his time, largely because of his view that excess engenders excess—it is not a trivial point that he was much attracted to the recently introduced phrases "balance of

---

⁴¹ *De Officiis* 1. 40. 142.
⁴² *Characteristics*, pp. 288-89, 325-27.
⁴³ "Of Superstition and Enthusiasm," *Works*, 3:149, for example.
⁴⁴ "Of the Original Contract," *Works*, 3:452.
⁴⁵ "Of Parties in General," *Works*, 3:127.
⁴⁶ "Of the Immortality of the Soul," *Works*, 4:403; "Of the Coalition of Parties," ibid., 3:464.
⁴⁷ "That Politics may be reduced to a Science," *Works*, 3:98, 106-7.
⁴⁸ "Of the Independency of Parliament," *Works*, 3:119; see "Idea of a Perfect Commonwealth," ibid., 480ff.

trade" and "balance of power,"⁴⁹ to denote appropriately moderate notions.⁵⁰

Hume freely concedes that "all questions concerning the proper medium between extremes are difficult to be decided; both because it is not easy to find *words* proper to fix this medium, and because the good and ill, in such cases, run so gradually into each other, as even to render our *sentiments* doubtful and uncertain."⁵¹ This difficulty, combined with our ignorance of the future,⁵² leads to reliance on the past and on what is established and therefore known; that is largely why "antiquity always begets the opinion of right."⁵³ Moreover, "human society is in perpetual flux, one man every hour going out of the world, another coming into it," and stability can be maintained only by gradual innovations.⁵⁴ It is important to note that Hume does not use the notions of inertia and equilibrium to argue for a static and unchanging society; rather, he subscribes to a dynamic model of a complex machine that can easily go wrong, needs the most tender care and maintenance, but that certainly needs to be kept moving: "Rust may grow to the springs of the most accurate political machine, and disorder its motions."⁵⁵ At this stage, however, advocacy of moderation threatens, once again, to dissolve into a vague and uninteresting recommendation to exercise judgment and common sense.

In order to bring the discussion into focus, therefore, it will be instructive to look briefly at a quartet of essays in the 1742 edition that were designed, Hume tells us, "to deliver the sentiments of sects that naturally form themselves in the world, and entertain different ideas of human life and happiness."⁵⁶

III

In "The Epicurean" we read that although "the health of my body consists in the facility, with which all its operations are performed," my

---

⁴⁹ "Of the Balance of Trade," *Works*, 3:330; "Of the Balance of Power," ibid., 348.
⁵⁰ And see "Of Essay Writing," *Works*, 4:368, dating from 1742.
⁵¹ "Of the Independency of Parliament," *Works*, 3:121.
⁵² See "Of the Protestant Succession," *Works*, 3:475.
⁵³ "Of the First Principles of Government," *Works*, 3:110.
⁵⁴ "Of the Original Contract," *Works*, 3:452; see also "Of the Coalition of Parties," ibid., 465.
⁵⁵ "Idea of a Perfect Commonwealth," *Works*, 3:493.
⁵⁶ "The Epicurean," *Works*, 3:197n.

will has little power over its internal condition. Worthwhile and lasting pleasure cannot result from self-absorption, because pleasure depends on both internal and external factors over which we have little control. Pride can beget only "*artificial happiness*." In the next essay, the Stoic underlines the implication of this remark by stressing that man is a social being, but he denies the Epicurean's claim that we can justifiably ignore the past and the future while enjoying the present.[57] On the contrary, we can attain happiness only if we are historically conscious, noting our mistakes and seeking their causes and their remedies. Chance can be combatted only by a knowledge of causes, and such knowledge is a necessary condition for attaining sustained happiness: "happiness cannot possibly exist, where there is no security; and security can have no place, where fortune has any dominion." The Epicurean failed to see that a social environment was necessary to the enjoyment of his debauching and that such an environment itself requires the exercise of social virtues, for these alone are sustaining: "As sorrow cannot overcome them, so neither can sensual pleasure obscure them." The Stoic here introduces another note into the discussion, for he asserts that a mind properly sensitive to social virtues will view "liberty and laws as the source of human happiness" and devote itself "to their guardianship and protection." The Stoic, in effect, articulates a secular morality rooted in social virtues, as distinct from the egotistical, sensual indulgence and "lethargic indolence" of the Epicurean.[58]

Leaving aside "The Platonist," we may turn to "The Sceptic." In "their reasonings concerning human life, and the methods of attaining happiness"—the topic of the preceding essays—philosophers commonly overwork or misapply their favorite principles. The skeptic claims that men are governed by the narrowness not only of their understanding but of their passions and that most of us are influenced by "a predominant inclination" to which our other desires submit. Once we realize that there is a "vast variety of inclinations and pursuits among our species," we may discern that one man "may employ surer means for succeeding than another" by "employing his reason to inform him what road is preferable." To the objection that this is no more than "common prudence, and discretion," and that a philosopher might be expected to advise on

---

[57] Ibid., 198; and "The Stoic," ibid., 205; on p. 203 the Stoic follows Cicero's comparisons between man and other animals.
[58] "The Stoic," *Works*, 3:205-9.

ends rather than means, the skeptic replies that such a request rests on philosophical confusion. First, "objects have absolutely no worth or value in themselves" such as could be discerned by reason; on the contrary, "beauty and worth are merely of a relative nature, and consist in an agreeable sentiment, produced by an object, according to the peculiar structure and constitution of that mind." The sentiment itself determines the mind "to affix the epithet *beautiful or deformed.*" In an important footnote Hume asserts that a property is no less real for being a dependent or relational property, and that a relational property can be reasoned about in the same way as other properties: beauty and virtue are simply like colors in this respect, and "there is sufficient uniformity in the senses and feelings of mankind, to make all these qualities the objects of art and reasoning, and to have the greatest influence on life and manners."[59] This passage, of course, echoes the well-known discussion at the beginning of Book 3 of the *Treatise* and in Hume's letters to Hutcheson of 1739 and 1740;[60] moreover, the passage is reiterated in both *Enquiries*, and yet again, in 1757, in the essay "Of the Standard of Taste."[61]

The second point is this: it is a mistake to think of a philosopher as being in possession of special knowledge, as if he were an expert in "magic or witchcraft"; he is not "a *cunning man*" in this sense.

Thirdly, the skeptic claims that because "there is something approaching to principles in mental taste," and because taste is subject not only to custom, prejudice, and humor but also to "education," one can make some general observations about reliable grounds for happiness. "To be happy, the *passion* must be" moderate, social, cheerful, and, in order to sustain it over any length of time, appropriate to the facts of the situation; for the last, historical reflection is necessary. A mind possessing these traits is said to be not a properly *rational* mind, as the reader might expect, but a *virtuous* mind. The two notions, however, are no longer separable, as the summary of the skeptic's argument at this stage of the essay shows: a virtuous mind is "that which leads to action and employment, renders us sensible to the social passions, steels the heart against the assaults of fortune, reduces the affections to a just moderation, makes our own thoughts an entertainment to us, and inclines us rather to the pleasures of society and conversation, than to those of the senses." The

---

[59] "The Sceptic," *Works*, 3:213-19.

[60] See especially *Treatise*, III, I, I, p. 469; and *Letters*, 1:39.

[61] First *Enquiry* (ed. C. W. Hendel [Indianapolis: Bobbs-Merrill, 1955]), p. 23n.; second *Enquiry*, app. 1, pp. 291-92; "Of the Standard of Taste," *Works*, 3:268, 272.

skeptic adds that because "nature has a prodigious influence" over all men, rules of morality, and philosophical reflections generally, can aid only those who already have a "lively sense of honour and virtue"; philosophy can be no *"medicine of the mind"* to the perverse. What philosophy, broadly conceived, can do is to harness antecedent dispositions and inculcate habits.

One claim is important for our purposes: "It is certain, that a serious attention to the sciences and liberal arts softens and humanizes the temper, and cherishes those fine emotions, in which true virtue and honour consists."[62]

There is no clue in the three preceding essays that the skeptic's discussion will be so sustained and condensed — we are still little over halfway through. But now the skeptic repeats one of his central claims, as a prelude to further refinement. "No direct arguments or reasons" can be used "to excite or moderate" a man's passion or his value for an object; but "the passion, in pronouncing its verdict, considers not the object simply, as it is in itself, but surveys it with all the circumstances, which attend it." Here, a philosopher may intervene and "suggest particular views, and considerations, and circumstances, which otherwise would have escaped us; and, by that means, he may either moderate or excite any particular passion." It must be conceded, however, that the *"artificial* arguments" of philosophy "will never produce those genuine and durable movements of passion, which are the result of nature and the constitution of the mind";[63] indeed, there is a danger that "refined reflections," if they influence the passions at all, will entirely extinguish them, "rendering the mind totally indifferent and unactive."[64] After observing that a familiar "disdain towards human affairs," found so often among philosophers, lasts only "as long as nothing disturbs him or rouses his affections," the skeptic suggests that philosophers could usefully remind men of the transcience of life and of the fact that there is generally someone worse off than oneself.[65] A footnote at this point adds a number of other homilies designed to "tranquilize and soften all the passions"; and the essay rapidly concludes with the observation that philosophical reflection might be construed as overvaluing life, "were it

---

[62] "The Sceptic," *Works*, 3:215-24.
[63] Ibid., 224-25.
[64] Ibid., 225; cf. "Of the Original Contract," ibid., 456.
[65] "The Sceptic," *Works*, 3:227; cf. second *Enquiry*, VI, II, p. 245n.

not that, to some tempers, this occupation is one of the most amusing, in which life could possibly be employed."[66]

It is important to ask ourselves why the fourth essay of the quartet is entitled "The Sceptic." Skepticism was commonly taken to involve the denial of something—the existence of some allegedly real property, the extent of some method of enquiry, the possibility of knowing something.[67] In this sense, almost any denial of or doubt concerning an assertion by a dogmatist, religionist, enthusiast, or fanatic (to use Hume's terms) might be branded, loosely, as skeptical. In this essay the role of reason in the realm of value has been diminished, and a quite unpretentious task has been assigned to philosophy—or so it seems: "Here then is the chief triumph of art and philosophy: It insensibly refines the temper, and it points out to us those dispositions which we should endeavour to attain, by a constant *bent* of mind, and by repeated *habit*. . . . The reflections of philosophy are too subtle and distant to take place in common life, or eradicate any affection."[68] Another reason for the title of the essay may have been equally obvious to Hume's readers. The quartet of essays, taken as a group, constitutes one of Hume's earliest attempts at the dialogue form, in which arguments are skillfully distributed among dramatically contrasted characters. Hume's immediate model was Cicero, who, having outlined and rejected Epicureanism, Stoicism, and Platonism, presented his own skeptical position.[69] There are two more important points, however. First, a skeptic's position does not consist wholly of questions, doubts, and denials, and we should note that the positive attitude to life advocated by the skeptic in the fourth essay of the quartet is none other than that of moderation, which we discussed earlier. All its dimensions are discernible in "The Sceptic": moderation is a condition of understanding (the Epicurean, Stoic, and Platonist are immoderate in confining their principles); it is a condition of communication; and, without requiring us to adopt a weakly compromising attitude toward our adversaries, it has moral and political dimensions in connection with social cohesion and stability. The second point can be brought

---

[66] "The Sceptic," *Works*, 3:229n., 231.

[67] Hence the description of the *Treatise* in the *Abstract*. Bayle had characterized Pyrrhonism as mainly a challenge to religion. Cf. *Dialogues concerning Natural Religion*, ed. N. Kemp Smith (Indianapolis: Bobbs-Merrill, 1947), p. 139; *Works*, 2:388.

[68] "The Sceptic," *Works*, 3:224-25.

[69] For example, *De Finibus*, *De Natura Deorum*. See "Of the Rise and Progress of the Arts and Sciences," *Works*, 3:189n.

out by reminding ourselves of the conclusion to the first *Enquiry*, published in 1748, seven years after the essay we have been discussing.

Hume argues that everyone wants to "attain a proper stability and certainty" in his "determinations" but that we cannot determine a priori "the proper criteria of truth and falsehood" for every "sphere" of inquiry.[70] That is why an exclusive attitude of doubt, before and during every investigation, and toward every conclusion we reach, is radically misconceived. The exclusive use of doubt is as inappropriate as the exclusive use of reason: both are excesses typical of philosophers who "confine too much their principles."[71] If we are genuinely interested in the foundations of man's capacities to "act and reason and believe" — the phrase echoes a passage in the first section — we have to recognize that man is a social animal whose complex mechanisms are inexplicable by reason alone.[72] At least "a *Stoic* or *Epicurean* displays principles which . . . have an effect on conduct and behaviour," whereas the *antecedent* and *consequent* species of skepticism, associated with *Pyrrhonism*, can have no influence "beneficial to society." In fact, "action, and employment, and the occupations of life" subvert "the excessive principles of scepticism."[73] In Hume's eyes a properly functioning machine is one in which none of the constituent parts idles or runs out of control. Insofar as man is a balanced organism or machine, his "reasonable . . . sociable . . . active" sides will act as mutual checks.[74] The *mitigated* skepticism of the first *Enquiry* is none other than the moderation we have discussed.

There is, however, a rider. "Moral reasoning," Hume tells us, "forms the greater part of human knowledge and is the source of all human action and behaviour," and "moral reasonings are either concerning particular or general facts."[75] If we examine the list, which includes history, geography, and astronomy under the former heading, and politics, physics, and chemistry under the latter, we find no reference to philosophy. In the penultimate paragraph we are reminded that "morals and criticism

---

[70] First *Enquiry*, XII, I, pp. 150-51.
[71] "The Sceptic," *Works*, 3:213.
[72] First *Enquiry*, XII, II, p. 160. The phrase echoes a passage in the first section, p. 8.
[73] Ibid., pp. 159-60.
[74] Ibid., I, p. 8.
[75] Ibid., XII, III, p. 164. See Cicero, *De Officiis*: "Those duties are closer to Nature which depend on the social instinct than those which depend upon knowledge. . . . Service is better than mere theoretical knowledge, for the study and knowledge of the universe would somehow be lame and defective, were no practical results to follow" (XLIII). "Every duty,

are not so properly objects of the understanding as of taste and sentiment"—the tenet that underpinned the skeptic's denial that a philosopher could issue guidance on the ends of life, on "what desire we shall gratify, what passion we shall comply with, what appetite we shall indulge."[76] Inquiries traditionally undertaken by philosophers, or at least philosophers of a rationalist persuasion, will be undertaken by others— by scientists and by historians. All that remains is to realize that "philosophical decisions are nothing but the reflections of common life, methodized and corrected."[77] At the opening of the first *Enquiry* Hume observed that "nature has pointed out a mixed kind of life as most suitable to the human race," and that the goal of discovering "the proper province of human reason" is "to live at ease ever after."[78] Any "reasonings lose their force by being carried too far," however, whether in a political or a philosophical context; indeed, "there is no virtue or moral duty, but what may, with facility, be refined away, if we indulge a false philosophy, in sifting and scrutinizing it, by every captious rule of logic, in every light or position, in which it may be placed."[79] The philosopher's tasks vary. After "exact analysis," in the manner of an "anatomist," it would be proper "to represent the common sense of mankind in more beautiful and engaging colours,"[80] although, as the beginning of the *Abstract* makes clear, it is no longer satisfactory to do the latter without the former—as Cicero did. Often a philosopher has the task of "extricating" us from "uncertainty" brought about by "abstruse philosophy,"[81] and there is no guarantee that the results will always mirror the opinion of the common man. But there are no special sources of knowledge available only to a philosopher, nor any special areas of concern to him alone. In what may have been intended as a preface to the 1742 essays, Hume wrote: "learning has been [a] great . . . Loser by being

---

therefore, that tends effectively to maintain and safeguard human society should be given the preference over that duty which arises from speculation and science alone" (XLIV). "The following question should, perhaps, be asked: whether this social instinct, which is the deepest feeling in our nature, is always to have precedence over temperance and moderation also. I think not" (XLV).

[76] "The Sceptic," *Works*, 3:215.

[77] First *Enquiry*, XII, III, p. 162.

[78] Ibid., I, pp. 9, 12.

[79] "On the Independency of Parliament," *Works*, 3:118n.; "Of the Original Contract," ibid., 456.

[80] First *Enquiry*, I, pp. 12, 10, 7. For other tasks, see my "Strains in Hume and Wittgenstein," in *Hume: A re-evaluation*, pp. 196-97.

[81] "Of the Standard of Taste," *Works*, 3:279; first *Enquiry*, I, p. 16.

shut up in Colleges and Cells, and secluded from the World and good Company. . . . Philosophy went to Wrack by this moaping recluse Method of Study, and became as chimerical in her Conclusions as she was unintelligible in her Stile and Manner of Delivery. And indeed, what cou'd be expected from Men who never consulted Experience in any of their Reasonings."[82] In the first volume of his essays, he contrasted the philosopher, whose "general abstract view of the objects leaves the mind so cold and unmoved," and the "man of business," who "has his judgment warped on every occasion by the violence of his passion," with the historian: "history keeps in a just medium betwixt these extremes, and places the objects in their true point of view."[83]

In brief, the attitude of mind characterized in the essay "The Sceptic" is precisely that attitude enacted in the first *Enquiry*.

IV

The conclusion can be as short as the exposition has been long. Hume conceives pleasure as a necessary constituent of human happiness, and art as a means of providing it. Art probably arose only when men had time to relax from their pursuit of the bare necessities of life, but it flourished only when men gained sufficient control of themselves and their fellows to realize that no pleasure should be indulged to excess. The physical health of the individual and the political stability of society required an attitude of moderation in all things; the democratic functioning of the body as of the state required the proper representation of all the constituent members. Moderation was to be understood as the set of Ciceronian virtues, underpinned by Newtonian assumptions, and the necessary laws of physics were taken to justify certain procedures in the social and political realm. It was a mistake to think that a philosopher had special insight into the secret paths to happiness; there are no secret paths, and the philosopher has no special knowledge entitling him to pre-eminence among men. Those who prosecute abstract reflection beyond the contexts in which it serves the public good do so for essentially aesthetic reasons. The whole man is a healthy man, and moderation is constitutive of being healthy, social, and fully human.[84]

---

[82] "Of Essay Writing," *Works*, 4:368.
[83] "Of the Study of History," *Works*, 4:391. In "Of the Coalition of Parties," ibid., 3:464, Hume distinguishes *philosophical* and *practical* controversies from *historical*.
[84] See Cicero, *De Finibus* 4. 14. 36.

I have discussed elsewhere Hume's account of aesthetic judgments,[85] but there are many questions that need to be asked of the present account. How are the criteria of moderation in a given context determined?[86] Are problems concerning the different media of the arts and the quality of individual works illuminated by these remarks? What is the precise effect of Newtonian assumptions on Hume's thinking in these domains, and how are the themes of the essays related to those of the official philosophical works?[87] To these, and other important issues, however, I must address myself on another occasion.

---

[85] See n. 24 above. It should be observed that, for Hume, art arises only under conditions of moderation, and that the criteria of merit are to be found in moderation. The importance of rhetoric to Hume's views must not be overlooked, and I discuss it in my forthcoming *Aspects of Hume*.

[86] See "Of the Balance of Trade," *Works*, 3:333: "All water, wherever it communicates, remains always at a level. Ask naturalists the reason; they tell you, that, were it to be raised in any one place, the superior gravity of that part not being balanced, must depress it, till it meet a counterpoise; and that the same cause, which redresses the inequality when it happens, must for ever prevent it, without some violent external operation."

[87] See the concluding sentence of *A Dissertation on the Passions*, *Works*, 4:166: "In the production and conduct of the passions, there is a certain regular mechanism, which is susceptible of as accurate a disquisition, as the laws of motion, optics, hydrostatics, or any part of natural philosophy."

Time and Value in Hume's Social and Political Philosophy

Donald W. Livingston

HUME COMMENTATORS HAVE PAID INSUFFICIENT ATTENTION, I think, to the way in which the concept of time shaped Hume's social and political philosophy. Social and political order is constituted by standards, and on Hume's view these standards have a temporal structure conceived of as a certain relation between present and past existences. In this, Hume's theory differs fundamentally from two types of social and political theory held by most of his contemporaries. The first sort of theory holds that social and political standards have no essential temporal content. I shall call this the *rationalist theory*; it includes most versions of the social-contract theory and the theory of natural law current in Hume's time. The other sort of theory holds that social and political standards *do* have an essential temporal content, but this purely temporal authority is conceived of as a relation between present and future existences. I shall call this the *providential theory*; it was a common way of thinking among such eighteenth-century radical reformers as Dr. Richard Price and Catharine Macaulay. In what follows I shall compare Hume's social and political philosophy with both of these theories, having the goal in mind of uncovering the rationale for his qualitative conception of present and past time and of showing how this qualitative conception of time is rooted in his theory of the understanding.

I

We may begin with the rationalist theory. The concept of reason presupposed in this theory was first stated in Descartes's *Discourse on Method*. Descartes laid it down as a principle of reason that all former opinions should be considered false until they can be made to "conform to the uniformity of a rational scheme."[1] By a rational scheme he meant a set of propositions that are intuitively certain or are deduced from propositions intuitively certain. Applied to social and political philosophy (although Descartes did not so apply it) this principle entails that it

---

[1] *The Philosophical Works of Descartes*, trans. E. S. Haldane and G. R. T. Ross, 2 vols. (New York: Dover, 1955), 1:89.

is analytic to the concept of reason to treat the standards governing existing social and political institutions as false until they can be shown to be in accord with intuitively certain propositions. Since the standards that make up existing social and political institutions are traditional, temporal, and contingent, they cannot be the objects of self-evident propositions. The conceptual effect of Cartesianism in politics, then, is to deny prima facie the authority and, hence, the reality of all existing social and political order. This way of thinking easily leads to a frame of mind that I shall call *metaphysical rebellion*. It is metaphysical because in methodologically rejecting the whole order of historical social and political standards it is no longer possible to make distinctions between good and evil *within* that order. The historical order itself is viewed not in terms of the *moral* categories of good and evil but in terms of the metaphysical categories of reality and illusion. By the rationale of the evil-demon hypothesis, the historical social and political order is thought of methodologically as a grand hoax. True social and political order is viewed as an order of nature: a timeless object of reason existing independent of the historical process. Moreover, we constantly confuse the historical order with the natural order in roughly the same way that (as Descartes and other modern philosophers taught) we confuse the sensory order with the physical order. This familiar modern teaching Hume dryly described in the *Treatise* as the doctrine of "double existence."[2] It is important to appreciate that the doctrine of double existence is not an accident of Descartes's analysis of our knowledge of the physical world but is entailed in the Cartesian conception of reason, which, when applied to our understanding of the moral world, must yield a corresponding doctrine of double existence. Cartesianism in politics, therefore, requires that we think of two societies: the historical society, an interconnecting web of illusion and contingency, and the timeless and rationally ordered society of nature, with which the first is conceptually confused. But whereas emancipation from sensory illusion can be achieved by philosophical reflection alone, emancipation from historical, social, and political illusions requires more sanguinary methods.

Descartes did not apply his revolutionary conception of reason to politics, but others did so, and there soon developed what might be called a movement of left-wing Cartesianism that includes such thinkers as Jean

---

[2] *A Treatise of Human Nature*, ed. L. A. Selby-Bigge (Oxford, 1888), I, IV, II, p. 215 (hereafter cited as *Treatise*).

Meslier, Morelly, the Abbé de Mably, and Rousseau.³ The doctrine of double existence is behind Morelly's yearning for metaphysical revolution in the *Code de la Nature*, where he writes: "since I maintain that vulgar morality [historical morality] has been established on the ruins of the laws of nature, one must wholly overturn the former in order to reestablish the latter."⁴ The same doctrine of double existence is expressed by Rousseau's famous statement that "man is born free but everywhere he is in chains" and in a later and different philosophical context by Proudhon's paradoxical statement that "property is robbery." These are ringing phrases and are perhaps splendid cases of Hume's complaint in the *Treatise* that "whatever has the air of a paradox, and is contrary to the first and most unprejudic'd notions of mankind is often greedily embrac'd by philosophers, as shewing the superiority of their science, which cou'd discover opinions so remote from vulgar conception."⁵

Cartesianism is not confined to the rationalist tradition, narrowly conceived as a doctrine of self-evident truths. What is essential is the method of doubt: the presumption that all historical standards are to be thought of as false until brought into conformity with something called *reason*. And the conception of reason can vary. Bentham held to a utilitarian conception of reason, but he is still following the Cartesian method when he says that "rude establishments" must be brought "to the test of polished reason."⁶ Marx also is in command of the heroic conception of reason, so compellingly stated by Descartes in the *Discourse* and *Meditations*, when he writes in a letter to Ruge: "what we . . . have to achieve . . . is the ruthless criticism of all that exists. . . . Reason has always existed, but not always in reasonable form."⁷

Cartesianism in politics, and the metaphysical rebellion that follows

---

³ The expression "left-wing Cartesianism" is a valuable one, taken from Gerhardt Niemeyer, *Between Nothingness and Paradise* (Baton Rouge, La.: Louisiana State University Press, 1971), p. 8.

⁴ Ed. Gilbert Chinard (Paris, 1950), p. 180.

⁵ *Treatise*, I, II, I, p. 26.

⁶ According to Mill, it was Bentham's method, not his opinions, that constituted the novelty and value of his work: "He begins all his inquiries by supposing nothing to be known on the subject, and reconstructs all philosophy *ab initio*, without reference to his predecessors" (*Mill on Bentham and Coleridge*, ed. F. R. Leavis [New York, 1950], p. 57). The method described here is clearly Cartesian as is Proudhon's: "If your will is untrammelled, if your conscience is free, if your mind can unite two propositions and deduce a third therefrom, my ideas will inevitably become yours" (*What is Property?*, p. 13).

⁷ *Karl Marx on Revolution*, in *The Karl Marx Library*, ed. and trans. Saul K. Padover, 13 vols. (New York, 1971), 1:516–17.

from it, was well established in Hume's time, nor was it simply an amusing error of closet philosophers. Hume was the first philosopher to recognize it as a conceptual structure of political parties and so as a civic danger as well as an absurdity. In "Of Parties in General" he distinguished two sorts of political parties: those of interest and ambition and those of metaphysical principle. The former are the more excusable and reasonable, but parties of metaphysical principle are conceptual absurdities and, moreover, are unique to modern times:

> Parties from *principle*, especially abstract speculative principle, are known only to modern times, and are, perhaps, the most extraordinary and unaccountable *phaenomenon*, that has yet appeared in human affairs. Where different principles beget a contrariety of conduct, which is the case with all different political principles, the matter may be more easily explained. . . . But where the difference of principle is attended with no contrariety of action . . . what madness, what fury, can beget such unhappy and such fatal divisions?[8]

The argument here against metaphysics in politics is the same that Hume has urged elsewhere against metaphysics generally, namely, that contrary metaphysical principles do not entail contrary propositions that can be tested empirically and so are vacuous.

The metaphysical political parties that Hume has chiefly in mind in this essay are religious parties, but his criticism applies equally to the secular parties that were beginning to appear in his time and have increased since the French Revolution. This point may be easily obscured by Hume's famous remark in the *Treatise* that "errors in religion are dangerous, those in philosophy only ridiculous."[9] But as the remainder of the essay shows, the errors that make religious parties dangerous are *philosophic*. Hume did not think there was anything intrinsically dangerous about religion. In barbarous times, he argues, before the appearance of philosophy, religious sects consisted mainly of "traditional tales and fictions," which may be different without being contrary, and even when contrary,

> every one adheres to the tradition of his own sect, without much reasoning or disputation. But as philosophy was widely spread over the world, at the time when Christianity arose, the teachers of the new sect were obliged to form a system of speculative opinions. . . .

---

[8] *The Philosophical Works*, ed. T. H. Green and T. H. Grose, 4 vols. (London, 1886), 3:130-31 (hereafter cited as *Works*).
[9] I, IV, VII, p. 272.

Hence naturally arose keenness in dispute, when the Christian religion came to be split into new divisions and heresies: And this keenness assisted the priests in their policy, of begetting a mutual hatred and antipathy among their deluded followers. Sects of philosophy, in the ancient world, were more zealous than parties of religion; but in modern times, parties of religion are more furious and enraged than the most cruel factions that ever arose from interest and ambition.[10]

When Hume speaks of religion he usually has in mind the modern conception of religion, which has philosophy analytically built into it, and it is this conception that enables him to say in the first *Enquiry* that religion is "nothing but a species of philosophy."[11] So, metaphysical religious parties are dangerous because they are metaphysical and not because they are religious. Moreover, in Hume's day the religious element in metaphysical political parties was fading out in favor of the philosophical element, and it would not be long before men and armies would be moved by purely secular philosophical concepts such as liberty, equality, the rights of man, and the historical class struggle.

The metaphysical political parties that Hume dealt with were conceptually governed mainly by some version of the social-contract theory or the theory of natural law. Both were based on timeless principles known through reason: the natural law was grounded on the intuition of an eternal fitness between natural situations and acts, the social contract on a timeless obligation to keep promises. Neither theory, however, provided an account, nor saw the need to provide an account, of how historical institutions as such can be thought of as having rational authority. On both theories, historical institutions have authority only because and to the extent that they conform to the natural law or to the social contract. Both theories, therefore, are open to Cartesianism in politics: the methodological presumption that all historical institutions are illusory unless certified by atemporal principles independent of the historical order. Natural-law theorists, of course, did not entirely reject historical considerations; many held that the utilities framed in long-established institutions *confirmed* the natural-law. But again historical institutions themselves were thought of as having no authority in their own right. So conceived, natural law theory can be used as a ruthless measuring rod to which all historical institutions must conform on pain of being declared

---

[10] *Works* 3:132-33.
[11] *An Enquiry concerning Human Understanding*, ed. L. A. Selby-Bigge, 2nd ed. (Oxford, 1902), XI, p. 146 (hereafter cited as first *Enquiry*).

illusory. Similarly, Hume rejected the social-contract theory, among other reasons, on the ground that if it were correct, no exercise of political authority in history has been legitimate.[12] Hume's argument here may be easily underrated because it looks like an empirical argument by counterexample and so logically irrelevant to the normative question of what constitutes legitimate authority. But Hume is not offering an empirical argument; he is arguing for a different conception of reason, one with a historical content capable of explaining how historical social and political institutions as such can be legitimate. His appeal to history has force only if we view it as a way of showing that the possibility of metaphysical rebellion is entailed in the social-contract theory and for that reason should be rejected.

II

I turn now to an analysis of Hume's historical conception of reason. What Hume called his "first principle" of the understanding is a theory of what it means to have a concept of something and can be stated in two propositions: (1) that every simple idea is derived from exactly corresponding impressions, and (2) that every idea, simple or complex, is derived from past impressions.[13] I shall call (1) the *copy principle* and (2) the *past-entailing principle*. Although most commentators have taken the copy principle to be the most important part of the theory, the past-entailing principle is really its essence.[14] The reason is that, as a moral philosopher, Hume is mainly concerned to examine complex ideas of reflection, which, as he says, need not *copy* past complex impressions.[15] So, even if the copy principle were rejected, the most important part of the theory would remain.

Hume's is the only theory in the empirical tradition that attempts to explicate meaning in terms of a relation between present and past existences. Three forms of empiricism have dominated: phenomenalism, pragmatism, and logical empiricism. Each is built around a theory of meaning that entails that expressions purportedly about the past must be

---

[12] "Of the Original Contract," *Works*, 3:447ff.

[13] *Treatise*, I, I, I, pp. 4–5; III, V, p. 85.

[14] See for example A. H. Basson, *David Hume* (Harmondsworth: Penguin Books, 1958), p. 37.

[15] *Treatise*, I, I, I, p. 3; II, p. 8.

recast into some non-past-tense idiom or be declared meaningless.[16] According to most forms of phenomenalism, sentences purportedly about the past are either meaningless or must be taken to refer to sets of actual or possible present experiences. Likewise, pragmatism is the doctrine that the meaning of descriptive expressions is grounded in reference to present and future experiences. C. I. Lewis writes: "To ascribe an objective quality to a thing means implicitly the prediction that if I act in certain ways, specifiable experiences will eventuate." And the "whole content of our knowledge of reality is the truth of such 'if-then' propositions."[17] If this account is right, expressions purportedly about the past must be recast somehow into expressions about the present and future or be declared meaningless. Phenomenalism and pragmatism may be read as *tensed* theories of meaning insofar as they typically require the use of tensed expressions. But not all forms of empiricism are tensed. Various forms of logical empiricism explicate descriptive meaning by reference to tenseless expressions. Again, expressions normally taken to be about the past are either meaningless or must be recast into some tenseless idiom. A. J. Ayer, for instance, once argued that "no sentence as such is about the past," on the ground that all tensed expressions must be reducible to tenseless expressions.[18]

Although quite different in other respects, absolute idealists share with logical empiricists the view that reality can be understood only through tenseless language and that statements purportedly about the past are philosophically defective. Thus Bosanquet thought that history, because it purports to be about the past, is "a hybrid form of experience incapable of any degree of 'being or trueness'."[19] Similarly, Michael Oakeshott writes that "no fact, truth or reality is, or can be past" and that "there are no facts at all which are not present absolutely."[20] More recently, Jack Meiland has defended a version of the idealist view that he calls the "construction" theory of history, which holds that historians should not be thought of as making statements about the past, because there is no past reality for their statements to be about. Rather, history is

---

[16] A. J. Ayer, *Language, Truth, and Logic* (London, 1951), preface to the 2nd ed., pp. 18-19.
[17] *Mind and the World Order* (New York, 1956), pp. 140, 142.
[18] *The Problem of Knowledge* (Harmondsworth: Penguin Books, 1956), p. 160.
[19] Bernard Bosanquet, *The Principle of Individuality and Value* (London, 1912), pp. 146-47.
[20] *Experience and Its Modes* (Cambridge, 1933), pp. 108, 146-47.

a study of the present understood in a tenseless way, the task of history being "to give a coherent account of the present world as a whole."[21]

These empirical and idealistic theories of past-tense language are profoundly counterintuitive. If they are correct, we simply cannot *say* anything about the past at all, much less anything true; any attempt to talk about the past turns out to be talk about something else on pain of not being about anything. Hume's theory, however, takes reference to the past as primitive and so is much more in line with our common way of thinking. But there is a deeper argument to be made for Hume's theory. Whatever difficulties it may have, it is the only theory in the empirical tradition and in most of the idealist tradition that makes possible a very important class of concepts that I shall call *past-entailing concepts*.[22] These are tensed concepts that apply to present existences on condition that certain sentences about the past are true. They can best be introduced by comparison with concepts that are not tensed. Many of the concepts we use are tenseless; examples of these are "is a man," "is red," "is elastic," "is a person," and so on. These concepts can be correctly applied to present existences even if no sentence about the past is true. *Logically* the present existences picked out by these concepts need have no past even if they in fact have one. But not all concepts are of this sort: "is a nephew," "is a U.S. senator," "is a friend," "is a priest," "is a Rembrandt" are concepts that logically cannot be applied to present existences unless certain sentences about the past are true. Since "is a man" is a tenseless concept, it is logically possible that God could have created Adam without a past from the dust of the earth. But not even God could create a nephew or a U.S. senator without also creating a past of the appropriate length. Ontologically, there cannot be any U.S. senators without a past stretching back at least to 1789 when the U.S. Constitution was ratified; and the concept of a U.S. senator is unintelligible unless it is possible for sentences purportedly about the past to be true.

Empiricists and idealists have tended to take as their paradigm of language the language of theoretical science, which, whatever else it is, is not a past-entailing language. Hume, however, takes as his paradigm the language of history, which is very much a past-entailing language and which is necessary for understanding the moral world. We can no more

---

[21] *Scepticism and Historical Knowledge* (New York, 1965), p. 192.

[22] The idea of past-entailing concepts and the idea of narrative associations developed later are based on Danto's profound discussion of historical language in his *Analytical Philosophy of History* (Cambridge, 1965).

understand the moral world without past-entailing concepts than we can understand the physical world without tenseless concepts. It should be pointed out, however, that all past-entailing concepts presuppose tenseless concepts: if x is a senator, then x is a man. So the individuals and institutions that make up the moral world have a tenseless content, but in our common way of thinking they are of interest to us only under some past-entailing conception of them.

III

But there is another feature of Hume's past-entailing theory of meaning that must be mentioned, namely, its *narrative* character. Events take on narrative significance in a story when we view them in the light of temporally later events. To celebrate the birth of a great man is, at the very least, to read a meaning into the event that those who lived through it could not have experienced. Similarly, a Humean impression of red on its first appearance is unintelligible because we have no idea of it at all. It is only after the impression has occurred that we can have its idea. So the meaning structure of a simple Humean idea is narrative in form: a past existent is viewed in the light of a later existent that conveys narrative significance to it and *because* of that fact is called an idea. Once we have a set of simple narrative ideas we can, by ignoring their temporal features, construct, in the standard Humean way, an abstract, tenseless idea of simple impressions. But our primordial way of conceptualizing the world is narrative: all Humean ideas, we may say, are story-laden. Hume appears to be the first modern philosopher to have thought of understanding in terms of narrative categories. But it was not until Hegel that the categories of narrative thinking were systematically ordered and made into a theory of understanding and reality. Hume and Hegel are, of course, vastly different philosophically, but the rationale locked into Hume's narrative theory of concept formation is virtually the same as that built into Hegel's conception of philosophy: "When philosophy paints its gray in gray, a form of life has become old, and this gray in gray cannot rejuvenate it, only understand it. The owl of Minerva begins its flight when dusk is falling."[23] Similarly, Hume holds that only when impressions are faded and safely in the past can we have ideas of them.

---

[23] G. W. F. Hegel, *Philosophy of Right and Law*, trans. J. M. Sterret and C. J. Friedrich, in *The Philosophy of Hegel*, ed. Carl J. Friedrich (New York, 1954), p. 227.

Whether adequate or not, Hume's narrative account of *simple* ideas is counterintuitive. Concepts such as "is red" certainly appear to be tenseless and not at all explicable in narrative categories. But the narrative paradigm of concept formation is much more in order with ideas of reflection, which constitute the moral world and which, as Hume explains, are the main object of investigation in the *Treatise*.[24] In Book II, Part III, Sections VII–VIII where Hume discusses the influence of the ideas of space and time on the passions, we learn (1) that every idea of reflection makes reference to the self and (2) that the self is essentially temporally reflective, being every moment aware of its location in the present and of its relation to ideas of temporally distant objects. From (1) and (2) it follows that every idea of reflection is *temporally complex*. But most important, every temporally complex idea is the result of what I shall call a *narrative association*. According to Hume, when we think of an object in time, we never conceive it in isolation from other objects but always think of it as being *significant* in the light of some temporally distant object. To say that in 1809 the man who wrote the Gettysburg Address was born is to conceive of Lincoln's birth under a narrative association where the birth is viewed as significant in the light of a temporally later event.[25] Temporally complex ideas, then, are to be thought of, on Hume's view, not merely as logical conjunctions of tenseless ideas set in a temporal order but as narrative associations whereby events take on significance by being viewed in the light of temporally distant events. But why, one might ask, should events be viewed as significant just because they are separated in time from other events? To ask this question is simply to ask how narrative significance is possible. Philosophers generally have shown little interest in raising this question, and I cannot deal with it here. But it is worthwhile to point out that Hume was the first to raise it: he is working at it in the two sections we are examining of Book II of the *Treatise* and even more clearly in editions K, L, and N of the first *Enquiry* where the section entitled "Of the Association of Ideas" is virtually nothing but a discussion of how the theory of association can explain the nature of narrative significance in history and epic poetry.

Although Hume is committed to the view that all ideas are narratively structured, he does not think that the existences corresponding to these ideas need be narratively structured. The tenseless idea of red (which we abstract from the particular past-entailing idea of red) refers to red things

---

[24] *Treatise*, I, I, II, p. 8.

[25] Compare this example with Hume's account of the significance we read into a "*Greek medal* ... in our cabinet," in *Treatise*, II, III, VIII, p. 433.

that are thought of as having no tensed properties. Similarly, the abstract idea of time presented in *Treatise* I, II, III refers to a tenseless order of successive objects, and in Section IV Hume holds explicitly that *real* time exists under this tenseless conception of it. Indeed, his view appears to be that the entire physical world is to be thought of as ontologically tenseless. But the case is otherwise with the moral world. The idea of the moral world is structured by the narrative associations of the temporally reflective imagination, which necessarily conceives of objects in relation to the self's awareness of its position in tensed time. The conception of moral entities is therefore essentially tensed and narrative, and Hume appears willing to ontologize these narrative ideas. Thus corresponding to past-entailing ideas such as "is a senator" and "is a Tudor rose" are what we might call *past-entailing existences*, that is, real senators and Tudor roses that have the past built ontologically into their present existence. But such entities are real only in the moral world, which itself is mind-dependent (in roughly the same way that secondary qualities are mind-dependent) since temporally complex ideas of reflection require reference to the self for their existence. Independent of the temporally reflective self, there are no tensed ideas, no narrative orders of existence, and no moral world.

In these same sections of Book II, Hume gives an account of the qualitative differences between the modes of tensed time. We should recall that the idea of time explained in Book I is a tenseless concept — the idea of objects in succession — and Hume holds that time as it is in itself conforms to this tenseless conception of it. For Hume, then, past, present, and future are experienced not as objective features of real time but as certain relations of real time to self-awareness. Because of certain propensities of the imagination (which we shall examine shortly) the quantitative units of real time take on a qualitative character. Hume explains this doctrine by working through two questions. The first is why, all things equal, we have a more lively conception of and a great passion for objects removed in the future over those removed an equal distance in the past. Hume's answer is derived from three properties of the fancy.

(1) The imagination is essentially present-oriented: "However it may turn its attention to foreign and remote objects, it is necessitated every moment to reflect on the present."[26]

(2) In reflecting on temporally remote objects, "we take them in their

---

[26] Ibid., VII, p. 428.

proper order and situation, and never leap from one object to another . . . without running over, at least in a cursory manner, all those objects, which are interpos'd betwixt them. When we reflect, therefore, on any object distant from ourselves, we are oblig'd not only to reach it at first by passing thro' all the intermediate space betwixt ourselves and the object, but also to renew our progress every moment; being every moment recall'd to the consideration of ourselves and our present situation.''[27]

(3) "Besides the propensity to a gradual progression thro' the points of . . . time, we have another peculiarity in our method of thinking. . . . We always follow the succession of time in placing our ideas, and from the consideration of any object pass more easily to that, which follows immediately after it, than to that which went before it. We may learn this, among other instances, from the order, which is always observ'd in historical narrations.''[28]

Using propensities (1)–(3) we can now state Hume's answer to the question of why we have a more lively conception of future objects than of those removed an equal distance in the past. The "present situation of the person is always that of the imagination, and . . . 'tis from thence we proceed to the conception of any distant object." When the object is past, the progression of thought in passing to it from the present "is contrary to nature, as proceeding from one point of time to that which is preceding, and from that to another preceding, in opposition to the natural course of the succession." But when we turn our thought to the future object, the "fancy flows along the stream of time" and arrives at the object by an order that seems natural, "passing always from one point of time to that which is immediately posterior to it." This "easy progression of ideas" gives us a stronger conception of future tense ideas than we have of past tense ideas where "we are oblig'd to overcome the difficulties arising from the natural propensity of the fancy." Moreover, this future-referring propensity of the fancy is brought into play, to some degree, upon the conception of *any* temporally disposed object. Past and present objects are always narratively associated with some idea of the future: "The fancy anticipates the course of things, and surveys the object in that condition to which it tends, as well as in that, which is regarded as the present." We "advance, rather than retard our existence. . . .

---

[27] Ibid.
[28] Ibid., p. 430.

By which means we conceive the future as flowing every moment nearer us, and the past as retiring." In this way, Hume provides a ground for explicating such future-referring passions as anticipation, hope, anxiety, destiny, and fate—passions generated to some degree by the conception of any temporally disposed object.[29]

The second question to be considered is why we have a greater veneration and esteem for an object in the remote past than for one an equal distance in the future. To answer this question, Hume uses the three propensities mentioned above along with two more.

(4) "'Tis a quality very observable in human nature, that any opposition, which does not entirely discourage and intimidate us, has rather a contrary effect, and inspires us with a more than ordinary grandeur and magnanimity."[30]

(5) "'Tis evident that the mere view and contemplation of any greatness, whether successive or extended, enlarges the soul, and give it a sensible delight and pleasure. A wide plain, the ocean, eternity, a succession of several ages; all these . . . excel every thing, however beautiful, which accompanies not its beauty with a suitable greatness."[31] Now although it is difficult to conceive of a past object owing to the propensity of the imagination to conceive of future objects that extend our existence, this propensity can be overcome. The "difficulty, when join'd with a small distance, interrupts and weakens the fancy: But has a contrary effect in a great removal. The mind, elevated by the vastness of its object, is still farther elevated by the difficulty of the conception; and being oblig'd every moment to renew its efforts in the transition from one part of time to another, feels a . . . vigorous and sublime disposition," which by narrative association is transferred to the idea of the distant past object and "gives a proportionable veneration for it."[32] It is "as if our ideas acquir'd a kind of gravity from their objects" so that the remote past is seen as a realm of monumental greatness, a source of authority and standards: "Hence we imagine our ancestors to be, in a manner, mounted above us, and our posterity to lie below us."[33] On this rudimentary passion of temporal piety are grounded the passions of veneration, love of antiquity, and, most important, the passions that give

---

[29] Ibid., pp. 430–32.
[30] Ibid., VIII, p. 433.
[31] Ibid., p. 432.
[32] Ibid., p. 436.
[33] Ibid., pp. 435, 437.

authority to purely temporal standards framed in traditions, customs, precedent, and prescription. Indeed, even the standards of causal inference derive much of their authority from this *normative* manner of conceiving the past.

We are now in a position to construct a Humean answer to our original question, How is it possible for historical institutions *as such* to have rational authority? For Hume, reason has a historical content. His past-entailing theory of meaning treats conceptualization itself as having narrative form. From simple narrative ideas we can, by ignoring their temporal features, form abstract, tenseless ideas. But such ideas always have a narrative content that constitutes part of their meaning and is a limit on their applicability. The moral world is a mind-dependent order woven together by the narrative associations of the temporally reflective imagination. The individuals and institutions that constitute this world may be thought of as past-entailing existences that have the past ontologically built into their present existence. To understand this world and to evaluate it we must, at the very least, think in a tensed and narrative way. When we think in this way the past, owing to an original propensity of the fancy (explained above), is viewed *normatively*. Entire social and political orders are grounded in traditions, and at the root of these traditions are what might be called normative institutions and individuals: the Magna Carta, the Glorious Revolution of 1688, the Bill of Rights, the Founding Fathers, the Last Supper, and so on. For these entities men have a purely temporal affection and piety, and it is this *temporal passion* of reflection that transforms them into normative entities from which flow, by the narrative association of ideas, a great variety of legal, political, and social standards of varying degrees of authority. To operate in common life these standards, logically, and in fact, need have no temporally neutral justification. Hume, of course, recognized the existence of temporally neutral standards and the necessity of using them to evaluate and discipline the traditions that constitute common life. But he conceived of them as abstractions from narrative associations and so as having an irreducible historical content that requires an affirmation of the existing historical order as a whole. In this way Hume's temporally neutral standards logically avoid the historical vacuity characteristic of the social contract and natural-law theories of his time. This can be seen in Hume's use of the concept of utility. Ultimately, it is for utility that men form society and institute government; and the moral approval, by sympathy, of this utility is the ground of our obligation to obey government. Utility so conceived is a temporally neutral standard, applying to any government at any time; but it is also, and primarily, a value immanent in existing social and political order. Hume did not think of utility, as later utilitarians were to do, as a transcendent standard contrived to reveal the inadequacies of historical institutions. When government breaks down utility can be used to understand the *failure* historically, but it cannot be used as the standard of a project to reconstruct society.

Turning from the general obligation to obey government to the obligation to obey particular governments, the historical-narrative character of utility is even more marked. Our obligation to obey particular governments presupposes the obligation to government as such; within that framework, the question of allegiance is no longer a question of interest and utility: "The same interest, therefore, which causes us to submit to magistracy, makes us renounce itself in the choice of our magistrates, and binds us down to a certain form of government, and to particular persons, without allowing us to aspire to the utmost perfection in either."[34] As in the case of determining Justice (which, for Hume, is basically the question of who is to own what), the question is not determined by timeless reflections on the general interest but by more "frivolous" considerations, for example, by the normative principles of the temporally reflective imagination: long possession, present possession, conquest, succession, and the like. Arguments from these principles are possible, but they are arguments about historical facts, not arguments about instantiating some timeless structure of utility.[35]

In holding that the rationality of historical institutions consists in their utility and in giving utility a historical content, Hume laid down a conceptual barrier to all forms of Cartesianism in politics. The moral world is the product of thought and particularly of narrative associations. The entities that populate this world such as nephews, senators, and thieves are thought of as existing under past-entailing conceptions; by virtue of narrative associations, the idea of the past is logically written into the idea of the present existence of these entities. Moreover, the past that is

---

[34] Ibid., III, II, X, p. 555. Consider also Hume's remark that "any one, who finding the impossibility of accounting for the right of the present possessor, by any receiv'd system of ethics, shou'd resolve to deny absolutely that right, and assert, that it is not authoriz'd by morality, wou'd be justly thought to maintain a very extravagant paradox, and to shock the common sense and judgment of mankind" (ibid., p. 558). Proudhon's statement that "property is theft" is just such a paradox.

[35] Ibid., pp. 562-63.

built into their present is *normative*. Thus merely to describe something as a senator, nephew, or thief is already to be logically committed to the order of rights and duties internal to that historical order; and we are all part of *some* historical order. Cartesianism in politics, therefore, is an attempt to be logically emancipated from the temporal cords woven by the narrative imagination. Instead of being viewed as past-entailing existences, the moral world is now viewed as being populated with individuals thought of in a tenseless way: rational agents, moral agents, persons — governed exclusively by timeless principles and undisciplined by past-entailing normative concepts. In this way Cartesianism in politics *conceptually* destroys the moral world as normally conceived by eliminating all past-entailing concepts, and this purely logical destruction is viewed as a demand of reason itself. But then distinctions of good and evil *within* the moral world cease to exist and rational evaluation is impossible. The whole then must be seen as illusory and in need of being totally replaced. As Hume remarked in *A Dialogue*, "There are no manners so innocent or reasonable but may be rendered odious or ridiculous, if measured by a standard unknown to the persons."[36] But if Hume is right, any Cartesian-type tenseless order that replaces the historical one will immediately become the object of the narrative imagination, and soon there will be a new order of past-entailing normative existences, for "time and custom give authority to all forms of government . . . and that power, which at first was founded only on injustice and violence, becomes in time legal and obligatory."[37] And when this happens Cartesianism in politics and the metaphysical rebellion attendant upon it will, senselessly, once again appear as a demand of reason itself.

IV

I turn now to an examination of the providential theory of social and political norms. This theory, like Hume's, locates social and political standards not in a timeless order independent of history but in the historical process itself. A contemporary version of the theory is defended by Herbert Marcuse: "Ethical standards by virtue of their imperative claim transcend any given state of affairs, and they transcend it, not

---

[36] *Enquiries concerning the Human Understanding and concerning the Principles of Morals*, ed. L. A. Selby-Bigge, 2nd ed. (London, 1902), p. 330.
[37] *Treatise*, III, II, X, p. 566.

to any metaphysical entities but to the historical continuum in which every given state of affairs has emerged . . . and in which every given state of affairs will be altered and surpassed by other states."[38] This, of course, sounds very much like Hume, but there is a fundamental difference: Hume explicates historical standards as a relation between the normative past and the present, whereas Marcuse (and the providential theory generally) explains them as a relation between the normative *future* and the present. The providential theory is deeply rooted in the Hebrew-Christian tradition. Its main tenets are that, through the revelation of God's acts in history or through natural theology or both, one can know that God has certain properties such that one can infer the existence of a future state of perfection in the light of which the present can be judged to be a passing, inadequate stage of existence. Secular versions of the providential theory were already beginning to appear in Hume's time. The first such theory appears to have been worked out by Turgot in two addresses given in 1750 when he was Prior of the Sorbonne: "Discourse on the Advantages which the Establishment of Christianity has Procured for Mankind" and "Philosophical Tableau on the Successive Advancements of the Human Mind." In these addresses Turgot interpreted history as a causal mechanism moving toward a future state of perfection without the benefit of either Divine or conscious human guidance. Building on Turgot's theory, Condorcet, in his *Sketch of a Historical Picture of the Progress of the Human Mind* (1795), claimed to have discovered ten stages through which the historical process must pass. But neither Turgot nor Condorcet formulated laws capable of explaining the necessity of the progressive process. In 1784 Kant published "Idea of a Universal History from a Cosmopolitan Point of View," in which he sketched out an analysis of the categories of progressive history and expressed the hope that nature would one day bring forth a Newton to discover its laws. In 1808 Charles Fourier published *Theory of the Four Movements*, in which he explicitly claimed to be the Newton of history; and by the time of Comte and Marx, the idea of a science of the whole of history was well established.

Hume, of course, was not familiar with these purely secular providential theories (with the exception of Turgot's theory). But he was quite familiar with the sacred version of the theory that, moreover, had already

---

[38] "Ethics and Revolution," in *Ethics and Society*, ed. Richard T. De George (New York, 1966), p. 134.

taken on secular form insofar as it was presented as a theory having scientific support. Hume thoroughly criticized it in the *Dialogues* and in the first *Enquiry* under the concept of "the religious hypothesis." It was part and parcel of the theoretical baggage of eighteenth-century radical reformers with a religious bent, the sort of individual Hume memorably described in the *Treatise* as a "seditious bigot."[39] The frame of mind is well expressed by Catharine Macaulay in a pamphlet critical of Burke's *Reflections on the Revolution in France* and written about thirteen years after Hume's death:

> The events of human life, when *properly* considered, are but a series of *benevolent providences*: many of them, though very important in their consequences, are too much confounded with the common transactions of men to be observed; but whenever the believer thinks he perceives the *omnipotent will* more immediately declaring itself in favour of the future *perfection* and happiness of the moral world, he is naturally led into the same ecstasies of hope and *gratitude*, with which Simeon was transported by the view of the infant messiah. Has Mr. Burke never heard of any millenium, but that fanciful one which is supposed to exist in the Kingdom of Saints? If this should be the case, I would recommend to him to read *Newton* on *the prophecies*.[40]

We have here a form of metaphysical rebellion different from that following upon Cartesianism in politics. The present is viewed as unreal not because it has a historical character that alienates it from the timeless order of nature but because it has the *wrong* sort of historical character. The historical standard for judging the present society is not the normative past as it is for Hume, but a set of future events known to be inevitable either through revealed or empirical knowledge of God's properties or through purely secular laws of history. The mark of reality is given only to the set of future events, the past-entailing order of present society being unreal to the degree that it is temporally distant from the inevitable future society. Such a frame of mind, logically, cannot find itself at home in any sort of present. Charles Fourier, who thought of himself as the Newton of history, was forced to view the social and political order of the entire human present and past as total illusion:

---

[39] III, II, II, p. 497.

[40] *Observations on the Reflections of the Right Hon. Edmund Burke, on the Revolution in France in a Letter to the Right Hon. The Earl of Stanhope* (London, 1790), pp. 20-21.

"The vice of our so-called reformers is to indict this or that defect, instead of indicting civilization as a whole, inasmuch as it is nothing but a vicious circle of evil in all its parts; one must get out of this hell."[41] The same sort of alienation governs Marcuse's total rejection of the present: "The true positive is the society of the future and therefore beyond definition and determination, while the existing positive is that which must be surmounted."[42]

In the first *Enquiry* Hume raised a rhetorical question that applies to all providential theories of social and political order whether sacred or secular:

> What must a philosopher think of those vain reasoners, who, instead of regarding the present scene of things as the sole object of their contemplation, so far reverse the whole course of nature, as to render this life merely a passage to something farther; a porch, which leads to a greater, and vastly different building; a prologue, which serves only to introduce the piece, and give it more grace and propriety?[43]

Hume's answer is that reasoners of this kind gain their ideas of providential order from their "own conceit and imagination." His strategy is to show that experience provides no reason to infer the existence of a normative future state relative to which the present can be viewed as an inferior passing stage. There is little doubt that Hume would have rejected the secular providential theory if he had been aware of it. What a Humean-type criticism might look like can be inferred from his analysis of the narrative structure of the moral world along with his criticism of the sacred providential theory.

The moral world is the result of narrative associations between ideas of present and past existences, where the past existent is viewed normatively. The moral world, on the providential theory, is also the result of narrative associations, but of those holding between ideas of present and future existences, where the future existent is viewed normatively. We may call these *providential narrative associations*. But according to Hume's theory of the temporal passions, only the past can be normative and constitutive of the moral world. To think of the future as normative is not only to reverse our temporal passions and to think of our posterity

---

[41] *Oeuvres complètes*, 6 vols. (Paris, 1848), 6:xv.
[42] "Repressive Tolerance," in R. P. Wolff, B. Moore, Jr. and H. Marcuse, *A Critique of Pure Tolerance* (Boston: Beacon Press, 1965), p. 87.
[43] First *Enquiry*, XI, p. 141.

as mounted above us and of our ancestors as lying below us, it is also to think of the future as in some way already past. It would be, as Hume says in criticizing the sacred version of the providential theory, to "reverse the whole course of nature." If so, then, the providential theory is impossible because it contradicts the nature of things. The logical structure of Hume's intuition can be analyzed as follows.

Narrative associations of ideas may be thought of propositionally. A narrative proposition would be a temporally complex proposition that refers to two time-separated events but describes only one of those events. A narrative proposition, then, is at the very least a truth-functional conjunction of two or more propositions all of which must be true for the proposition as a whole to be true. Let us see how narrative propositions can be used to evaluate some present social and political order. Suppose we say that we are oppressed in the present, meaning that our freedom of speech, for example, is being ignored by a certain state law. Such a statement expresses a narrative proposition; it describes an event in the present (the state action) in the light of past normative events, in this case ratification of the Bill of Rights in 1789 and certain interpretations of that Bill in the tradition of law that is based on it. In order for it to be true that we are oppressed in the way described, a set of propositions about the present must be true in conjunction with a set of propositions about the past. Since propositions about the present and past can be true or false, narrative propositions as a whole can be true or false, and so it can be true or false that we are oppressed in the present. Narrative propositions, then, make possible rational criticism of the present social and political order, but only on condition that we accept the normative past that constitutes the order. Suppose now that we try to evaluate the present with providential narrative propositions. These would amount to truth-functional conjunctions of present-tense and future-tense propositions. But there is a venerable tradition going back to Aristotle that teaches that future-tense propositions cannot be true on pain of fatalism.[44] If this is right and if fatalism is false, then no conjunction of a future-tense and present-tense proposition can be true, and, consequently, no providential narrative proposition about the present can be true. If so, then, we cannot rationally evaluate the present using the future as a standard because nothing we could say about the present could be true.

---

[44] Aristotle, *Int.* 19a, and Danto, chap. 9.

Hume's social and political philosophy is just part of his wider program of purging common life of metaphysical thinking. "The political interests of society have no connexion with the philosophical disputes concerning metaphysics and religion."[45] The radically secular and empirical structure of Hume's social and political philosophy is a commonplace. But what is not so widely appreciated is the peculiar *historical* shape that Hume gives to the ideas of the secular and the empirical. It is this aspect of Hume's thought that I have tried to focus on. The past-entailing theory of concept formation, the narrative conception of understanding, the narrative structure of the moral world and of the social and political standards that constitute it, are not only essential features of the special sort of historical empiricism Hume worked out, they are also philosophically suggestive, and they can and should be developed further.

---

[45] First *Enquiry*, XI, p. 147.

The Nature of Hume's Skepticism

D. C. Stove

> *If I can make it appear, that the conclusion is not so certain as is pretended . . . it is all I aspire to.*
>
> Hume, "On The Populousness of Ancient Nations"

I

HUME'S PHILOSOPHY HAS ALMOST ALWAYS MADE ON ITS READERS a certain strong impression, of a kind that has led many of them to describe it as being on the whole a "skeptical" or "negative" or "destructive" philosophy. In this essay it will be taken for granted, because it seems to me to be evident, that these descriptions are true. It is not evident, however, exactly what it is about Hume's philosophy that makes them true. It should be possible, and would certainly be worthwhile, to make this evident. Taking in particular the most important of these descriptions, that of his philosophy as "skeptical," it should be possible to state in what exactly Hume's characteristic skepticism consists. This is what I aim to do.

I do not think that every part of Hume's philosphy is skeptical, or even that there is a skeptical aspect to every part of it. Hence I do not suppose that, if I succeed in explaining what his skepticism consists in, I will have said all there is to say about the nature of his philosophy. Still, Hume's skepticism is so prominent a feature of his philosophy that an account of the former, if correct, should go at least a considerable way toward being an account of the latter. And it will, I think, be found surprising just how much of Hume's philosophy can in fact be comprehended in an account of his skepticism.

II

There is nothing that a philosopher or a logician has more occasion to do, or that is more essential to his calling, than assessing the conclusiveness of arguments, or, in other words, assessing the probability of their conclusions in relation to their premises.

Suppose an argument is from premise E to conclusion H. One possible assessment of its conclusiveness is a judgment that the falsity of H is impossible, or that H is certain, in relation to E. This kind of assessment of conclusiveness I shall call a "judgment of deducibility." Another possible assessment of its conclusiveness is a "judgment of nondeducibility," that is, a judgment that the falsity of H is possible, or that H is less than certain, in relation to E. Since the certainty of a proposition in relation to another proposition is identical with its having the highest possible degree of probability in relation to that other, a judgment of deducibility is a judgment that the probability of the conclusion H in relation to the premise E is the highest possible; and a judgment of nondeducibility is a judgment that the probability of H in relation to E is less than the highest possible. Since the highest possible probability is 1, a judgment of deducibility and a judgment of nondeducibility can be properly abbreviated respectively as $P(H/E) = 1$ and $P(H/E) < 1$.

Judgments of deducibility and nondeducibility are two kinds of assessment of the conclusiveness of arguments that are made very often by philosophers and logicians. But these are not the only such assessments they make. For any philosopher or logician often has occasion to *compare* two arguments with respect to their degree of conclusiveness. He often judges that two arguments are equally conclusive, or unequally so. That is, he often assesses the probability of the one conclusion H, in relation to its premise E, as being equal to, greater than, or less than the probability of the other conclusion H', in relation to its premise E'. Or, abbreviated, he often judges that $P(H/E) = P(H'/E')$, or, say, that $P(H/E) > P(H'/E')$.

Among such comparative assessments of conclusiveness or of probability there are two kinds that are especially noteworthy. One of these consists of what (following Keynes) I call "judgments of relevance" or of "irrelevance." Let two arguments have the same conclusion H, and let the premise of one be E while the premise of the other is $E.E'$. Then the judgment $P(H/E.E') = P(H/E)$ is a judgment of irrelevance. It asserts that E' is irrelevant to H in relation to E, in the sense that the addition of E' to the premise E leaves H neither more nor less probable, or leaves the argument to H neither more nor less conclusive, than it is in the absence of that addition. The contrary inequalities $P(H/E.E') > P(H/E)$ and $P(H/E.E') < P(H/E)$ are judgments of favorable relevance and of unfavorable relevance, respectively.

The other kind of comparative assessment consists of what (again following Keynes)[1] I call "judgments of indifference" or of "preference." Let two arguments have the same premise E, and conclusions H and H', respectively. Then the equality $P(H/E) = P(H'/E)$ is a judgment of indifference. It asserts that E is indifferent as between H and H', in the sense that H is neither more nor less probable in relation to E than H' is, or that an argument from E to H is neither more nor less conclusive than one from E to H'. The contrary inequalities, for example, $P(H/E) > P(H'/E)$, are judgments of preference.

Any philosopher or logician knows a great many comparative assessments of conclusiveness. In some cases this knowledge is derivative, at least in part, from knowledge of judgments of deducibility. Thus, from $P(H/E) = 1$ conjoined with $P(H'/E') = 1$ it follows trivially that $P(H/E) = P(H'/E')$, and from $P(H/E) = 1$ conjoined with $P(H'/E') < 1$ it follows that $P(H/E) > P(H'/E')$. But not all of our knowledge of comparative assessments of conclusiveness is derivative, even in part, from our knowledge of deducibility. For we all know a great many comparative assessments in cases where neither H is deducible from E nor H' is deducible from E'. For example, let E be "All men are mortal and Socrates is mortal," and H be "Socrates is a man"; and let E' and H' be the same as E and H, except that "Socrates" is uniformly replaced by "Plato." Then any philosopher or logician knows that $P(H/E) = P(H'/E')$, and so does any layman, I should think, though he may not know that he knows it. Or take the judgment of irrelevance $P(H/E.E') = P(H/E)$, where E and H are as in the previous example, but E' is now some tautology: any philosopher or logician, and, I should think, any layman, knows the truth of this comparative assessment. Yet in each of these examples neither of the two arguments being compared has its conclusion deducible from its premise. Similar examples, as will be evident, could be multiplied indefinitely.

This fact, although obvious enough, is rather important. For whereas all philosophers or logicians are, and always have been, professionally engaged in making judgments of deducibility and of nondeducibility and hence in calling on their knowledge of "deductive logic," it is often

---

[1] For the terminology of both "irrelevance" and "indifference," see John Maynard Keynes, *A Treatise On Probability* (London: Macmillan, 1921), p. 54.

supposed that "inductive logic" (in Carnap's sense) is something of which a philosopher or logician *may* have no knowledge, perhaps *ought* to have no knowledge, and, at least if he is long dead, *can* have had no knowledge. Yet, as we have just seen, many comparative assessments of the conclusiveness of two arguments, the conclusion of neither of which is deducible from its premise, are known to all philosophers and logicians at any time. Now, such comparative assessments of conclusiveness are quite as "nondeductive," quite as typical of the contents of "inductive logic" in Carnap's sense, as assessments of the more publicized $P(H/E) = ½$ kind, that is, as the nonextreme numerical equalities $P(H/E) = r$, where $0 < r < 1$. The fact is, then, that all philosophers or logicians, now and in the past, know, or at any rate believe, a great many propositions that belong to inductive logic.

Assessing the conclusiveness of arguments, although it is essentially the business of philosophers and logicians, is not only *their* business. On the contrary, it is everyone's business. Even in the commonest affairs of practical life everyone has constantly to be assessing how conclusive arguments are. At this moment many a postman is engaged in assessing how probable is the conclusion H, "That dog will bite me," in relation to premises E that include his observational knowledge about the dog. And in this respect the postman's situation is a paradigm of waking human life.

Between lay and professional assessments of the conclusiveness of arguments there are indeed characteristic differences. One such difference, as I have already implied, is that professional assessments are more likely to be *consciously* made. Another difference, and perhaps the most important one, is the *generality* of many professional assessments. No layman needs any prompting in order to make some assessment of the conclusiveness of the argument from E, "All the passengers died in the crash, and your son was one of the passengers," to H, "Your son died in the crash." But typically, at any rate, the layman assesses that argument and any other particular arguments one at a time, just as they arise. His assessments of conclusiveness, then, are typically *singular*. By contrast, what an Aristotle or a Russell does is to subsume the layman's singular assessment (if it is a true one) under some assessment that is *general*—that at one stroke assesses every member of a certain *class* of arguments; that judges, for example, not only that $P(H/E) = 1$, where E and H have the particular values just mentioned, but that for any x, any F, and any G, P (x is G/All F are G and x is F) = 1.

Assessing the conclusiveness of arguments is, then, a natural or spontaneous human activity. Now, as the example just mentioned will suggest, it is a further fact—of the utmost importance—that men's untutored assessments of conclusiveness are, at least over a very wide range of arguments, almost or even entirely *unanimous*. Consider again the argument about the son killed in a crash. No teacher of elementary logic ever had a class so bad that just one-eleventh of them would assess this argument by $P(H/E) = 1$, while another eleventh would assess it by $P(H/E) = .9$, and so on, down to $P(H/E) = 0$. In fact, no teacher ever had even one student who did not, even prior to instruction, assess this argument by $P(H/E) = 1$. Or again, consider judgments of favorable relevance. Among comparative assessments of conclusiveness belonging to this kind there are countless ones that everyone makes quite spontaneously; for example, $P(H/E.E') > P(H/E)$, where H is "Tom is rich," E is "Tom is a Texan," and E' is "Almost all Texans are rich." Indeed, this is a case in which the giving of examples is absurdly easy, so much so that it is even apt to be misleading. Just as the mass of the Australian continent is so enormous that I cannot easily suggest it to someone, and may well mislead him, by putting in his hand a few stones from the road, similarly, the mass of unanimous lay opinion about the conclusiveness of arguments is so enormous that it is not easily suggested by giving a few examples of it. Still, I do not see what else can be done to suggest it.

There are, then, at least very many assessments of the conclusiveness of arguments that are "natural," in the sense that everyone, or almost everyone, makes them. A natural assessment of conclusiveness need not be true. I think that in fact most of them are true and (with Locke) that God did not deal so sparingly with men as to make them barely two-legged, leaving it to Aristotle to make them rational. But it is not part of my meaning, in calling a certain assessment of conclusiveness natural, that it is true. Not only could there have been assessments of conclusiveness that are natural yet false: in fact there are in men permanent tendencies, at least, toward making such assessments. The so-called fallacies show this. Not every argument from E to H such that $P(H/E) < 1$, although *someone* thinks mistakenly that $P(H/E) = 1$, is an instance of some fallacy. Fallacy ("undistributed middle," for example) exists only where, although $P(H/E) < 1$, there is some tendency *more or less common to all men* to think mistakenly that $P(H/E) = 1$. Thus, since there are fallacies, there are at least tendencies in men in general to make false assessments of conclusiveness. And it is, of course, part of the duty of a philosopher or logician to try to correct such assessments, or incipient assessments, *downward*.

Let us call an assessment of the conclusiveness of an argument or of a class of arguments "skeptical" if it is less favorable than the natural assessment (where such exists) of that argument or class of arguments; that is, if it ascribes to the argument(s) in question a *lower* degree of conclusiveness than the natural assessment does. Thus, for example, if the judgment of deducibility $P(H/E) = 1$ is natural, then the contrary judgment of nondeducibility $P(H/E) < 1$ will be skeptical in my sense. Again, the judgment of irrelevance $P(H/E.E') = P(H/E)$ will be skeptical if it is natural (in my sense) to believe that, on the contrary, E' is favorably relevant to H in relation to E. The judgment of indifference $P(H/E) = P(H'/E)$ will be skeptical if $P(H/E) > P(H'/E)$ is natural. And so on. A skeptical assessment need not, of course, be a false one, since a natural assessment need not be true.

Arguments, in the sense in which philosophers or logicians are interested in them, are as numerous as ordered pairs of propositions E, H — and that is very numerous indeed! Consequently, most arguments have never had any assessment of their conclusiveness made by anyone at all; still less, the *same* assessment made by *everyone*. For most arguments, therefore, there simply is no natural assessment of how conclusive they are. And where that is so there can be (by the above definition) no skeptical one either.

Even where no natural assessment exists for the argument from E to H, there may nevertheless be an assessment of it that prevails among all or almost all persons at a certain time and place; or prevails among most of those, even if they are a minority, who assess that argument at all; or prevails among some numerous, important, interested, or qualified class of people (say, Christians, or the educated, or philosophers); or prevails at any rate among *some* people. An assessment of the conclusivesness of the argument from E to H may, then, without being actually a natural one, be a more or less *prevailing* one in particular circumstances. For example, it is clear that among the educated in the West, especially between 1690 and 1860, there prevailed some very favorable (even if vague) assessment of the conclusiveness of the argument from E to H, where H is "Adaptation in organisms is caused by a single very powerful intelligence," and E is a summary of all the then known phenomena of organic adaptation.

Accordingly, let us widen the concept of a skeptical assessment of conclusiveness and call an assessment skeptical as long as it conflicts either with a natural assessment or with some more or less widely prevailing one and ascribes to the argument(s) in question a lower degree of conclusiveness than that assessment does.

This requires us to call an assessment skeptical and to call a more favorable contrary of it prevailing, even if there should happen to be in fact just one person on either side of the question — which is, admittedly, artificial. But this consequence does not matter, for disagreements about the conclusiveness of arguments are hardly ever in practice so esoteric as that, even among philosophers. And on the other hand we are now able, without requiring that the more favorable assessment be so very widely prevailing as to be actually natural in my sense, to identify just one opinion, in every (two-sided) disagreement about conclusiveness, as being skeptical; and this is a useful piece of terminology.

Among assessments that are skeptical in this widened sense, one will be *more* skeptical than another if it conflicts with a *more* widely prevailing opinion than the other does. Thus an assessment that "underbids" another prevailing among *all* theists, for example, is more skeptical than one that underbids just an assessment prevailing among all *Christian* theists; and so on. An assessment that underbids a *natural* assessment, consequently, is as skeptical as one can be.

Now there is an ancient libel on our profession, according to which there is no question on which all philosophers agree; but it is not true. There are disagreements about the conclusiveness of arguments in which all philosophers and logicians are to be found on the same side of the question, and that the skeptical side. (Witness, again, the fallacies, such as undistributed middle. The argument from E, "All men are mortal and Socrates is mortal," to H, "Socrates is a man," is fallacious, as distinct from simply invalid, because all men have at least some tendency to judge mistakenly that $P(H/E) = 1$; but all philosophers and logicians agree that $P(H/E) < 1$.) However, there are some philosophers who display, whether from temperamental or other causes, the following curious characteristic: in any disagreement about the conclusiveness of arguments they are *always* to be found on the skeptical side of the question.

I believe that Hume is one of these, and my thesis is that his skepticism is, without important remainder, skepticism of the particular kind explained above. He is skeptical precisely, and almost exclusively, in maintaining that a certain argument, or (more usually, since he is a professional assessor) a certain class of arguments, is less conclusive than it is thought to be by everyone else (and, indeed, by Hume himself most of the time); or less conclusive than it is thought to be by most philosophers; or by rationalist philosophers, at any rate; or by scientific optimists, Cartesian or Newtonian; or by Baconian empiricists; or by rationalistic moralists; or by Christian theists; or by deists; or by atheists; or at any rate by *some* school of thought or other. These assessments of his are skeptical in different degrees, according as the school of thought maintaining a more favorable assessment of the arguments in question happens to be more or less numerous. But (I maintain) all of what have always been felt to be the characteristically skeptical theses of his philosophy are in fact assessments of the conclusiveness of arguments, and ones that are skeptical in the sense I have explained. The general nature of Hume's skepticism, then, is this: whenever the conclusiveness of arguments is up for assessment and there are two opinions on the matter, of which Hume's is one — conditions that, it will soon be shown, are satisfied extremely often — then *Hume's bid is the lower.*

III

Now to provide textual evidence for this thesis. Part of this evidence is arranged below in three columns. In the first I give a typical and important thesis of Hume's philosophy. In the second I give an assessment of the conclusiveness of some argument or class of arguments that is at least part of the content of the Humean thesis given on the left and that is at the same time skeptical in the sense I have explained. In the third column I mention someone whose assessment of the conclusiveness of the argument(s) in question is more favorable than this Humean assessment.

It is clear that in order to establish my thesis I need a large number of examples. Equally clearly, in a short essay it is impossible to defend a large number of the interpretations, implicit in my second column, of the Humean theses mentioned in the first. Fortunately, however, there happens to be one question of interpretation that is a key to nearly all the others for which I need to assume an answer and that itself is not hard to answer. This is the question of what Hume means when he calls an argument "demonstrative" or a "demonstration."

Applied to arguments these words are now somewhat archaic and unclear. If we do nowadays call an argument from E to H demonstrative, the only thing that our hearers will be *sure* we intend to convey is that H is deducible from E. This is not Hume's meaning, or rather, it is only part of it. His meaning of the word is an older one, of which the only definite trace now remaining is the name (itself archaic), for logic and mathematics, of "demonstrative sciences." It is this: an argument from E to H is "demonstrative" if and only if H is deducible from E *and E is a necessary truth*.

This is the only interpretation of Hume's use of the word that can explain his identification of demonstrative argument with "abstract reasoning *a priori*" or his constantly reiterated thesis that "there can be no demonstrative argument for a matter of fact and existence." If, however, it is not clear almost at once that this interpretation is correct, I must refer to what I have written elsewhere in support of it.[2] Fortunately for the present essay, this is one of my interpretations of Hume that has, so far as I know, met with complete agreement.

The second column below will contain, as a consequence of what was said earlier, major fragments of *Hume's inductive logic*. It is worthwhile to emphasize this, because so influential a philosopher as Popper believes that Hume had no commitments of his own in inductive logic and even, what is still more groundless, that Hume anticipated one of his criticisms of inductive logic.[3] This latter belief, as I have pointed out elsewhere,[4] rests on nothing but Popper's ignorance of Hume—his ignorance, in particular, of what is meant in the *Treatise*, the *Abstract*, and the first *Enquiry* by the phrases Hume regularly puts in opposition to "demonstrative arguments," namely, "probable arguments" and "probability." And as to the former belief, *all* philosophers and logicians have commitments in inductive logic (as I have already pointed out) if only because they all make comparative assessments of the conclusiveness of arguments in cases where the conclusion of neither argument is deducible

---

[2] In my *Probability and Hume's Inductive Scepticism* (Oxford: Oxford University Press, 1973), pp. 35-36 (hereafter cited as *Probability*).
[3] See his *Logic of Scientific Discovery* (London: Hutchinson, 1959), pp. 265, 365; and *Conjectures and Refutations* (London: Routledge and Kegal Paul, 1963), pp. 192-93, 289.
[4] First in *The Philosophical Review* 74 (1965): 160-77.

from its premise. Hume has in fact even more such commitments than most philosophers, as will soon appear evident. Of course his inductive logic is fragmentary; that was to be expected. It is also eccentric: that is owing precisely to its constant bias toward skepticism in the sense I have introduced. It is even internally inconsistent, as I have pointed out elsewhere.[5] But all of this shows, of course, not that Hume had no inductive logic but only that the inductive logic he had was not good.

Some of the assessments of conclusiveness given in the second column below are as skeptical as an assessment can be, but others may seem to be skeptical only in a very attenuated degree or even not at all. Now, I have already admitted that some of them are more skeptical than others; that is, some of them underbid a more widely prevailing assessment than others do. Still, so long as it is possible to make a true entry in the third column the thesis in the second column is a skeptical one in my sense. And as to *how* skeptical some of these theses are, there are two sources of error that it is imperative we be on our guard against. One is the provincialism of supposing, in effect, that all philosophers are and always have been British empiricists. The other is the tendency for us to have adopted as our own some assessment of conclusiveness (of the design argument, say, or of induction) that we really owe not even to British empiricism at large but specifically to Hume himself, and as a result to imagine that Hume's assessment is a truth that everyone knows, or even an analytic truth of common English. Unless we succeed in guarding against both of these temptations, we will not only make historical mistakes but ignorantly repudiate debts that we owe to Hume's philosophy.[6]

Entries in the first column are either simply quotations or else paraphrases of theses unmistakably Humean, accompanied by a reference to the text. In each case I give only one quotation, or for a paraphrase, only one reference. Hume is so repetitive a writer that in most cases the quotation or the reference given could easily be backed up by ten others.

In the second column, H and H' are simply abbreviations for such concrete propositions as are explained in each case; h and e are variables, ranging over such classes of propositions as are specified in each case. But I had so much occasion to say "for any *necessarily true* proposition e" that it seemed better to appoint a particular letter to express this, and to

---

[5] *Probability*, pp. 71–73.
[6] Ibid., pp. 98–110.

leave the quantification implicit. Accordingly, *n* is always to be read "for any necessary truth *n*."

Humean Thesis	An Assessment of the Conclusiveness of Arguments that is at Least Part of the Content of this Thesis	Someone whose Assessment of the Same Arguments is More Favorable than Hume's
1. There can be no demonstrative arguments to prove that whatever begins to exist must have a cause of existence.[7]	$P(H/n) < 1$, where H is the "causal principle" just mentioned.	Hobbes, Locke, Clarke, among others.
2. "There can be no *demonstrative* arguments to prove, *that those instances, of which we have had no experience, resemble those, of which we have had experience.*"[8]	$P(H/n) < 1$, where H is the "resemblance thesis" just mentioned.	Any inductive infallibilist. See this column below, opposite theses 9 and 10.
3. The connection between causes and effects is never necessary. Causal laws can never be discovered by abstract "reasonings *a priori.*"[9]	$P(h/n) < 1$, for any causal law h.	All aspirants to armchair-science-with-certainty; e.g., the Cartesians.

---

[7] See, e.g., *A Treatise of Human Nature*, ed. L. A. Selby-Bigge (Oxford, 1888), I, III, III, pp. 79–80 (hereafter cited as *Treatise*).

[8] Ibid., VI, p. 89.

[9] *An Enquiry concerning Human Understanding*, ed. L. A. Selby-Bigge, 2nd ed. (Oxford, 1902), IV, I, p. 27 (hereafted cited as first *Enquiry*).

The Humean theses 1, 2, and 3 are all subsumed by the more general thesis 4. Accordingly, the assessment corresponding to 4 assesses a class of arguments that properly includes the classes of arguments assessed by the entries in the second column opposite 1, 2, and 3.

| 4. There can be no demonstrative arguments for any matter of fact and existence.[10] | For any contingent h, $P(h/n) < 1$. | Anyone already referred to in this column. |

The entry in the second column opposite 4 is a particularly interesting one. Carnap held, surely rightly, that measures of logical probability, to be adequate, must at least satisfy the condition he called "regularity": the condition, that is, that for any contingent h and tautological e, $P(h/e) < 1$. (At least, he held this subject to a certain restriction that need not concern us here.) We now see that Hume maintained the same thesis, and indeed (since tautologies are included in necessary truths) a stronger version of it. Hume's inductive logic, then, has at least the merit of being "regular" in Carnap's sense. (It is another question, though, whether it is *consistently* so.)

Another thesis that Hume sometimes maintained concerning "initial" probabilities, that is, probabilities in relation to necessarily true premises, is 5.

| 5. A priori, a man would be "altogether incapable . . . [of determining] what kind of scene the universe must be, or [of giving] the preference to one state . . . of things above another. . . . every chimera of his fancy | $P(h/n) = P(h'/n)$ for any contingent h and h'. Or at least, $P(h/n) = P(h'/n)$ for any h and h' that are (Carnapian) state-descriptions of the universe. | Carnap, and indeed anyone who knows, where H is "Socrates is a man" and H' is "Plato is a man," the judgment of preference $P(H/n) > P(H.H'/n)$; which is, I think, *everyone*. |

---

[10] Ibid., pp. 25-26.

would be upon an
equal footing; nor
could he assign any
just reason, why he
adheres to one . . .
system, and rejects
the others, which are
equally possible."[11]

The assessment corresponding to 5 is, as it happens, a thesis of which Carnap pointed out, in a famous passage, a skeptical consequence concerning inductive arguments.[12]

All the theses listed so far concern contingent conclusions or hypotheses in relation to premises or evidence necessarily true; and they are all, evidently, variations on the theme of the impotence of evidence of that kind to support such contingent conclusions. What is there, then, that *does* enable us "ever [to] draw any inference concerning real existence and matter of fact"? What is that evidence e that can make a contingent hypothesis h either certain or, at any rate, more likely than it is a priori? Why, answers Hume, *nothing but experience*, of course.

I put "of course" into Hume's mouth here because he makes it perfectly clear that he regards this thesis as a commonplace among his readers, as indeed it was, and still is. It was and is so because most of his readers were (and still are), like Hume himself, Baconian empiricists. But the familiarity of the thesis should not disguise from us its skeptical, indeed, its revolutionary, character. For this thesis is no other than "Bacon's bell": the famous bell that, in Bacon's own proud yet truthful words, "called the wits together," in the Royal Society and elsewhere. In the entire history of thought there is scarcely a more decisive new departure than this emphatic repudiation of every authority—scriptural, papal, Aristotelian, or other—except the authority of experience, in contingent enquiries. This thesis, then, despite its banal sound, was and is in reality a prodigious self-denying ordinance; far more self-denying in fact

---

[11] *Dialogues concerning Natural Religion*, ed. N. Kemp Smith (Indianapolis; Bobbs-Merrill, 1947), II, p. 145 (hereafter cited as *Dialogues*).

[12] See his *Logical Foundations of Probability* (Chicago: University of Chicago Press, 1950), pp. 564–65.

(far more destructive, for example, of Protestant "Bible-Christianity") than Bacon himself, or indeed anyone before Hume, realized.

As an assessment of conclusiveness, Bacon's bell is clearly enough, at least in part, a judgment of *irrelevance*: it says that every premise e, *except* a certain kind, is irrelevant to any contingent hypothesis h. It would not do, however, to interpret it as asserting that, for any contingent h and *any nonobservational e*, $P(h/n.e) = P(h/n)$. For Bacon's bell is not obviously false, whereas that assessment is: for example, let h be "a is hot" and e be "All flames are hot and a is a flame." To exclude such cases — and to exclude along with them the suggestion (which Bacon most specifically and emphatically intended to exclude) that syllogism is a substitute for science — what is needed, and is perhaps sufficient, is to impose on the range of values of e a further restriction, the general nature of which will readily suggest itself. Let us call a proposition "directly accessible" if and only if, if it were true, it would be possible in principle to learn its truth without reliance on inference. Then at least part of the content of Bacon's bell can be captured without obvious falsity, as in the second column below.

6. "Nor can our reason, unassisted by experience, ever draw any inference concerning real existence and matter of fact."[13]	$P(h/n.e) = P(h/n)$ for any contingent h and any e that is directly accessible but not observational.	Anyone who thinks Baconian empiricism is false.

Experience just of *one* instance, however, is no use at all, Hume insists. That we have found something by observation to be a flame gives us no more reason than we had prior to all experience to anticipate that it is hot. One instance is no better than no instance.

7. "Adam, though his rational faculties be supposed, at the very first, entirely perfect, could not have inferred from	(Changing the example slightly, and abbreviating "a is a flame" and "a is hot" respectively as Fa and Ha),	All of us, as Hume points out, in cases where familiarity with a certain conjunction of properties has bred contempt of our debt

---

[13] First *Enquiry*, IV, I, p. 27.

the fluidity and transparency of water that it would suffocate him, or from the light and warmth of fire that it would consume him."[14]	$P(Ha/n.Fa) = P(Ha/n)$.	to experience; as it has done, e.g., in the case of flame and heat.[15]

Our experience must be *long* (as well as uniform or nearly so) before it entitles us to generalize or predict beyond it.

8. "It is only after a long course of uniform experiments . . . *that we attain a firm reliance and security with regard to a particular event.*"[16]	For example (abbreviating as before), $P(Hz/n.Fz.e) = P(Hz/n.Fz)$, for any *e* that is directly accessible, but not a long conjunction of pairs of observation statements $(Fa.Ha).(Fb.Hb).(Fc.Hc)\ldots$	Same as the preceding entry in this column.

But even given experience, however long and uniform, Hume insists that no conclusion that extends the observed conjunction to unobserved instances is *deducible* from that experience. (Or, as we would say, any such conclusion is at best probable in relation to such evidence.)

9. "When a man says, *I have found*, in all past instances, *such sensible qualities* [as flame, e.g.,] *conjoined with such secret powers* [as to	(Abbreviating "*z* possesses the secret powers that produce heat" as Gz), $P(Gz/n.Fz.e) < 1$, for any *e* that is a conjunction, however	Everyone; since we all believe, and on no other foundation than experience, that a lighted match on which we put a finger tomorrow will be

---

[14] Ibid.
[15] Ibid., pp. 27–29.
[16] Ibid., II, p. 36.

produce heat]: And when he says, *Similar sensible qualities will always be conjoined with similar secret powers*, he is not guilty of a tautology...."[17] long, of pairs of observation statements $(Ga.Fa).(Gb.Fb)$... (where the individual constants do not include z). hot, and believe it with a degree of belief no different from what it would be if we thought that this prediction was *deducible* from our past experience.

Much more generally, subsuming 9 and many other specific assessments, the conclusion of an inductive argument is *never* deducible from its premise.

10. "As to past *experience*, it can be allowed to give *direct* and *certain* information of those precise objects only, and that precise period of time, which fell under its cognizance.... [For example,] the bread which I formerly eat, nourished me... : but does it follow, that other bread must also nourish me at another time...? The consequence seems nowise necessary."[18] For any h and e such that the argument *from e to h* is inductive, $P(h/e) < 1$. Bacon, Mill, and their followers. "We can hardly conceive men of science commonly speaking of the most firmly established generalisations of mechanics, optics, or chemistry, simply as conclusions possessing a high degree of probability."[19]

The assessment corresponding to 10 is what I call the thesis of inductive fallibilism. In it, it must be understood, the word "inductive" occurs

---

[17] Ibid., p. 37.
[18] Ibid., pp. 33-34.
[19] T. Fowler, *The Elements of Inductive Logic*, 3rd ed. (London, 1876), Preface.

with the sense of arguments from observed to unobserved instances of empirical predicates. This is, of course, the sense in which the word has most often been used in the last four centuries. When it is so used the thesis of inductive fallibilism is not at all a truism, and still less is it (as some now suppose) an analytic truth of ordinary English. It is a substantial logico-philosophical thesis and even one that, as the quotation from Fowler may serve to remind us, has often, by implication at least, been denied within the last hundred years.[20]

To return to Hume. Concerning, for example, a prediction such as "z is hot," he has so far said (4) that we can have no completely conclusive reason to believe it prior to experience; that, indeed (6), we can have no reason at all to believe it other than what experience can provide; that, even given "z is a flame," we still have (4 and 7) no completely conclusive (or indeed any) reason to believe it, even though that premise *is* given only by experience; that (8) a long experience of flames as hot is needed to give us any reason to believe it; that (10) even such experience, however long, does not give us a completely conclusive reason to believe it.

He now adds that even such experience still does not give us any reason at all to believe it. From the point of view of reason, a thousand flames all observed to be hot are no better than one.

11. "[There is a] difficulty why we draw, from a thousand instances, an inference which we are not able to draw from one instance. . . . Reason is incapable of any such variation."[21]	$P(Hz/n.Fz) =$ $P(Hz/n.Fz.(Fa.Ha).$ $(Fb.Hb) \ldots$ (1000 instances)).	Everyone, since the contrary judgment of favorable relevance is natural.

But one instance, Hume had said (7), is no better than no instance. That a thousand flames, then, have all been observed to be hot is really

---

[20] Of course, as Carnap uses the word "inductive," inductive fallibilism *is* a pure tautology, since to call an argument from E to H "inductive" simply *means*, with him, that H is not deducible from E (see his *Logical Foundations*, p. 580). But this is no more than a neologism of the 1940s, and a singularly unfortunate one (see *Probability*, chaps. 7, 8).

[21] First *Enquiry*, V, I, p. 43.

irrelevant to "z is hot," just as "z is a flame" is. Similarly, of course, for all inductive arguments whatever.

12. "*Even after the observation of the frequent or constant conjunction of objects, we have no reason to draw any inference concerning any object beyond those of which we have had experience.*"[22]	For any h and e such that the argument from e to h is inductive, $P(h/n.e) = P(h/n)$.	Same as the preceding entry in this column.

This assessment of the conclusiveness of inductive arguments is the famous skepticism of Hume concerning induction. As we called 6 (the thesis that in contingent enquiries we can learn from *nothing but* experience) "Bacon's bell," we should call 12 "Hume's bell": it adds to Bacon's thesis the simple but appalling rider that we cannot learn *even from* experience.

Bacon's bell called the empiricist wits together. Hume's bell must infallibly have dispersed them again, had they paid any attention to it. Fortunately they did not, at least in the eighteenth and nineteenth centuries. In our own more enlightened age, of course, Hume's bell has been much more attended to and has contributed significantly, chiefly via the irrationalist philosophies of science of Popper and his school, to the decay of confidence in empirical science that is very visible, even among scientists themselves, in the present century.

All the examples so far have been drawn from Hume's philosophy of the understanding. However, my thesis requires that other branches of his philosophy, for example, his philosophy of morals and of religion, should likewise be replete with skeptical assessments of the conclusiveness of arguments. And so they are.

Here are two examples from Hume's moral philosophy, the second of them being especially famous. Both, of course, are from Book III, Part I, Section I of the *Treatise*—"Moral Distinctions not deriv'd from Reason."

---

[22] *Treatise*, I, III, XII, p. 139.

13. "[The] opinion very industriously propagated by certain philosophers, that morality is susceptible of demonstration," is false.[23]	For any ethical h, $P(h/n) < 1$.	Any rationalist in the philosophy of morals.
14. The famous paragraph about "is" and "ought."[24]	For any ethical h and factual e, $P(h/e) < 1$.	Any "naturalist" in moral philosophy who supposes that some ethical conclusions are deducible from factual premises.

Most of the examples so far have been judgments of nondeducibility; and all of these have been from the *Treatise* or first *Enquiry*. This is not a coincidence. Those books are, in the strict chronological sense, *juvenilia*. It was therefore to be expected, and it is a fact, that the assessments of conclusiveness most abundant in them should be of that particular kind that undergraduates and *enfants terribles*, even ones of surpassing genius, are fondest of: judgments of nondeducibility — "It does not *follow!*"

On the other hand, in the incomparable masterpiece of Hume's maturity, the *Dialogues*, a different kind of skeptical assessment of conclusiveness predominates; and the reason for this change is easily seen. Concerning the main argument up for assessment there, namely, the design argument for the existence of God, a judgment of nondeducibility would have been quite nonskeptical, and indeed pointless, because a more favorable assessment of it was not maintained by anyone. No theist, or at least no intelligent one, has ever maintained that the existence of God is actually *deducible* from the observable phenomena of organic adaptation, or of the solar system, and so on. Accordingly, we find that judgments of nondeducibility are relegated in the *Dialogues* to a very minor role; in fact, they are directed only at a priori arguments for theism, which are

---

[23] Ibid., III, I, I, p. 463.
[24] Ibid., p. 469.

discussed only very briefly, and by way of digression, in Part IX. Also conspicuous by its absence from the *Dialogues* is the most *enfant terrible* of all Hume's judgments of irrelevance: the inductive skepticism of 12. And again, it is very easy to see why. How perfectly it would have suited Cleanthes, and all those who share his favorable assessment of the design argument, to find that its skeptical assessor, Philo, made his own position incredible from the outset by being equally skeptical about all ordinary scientific arguments from experience as well! That, indeed, is precisely the position that, throughout Parts I and II, Cleanthes tries to fasten on Philo, but without success; whereas he must have succeeded had Philo espoused inductive skepticism.

By contrast, what are conspicuously present, indeed superabundant, in the *Dialogues* are judgments of *indifference*.[25] In fact, almost everything that Philo says about the conclusiveness of the design argument, or of closely related arguments, terminates in a judgment of indifference — one that is, of course, skeptical by comparison with the judgments of preference that Cleanthes and most of Hume's contemporaries made concerning the arguments in question.

Here is one of Hume-Philo's judgments of indifference.

| 15. "If *reason* (I mean abstract reason, derived from inquiries *a priori*) be not alike mute with regard to all questions concerning cause and effect; this sentence at least it will venture to pronounce, That a mental world or universe of ideas requires a cause as much as does a material world or universe of objects...."[26] | $P(H/n) = P(H'/n)$, where H is "A mental universe, if it exists, has a cause" and H' is "A material universe, if it exists, has a cause." | All the many theists who suppose that orderliness, in itself, warrants a judgment of preference in favor of an intelligent cause. |

---

[25] See, e.g., pp. 145–46, 160, 162, 164, 167–69, 175, 178–83. These references span exactly the main body of the *Dialogues*, viz., Parts II–VIII.

[26] Ibid., IV, p. 160.

A second judgment of indifference, equally characteristic of the *Dialogues*, is the following.

16. "Nor is it less intelligible, or less conformable to experience to say, that the world arose by vegetation from a seed shed by another world, than to say that it arose from a divine reason or contrivance. . . ."[27]	$P(H/n.e) = P(H'/n.e)$, where H and H' are the two cosmogonic hypotheses just mentioned, and e is any observation statement known to be true.	Everyone who makes the usual Christian assessment of the design argument.

Philo, however, even before his apparent *volte-face* in Part XII of the *Dialogues*, is not always content to settle for a judgment of indifference. He sometimes ventures a judgment of preference, where it is skeptical to do so. For example, he is much more negative concerning the hypothesis of divine benevolence in relation to natural evil than he ever is about the hypothesis of divine intelligence in relation to the evidence of organic adaptation. Moreover, he remains so even in Part XII. (This fact is overlooked by those who would have us regard Part XII as insincere wherever it is at all possible to do so.) Accordingly, at the end of the two parts (X–XI) concerned with natural evil he does not hesitate to conclude with a judgment of preference that is explicit enough, and skeptical enough, even to awaken Demea.

17. "There may *four* hypotheses be framed concerning the first causes of the universe: *that* they are endowed with perfect goodness, *that* they have perfect malice, *that* they are opposite and have both goodness and malice, *that*	$P(H/E) > P(H'/E)$, where H and H' are respectively the fourth and first of the theodicies just mentioned and E is a summary of the phenomena of natural evil and its opposite.	Most Christian theists.

---

[27] Ibid., VII, p. 178.

they have neither goodness nor malice. Mixed phenomena can never prove the two former unmixed principles. And the uniformity and steadiness of general laws seem to oppose the third. The fourth, therefore, seems by far the most probable."[28]

It would be very easy to make this list of examples four times as long. In order to suggest just how easy this would be, I will briefly indicate, without quotation, some fertile sources of other skeptical assessments in Hume.

In the first *Enquiry*, Section X ("Of Miracles"), Hume was engaged — as is indeed quite obvious — in assessing the conclusiveness of arguments, namely, of arguments to the miraculous from testimony-to-the-miraculous. It is equally obvious that his assessment of them was skeptical by comparison with the assessment then generally prevailing among Christians.

In *Treatise*, I, IV, II ("Of scepticism with regard to the senses"), there is a great deal of scepticism in my sense, principally by way of judgments of nondeducibility or of irrelevance.

A thesis that two propositions are *compatible* is a judgment of nondeducibility, namely, that from one of the two propositions the negation of the other is not deducible. Hence my view of Hume's skepticism would lead us to expect that he will often maintain compatibility theses, at any rate where it is skeptical to do so. And so he does. An important example is the compatibility of freedom with determinism,[29] which is skeptical by comparison with the "incompatibilism" espoused both by most philosophers and by most laymen. A still more important example is the compatibility of evil with a perfect, omnipotent creator.[30] This assessment is

---

[28] Ibid., XI, p. 212.
[29] First *Enquiry*, VIII.
[30] *Dialogues*, X-XI.

skeptical by comparison with the judgment of deducibility (that the nonexistence of such a creator is deducible from the existence of evil) that was made, if not by Lucretius himself, then at least by many neo-Lucretians.[31]

More fundamental in Hume's philosphy than any thesis I have mentioned, and constituting the very roots of his antirationalism, are his various theses of the "looseness," or "separability" from one another, of all "objects," or of all "beings," or at least of all "simple qualities," or of all "simple ideas."[32] It is evident that these are all theses of at least *logical* separability. In that case they are all judgments of nondeducibility. And many of them, at least, are, and are expressly put forward as being, contrary to natural assessments.

Enough evidence to establish my thesis has now, I think, been offered. Skeptical judgments of nondeducibility, we have seen, are extremely abundant in Hume's philosophy. Now suppose that it is true, as I along with many others have maintained, that Hume, at least in the *Treatise* and first *Enquiry*, is a "deductivist." In that case he is committed *by implication* to a great many skeptical assessments of conclusiveness, over and above those that he himself actually makes. For deductivism is the thesis that, if *H is nondeducible from E*, then (in relation to necessary truths) *E is irrelevant to H*. And if the former assessment is a skeptical one in my sense, then the latter must be more skeptical still.

Many scholars have had in their hands the key to the nature of Hume's skepticism without realizing it. For many scholars have more or less clearly recognized that the kind of question with which Hume is characteristically concerned is not whether it is *true* that the next flame will be hot, or that every event has a cause, or that God exists. Rather, he is concerned with the question of how conclusive the commonly received *arguments for* those propositions are. And once this fact is recognized, it is no great further step to perceive that his characteristic skepticism resides in his regularly answering these questions by saying that those arguments are less conclusive than they are widely judged to be. Still, this further step has not been taken by anyone, as far as I know, before now.

---

[31] Among them J. L. Mackie and H. J. McCloskey, who, through being less cautious than Hume was on this matter, have recently suffered the mortification of finding themselves successfully underbid by a mere theist, A. Plantinga. The three articles in question are all reprinted in B. Brody, ed. *Readings in the Philosophy of Religion* (Englewood Cliffs, N.J.: Prentice-Hall, 1974).

[32] *Treatise*, I, I, IV, p. 10; VII, pp. 18, 24; II, III, p. 36; V, p. 54; III, VII, p. 97; VIII, p. 103; IV, II, p. 207; first *Enquiry*, IV, I, p. 29; VII, II, p. 74.

A Skeptic's Progress:
Hume's Preference for the First Enquiry

John Immerwahr

THIS PAPER IS AN INVESTIGATION OF HUME'S SKEPTICISM in Book I of the *Treatise* and in the first *Enquiry*.[1] I hope to show that in each of these works Hume distinguishes between two types of skepticism, Pyrrhonism and Academic skepticism. I will also argue that the Academic skepticism of the *Enquiry* differs significantly from the Academic skepticism of the *Treatise*[2] and that this difference accounts, in part, for Hume's preference for the *Enquiry*.

ACADEMIC AND PYRRHONIAN SKEPTICISM IN *Treatise I*

Let us begin by examining the discussion of skepticism with regard to reason in the *Treatise*.[3] Few arguments in Hume have been as poorly received as this one; D. C. Stove recently described it as "one of the worst arguments ever to impose itself on a man of genius."[4] Although I do not wish to defend Hume's arguments, I will claim that we can learn something useful from this chapter. In the rush to point out the fallacies of the arguments found here, commentators have not always stopped to ask what the purpose of the chapter is.

In examining this chapter it will be helpful to keep in mind the fact that Hume was aware of at least two distinct versions of skepticism as a historical position.[5] Academic skepticism rejects dogmatism (the view that we can know anything with certainty), but it holds that men can have *probable* knowledge and that this probability should be the guide to life.

---

[1] I am indebted to a number of people for remarks about earlier drafts. William Alston, Nathan Brett, and John Fielder all gave especially helpful comments.

[2] I disagree, therefore, with Jan Wilbanks, who holds that "the differences, if any, between the scepticism of *Treatise I* and that of *Enquiry I* lie in the manner of its expression, not in its nature" (*Hume's Theory of Imagination* (The Hague: Martinus Nijhoff, 1968), p. 89).

[3] *A Treatise of Human Understanding*, ed. L. A. Selby-Bigge (Oxford, 1888), I, IV, I, pp. 180-87 (hereafter cited as *Treatise*).

[4] *Probability and Hume's Inductive Scepticism* (Oxford: Clarendon Press, 1973), p. 132.

[5] For Hume's awareness of the skeptical tradition see B. M. Laing, *David Hume* (London: Ernest Benn, 1932), pp. 72-85, or John Laird, *Hume's Philosophy of Human Nature* (London: Methuen, 1932), pp. 180-84. For the distinction itself see Sextus Empiricus, *Outlines of Pyrrhonism*, trans. R. G. Bury, 4 vols. (New York: G. P. Putnam & Sons, 1933), 1:139ff.

Pyrrhonism rejects both dogmatism and Academic skepticism. According to the Pyrrhonians we can have neither certain knowledge nor probable knowledge; the Academic acceptance of probable knowledge is only a concealed dogmatism. For the Pyrrhonian skeptic we must totally suspend judgment and let our lives be guided by nature and custom.

The terms "Academic" and "Pyrrhonian" are not explicitly used by Hume in the *Treatise*. I will argue, however, that in the section "Of scepticism with regard to reason" Hume is distinguishing between these two positions and arguing for Academic skepticism.[6] The section actually contains two separate arguments. The first argument (paragraphs 1-3) is an argument for Academic skepticism and is accepted by Hume; the second argument (paragraphs 5-6) is an argument for Pyrrhonism that Hume subsequently rejects.

The first argument is directed specifically against deductive reasoning, and Hume tries to show that all deductive reasoning "degenerates into probability." Since there is a possibility of error in the simplest deductive judgment, Hume argues, all deductive judgments are only probable. He has already shown elsewhere that all inductive judgments are judgments of probability; hence the conclusion of the first argument is that there is no certain knowledge, only judgments of probability.[7] This, of course, is exactly the position held by Academic skepticism.

The second argument is an attack on probable reasoning in general and is thus directed at both inductive and deductive reasoning.[8] Hume

---

[6] There is considerable disagreement in the literature about whether two versions of skepticism can be isolated in the *Treatise*. Daniel Breazeale implies that no distinction between moderate and extreme skepticism can be found in the *Treatise*, and that this distinction appears only in the *Enquiry* ("Hume's Impasse," *Journal of the History of Philosophy* 13 (July, 1975):321). Others have argued that Hume is working in the *Treatise* in the direction of two forms of skepticism but that no clear distinction is made. See James Noxon, *Hume's Philosophical Development* (London: Oxford University Press, 1973), p. 15, and Anthony Flew, *Hume's Philosophy of Belief* (London: Routledge and Kegan Paul, 1961), p. 267. I am in closer agreement with Wilbanks, who sees Hume as making a distinction between two versions of skepticism in both the *Treatise* and the first *Enquiry* (pp. 88ff.). As will become clear later, however, I disagree with Wilbanks on other grounds.

[7] *Treatise*, I, III, VI, p. 90.

[8] This chapter is sometimes taken as an argument directed exclusively against deductive reasoning. Although the first argument is directed against deductive reasoning, the second argument concerns all probable reasoning. Critics who took the chapter as an attack on deductive reasoning alone include Richard Popkin, "David Hume: His Pyrrhonism and His Critique of Pyrronhism," in *Hume*, ed. V. C. Chappell (Garden City, N.Y.: Anchor Books, 1966), pp. 62ff., and Farhang Zabeeh, *Hume: Precursor of Modern Empiricism* (The Hague: Martinus Nijhoff, 1960), pp. 145ff.

reasons that every judgment of probability has a margin of error and thus must be corrected by another judgment of probability. This second judgment must also be corrected by another judgment of probability, and so on, ad infinitum. Multiplying all of the probabilities together, it is claimed, reduces the probability of the original judgment to nothingness, resulting in a "total extinction of belief and evidence."[9] The conclusion of the second argument is thus the Pyrrhonian position that we must suspend all judgment. The conclusion of the first argument is Academic skepticism, then, in that all knowledge is reduced to probability; the conclusion of the second argument—the destruction of all probable judgments—is, again, Pyrrhonian skepticism.

Although Hume accepts the logic of the second argument, he finds fault with it on psychological grounds. The reiterated judgments of probability are too subtle and "remote" to have any influence on the imagination, which is, after all, the ultimate source of belief. The argument for Pyrrhonism has, therefore, no psychological force for individual human judgments. "Nature," Hume writes, "has determin'd us to judge as well as to breathe and feel."[10] In the *Abstract* he says that "philosophy wou'd render us entirely Pyrrhonian, were not nature too strong for it."[11]

Although Hume rejects the argument leading to Pyrrhonism, he does not reject the argument leading to Academic skepticism. The difficulty with the argument for Pyrrhonism is that "after the first and second decision" of probability the reasoning involved becomes too subtle to have any motivating force upon the imagination.[12] The argument for Academic skepticism (that all knowledge is a species of probability) does not depend on the reiterated judgments of probability involved in Pyrrhonism; it involves only the *first* judgment of probability and is thus immune to the problems of the argument for Pyrrhonism.

Hume's final position in Book I of the *Treatise* is an uneasy acceptance of Academic skepticism. Although he sometimes expresses reservations concerning this version of skepticism, he for the most part adopts it. Dogmatism is clearly rejected by Hume since it ignores the obvious fallibility of human reasoning. He describes as fools "all those who reason

---

[9] *Treatise*, I, IV, I, p. 183.
[10] Ibid.
[11] *An Abstract of A Treatise of Human Nature,* intro. J. M. Keynes and P. Sraffa (Hamden, Conn.: Archon Books, 1965), p. 24.
[12] *Treatise* I, IV, I, p. 185.

or believe any thing *certainly*,"[13] and he apologizes for having used "such terms as these, *'tis evident, 'tis certain, 'tis undeniable*." These expressions, he assures us, "imply no dogmatical spirit" since such sentiments would be appropriate for "a sceptic still less than any other."[14] Hume also rejects Pyrrhonism, or "total scepticism," as a view lacking psychological force and held only by a "fantastic sect."[15] We are left with an Academic or moderate skepticism that Hume characterizes as the position of "true philosophers."[16]

THE FACULTIES OF THE IMAGINATION

The distinction between extreme and moderate skepticism is rooted in another distinction that runs through Book I of the *Treatise*. Hume repeatedly distinguishes two separate faculties of the imagination.

1. The "general and established properties" of the imagination. Hume argues that the imagination has certain universal, permanent, and irresistible tendencies that are most clearly seen in *causal* judgments. This faculty of the imagination is the basis of all scientific and inductive reasoning. The basic operation of this faculty is to bring forward the idea of an effect when we have the impression or idea of its cause (and vice versa).

2. The "trivial qualities of the fancy."[17] Hume thinks that our imagination also causes us to make judgments based on relationships other than cause and effect. The trivial qualities produce *noncausal* judgments that are most typically at work in credulity, prejudice, superstition, belief in "prodigies and apparitions," education, and other philosophical undesirables.[18] Many judgments based on trivial qualities have as their root the relations of resemblance and contiguity (rather than cause and effect), but the most general way of characterizing these judgments would be simply as noncausal judgments of factual matters.

---

[13] Ibid., VII, p. 270.

[14] Ibid., p. 274.

[15] Ibid., I, p. 183.

[16] Ibid., III, p. 224.

[17] For the labels see *Treatise* I, IV, II, p. 217. Causal reasoning, which is based on the general properties, is discussed throughout the *Treatise*. Some places in Book I of the *Treatise* where the trivial qualities are discussed are the following: II, V, pp. 60-61; III, IX, pp. 109-10; III, XIII, p. 150; IV, II, p. 217; IV, pp. 225-26; V, p. 238 (reading "imagination" here in the "more limited sense" as being only the trivial qualities of III, IX, p. 118n.); VII, p. 254n.; VII, p. 267.

[18] Ibid., I, III, IX, pp. 101ff.

One of Hume's ways of illustrating the trivial qualities is the following example: "A drunkard, who has seen his companion die of a debauch, is struck with that instance for some time, and dreads a like incident for himself: But as the memory of it decays away by degrees, his former security returns, and the danger seems less certain and real."[19] The drunkard's beliefs are obviously not based solely on causal judgments arising from the general properties. If one were motivated by scientific reasoning alone, the amount of time between the experiment and the conclusion drawn from it should have no great significance. The drunkard's reasoning, however, is based instead on the trivial qualities, where non-causal relations (in this case, contiguity of time) are what produces belief.

A constant theme of the *Treatise* is the conflict between the general properties and the trivial qualities. If the general properties are followed to their logical outcome, the result is total Pyrrhonism, which denies the possibility of human judgment, the existence of an external world, and personal identity. What saves us from this total skepticism is the operation of the trivial qualities, which lead us to the comparatively safe harbor of Academic skepticism.

In his summary of the discussion of skepticism regarding reason, Hume makes it very clear that it is precisely this conflict that is involved. He claims that adherence to

> the general and more establish'd properties of the imagination . . . if steadily executed, wou'd be dangerous, and attended with the most fatal consequences. . . . The understanding [i.e., the imagination], when it acts alone, and according to its most general principles, entirely subverts itself, and leaves not the lowest degree of evidence in any proposition. . . . We save ourselves from this total scepticism only by means of that singular and seemingly trivial property of the fancy, by which we enter with difficulty into remote views of things.[20]

Following the trivial qualities (which we cannot avoid doing) thus brings us away from Pyrrhonism; however, the end of this process is not dogmatism but a moderate Academic skepticism.

Following the general properties, in other words, leads us into the Pyrrhonistic conclusion that we must suspend all judgment. If we observe human reasoning scientifically (following the general properties),

---

[19] Ibid., XIII, p. 144.
[20] Ibid., IV, VII, pp. 267-68.

we see that we should treat human reason as a cause and truth as an effect.[21] A proper investigation, however, shows us that this cause is not invariably followed by truth as an effect, so causal reasoning indicates that we should make judgments of probability concerning the accuracy of all human judgments. The reasoning here is primarily causal and involves the empirical observation of human reason. The same causal, or general-property, reasoning leads us to correct our additional judgment of probability, and so on, ad infinitum—a process that would ultimately, according to Hume, destroy all belief.

What prevents this destruction of all belief is the operation of the trivial qualities. Other noncausal factors interrupt this perfectly "reasonable" causal argument and prevent us from actually extinguishing belief because of this argument. The laziness of the mind (a typical trivial quality) robs the general-property argument of its force and thus saves us from skepticism.[22]

Hume finds the same process in a number of other places, for example, in the discussion of the external world. If we were to follow causal reasoning alone we would be led to the conclusion that the objects of perception do not have a continuous and distinct existence. What convinces us of the existence of the external world is not causal reasoning but noncausal reasoning based primarily on resemblance. The similarity of our perceptions causes the mind to feign the continued existence of external objects, a process Hume describes as involving the "trivial qualities of the fancy."[23]

The message of the first book of the *Treatise* is that the general properties lead us into a total skepticism where human reason is completely unreliable and there is no ground for belief in personal identity or an external world. The "trivial suggestions of the fancy" moderate this skepticism and leave us with a common-sense version of Academic skepticism. I describe this version of skepticism as "common sense" since it

---

[21] Ibid., I, p. 180.

[22] The discussion of skepticism regarding reason is a good example of the principles Hume illustrates in the discussion of philosophical and unphilosophical probability. The idea of applying correction factors is a typical operation of philosophical (based on the general properties) probability (ibid., III, XII, p. 133). What saves us from the resulting Pyrrhonistic infinite regress is unphilosophical probability (a trivial quality); Hume connects the discussion of skepticism with the discussion of unphilosophical probability in a number of places (ibid., XIII, p. 146n.).

[23] Ibid., IV, II, pp. 208, 217.

includes a commitment to the reliability (in probable terms) of human reason and to the self and the external world.[24]

Hume starts out by describing the trivial qualities as unnecessary and avoidable elements in human reasoning.[25] As the *Treatise* develops they take on an increasingly more important role. In the section on general rules they are seen as an important element in thinking, and by the discussion of skepticism they emerge as the only thing that saves us from Pyrrhonism.[26] Hume's final position is that the trivial qualities are an essential part of almost all human judgments; significantly he modifies his description of the trivial qualities toward the end of Book I by describing them as being only "*seemingly* trivial."[27] The "trivial suggestions of the fancy" are not really *trivial* at all but are the basis for universal and unavoidable human judgments.[28]

ACADEMIC SKEPTICISM IN THE FIRST *Enquiry*.

In the first *Enquiry* Hume explicitly distinguishes between Academic and Pyrrhonian skepticism. But two important differences stand out between the Academic skepticism presented in the *Treatise* and that presented in the *Enquiry*.

1. In the *Treatise* Hume rejects all claims to certainty and takes the traditional Academic view that we can have only probable knowledge. In the *Enquiry* certainty is permitted to the skeptic so long as it is limited to relations of ideas.[29]

2. The Academic skepticism of the *Treatise* is founded on the trivial qualities. Although the distinction between trivial qualities and general properties does not appear so clearly in the *Enquiry*, Hume makes it apparent that the mitigated skepticism of the *Enquiry* is based upon causal rather than noncausal operations of the mind.

---

[24] For Hume as a common-sense philosopher see Nicholas Capaldi, *David Hume: The Newtonian Philosopher* (Boston: G. K. Hall, 1975), pp. 30ff.

[25] *Treatise*, I, III, IX, p. 109.

[26] Ibid., XIII, p. 150.

[27] Ibid., IV, VI, p. 254; VII, pp. 265, 268, emphasis mine.

[28] The only real exception to this pattern is the puzzling position taken in the *Treatise*, I, IV, IV, pp. 225–26. Here Hume still describes the trivial qualities as unnecessary and avoidable, although it is hard to see how he could say this after what he has said in I, IV, I, about the role of the trivial qualities in saving us from Pyrrhonism.

[29] Hume does present some arguments to cast doubt on "all abstract reasonings" in *Enquiry* I, but in a footnote he offers a solution to these problems (*An Enquiry concerning Human Understanding*, ed. L. A. Selby-Bigge, 2nd ed. (Oxford, 1902), XII, II, pp. 156, 158n. (hereafter cited as first *Enquiry*)). In general, he maintains his original claim that relations of ideas are "either intuitively or demonstratively certain" (ibid., IV, I, p. 25).

What accounts for this change in Hume's moderate skepticism? Two questions must be answered. First, why does he feel that the same faculty (the general properties) that led to Pyrrhonism in the *Treatise* will yield Academic skepticism in the *Enquiry*? Second, what philosophical task does the later version of Academic skepticism perform that the earlier did not?

There are two main reasons for Hume's belief in the *Treatise* that the general properties lead to Pyrrhonism. First of all, an exclusive reliance on the general properties is destructive of all human reasoning because of the declining probability that results from the reiterated calculations required by strict general-properties reasoning. By the time he comes to the first *Enquiry*, however, Hume's view of this problem appears to have changed. He seems to have rejected the argument for the self-destructiveness of reason. Aside from its inherent weakness, the best reason for thinking that Hume is dissatisfied with this argument is that it is the only major argument of Book I of the *Treatise* not repeated in his later writings.[30] If Hume still found the argument compelling, one would expect him to have at least mentioned it in the catalogue of skeptical arguments given in the *Enquiry*.[31] I will assume, then, that by the time Hume writes the *Enquiry* he no longer believes that all human reasoning is ultimately self-destructive.

A second skeptical feature of the general principles in the *Treatise* is that they lead to counterintuitive metaphysical claims, namely, the denial of the external world and of personal identity. In the *Treatise* Hume feels that any faculty that leads to these absurd conclusions should be rejected as being impossibly Pyrrhonistic.

Hume's approach to these metaphysical problems in the *Enquiry* is interestingly different. In the *Treatise* he solves these difficulties by bringing in a new operation of the imagination, the trivial qualities, to protect

---

[30] See Stove, p. 132. The discussion of the immateriality of the soul reappears in "Of the Immortality of the Soul" (*The Philosophical Works*, ed. T. H. Green and T. H. Grose, 4 vols. (London, 1886), 4:399 (hereafter cited as *Works*)). And the discussion of personal identity appears again in the *Dialogues concerning Natural Religion* (ed. Norman Kemp Smith (Indianapolis: Bobbs-Merrill, 1947), IV, p. 159). Douglas Lewis has argued in correspondence that this argument is mentioned again in the *Dialogues* where Hume speaks of reason's furnishing "invincible arguments against itself" that are "too refined and subtle" to counterpoise the senses and experience (*Dialogues*, I, p. 135). I read this passage as a reference to skeptical arguments generally rather than to the argument of *Treatise*, I, IV, I in particular.

[31] First *Enquiry*, XII, I-II.

us from these skeptical results. In the *Enquiry* we are saved from Pyrrhonism not by a new operation of the mind but by limiting the general properties to the subjects appropriate for human investigation.[32] Since human knowledge is "by no means fitted for such remote and abstruse subjects," the fact that the general properties lead to strange metaphysical conclusions regarding the soul and the external world is no reason to reject them as the basis of human reasoning.[33] In the *Enquiry* Hume seems to be ready to take his own advice and to commit all metaphysics of this type (even his own) to the flames.[34]

Hume's lack of concern with metaphysics is hardly surprising given that from the very first he always claimed that his major interest was what he called "moral subjects." During the period when Hume wrote the *Enquiry* he was deeply involved in work on politics, criticism, and especially religion.[35] The real attraction of the *Enquiry* version of moderate skepticism is its superior advantage in working with these practical problems, particularly with religion. Hume's focus of interest has thus shifted from abstract metaphysical questions such as the nature of the self and the external world, and the metaphysical paradoxes to which the general properties lead no longer seem as important to him. What does loom as important is the power of the *Enquiry* version of Academic skepticism in establishing a foundation for these practical concerns and in providing a critique of superstition.

From Hume's point of view, at least four areas of human interest must be clearly distinguished: rationalistic metaphysics and theology, natural science, moral subjects, and superstition and vulgar religion. Let us examine the Academic skepticism of the *Treatise* in regard to these four areas. Presumably this skepticism will eliminate rationalistic metaphysics. The difficulty is that this version of skepticism does not offer any way of eliminating superstition or even of distinguishing it from science and the moral subjects. Hume sometimes talks in *Treatise* I as though he can make such a distinction by showing that superstition is founded on the trivial qualities, whereas science and the moral subjects are founded

---

[32] Ibid., III, p. 162.

[33] Ibid., I, p. 12.

[34] For Hume's antimetaphysical bias in the *Enquiry* see John O. Nelson, "Two Main Questions Concerning Hume's *Treatise* and *Enquiry*," *Philosophical Review* 81 (July, 1972):349. Nelson's views are criticized by Phillip D. Cummins in "Hume's Disavowal of the *Treatise*," *Philosophical Review* 82 (July, 1973):371–79.

[35] Ernest Campbell Mossner, *The Life of David Hume* (Austin, Texas: University of Texas Press, 1954), pp. 319ff.

on general properties.³⁶ His final position, however, turns out to be that science, moral subjects, and superstition all have a common foundation in the trivial qualities.

The idea that science and superstition could have the same basis is something that upsets Hume even in the *Treatise* and that becomes still more intolerable later on. One of the chief attractions of philosophy for the mature Hume is its power against superstition, prejudice, and false religion.³⁷ In the essay "Of Suicide," Hume observes that "one considerable advantage that arises from Philosophy, consists in the sovereign antidote which it offers to superstition and false religion. All other remedies against that pestilent distemper are vain, or at least uncertain."³⁸ No form of skepticism would be acceptable that did not provide a critique of superstition.

In fact, Hume's anticipation of this problem in the *Treatise* seems to be one of the major causes of the forlorn desperation of the conclusion of Book I. Hume sees that if we "assent to every trivial suggestion of the fancy . . . they lead us into such errors, absurdities, and obscurities, that we must at last become asham'd of our credulity."³⁹ Presumably, he sees here that relying on Academic skepticism involves basing human reason on the same faculty of the imagination that leads to superstition and other undesirables. On the other hand, he sees that if we abandon the trivial qualities, "we subvert entirely the human understanding."⁴⁰ He finds himself trapped between "a false reason [the trivial qualities] and none at all [the general properties]."⁴¹

What Hume needs is a version of skepticism that will eliminate rationalistic metaphysics and theology without letting superstition and popular religion in by the back door. The moderate skepticism of the *Treatise* is itself based on the trivial qualities and is thus unable to provide such a critique.

The Academic skepticism of the *Enquiry* can now be seen as a solution

---

³⁶ *Treatise*, I, IV, IV, pp. 225-26. Thomas K. Hearn discusses Hume's attempt to make this kind of distinction in "'General Rules' in Hume's *Treatise*," *Journal of the History of Philosophy* 7 (October, 1970): 405-22. Although Hume is hopeful, in the passages Hearn discusses, that the distinction can be drawn (mostly in I, III), by the time he comes to I, IV he feels that such a distinction cannot be drawn.
³⁷ First *Enquiry*, I, pp. 11-12.
³⁸ "Of Suicide," *Works*, 4:406.
³⁹ *Treatise*, I, IV, VII, p. 267.
⁴⁰ Ibid., p. 268.
⁴¹ Ibid.

to the dilemma posed in the conclusion of *Treatise* I. In the *Enquiry* Hume offers a version of skepticism that can be used to attack both metaphysics and superstition, while leaving science and the moral subjects as appropriate subjects of human reasoning having a similar foundation. This double aspect of Hume's new, mitigated skepticism is nicely illustrated by the two chapters in the *Enquiry* dealing with religion; the same skepticism provides an attack against both natural theology and superstition.

In Section XI Hume attacks philosophical theology by showing that it has no consequences for ethics. By an analysis of the argument from design he shows that no ethical conclusions can be derived from knowable facts about God. The point of the argument is to show that, since human knowledge can never go beyond the realm of causal judgments, it is too weak to make any strong conclusions in natural theology. Rationalistic theology would appear to be outside the proper scope of human judgment.

The same principles are used in Section X of the *Enquiry* to attack the belief in miracles, thus providing an "everlasting check to all kinds of superstitious delusion."[42] For Hume, belief in miracles follows not from the "maxim by which we commonly conduct ourselves in reasoning" (causal reasoning) but from certain *noncausal* influences on belief — in this case "*surprise* and *wonder*."[43] Since the belief in miracles is not based on causal principles of judgment it must be rejected. "The wise," according to Hume, "lend a very *academic* faith" to reports of miracles.[44]

Hume could not have used the moderate skepticism of the *Treatise* to criticize the belief in miracles, because there both moderate skepticism and the belief in "whatever is reported, even concerning apparitions, enchantments, and prodigies" are both based upon the trivial qualities.[45] We know that an early version of the *Treatise* contained a chapter on miracles, but this was probably similar to the discussion in the *Enquiry*, which attacks the belief in miracles because it cannot be supported by causal reasoning.[46] In terms of the *Treatise* this would have been a Pyrrhonian attack on miracles and hence ultimately unsatisfactory for

---

[42] First *Enquiry*, X, I, p. 110.
[43] Ibid., II, p. 117.
[44] Ibid., p. 125, emphasis mine.
[45] *Treatise*, I, III, IX, p. 113.
[46] Mossner, p. 111.

Hume's purposes. Since Pyrrhonism is a psychologically untenable position, a Pyrrhonistic critique of miracles does not do much to advance the battle against superstition. What Hume needs, and what the *Enquiry* version of Academic skepticism gives him, is a way to criticize superstitious beliefs from within the stance of moderate skepticism.

By freeing moderate skepticism from the trivial qualities and basing it on the general properties instead, Hume is able to use this skepticism as a weapon against both superstition and metaphysical theology. Human reason is too weak to permit any interesting conclusions in metaphysics and theology, but it is strong enough to rule out superstition and vulgar religion. The moderate skepticism of the *Enquiry* is precisely what Hume needs to carry out his investigation of the moral subjects — a double-edged sword to be used against metaphysics, on the one hand, and superstition, on the other.

CONCLUSION

There has been considerable discussion of Hume's clearly stated preference for the first *Enquiry* over the *Treatise*.[47] If I am correct, one major difference between the two works is that the *Enquiry* presents a version of moderate skepticism that lends itself more readily to the critique of both superstition and metaphysics. It is tempting to see this difference as a ground for Hume's preference.

Late in life Hume described the *Enquiry* as a "compleat Answer to Dr Reid and to that bigotted silly Fellow, Beattie."[48] A natural reaction to this remark is to look for some improvement in the *Enquiry* that could properly be supposed to be such an answer. Both Reid and Beattie attack the *Treatise* for its skepticism, and, I have argued, Hume himself was dissatisfied with both of the versions of skepticism discussed in the *Treatise*.[49] In the dialectic between skepticism and the antiskeptical thoughts of the common-sense philosophers, Hume surely would have wanted to present his most defensible version of skepticism. It is thus reasonable to suppose that it is the improved version of skepticism in the *Enquiry* that Hume sees as the "compleat Answer."

---

[47] First *Enquiry*, "Advertisement" (p. 2).

[48] *The Letters of David Hume*, ed. J. Y. T. Greig, 2 vols. (London: Oxford University Press, 1932), 2:301. I accept Nelson's view in "Two Main Questions" that Hume had other than purely literary reasons for rejecting the *Treatise*.

[49] See Nelson, "Two Main Questions."

The Dialogues as Original Imitation: Cicero and the Nature of Hume's Skepticism

Christine Battersby

"THE FAME OF CICERO FLOURISHES AT PRESENT; but that of Aristotle is utterly decayed."[1] In thus selecting Cicero as an example of the inevitable and deserving popularity of "easy" philosophy over "abstract" philosophy, Hume reflects the partiality of eighteenth-century audiences for Cicero's writings. Of Cicero's works the dialogue *The Nature of the Gods* was a particular favorite. Voltaire described it and another work of Cicero's as the two best works "ever penned by mere human wisdom"; and such writers as Gibbon, Rousseau, Diderot, and Montesquieu were among its admirers.[2] In the eyes of the latter, Cicero's dialogue represented a triumph for religious skepticism, with all "systems" fading into nothingness and their "champions" destroying one another.[3] The dialogue was not always interpreted so negatively, however. For some it was reason, not skepticism, that triumphed and natural religion that won the day. When Hume came to scrutinize the foundations of natural religion he used Cicero's dialogue as a model for his own *Dialogues concerning Natural Religion*. The divergent interpretations of Cicero and the fact that various seventeenth-century divines had extracted its argument from design to buttress their own religious position made this choice of a model ironically appropriate.

Hume no doubt relied on the popularity and previous religious use of the Ciceronian dialogue to guarantee his readers' recognition of the similarities with his model. The two prefaces and endings are, for example, similar. In each case we are introduced to a youthful narrator who

---

I am grateful to Professor Edmund Howells and to participants in the McGill Bicentennial Hume Conference for comments on this paper.

[1] *An Enquiry concerning Human Understanding*, ed. L. A. Selby-Bigge, 2nd ed. (Oxford, 1902), I, p. 7 (hereafter cited as first *Enquiry*).

[2] For a fairly full account of Cicero's popularity in the eighteenth century and a bibliographical essay see Peter Gay, *The Enlightenment: An Interpretation*, 2 vols. (London: Wildwood House, 1973), vol. 1.

[3] Montesquieu, "Discours sur Cicéron," in *Oeuvres complètes*, ed. André Masson, 3 vols. (Paris: Nagel, 1950-55), 3:17. And see J. M. Ross's introduction to Cicero's *Nature of the Gods*, trans. Horace C. P. McGregor (Harmondsworth: Penguin, 1972), for information on the differing uses to which the dialogue was put (hereafter cited as *Nature of Gods*).

claims that his function is merely to listen and record, without taking part in the dispute. However, at the end the narrator abandons the role of a mere observer to judge who has won the argument. Both narrators decide against the skeptic; the closing words of Hume's narrator deliberately echo those of Cicero's. Hume's work is not, however, a slavish copy of Cicero's: it departs from the original in several important respects, falling into the category of eighteenth-century "original imitation."[4] In this type of imitation the parent work is used as a norm in such a way that deviations from the original are highlighted and stand out as significant.

To understand Hume's *Dialogues* we need to understand how and why they depart from the Ciceronian prototype. One such departure has already received some attention from commentators: it is the introduction of an extra narrator, Pamphilus, into the Humean dialogue—a narrator who is sharply distinguished from Hume, the author. Thus, whereas the Ciceronian original ends with an authorial judgment, the Humean imitation ends with the unauthoritative voice of Pamphilus. Kemp Smith has suggested that the introduction of Pamphilus is to preserve Hume's "anonymity."[5] But although this seems prima facie the main reason for Pamphilus's introduction, a consideration of the history of the reaction to Cicero's dialogue makes this explanation seem far from convincing. The lengthy dispute over Cicero's sincerity shows that an interposed narrator is not necessary to preserve "anonymity."

The dispute among critics arises in part because, structurally, Cicero's dialogue is balanced toward the Skeptic. The Skeptic has two separate occasions on which to impress the audience with his ingenious objections. He is also the last speaker to get the chance to refute his opponent point by point. There is a suggestion at the end that the Stoic could defeat the Skeptic if the argument continued; but, in the form in which the dialogue has come down to us, at least, the Skeptic has the upper hand by having the last long speech. This balance has led many (including Hume) to suppose that, despite the final authorial judgment, Cicero meant the Skeptic to triumph.[6]

---

[4] See Howard J. Weinbrot, "Augustian Imitation: The Role of the Original," *Proceedings of the Modern Language Association Neoclassicism Conferences 1967-68*, ed. Paul J. Korshin (New York: A. M. S. Press, 1970), pp. 53-70.

[5] *Dialogues concerning Natural Religion*, ed. N. Kemp Smith (Indianapolis: Bobbs-Merrill, 1947), p. 60 (hereafter cited as *Dialogues*).

[6] This, at least, seems to be the implication of Hume's remarks on Cicero's strategy in *The Natural History of Religion*, in *The Philosophical Works*, ed. T. H. Green and T. H. Grose, 4 vols. (London, 1886), 4:352 (hereafter cited as *Nat. Hist. Rel.* and *Works*,

Some of Cicero's own comments in the preface also undermine the final judgment. Instead of instructing his readers to take careful note of the final authorial judgment, Cicero suggests that authorial judgments are both unimportant and irrelevant. Those who want to know his opinion show "excessive curiosity"; the reader's interest should be centered not on the "weight of the authority" but on the "weight of the argument." His readers should not follow chosen teachers: "the authority of those who set out to teach is often an impediment to those who wish to learn." Instead, everyone should "come into court, weigh up the evidence, and return their verdict as to what we are to say about religion."[7] In this way, then, the authority of the author is questioned, and Cicero leaves the way open for those who claim that the Skeptic's arguments carry the greatest weight. "Anonymity" has been preserved without an intrusive nonauthorial narrator.

For the purposes of "anonymity" Hume requires even less than Cicero the intervention of a nonauthorial narrator. The mere fact that Hume imitated a work that is only problematically sincere is grounds enough for suspecting guile. We must look for an additional reason for the introduction of Pamphilus into the dialogue. Michael Morrisroe suggests one possibility:

> Pamphilus is a *naif*, a tool of Hume, who misunderstands both the issues and outcome of the argument. His conclusion proclaims Cleanthes the winner of the debate, and his introductory statement advises that the subject of discussion is the attributes of God. However, it is Philo who wins the argument, and the subject is whether God's existence can be proven by the design argument.[8]

Pamphilus is certainly a tool, but not quite in the way Morrisroe suggests. The tension between a discussion of the attributes and a discussion on the existence of God is in the text, quite apart from the introductory

---

respectively). This also seems to be the rationale behind some simplistic remarks (deservedly deleted from most later editions) in the essay "Of the Rise and Progress of the Arts and Sciences." Here, in addition to describing Cicero as "a great sceptic in matters of religion," Hume does not even acknowledge the existence of Ciero's final authorial judgment. He seems to take the presumed insincerity of Cicero's ending as an indication that Cicero did not himself say "something decisive on the subject" (*Works*, 3:189n.).

[7] *Nature of Gods* 1. 10, p. 73; 1. 13–14, p. 75.

[8] Michael Morrisroe Jr., "Rhetorical Methods in Hume's Works on Religion," *Philosophy and Rhetoric* 2 (1969):134.

letter by Pamphilus. This tension was also present in Cicero's work without the offices of an extra narrator. His speakers, like Hume's, claim that they are not casting doubts on the existence of God at the very same time as the discussion undermines it. We might agree with Cleanthes that Philo is merely uttering "pious declamations" when he says, "the question can never be concerning the *being*, but only the *nature* of the Deity," but Pamphilus is in no way necessary for the introduction of this tension.[9] Neither can Pamphilus's judgment at the end be simply reversed in the way that Morrisroe suggests. If, as Philo says, the atheist "is only nominally so and can never possibly be in earnest," and if the dispute between Philo and Cleanthes is one "which admits not of any precise meaning, nor consequently of any determination," then Pamphilus is certainly wrong to attempt a verdict at the end.[10] But his verdict is no more wrong for deciding in favor of Cleanthes.

One of the Ciceronian features that Hume omits from his dialogue is the appeal to the reader to "weigh up the evidence." Hume seems to be more consistently skeptical than Cicero of man's ability to reach reasonable conclusions on matters such as the argument from design. The mitigated skepticism that Hume recommends as "durable and useful" at the end of the first *Enquiry* places two important limitations on those who attempt to reason: first, they should never aim at dogmatism, and, secondly, they should limit their inquiries to subjects in which we have "daily practice and experience." If the reason is so weak that we cannot even "give a satisfactory reason, why we believe, after a thousand experiments, that a stone will fall, or fire burn," then we are even more at risk when we go beyond "common life" and give answers on subjects where there is no "daily practice and experience" to guide us. In a phrase almost exactly echoed by Philo in the *Dialogues*, Hume mentions questions concerning "the origin of worlds, and the situation of nature, from, and to eternity" as beyond the "narrow reach" of "correct *Judgement*." Such inquiries are too "distant" and "high" or, as Philo says, too "subtile" and "refined."[11]

On the question of dogmatism Hume speaks scathingly in the first *Enquiry* of those who "have no idea of any counterpoising argument" and have no "indulgence for those who entertain opposite sentiments."

---

[9] *Dialogues*, II, pp. 142, 143. And see, for example, *Nature of Gods* 2. 13, p. 128; 3. 10, p. 196.

[10] *Dialogues*, XII, p. 218.

[11] First *Enquiry*, XII, III, pp. 161, 162; *Dialogues*, I, pp. 132, 135.

Lacking a proper appreciation of the "strange infirmities of human understanding," they also lack "doubt, and caution, and modesty." They hate being in a state of hesitation or balance, since "to hesitate or balance perplexes their understanding, checks their passion, and suspends their action."[12] Hume's own appreciation of the weaknesses of reason, on the other hand, causes him to admire hesitation, counterpoising arguments, and balance.

This concern with balance can be seen in the preface to the *Dialogues* where Pamphilus talks of "preserving a proper balance among the speakers." Similarly, in the *Essays* Hume criticizes Cicero's method of writing dialogues as not balanced enough. Cicero's dialogues are seen to suffer from the fault, which Hume talks about in a letter to Elliot, "of putting nothing but Nonsense into the Mouth of the Adversary." He is said to introduce his friend Atticus as "a humble admirer of the orator" who "pays him frequent compliments, and receives his instructions, with all the deference which a scholar owes to his master."[13] Although *The Nature of the Gods* cannot be criticized for introducing this type of master-student relationship, the dialogue is less well-balanced than its Humean counterpart. The tendencies toward lengthy monologues, lack of conversational interchange, and lack of narrational interruption mean that there is a definite structural bias toward the interlocutor with the last long speech—the Skeptic. Conversely, Hume's use of short sections containing more than one speaker, the frequent conversational exchange, and the interruptions of Pamphilus serve to balance Hume's protagonists more evenly.

Pamphilus helps maintain equilibrium not through the frequency of his interjections but because (from the start) he seems to be biased in favor of Cleanthes. He tells us that Cleanthes has an "accurate philosophical turn," whereas Philo has merely a "careless scepticism." Philo's manner is "vehement," "somewhat between jest and earnest," causing impatience in Cleanthes. The only reference to Philo's victory carries with it the unpleasant suggestion of "an air of alacrity and triumph."[14] The characterization of Cicero's protagonists is similar; but it is made by the author, who declares himself to be "impartial" and "unprejudiced" and

---

[12] First *Enquiry*, XII, III, pp. 161, 162.

[13] "Of the Rise and Progress of the Arts and Sciences," *Works*, 3:189. And see *Dialogues*, p. 127. Also, *The Letters of David Hume*, ed. J. Y. T. Greig, 2 vols. (Oxford: Clarendon Press, 1932) 1:154 (hereafter cited as *Letters*).

[14] *Dialogues*, p. 128; II, p. 150; V, p. 166.

provides evidence for this assessment by awarding the final decision to a member of an opposing school. Pamphilus, on the other hand, makes no such explicit claim that he has not come "to be anyone's ally." His decision at the end is in favor of his own teacher, and there is thus, throughout, a question about the reliability of Pamphilus's own comments on the progress of the discussion.[15]

The most flagrant example of biased recording has already been noted by Kemp Smith. After Cleanthes has used the analogies of an intelligible voice from the clouds and a world peopled by intelligible volumes, Pamphilus reports, "PHILO was a little embarrassed and confounded: But while he hesitated in delivering an answer, luckily for him, DEMEA broke in upon the discourse, and saved his countenance." Here it seems to be only Pamphilus's narration that makes us suppose that Cleanthes is winning the argument. Demea (quite correctly) points out that Cleanthes' analogies will not work. An argument of the form "A causes B, therefore X causes Y" will work only where either A and X or B and Y are known to be similar. Divine intelligence is not known to be similar to human intelligence; and "this volume of nature" is not similar to "any intelligible discourse or reasoning."[16]

There seems no reason why Philo (who is normally quicker than Demea) could not have made this point himself. The reader who misses the master-student relationship between Cleanthes and Pamphilus might well be puzzled at Pamphilus's claim that Philo is confounded. There can

---

[15] J. M. Ross's précis on the characters in *The Nature of the Gods* reveals how close a match there is between Cicero and Hume (*Nature of Gods*, p. 27). Velleius, the "dogmatic convert," corresponds to Demea with his "rigid inflexible orthodoxy." Philo's careless skepticism is an echo of Cotta, "the urbane man of the world"; and Cleanthes' accurate philosophical turn correponds to Balbus, "the warm-hearted preacher aflame with admiration for the harmony of the universe," who is also a "logical thinker who has worked out for himself a rational explanation of his beliefs."

To underline Hume's extensive use of the Ciceronian model, I would point out that there are nominal links between Philo, Cleanthes, Pamphilus, and Cicero's characters. Cotta and Cicero (the Skeptics) were taught by Philo; Balbus (the Stoic) refers to "our own Cleanthes"; Pamphilus is a student of Plato, and the Platonists are attacked as friends of the Stoics. Thus the very choice of the name "Pamphilus" indicates an alliance with Cleanthes (*Nature of Gods* 1. 17, p. 76; 1. 19, p. 77; 1. 72, p. 98; 2. 13, p. 128.)

[16] *Dialogues*, III, pp. 152-56, 65-66, 104. Because of the characterization of Demea as shortsighted and narrow-minded, it is frequently difficult to recognize that some of the most telling attacks on Cleanthes' reason-based Christianity come through his mouth (e.g., that agreement on the existence of God is "useless" without agreement on his nature, VI, p. 170). Kemp Smith's commentary on Philo's confusion underestimates Demea and merely reports that his comments redirect the discussion.

be no doubt that Philo breaks off the discussion. But that he was confounded rather than taken aback by Cleanthes' flattering (though pointed) eulogy on the powers of his imagination might well be wishful thinking on the part of Pamphilus. The relationship of Pamphilus and Cleanthes is a device that enables Hume to distance himself from the final decision and at the same time to preserve the structural balance between the two main speakers within the body of the text. Philo has superior skill in argument; but we are told that it is Cleanthes who has the "accurate philosophical turn." Philo has the last word in the majority of sections and dominates increasingly toward the end. Nevertheless, Pamphilus's judgments have led many to suppose Cleanthes the winner. In the *Dialogues* the speakers are counterbalanced, and Pamphilus helps to maintain equilibrium.

There is thus a major structural difference between Hume's *Dialogues* and *The Nature of the Gods*. In terms of balance, the latter resembles less the *Dialogues* and more Hume's four essays "The Epicurean," "The Stoic," "The Platonist," and "The Sceptic." These essays (which also clearly owe much to Cicero) are what *The Nature of the Gods* tends toward—a series of monologues. The fact that the final of these four essays is "The Sceptic" means that it is difficult not to identify Hume with the skeptic, despite the footnote he uses to dissociate himself from this position. There is a dispute as to whether or not a similar distancing footnote is used in the *Dialogues* itself.[17] Structurally, however, no such note is required to achieve dissociation. The mere fact of balanced conversation is enough to prevent an automatic equation of Hume with the skeptic.

Conversation is a distancing device; but it also has important roots in

---

[17] For the disputed footnote see *Dialogues*, XII, p. 219n. Until recently the dispute was about whether or not the note is distancing. Morrisroe, for example, claims that the words "come from the mouth of Philo," but that Hume would agree with them. James Noxon, on the other hand, claims that this is "the single occasion" in the *Dialogues* on which Hume speaks for himself, and that the footnote expresses a different order of skepticism from that of Philo. Compare Michael Morrisroe, "Linguistic Analysis as Rhetorical Pattern in David Hume," in William B. Todd, ed., *Hume and the Enlightenment: Essays Presented to Ernest Campbell Mossner* (Austin, Texas: University of Texas Press, 1974), p. 75, with James Noxon, "Hume's Agnosticism," in *Hume*, ed. V. C. Chappell (London: Macmillan, 1968), p. 379. However, a more fundamental problem has now been raised by J. V. Price, who, in his edition of the *Dialogues*, restores the footnote to the text as a part of Philo's speech on the grounds that neither the revised manuscript nor the structure of the *Dialogues* can justify a separate note (see *Dialogues concerning Natural Religion*, ed. J. V. Price [Oxford: Clarendon Press, 1976]).

Hume's conception of philosophy. In "Of Essay Writing" Hume makes a distinction between "learned" and "conversible" subjects similar to the distinction drawn between "easy" and "abstract" philosophy in the first *Enquiry*. The conversable involves an inclination to "the easier and more gentle Exercises of the Understanding, to obvious Reflections on human Affairs." Conversable subjects are too trivial to occupy the mind in solitude and "require the Company and Conversation of our Fellow-Creatures, to render them a proper Exercise for the Mind." Contrasted with these are the learned subjects, "the higher and more difficult Operations of the Mind, which require Leisure and Solitude," and hard labor. Hume claims that the separation of conversation and learning was the main drawback of the previous century. Conversation became trivial and consisted of no more than "gossiping Stories and idle Remarks." And learning suffered, too, "by being shut up in Colleges and Cells, and secluded from the World and good Company." The resulting philosophies suffered, for they were never brought to the test of experience. Hume sees experience and conversation to be closely connected; the learned philosophers "never consulted Experience" and "never search'd for that Experience, where alone it is to be found, in common Life and Conversation."

Hume sees his role as a mediator between the realms of the learned and the conversable. He describes himself as "a Kind of Resident or Ambassador from the Dominions of Learning to those of Conversation" and takes it to be his "constant Duty" to promote harmony between the two states. Accordingly, Pamphilus's justification for writing in dialogue form is also along these very lines. The study of the nature of God is "obscure" and "uncertain" and is thus best treated in "the style of dialogue and conversation." By such an approach the two "greatest and purest pleasures of human life, study and society," will be united in one work.[18] Pamphilus, like Hume, acts as an ambassador from the realms of learning to those of conversation. For Hume, and thus apparently for Pamphilus and the *Dialogues*, the dialogue form is closely connected with an empiricist concern to subject even the most abstract reasoning to the test of experience, to submit it to the test of "common Life and Conversation," where experience alone is to be found. There thus seems to be a philosophical reason for Hume's structural deviation from Cicero and his introduction of conversational interchange.

---

[18] *Dialogues*, p. 128; "Of Essay Writing," *Works*, 4:367-68.

For Hume, the dialogue form is not simply a device for hiding his own opinions. In addition to experiential testing there is a further philosophical reason for Hume's frequent use of dialogue instead of monologue to tackle the problems of natural religon.[19] If reason is so weak as to permit nothing but a mitigated skepticism, then there is a need for "counterpoising" arguments and an "indulgence for those who entertain opposite sentiments." Where nothing is certain, it is appropriate to maintain that hesitation or balance that the dogmatist so much dislikes. Accordingly, the "agreeable amusement" provided by "opposite sentiments" is precisely what Pamphilus promises the reader from the dialogue form: an amusement that will arise "even without any decision," even where the balance between counterpoising views is maintained until the very end.[20]

When Hume writes to Elliot in 1751 requesting help with strengthening Cleanthes' side of the argument, he shows clearly this concern with balance and the desire to reflect in dialogue real conversational interchange: "I have often thought, that the best way of composing a Dialogue, wou'd be for two Persons that are of different Opinions about any Question of Importance, to write alternately the different Parts of the Discourse, & reply to each other."[21] Hume suggests that his own propensity is to side with Philo but that he has tried to discipline himself against taking that side. Hume wishes that Elliot lived near so that they could act out the dialogue, Hume taking Philo's part and Elliot taking that of Cleanthes. He says that he has made Cleanthes the "hero" of the dialogue, despite his own propensities that "crept in upon me against my Will." On the subject of God and religion it appears that Hume is involved in "a perpetual Struggle of a restless Imagination against Inclination, perhaps against Reason." It seems likely that it is this struggle that makes it difficult for commentators to decide where Hume's sympathies lie in the *Dialogues*. The letters are of little help in this respect: some critics have used them to show that Hume identified with Philo, some to show that he sympathized with Cleanthes, some to show that he agreed with both or neither.[22]

---

[19] Hume lapses into dialogue form in first *Enquiry*, XI, the chapter entitled "Of a Particular Providence and of a Future State" (in 1748 it had been called, more revealingly, "Of the Practical Consequences of Natural Religion"). There is also, of course, "A Dialogue," appended to Selby-Bigge's edition of the two *Enquiries*.

[20] *Dialogues*, p. 128; first *Enquiry*, XII, III, p. 161.

[21] *Letters*, 1:154.

[22] Philo's case is argued by Kemp Smith in his introduction to *Dialogues*. Cleanthes' is put by B. M. Laing, "Hume's *Dialogues Concerning Natural Religion*," *Philosophy* 12

The problems that Hume commentators have in interpreting his letters are an interesting echo of Hume's own comments on Cicero in *The Natural History of Religion*. Hume notes that despite Cicero's presumed skepticism and irreligion, in everyday life and in letters—even in letters to his wife, whom he trusted—he appeared devoutly religious. Modern scholars would probably use such evidence to show that Cicero was not a skeptic at all. But Hume interprets this in the light of his own situation and philosophy. He still thinks of Cicero as a skeptic, but he claims that no man can ever be entirely serious in his skepticism. Hume seems to be talking about himself when he says that "men, on some occasions, might seem determined infidels, and enemies to the established religion, without being so in reality; or at least, without knowing their own minds in that particular."[23]

Hume's reason for saying this conforms with his claim in the first *Enquiry* that there is a difference in kind between the "distant" and "high" inquiries into the origin of worlds and questions about "common life" where we have "daily practice and experience" to guide us. It also fits in with Philo's division of subject matter into "subtile and refined" subjects such as theology, and experiential subjects such as speculations on trade, morals, politics, and criticism. For in the *Natural History* Hume talks about "the obscure, glimmering light" of the shadowy regions of religion and superstition where there is nothing "to equal the strong impressions, made by common sense and by experience," and where, as a consequence, both firm belief and firm disbelief are impossible.[24]

The belief that men have on religious matters is contrasted with "that solid belief and persuasion, which governs us in the common affairs of life." Men merely think that they believe in God "and disguise to themselves their real infidelity." Sustained belief is simply not possible on such subjects, for the mind of man has so "loose and unsteady a texture" that theological tenets cannot be retained "with any lasting impression." Religion does have an effect on the imagination; but the effect is "wavering and uncertain," subject to "every variety of humour" and to the caprices of the imagination.[25] Moments of impiety are concealed by

---

(1937): 175-90. And John Bricke uses three of the letters to argue that it is a mistake to identify Hume with any single character: "On the Interpretation of Hume's *Dialogues*," *Religious Studies* 2 (1975):1-18.

[23] *Nat. Hist. Rel.*, XII, *Works*, 4:348, 347.

[24] Ibid., p. 348; first *Enquiry*, XII, III, p. 162; *Dialogues*, I, p. 135.

[25] *Nat. Hist. Rel.*, XII, *Works*, 4:348, 349.

bigotry and hypocrisy. Elsewhere Hume makes it clear that his distrust of clergymen is due to their unnatural profession. They need a continuous belief in God; but this is something beyond the average human mind. As a result, Hume sees hypocrisy as the occupational disease of clergymen.[26] But just as consistent belief is not possible on such subjects, so is a consistent disbelief: "The most open impiety is attended with a secret dread and compunction." And just as hypocrisy is likely to be involved in the profession of clergymen, so, presumably, consistent and dogmatic atheism must also involve hypocrisy. Instead of certainty there is "some unaccountable operation of the mind between disbelief and conviction, but approaching much nearer to the former than to the latter."[27]

We learn from the *Treatise* that belief depends not upon reason but upon the conjunction of ideas in the imagination with the passions. However, as Hume explains in the *Natural History*, the problem is that, in the case of religion, the passions and the imagination force us in different directions. Passion inclines us to believe in God, but the imagination is unable to cope with the idea of an infinitely perfect God. And although primitive man starts off with polytheism and gods who are limited in their powers, passion (and, in particular, fear) forces man to magnify the powers of these limited gods into just that type of almighty and omnipresent God that the imagination is unable to cope with. On the question of God the imagination and passions are at war, and without the help of "daily practice and experience" no firm conclusion is possible. Whatever belief is upheld, the imagination or the passions are liable at any moment to force a recantation.[28]

---

[26] "Of National Characters," *Works*, 3:245-46n. On the unconscious and insidious nature of this hypocrisy see *The History of England*: "The religious hypocrisy, it may be remarked, is of a peculiar nature; and being generally unknown to the person himself, though more dangerous, it implies less falsehood than any other species of insincerity (8 vols. [London, 1778], vol. 7, chap. 62, "The Commonwealth: Manners and Arts" [in some early eds., chap. 63], p. 332 [hereafter cited as *History*]).

[27] *Nat. Hist. Rel.*, XII, XV, *Works*, 4:348, 362. Thus, in *History*, vol. 7, chap. 62, p. 346, Hobbes is criticized for partaking "nothing of the spirit of scepticism" and being "as positive and dogmatical as if human reason, and his reason in particular, could attain a thorough conviction" in matters of religion.

[28] For a clear statement of the conflict see *Nat. Hist. Rel.*, VIII, *Works*, 4:334-36. In this work Hume describes the type of religious belief that in the essay "Of Superstition and Enthusiasm" is given the technical name "superstition"—that which is a product of passion. Fear is the single most important passion in superstition, but (as required by his account of fear and hope as "mixed passions" that easily run into one another, in *Treatise*, II, III, IX) hope also plays an important role.

In the essay (and in *History*, vol. 7, chap. 62, pp. 332ff.) Hume does describe a

As Philo puts it in the *Dialogues*, the theist and atheist may well "insensibly change sides." Hume hints in the *Natural History* that the atheist is more likely to change sides in a theistic age than in a polytheistic age. This is not because theism is a better religion than polytheism; rather, it is because of its basis in fear. Polytheism sits "so easy and light on men's minds." It is "a true poetical religion"; the loves of the gods make men smile and the fables are "light, easy, and familiar; without devils, or seas of brimstone, or any object that could much terrify the imagination." According to Hume, polytheism is also based in fear; but not in that excess of fear that causes man to flatter and praise some particular god until he is sublimated into the all-powerful and all-perfect. In the case of theism the passions that the atheist has to fight are stronger than those in a polytheistic age. This seems to be Hume's reason for saying that "an ancient will place a stroke of impiety and one of superstition alternately, throughout a whole discourse: A modern often thinks in the same way, though he may be more guarded in his expression."[29]

Kemp Smith suggests a parallel between Hume and Cicero in their recognition that, despite the skeptic's right to criticize religion freely in his own thoughts, the skeptic still has certain duties toward the state religion to which he "is duty bound" to pay "outward deference." Noxon has already argued that Hume's vitriolic attacks on religious institutions count heavily against this interpretation of Hume. He disturbs Kemp Smith's parallel while still noting, "No doubt Cicero recognised a civic obligation to defer to the state religion." Noxon concedes more than he need to Kemp Smith. Hume admired Cicero's inconsistency not because he recognized the need to outwardly conform but

---

"contrary" type of religious belief—"enthusiasm"—that is a product of the imagination. The enthusiast sees visions, hears voices, and has "raptures, transports and surprising flights of fancy" that (because they are beyond his normal capabilities) he mistakenly ascribes to God, rather than to their real bodily causes. Hume does not detail the conflict between imagination and passion for enthusiasm. This is probably because, although fear is said to be a factor in all religious belief (even the most enthusiastic), visionary experiences are less common. Furthermore, the superstitious are led through fear to create an authoritative priesthood; but the enthusiasts have confidence in their own visions and hence have no priests to bridge the inevitable gaps in belief. Enthusiasm thus burns itself out more quickly than superstition, is less universal and less harmful.

There is nothing in the essay that contradicts the account of conflict between imagination and passion given in *Nat. Hist. Rel.* Indeed, the very fact that fear and hope are involved in enthusiasm as well as superstition is, according to the description of these passions in *Treatise*, II, III, IX, evidence that there is a conflict between imagination and passion. See both versions of the essay in *Works*, 3:144-50.

[29] *Nat. Hist. Rel.*, XII, *Works*, 4:352, 349, 349-50; *Dialogues*, XII, p. 218.

because, on matters of religion, a conflict between life, letters, and writings shows honesty and a lack of hypocrisy. On such subjects outward consistency is only a sign of inner hypocrisy. Philo's apparent inconsistency in Part XII of the *Dialogues* thus cannot be a reason for refusing to identify Hume and Philo. Inconsistency on such subjects is a consistent part of Hume's philosophy.[30]

Simply to identify Hume and Philo would, however, be an injustice to the caution and modesty of Hume's mitigated skepticism. The skeptic is skeptical about skepticism—and even skeptical about skeptics who are skeptical about skepticism. The balance between the protagonists is maintained until the very end, and Philo's admission of the inadequacy of his position means that he and Cleanthes are equal adversaries. We cannot doubt that Hume inclined more toward Philo's position than Cleanthes'; as witness to this we have the letter to Elliot and also the claim that in the "unaccountable operation of the mind between disbelief and conviction" the mind approaches disbelief more nearly than belief. But for Hume, the moderns' greater care in guarded expression and balancing speakers is not simply a matter of a stronger state religion but is a case of stronger passions at war with the imagination. Hume's own stylistic and structural deviations from Cicero's model tend toward counterpoise, balance, and concealment. This is the appropriate outward form for a work of mitigated skepticism. But it is also the appropriate outward form for a man trapped in his own epistemology—trapped in the struggle between passion and imagination, with reason too weak to determine belief.

The form and content of Hume's published writings on religion suggest that there was a real (if occasional) doubt in Hume's own mind on these matters. Skepticism is not a passive state of relaxation but a battle between opposing points of view. A total suspense of belief is not possible: this is Hume's criticism of Pyrrhonian skepticism. Neither does Hume's lifelong interest in religion suggest that he was an "acataleptic" who closes his mind to a subject once he has recognized that no certain answer is forthcoming. George Anderson, an eighteenth-century opponent of Hume, tells us that there is another sort of skeptic—men who "change sides, and become religionists, or atheists, by turns" as impelled by fear and passion.[31] All men (even believers) are, according to Hume,

---

[30] *Dialogues*, pp. 10, 41; Noxon, p. 375. Noxon, however, is among those who use Philo's inconsistency to argue against an equation of Hume with Philo (pp. 367, 380–81).

[31] Anderson distinguishes the three types of skeptic in *An Estimate of the Profit and Loss*

skeptics of this type—and this must include Hume himself. Since Hume came from a theistic culture, it would seem probable that the occasional, fleeting doubt in his mind had its base in fear. The scarcity of anecdotes or documentary evidence of religious belief in Hume suggests that he was generally successful in disciplining fear and passion. However, Hume's eighteenth-century critics were clearly wrong to seize upon anecdotal evidence of Hume's lapses into belief as a disproof of his system. The story of Hume's Italian madness of 1748, in which, "in the Paroxisms of his Disorder He often talked, with much seeming Perturbation, of the Devil, of Hell, and of Damnation," merely adds weight to Hume's claim that consistency on such subjects is not possible.[32] On matters of religion, belief and doubt are in precarious balance; it is this balance that is reflected in the very structure of the *Dialogues*.

---

of Religion, personally and publicly stated: Illustrated with Reference to "Essays on Morality and Natural Religion" (Edinburgh, 1753), pp. 64–65. Noxon treats Hume as an acataleptic who limits speculation to the subjects of "daily practice and experience" (pp. 381–82). This, however, overlooks Hume's personal inability to limit his inquiries in this way: "'Tis almost impossible for the mind of man to rest, like those of beasts, in that narrow circle of objects, which are the subject of daily conversation and action." Acatalepsy might be the ideal, but only the few—the beastlike "honest gentlemen" of England—can attain it (*A Treatise of Human Nature*, ed. L. A. Selby-Bigge [Oxford, 1888], I, IV, VII, pp. 271, 272).

[32] E. C. Mossner quotes Lord Charlemont's "Anecdotes of Hume" in *The Life of David Hume* (London: Thomas Nelson and Sons, 1953), p. 217.

Hume's Skepticism and the Dialogues

Terence Penelhum

THE QUESTON OF WHETHER HUME IS A SKEPTIC and, if he is, what sort of skeptic he is, is probably the most vexed problem of the subtle subscience of Humeneutics. I will say at the outset that I think Hume is a skeptic, but a skeptic of an aberrant kind. I shall try in what follows to indicate what I take the nature of his skepticism to be, the place that it has in his philosophical system in the *Treatise* and the first *Enquiry*, and the extent to which it leads him into inconsistencies. I shall then attempt to use the results to interpret the *Dialogues concerning Natural Religion.*

I

There are still well-informed philosophers who find it odd that anyone should even suggest that Hume is not a skeptic. To most students of philosophy the two paradigms of skepticism are the Descartes of the first *Meditation* and the Hume of the fourth and fifth sections of the first *Enquiry*. But it has come to be quite widely held that Hume's views, rightly understood, are not skeptical at all.

The former opinion is the one held by many of Hume's own contemporaries, particularly Reid and Beattie, and presented at length by T. H. Green in his introduction to the Green and Grose edition of Hume's Philosophical Works. It is taken as nearly self-evident by many students because they are confined in their studies of Hume to the first book of the *Treatise* and to Sections IV-VII of the *Enquiry concerning Human Understanding*, of which it is the most natural and obvious reading.[1] The attendant understanding of Hume represents him as the thinker who drew out the implications of Locke's "Way of Ideas" and showed how it leads inexorably to unanswerable doubts about induction, perception, and self-identity. The latter opinion of Hume is due primarily to the work of Norman Kemp Smith, who represents Hume as a *naturalist*: someone

---

[1] Hume discusses skepticism in the *Treatise*, I, IV, I and VII; in Section XII of the first *Enquiry*; in Part I of the *Dialogues*; in the essay "The Sceptic"; and in the *Letter from a Gentleman*. Some recent essays of particular interest on this theme are Wade Robison, "Hume's Scepticism," *Dialogue* 12 (1973):87-99; Nathan Brett, "Scepticism and Vain Questions," *Dialogue* 13 (1974):657-73; D. C. Stove, "Hume, the Causal Principle, and Kemp Smith," *Hume Studies* 1 (1975):1-22. The arguments in this essay are an extension of the interpretations offered in my *Hume* (London: Macmillan, 1975).

whose main objective is to reveal those forces in human nature that govern our factual beliefs, our emotions, and our moral lives, and to show the inadequacies of rationalist interpretations of them.[2] As seen in this interpretation, Hume becomes a common-sense philosopher, not a subverter of common sense; for he represents all of us, himself included, as inescapably committed by our very natures to certain beliefs and to certain emotional and evaluative responses to our physical and social environment.

The basis of a solution is surely that the Reid-Beattie interpretation and the Kemp Smith interpretation are not incompatible. If Hume's objective is to reveal the sources of our beliefs and evaluations in human nature, it is a perfectly proper part of such an inquiry to argue that these beliefs and evaluations do not result from our having discovered good reasons for them, and are unaffected by the subsequent revelation that no good reasons for them exist. Such a conclusion would imply that one should seek their causes elsewhere. Conversely, if Hume decides that our most basic beliefs concerning matters of fact are beliefs for which there are no good reasons, it is perfectly consistent with this to go on to ask what it is about us that makes us hold them nevertheless, and whether it is possible for us to suspend them or abandon them. I would suggest, then, that Hume is both a skeptic and a naturalist: that he does say that our basic beliefs about matters of fact are devoid of rational justification, that he offers us detailed accounts of how we come to hold them and why we cannot abandon them, and that these accounts are applications of a general understanding of human nature that is applied elsewhere to our emotional lives and to our moral and social evaluations. It is an integral part of such a position that this general understanding of human nature represents us as creatures of passion, not of reason; but since Hume says this over and over, there is surely no obstacle in the way of using this as the connecting link between the negative and the positive parts of his system. Hume's skepticism is not something incompatible with his naturalism. It is an integral part of it.

This position implies two propositions that I think are true but cannot argue here. The first is that Hume does indeed say that induction has no rational grounds, that our belief in distinct and continued existence cannot be given rational justification, and that our ascription of identity

---

[2] See his essays, "The Naturalism of Hume," *Mind*, n.s. 54 (1905): 147-73; 335-47; and *The Philosophy of David Hume* (London: Macmillan, 1941).

to ourselves is without foundation. The second proposition that my position implies is that Hume's primary aims are psychological rather than philosophical: that his complex and exciting arguments about the rationality of our beliefs are propaedeutic to a psychological examination of the sources of the cognitive and affective commitments our natures cause us to make. This does not imply that Hume *confuses* psychological and philosophical considerations with one another. On the contrary, his objectives cannot be stated without distinguishing them carefully; and he seems to me to be the first major philosopher to make the distinction between them. To argue that he confuses them on other than some individual occasions is to miss the whole point of what he is doing. Hume's naturalism is a combination or mixture of philosophy and psychology, with the latter predominating. The skepticism is the main thrust of the epistemological part of the philosophical propaedeutic to his psychological account of the sources of our cognitive commitments. Its purpose is to show us that it is not because we have good epistemological reasons to do so that we make these commitments, since ordinary men do not have such reasons, and philosophers have been unable to invent any.

II

So far I have been arguing that Hume's skepticism is closely integrated with his naturalism, but I have not said much about the nature of either. I now must do this, for one of Hume's best-informed interpreters, Richard Popkin, has identified them.[3] He reminds us that one of Hume's overt concerns is to define the relationship between his own skepticism and that of the Pyrrhonians; and he argues that Hume, partly through misinterpretation, arrives at a position that is in fact merely a consistent version of theirs. While I find this illuminating, I do not think it is quite right.

The major source for our understanding of ancient skepticism is the work of Sextus Empiricus, particularly his *Outlines of Pyrrhonism*. There is clear evidence that Hume was acquainted with Sextus. In spite of the title of his work, Sextus wrote about five hundred years after Pyrrho, and between them the Skeptical school had gone through more than one major cycle of change. In spite of these changes, the basic intent of

---

[3] "David Hume: His Pyrrhonism and his Critique of Pyrrhonism," *Philosophical Quarterly* 1 (1951), reprinted in *Hume*, ed. V. C. Chappell (New York: Anchor Books, 1966), pp. 53–98.

skepticism in the ancient world has to be seen as the same as that of the contemporary ethical schools of Epicureanism and Stoicism: that of cultivating an appropriate moral attitude in the face of a world in which happiness could no longer be identified with some objective that depended in any way upon external, social circumstance. Pyrrho's contribution was to urge the cultivation of noncommitment, or suspense of judgment, in the face of both the conflicting theoretical claims of competing schools of thought and the conflicting moral and religious claims of competing societies or creeds. This suspense of judgment would lead to unperturbedness, or *ataraxia*. Since this is the antithesis of the turmoil of the passions, the term *apatheia*, or absence of passion, appears to be more or less equivalent to it and is also used. When we come to the statement of the end of skepticism in Sextus, the objective is qualified significantly: "We assert still that the Sceptic's End is quietude in respect of matters of opinion and moderate feeling in respect of things unavoidable."[4] He explains the meaning of "things unavoidable" by saying that even the skeptic is sometimes cold or thirsty and cannot avoid being affected by such discomforts. But he is able to be less disturbed by them than his fellows because he makes no judgment about whether or not they are "evil by nature." This seems to mean that the skeptic cannot avoid committing himself on how things feel or seem to him, but he can avoid committing himself on how they really are. His commitment will therefore be to the moment, not to some dogma that attempts to judge the moment *sub specie aeternitatis*. Sextus recognizes (whether Pyrrho did or not) that nature gives us both sensations and intellectual responses to them, and that if the skeptic, like the Stoic, was to offer his way of life as living according to nature, then some assent to sensation would have to be allowed for—because the skeptic, unlike the Stoic, could not judge what nature required in terms of some cosmic metaphysic. The skeptic also has to recognize practical necessities and to participate in the daily affairs of society. Sextus sums up the life of the Skeptic as follows:

> Adhering, then, to appearances we live in accordance with the normal rules of life, undogmatically, seeing that we cannot remain wholly inactive. And it would seem that this regulation of life is fourfold, and that one part of it lies in the guidance of Nature, another in the constraint of the passions, another in the tradition of laws and customs, another in the instruction of the arts. Nature's

---

[4] *Outlines of Pyrrhonism*, trans. R. G. Bury (London: William Heinemann, 1967), p. 19.

guidance is that by which we are naturally capable of sensation and thought; constraint of the passions is that whereby hunger drives us to food and thirst to drink; tradition of customs and laws, that whereby we regard piety in the conduct of life as good, but impiety as evil; instruction of the arts, that whereby we are not inactive in such arts as we adopt. But we make all these statements undogmatically.[5]

This means, I think, that the skeptic as Sextus describes him accepts that he has to act, has to respond in some way or other to his sensations, and has to conform, or not to conform, to customs. In such a situation he will respond to his sensations with the natural or easy assent to which he, like all other men, is inclined, and he will conform to those customs and values he finds prevalent around him. But this will not be because he thinks, as other men do, that his sensations are appearances that reveal realities, or that the customs and values of his fellows embody moral truths. Nor does he think they do not: he suspends judgment either way. But since he suspends judgment either way, there is nothing to stop him from conforming in the easiest and most comfortable way possible. What is essential here is that the conformity, even if it does represent a change from the ascetic withdrawal that has sometimes been ascribed to Pyrrho himself, does not represent a departure from the basic thesis that quietude comes from suspense of judgment. It seems to me to depend upon it as much as ever; for only in the absence of judgment can one be confined to one's affections by the immediate exigencies of the moment.

To return to Hume: Popkin suggests that Hume misinterprets classical Pyrrhonism and that the position he himself adopts, though not identical with Pyrrhonism, is in fact a more consistent version of it than the one Sextus presents to us; and he says that his Humean skepticism is identical with what Kemp Smith calls naturalism.

Hume does indeed seem to misinterpret Pyrrhonism — if we take this to be the views of Sextus. At least he ignores the practical accommodations Sextus allows the skeptic, and the natural assent to appearances. But I do not see this as a fundamental misunderstanding. For Sextus's position still requires an inner suspense of judgment about the conformity of appearances to reality, and it is precisely this that Hume says we are not at liberty to exercise. "Nature, by an absolute and uncontrollable necessity has determin'd us to judge as well as to breathe and feel."[6] He does

---
[5] Ibid., p. 17.
[6] *A Treatise of Human Nature*, ed. L. A. Selby-Bigge (Oxford, 1888), I, IV, I, p. 183 (hereafter cited as *Treatise*).

not say that the Pyrrhonists' *arguments* are unsound; he even adds some of his own. But he insists that the suspense of judgment they recommend is beyond us. We cannot even say, with Sextus, "Yes, I realize that there is no good reason to suppose that my sensations are veridical, but I will do what comes naturally and act as though they are." Neither the plain man nor the philosopher can refrain from believing that they *are* veridical. We cannot make our assertions *un*dogmatically.

So I think that the form of skepticism Hume *does* adopt, though it is very close indeed to what Popkin finds in Hume, is more at variance than Popkin thinks it is with the views of Sextus. The Humean skeptic, according to Popkin, recognizes the psychological impotence of Pyrrhonian arguments and dogmatizes where it is natural to do so, in full recognition of his dogmatism and of the groundlessness of it. He also accepts that nature does, for some of us, encourage doubts and uncertainties at least for short periods, so that one is still following nature if one engages in the attendant suspense of judgment if one can. So the Humean skeptic is hesitant and dogmatic by turns, as nature encourages him. Such a thinker is bound to oscillate between a more suspenseful mood while he is doing philosophy, and a more dogmatic mood when playing backgammon. But he will follow nature more consistently than the classical Pyrrhonian, who will be trying to suspend judgment in the most unnatural way, both in his study and out of it. That way is not the way to *ataraxia*, but to madness.

This sort of skeptic, alternating from nature between suspense and dogmatism, is indeed the Hume of the seventh, and concluding, section of Book I of the *Treatise*: the Hume who is openly and endearingly, and I think unironically, torn between skeptical doubt and common-sense dogma. But there is one respect in which Popkin is superficial. He says that the classical Pyrrhonian will not achieve *ataraxia* by suspending judgment, because the attempt to suspend judgment constantly is unnatural. This may be so; but it does not seem to me to be this that Hume sees as the undesirable feature of skeptical doubt. He regards it as independently disturbing, even when it is the result of the indulgence of a natural inclination to philosophize. That sort of inclination *is* natural, but it is also hazardous. There is evidence that Hume did find philosophical perplexity conducive to exhaustion and melancholia. He says this, more or less, in the *Treatise*:

> But what have I here said, that reflections very refin'd and metaphysical have little or no influence upon us? This opinion I can scarce

forbear retracting, and condemning from my present feeling and experience. The *intense* view of these manifold contradictions and imperfections in human reason has so wrought upon me, and heated my brain, that I am ready to reject all belief and reasoning, and can look upon no opinion even as more probable or likely than another. Where am I, or what? From what causes do I derive my existence, and to what condition shall I return? Whose favour shall I court, and whose anger must I dread? What beings surround me? and on whom have I any influence, or who have any influence on me? I am confounded with all these questions, and begin to fancy myself in the most deplorable condition imaginable, environ'd with the deepest darkness, and utterly depriv'd of the use of every member and faculty.[7]

Consequently, I think that it is not the unnaturalness of skeptical doubts but their capacity to produce anxiety that makes Hume say the wise skeptic will keep them in their place. In the *Treatise* this seems mostly to amount to a decision to indulge in philosophy only when so inclined, and to escape from its tribulations into social life when they become too much. But this recognition of the hazardousness of philosophy leads him in the first *Enquiry* to a more formal attempt to limit skepticism, by limiting the subject matter of philosophical reflection as well as the psychological occasion of it. I refer, of course, to the introduction there of the concept of *mitigated skepticism*, which Hume recommends to us as a mode of thought whose virtues can be made obvious to us if we have learned humility about the powers of our reason from indulgence in the Pyrrhonian variety. I do not agree with Popkin that this later version of skepticism is the same as the earlier.[8]

Hume characterizes mitigated skepticism in three ways. First, it embodies a humility about the powers of reason, which may be a fruit of the study of Pyrrhonian arguments against it. Second, it "confines itself to common life," and its decisions are "nothing but the reflections of common life, methodized and corrected." The only argument he offers for this restriction is this one: "While we cannot give a satisfactory reason, why we believe, after a thousand experiments, that a stone will fall, or fire burn; can we ever satisfy ourselves concerning any determination, which we may form, with regard to the origin of worlds, and the situation of nature, from, and to eternity?"[9] Finally, he deduces from

---

[7] Ibid., VII, pp. 268–69.
[8] "Hume: His Pyrrhonism," p. 96.
[9] *An Enquiry concerning Human Understanding*, ed. L. A. Selby-Bigge, 2nd ed. (Oxford, 1902), XII, III, p. 162 (hereafter cited as first *Enquiry*).

this restriction that the skeptic will confine himself to "abstract reasoning concerning quantity or number" and "experimental reasoning concerning matter of fact and existence." This counsel of humility leads him to his final famous peroration about committing writings that are more ambitious than this to the flames.

I will try at this point to summarize what I take to be Hume's overall position with regard to skepticism. (1) He agrees with the Pyrrhonians that the beliefs of common life and the constructions of divinity and school metaphysics are devoid of rational justification. (2) He disagrees with the Pyrrhonian skeptics in their recommendation that the philosopher should in consequence withhold assent from the beliefs of common life and the constructions of divinity and school metaphysics alike. He has at least three reasons for saying this. (a) It is psychologically impossible for us *not* to assent to the beliefs of common life. (b) The skeptical attacks on these beliefs, though admitting of no answer, also produce no conviction: so not only is the assent to those beliefs something we are unable initially to withhold; it is also something that cannot subsequently be withdrawn. (c) Even if the assent could be withheld or withdrawn, to do so would produce not the inner calm and unperturbedness the Pyrrhonian pursues but the very anxiety he is seeking to avoid. In this respect, the questioning of the skeptic is in the same position as the constructions of the theologian and the metaphysician. Consequently, one is as hazardous to our peace of mind as the other. (3) The result of this is a recommendation to indulge our propensity to philosophical thought, if we personally have such a propensity, to the minimum. This recommendation takes different forms. (a) In the *Treatise* it amounts to a recommendation to indulge in philosophical speculation only on those occasions when we are minded to do so, and even then to treat it as a pastime in which nature has disposed us to participate. Its hazards are to be dealt with by making sure that we also participate actively in those social pursuits that will distract us from the rarefied doubts and wonders that beset us in our studies. What he says here has to be connected with his moral diatribes against the "monkish virtues" of the ascetic: the ascetic wantonly cuts himself off from those activities that are nature's cure for the mental distempers into which philosophy can lead us if we take it too seriously. (b) In the *Enquiry* this on-again-off-again policy is replaced by the positivist recommendations of mitigated skepticism: instead of trying to contain philosophy by rationing the amount of time we spend on it, we should contain it by confining its subject matter, so that it is critical and descriptive, not revisionary or speculative. Philosophy, thus understood, would become the journeyman study of those processes of reasoning we must use in common life and in science, where we presuppose and do not question the regularity of nature, the reality of the external world, and the identity of the self, and do not attempt to get above ourselves by treating of God, freedom, and immortality. Examples of this sort of activity would be his own comments on how we should estimate probabilities or judge of causes and effects.

III

The most obvious criticism of what Hume says concerns the consistency of mitigated skepticism. How can he recommend that we confine ourselves to the reflections of common life, when their presuppositions are as incapable of rational justification as the pretensions of metaphysics? Surely Hume should either indulge both or reject both? How can skepticism consistently *be* mitigated?[10]

I think Hume's answer is as follows. Although it is true that the natural beliefs of common sense and the speculative constructions of metaphysics and religion are alike devoid of rational justification; and although it is also true that human nature admits within it forces that make it natural, in some manner or other, to engage in both; the forces that impel us to adopt the beliefs of common life are found in all men, whereas those that lead us into metaphysics or into religion are found only in *some* men. Metaphysics is a relative rarity, indulged in only by philosophers. Religion is not a rarity in the same way, but the forces that produce it are *pathological* forces, such as the superstitious fear of the unknown, and fortunate men in civilized communities can be free from them. So the real reason for restricting philosophical thought to the affairs of common life is that our pursuit of those affairs is the result of beliefs that none of us can avoid having, whereas the fancies of the metaphysician and the theologian can be avoided with a bit of luck and judgment.

Offering this as Hume's answer is somewhat speculative. I do not mean by this that there is any lack of clear evidence that Hume regards the urges to metaphysics or religion as less than universal. He frequently indicates that our common beliefs owe nothing of their origin to the

---

[10] The best expression of this criticism is in G. E. Moore, "Hume's Philosophy," in his *Philosophical Studies* (London: Kegan Paul, 1922).

metaphysician. In the concluding passages of Book I of the *Treatise* he speaks somewhat enviously of those honest gentlemen who "in *England*, in particular . . . have carried their thoughts very little beyond those objects, which are every day expos'd to their senses."[11] The whole burden of the *Natural History of Religion* is to reveal the special psychopathology of religion as something we should evade if we can. What makes it speculative to offer this as Hume's answer to the common criticism that he has no grounds on which to distinguish the methodizing of natural beliefs on the one hand and the construction of metaphysical and theological systems on the other is that he does not explicitly offer this as his reason for recommending mitigated skepticism to us. On the contrary, the reason he gives is the strange one I have already quoted — that if we cannot give rational grounds for believing that a stone will fall, or fire burn, we cannot claim to settle problems about the origin or future of the world and ought therefore to have learned caution from our failure to justify our natural beliefs. Now this is an odd argument. Why should the failure to produce good reasons for thinking that fire burns teach us to be cautious? Since it shows us that we must inevitably ignore the absence of evidence and jump to conclusions without it, surely it should teach us that we have no sensible choice but to throw caution to the winds? But the moral looks different if we take into account what I have argued Hume believes about our psychological capacities. For the unjustifiability of our natural beliefs *can* teach us caution if it makes us see that we are so prone to believe unjustified propositions that we ought always to avoid intellectual commitments *where we can*. And nature does permit us to avoid them in the case of metaphysics or religion, by allowing us to be incurious or to suppress the curiosity we have. The evidence for our having the capacity to do this is that some men manage it.

If this is the right interpretation of what mitigated skepticism teaches us, then it is clearly not the same as the view Popkin finds, correctly, in the *Treatise*, where the wise philosopher philosophizes from time to time because it comes naturally to him to do so. Instead of saying, as he does there, that the best way to peace of mind is for those who like doing that sort of thing to do it, and the rest not, we now find Hume saying that everyone, however minded to philosophize, should keep to the "proper subjects of science and enquiry." The difficulty is that even though some men are incurious about metaphysics and are free of superstitious anxiety, it might still be impossible for *other* men, such as you or I or Hume,

---

[11] *Treatise*, I, IV, VII, p. 272.

to avoid wondering about the origin of the world or the immortality of the soul. Even though some commitments may be universal and some not, it might still be that those who are committed to the latter are as unable to avoid their commitment as they are to avoid the commitments that everybody else makes. Our inabilities may just vary; and the cautious advice of the mitigated skeptic may be advice that can be taken only by those who do not need it.

So the mitigated skepticism of the *Enquiry* accords less well with Hume's philosophical psychology than the quasi-Pyrrhonism of the *Treatise*, however much Hume the positivist and secularizer may wish to resort to it.[12] I shall suggest shortly that Hume modifies it in the *Dialogues*. For the moment, however, I must return to the position of the *Treatise*.

IV

I have so far suggested that Hume rejects the recommendations of classical Pyrrhonism for three reasons. (1) He does not think we are able to withhold assent from the beliefs of common life. (2) He does not think that anything Pyrrhonists may say can enable us to *withdraw* assent from these beliefs once we have acquired them. (3) Suspense of judgment leads not to peace of mind but rather to anxiety.

I have little to say about the third of these propositions. It seems to me that the effect of philosophical perplexity upon human nature is unlikely to be uniform, and that Hume may be right about its effect on some people and wrong about its effect on others. But for his opinion to be based on experience (as I have suggested it is), and for it to form the basis of a recommendation that we indulge ourselves in philosophy in modest doses, it is obviously necessary to modify the doctrine that we cannot withdraw our assent to the beliefs of common life. If we could not do it at all, we obviously could not be distressed by doing it, or be urged to do it only in moderation. What Hume has to say, and does say, is that those who can be afflicted by philosophical doubts can be spared their distressing consequences because these doubts are only short-lived and cannot survive the transition from the study to the world outside.[13]

---

[12] This is not to deny, of course, that Hume the positivist and secularizer is to be found in the *Treatise*!

[13] For example, see first *Enquiry*, XII, II, p. 160: "All human life must perish, were his principles *universally and steadily to prevail*" (my italics). The strongest statement of the

I turn now to the other two contentions. Hume has a moderately complex argument, I think, in support of the claim that we cannot *not* assent to the beliefs of common life.[14] I suggest that it goes as follows. There are no good reasons in favor of the beliefs of common life. Hence we do not hold those beliefs because we have such reasons. The only reasons that have been offered are all bad ones; they are known only to the philosophers who have invented them; and the philosophers themselves have held the beliefs they have attempted to justify before inventing their reasons. Hence not only is our assent to our natural beliefs not dependent on our having good reasons for them; it also is not dependent on our having bad reasons for them that we think are good. Therefore, we hold these beliefs not for reasons at all, but only because of *causes*, such as laziness, custom, or habit.

I think this argument is unsuccessful.[15] Hume is clearly right in insisting that philosophical arguments have no share in the genesis of our natural beliefs, but he does not succeed in showing that *reason* has no role in their genesis. Even if we agree that we have no good reasons for them, it might still very well be the case that we *thought* we had good reasons. To prove that to be untrue Hume would have to show, as he realizes, that the only reasons that have ever been thought of are those that the philosophers have thought of. But this is very implausible, even on Hume's own accounts of the origins of our beliefs. What Hume calls custom or habit is manifested in our inferences from the past to the future: right or wrong, surely our doing this is something that we *think* to be rational? Our belief in the distinct and continued existence of our perceptions may be due, as he says, to the constancy they show and the fact that assuming their continuance makes it easier to anticipate them: but right or wrong, surely we *think* this basis is rational? And our belief in personal identity may be due to our confusing successions of related perceptions with continuous unchanging ones, but surely the ascription of identity in such circumstances is *thought* to be rational when we make it?

Hume's argument in support of the claim that our assent to the beliefs of common life cannot be *withdrawn* is, I think, this. The Pyrrhonian skeptic shows us quite successfully that there are no good reasons in favor

---

view that skepticism is only skin deep is to be found in the (admittedly suspect) *Letter from a Gentleman*, where it is dismissed as a "jeu d'esprit."

[14] I am here extrapolating from many places, but especially from *Treatise*, I, IV, II.

[15] I am indebted here to some comments by Mr. Gary Colwell.

of these beliefs. But since these beliefs are not there because we have ever thought there are such reasons, we are naturally unaffected by the revelation that no such reasons exist. The Pyrrhonian's arguments are unanswerable, but they are also impotent, or "vain."

I think this, also, is a bad argument. Even if it were true that my beliefs are not due to my thinking they have good reasons, it by no means follows that when I am shown that they have no good reasons, they will remain unaffected. The discovery of their lack of epistemic respectability may nullify all the causes that have produced them. There is, in any case, some clear evidence that the encounter with Pyrrhonian arguments does at least have some shock value: even if we are no more rational than Hume says we are, we at least mildly aspire to be. Hume's recognition of this fact appears in his qualification, already noted, of the doctrine that skeptical doubts are ineffectual. He says instead that they produce only a "momentary amazement and confusion" and that involvement in daily affairs destroys their effects.[16]

V

I shall now try to explore the question of how correct Hume is in his negative estimate of the *efficacy* of Pyrrhonian doubts. Is he right to hold that they cannot cause us to withdraw our natural assent once it is given?

We must first put aside a number of irrelevant arguments. They all come from common, and reasonable, philosophical responses to the Pyrrhonian arguments as Hume himself presents them.

(1) There is, first of all, the common-sense response that comes from Reid and Moore. This consists of saying that because our common beliefs are true, and indeed because we *know* that they are true, the Pyrrhonian arguments Hume considers to reveal their lack of rational bases must be defective. For present purposes such arguments can all be admitted; yet they get us nowhere. For all they would show us is that the Pyrrhonian is engaged in producing arguments to undermine the status of propositions that he and we know quite well to be true. But this would not show, at all, that he and we could not be made doubtful about these propositions by these arguments. For we can be doubtful about things that we know perfectly well — even while saying too loudly, along with Moore, that we know that we know them. It is very likely, as Hume sees, that we may in

---

[16] First *Enquiry*, XII, II, p. 160.

such circumstances oscillate between two inconsistent attitudes—so that sometimes we really are quite doubtful and other times really are quite free of doubt. I defer for the moment the question of whether or not someone who oscillates like this can be said to know, or to believe, the propositions he oscillates in attitude toward, all the time. My point for the moment is the simple one that all that the arguments and asseverations of a Moore can do is prove that our doubts must be *mistaken*. This in no way shows that the doubt is *unreal*.

(2) Next, there are arguments deriving from Kant and Wittgenstein, which are designed to show that the doubts of the Pyrrhonian are *incoherent*. I shall follow a common practice and call these transcendental arguments, though I am not very clear what this title means. These arguments are supposed to show that there is something inescapably wrong with the Pyrrhonian's difficulties. They usually proceed by trying to persuade us that someone who worries about whether or not there is any good reason to assume that his sensory experiences correspond to realities implies, or presupposes, in posing his question, the ability to distinguish between mere sensations on the one hand and real things on the other; or that someone who wonders whether or not he is the same person that he was last week can wonder about this only if he is the same person and could not wonder about this if he were not. I find these arguments very difficult to assess. But I am willing to accept that they show what they are supposed to show. It just seems to me, once more, to be irrelevant to the questions of the efficacy of the Pyrrhonian skeptic's doubts. For this does not depend psychologically upon the coherence of the skeptic's reasons. If a transcendental argument succeeds, it presumably shows that the Pyrrhonian's doubts cannot be coherently argued for, or even expressed, unless the propositions he doubts are in fact true, *or* unless he is in some manner committed to them, *or* unless he already knows them. I am even willing to agree that if a Pyrrhonian were to concede that some such argument is successful, he would, in some cases at least, cease to doubt the things he doubts now. But none of this shows that before the incoherence is revealed (and if we need a transcendental argument to reveal it, it will not be obvious) we cannot genuinely doubt the propositions that the Pyrrhonian questions.

(3) Finally, very briefly, it has sometimes been argued that the doubts of the Pyrrhonian are really pseudodoubts for a linguistic reason. This reason is that when the propositions that the Pyrrhonian questions are subjected to philosophical analysis, they can be shown to be reducible to

propositions of an order that the Pyrrhonian has exempted from his questions. For example, it has been argued that the assertions about physical objects or persons that the Pyrrhonian says he is doubtful about can be translated into, and therefore are equivalent in meaning to, statements or sets of statements about sensory experiences to which the Pyrrhonian can assent. I think this sort of argument, even if it is successful, is also irrelevant to the question of the efficacy of the doubts the Pyrrhonian has. For it is quite possible for someone to be certain and doubtful about two propositions that are identical or logically equivalent, at least if he does not realize that they are. No doubt this will lead to inconsistencies in his actions and responses; but these can exist, and are in the circumstances quite intelligible.

VI

Having put these arguments aside, I return to the question of the efficacy, the psychological reality, of the doubts of the Pyrrhonian. Hume says that at best these doubts are very short-lived and are dispelled at once by the exigencies of common life.

We can all agree that in some sense it is true that philosophical doubts are much easier to sustain in the study than in the marketplace. The question is what this *shows*. To start with, it does not show that the doubts are not real ones while I nurse them in the study—unless one insists, questionbeggingly, that a doubt that is dispelled by a departure from the study is not a real doubt solely because of this. But let us make a minimal concession: let us admit that a real doubt has to affect our subsequent attitudes to some extent. The question is to what extent and in what ways. I would submit that a doubt that is conceived and nurtured in the study and then persists outside it, even in the form of an occasional question or hesitation, is still a real one, though a psychologically weak one—especially if a return to the study revives it readily.

Let us make a comparison with positive religious commitments, which I may regularly nourish in the church or the closet, and which may pale as I encounter the day-to-day demands of the secular world. Here I would suggest that the fact that I come to have my religious attitudes weakened, and come to have my doubts freshened, by these circumstances does not show that I did not really believe what I said to myself in the closet or in the church. I see no significant difference in the case of Pyrrhonian doubt. If I convince myself that it is doubtful that there are any real material objects while I am in the study and then find it difficult to feel doubtful for long about this while I am in the marketplace, the diminution of my hesitancies does not show that my doubts were unreal before I got there.

We can now add to *this*. Just as someone who has faith can, as a matter of personal policy, try deliberately to contend with the doubts that may flood in upon him when he leaves the closet or the church for the hurly-burly of the secular world, and can try to deepen and strengthen the attitudes that are the expressions of the convictions he has in faith, so one could (could one not?) deliberately sustain the doubts that one has argued oneself into in the study when one leaves the study for the backgammon table and the affairs of common life. Just as one can fight off doubts, so one could (could one not?) try to fend off convictions. After all, all one would need for a motive would be the reflection (true or false) that the best place to arrive at a knowledge of reality is in the calm and detached situation of the study, where one is capable of objectivity and able to apportion the impact of one's experiences to their epistemological status; or one might be swayed by the reflection (true or false) that the more involved in affairs one is, the more one is disturbed by them emotionally and intellectually. Reflections of this sort would be enough to supply one with a motive for not yielding to the blandishments of what other, less discriminating people call realities. After all, they do not have the benefit of reflection and study the way the philosopher does.

So far, then, I would suggest that the doubts the Pyrrhonian nourishes in the study need only a very limited persistence outside it to be classified as psychologically genuine; but they can in any case be sustained in the face of the impact of common affairs as a matter of deliberate policy, in the way in which someone who has a commitment of faith can sustain it in the face of those features of human life that serve to weaken the attitudes that faith generates, and to create doubts. I would now draw the conclusion that for as long as the skeptic is trying, with some success, to sustain his doubts in the face of the blandishments of common affairs, his situation is not the one that Hume suggests, in which he oscillates from skepticism to dogmatism between the study and the marketplace, but is one in which he remains doubtful, in a quite real sense, all along — one in which the common convictions are to some real degree fended off by the repetition of philosophical reflections. If this is true, then the skeptic's situation is the one that Sextus recommends to us, and that Hume seems to consider to be impossible, namely, one in which we suspend judgment on the very practices and commitments that other men make dogmatically, and with which we fall in on the surface.

This will no doubt immediately raise an objection: surely the so-called skeptic is really abandoning his suspense and hesitation altogether the first time he avoids an obstacle or sits on a chair or answers to his name in a roll call. For such actions would be things he would be *no more inclined to do than not* if he really had the doubts that he professes to have. Just to get into common affairs and to function within them is to abandon these hesitations. This objection is mistaken; and the mistake is one that Hume makes, but Sextus does not. Remember again that the question before us is not the overall consistency of the skeptic's opinions, but the reality of his doubts. For his doubts to be real, all that is necessary is for him to make the ordinary day-to-day responses to his situation without interpreting these responses in the common-sense manner. When it indeed appears to him that there is a bus approaching and that he is in its path, his response will be the same as everyone else's, but he will interpret it as one in which he controls the sequence of sensory experiences that he has, rather than as one in which he has stepped out of the way of a bus. For his doubts to be real, it is not necessary that the attempt to express what he thinks he is about be successfully made without confusions or inconsistencies. Nor is it in the least bit necessary, for his doubts to be real, that we, in talking about him, manage to describe what he is up to without committing ourselves to the reality of the external world, the rationality of induction, and the rest. All that is necessary is that the confusions he may be involved in, or the commitments we may have to make, are less than obvious *to him*.[17]

So Hume's denial of the reality of the skeptic's doubts is too hasty. It does seem possible for the doubts to persist, as a result of deliberate effort and reflection, into the affairs of common life, so that we are able to sustain the uninvolved participation in human affairs that Sextus recommends and that Hume says is beyond us. He may be right in suggesting that doubt and hesitation are worrisome and not liberating. But that would merely show that we would be imprudent to foster them. It would not show that he could avoid the worries by taking refuge in the supposed inability of human beings to sustain the doubts that lead to them.

---

[17] This objection is close, of course, to that dismissed in Section V.

VII

I turn now to the *Dialogues concerning Natural Religion*. It is my purpose here not to try to resolve all the calculated ambiguities of that work but merely to suggest that an understanding of the skeptical strain in Hume will assist us in resolving them. I must state at the outset that I agree with those scholars, from Kemp Smith on, who identify Hume with Philo. I do not agree, however, that such an identification makes the import of the *Dialogues* clear. He appears to change his position in Part XII in certain fundamental respects, and any interpretation of the *Dialogues* must either show that this change is only apparent and not real, or do something to explain it. My own view is that it is real enough and represents one more attempt on the part of Hume, as a skeptic, to assess the psychological weight of his own negative arguments. I shall try to make a case for this and estimate the success with which Hume has done it.

I can say nothing here about the detailed arguments of Parts II to XI. I follow most contemporary readers in thinking that in these arguments Philo demolishes the empirical or experimental theism that Cleanthes represents. He shows, in other words, that if one uses the evidential canons to which Cleanthes insists on appealing, there is no good reason to accept the theistic conclusions that Cleanthes finds so obvious. I will concentrate instead on Part I, which none of us seems to read, and on Part XII, which none of us seems to understand.

Philo comes on the scene in Part I agreeing with Demea about the "weakness, blindness, and narrow limits of human reason." He adds a skeptical turn of his own: since reason is prone to "uncertainty and needless contrarieties, even in subjects of common life and practice," it is clearly unable to decide "the origin of worlds." Cleanthes takes him to task for the implied suggestion that religious faith should be founded on philosophical skepticism and says that no philosophical skeptic can be in earnest. Pyrrhonians, he says, are like Stoics in assuming that "what a man can perform sometimes, and in some dispostions, he can perform always, and in every disposition." In making this criticism of Pyrrhonism Cleanthes is only repeating what Hume himself has said about it in the *Enquiry*. Unsurprisingly, if Philo is Hume, Philo agrees: the skeptic must engage in common life like other men, and if he should pursue his philosophical inquiries beyond the necessities of common life, this indulgence is excusable because it is based upon our universal urge to generality and principle. "What we call *philosophy* is nothing but a more regular and methodical operation of the same kind." But "when we carry our speculation into the two eternities . . . we have here got quite beyond the reach of our faculties." To depart from the topics of common life is to abandon the correctives that restrain the doubts of the skeptic; these doubts become at least as legitimate as the dogmatist's speculations once these correctives are removed.[18]

Thus far Philo is an exponent of the mitigated skepticism of the *Enquiry* who dissociates himself from Pyrrhonism and holds that philosophy should confine itself to the concerns of common life. He now has to face an obvious criticism from Cleanthes that such a restriction ought to restrain him from scientific inquiry as well as from metaphysics, since the plain man is as baffled by Newton as he is by Plato. He does not answer this immediately. The reason is obvious enough: the answer is to be found in the detailed arguments of Parts II to XI. These arguments show that the procedures of scientific inquiry cannot yield theological results, and that it is only scientific enquiry, not natural theology, that proceeds by methodizing and correcting the reflections of common life. What he does do immediately is comment on some historical remarks that Cleanthes has just made. Cleanthes has said that before the time of Locke, Christian apologists regarded reason as the enemy of faith and consequently were prone to find allies, however dubious, among the Pyrrhonists. Since Locke, however, skeptics have been assumed to be atheists, and faith has been held to be "nothing but a species of *reason*."[19] Cleanthes himself is patently a follower of Locke. Philo's comment is that "the priests" will always seek to consolidate the faith by any means that lies to hand, and that in recent ages they could no longer depend on "education" (indoctrination) to establish it; hence they now see reason not as a presumptuous enemy as before but as the only "principle to lead us into religion." I shall return to this passage shortly, but it does carry one obvious implication: if Philo can succeed, as he later does, in showing that Cleanthes is mistaken in believing reason to be the ally of priestly religion, then Locke's predecessors will have been right to think its natural ally to be skepticism.

Part XII opens after Demea's departure, with Philo retreating, at least nominally, from the "careless" skepticism of the previous ten parts.

---

[18] *Dialogues concerning Natural Religion*, ed. Norman Kemp Smith (Indianapolis: Bobbs-Merrill, 1947), 1, pp. 131-35 (hereafter cited as *Dialogues*).
[19] Ibid., p. 138.

Throughout Part XII he repeatedly asserts his acceptance of "a purpose, an intention, or design" and his "veneration for true religion." There is no denying that this is at least verbally inconsistent with the negativity of everything that he has said since Part I. Kemp Smith labors very hard to show that the inconsistencies can be dissolved and that Philo does not mean a word of it.[20] I think Nelson Pike has succeeded in showing that this line of argument is not wholly successful,[21] and I have tried elsewhere to steer a middle course between their interpretations.[22] I confine myself here to considerations that bear on the major theme of this paper.

Undoubtedly, Philo's protestations are expressed in language of carefully contrived ambiguity. Purpose and design strike everywhere "the most careless, the most stupid thinker"; the existence of God must be left undisputed since it is supported "by all the arguments which its nature admits of, even though these arguments be not, in themselves, very numerous or forcible . . . and no understanding [can] estimate their cogency."[23] Further, his final statement of the "whole of natural theology" is something he himself says is "somewhat ambiguous," namely, *"that the cause or causes of order in the universe probably bear some remote analogy to human intelligence."*[24] All of this must be emphasized. But it must also be emphasized that Philo does nevertheless accept *some* of what Cleanthes has been arguing for, namely, that the order in the universe does have a cause or causes that are somewhat like human intelligence—when he has shown decisively in what has preceded that Cleanthes' arguments do not show even this much to be a more likely view than any other. He still differs from Cleanthes, however, in three fundamental respects. First, he continues to deny that this proposition can be extended from human intelligence to other human qualities. Second, he insists that "it affords no inference that affects human life." Third, he spends a great deal of Part XII arguing that the evils of institutional and revealed religion set it apart from "the philosophical and rational kind—whereas Cleanthes obtusely continues to insist that

---

[20] Ibid., Introduction, pp. 120-23.
[21] See *Dialogues concerning Natural Religion*, ed. N. Pike (Indianapolis: Bobbs-Merrill, 1970), pp. 204-37. I am much indebted to Pike's argument throughout.
[22] See my *Hume*, pp. 189-96. For a well-argued statement of an interpretation different from the one offered there, and now extended, see J. C. A. Gaskin, "God, Hume, and Natural Belief," *Philosophy* 49 (1974): 281-94.
[23] *Dialogues*, XII, pp. 214, 216.
[24] Ibid., p. 227.

all "false" religion needs to bring it into conformity with "the true" is a little soap and water.

I incline to the view that these considerations show Philo (that is, Hume) to be genuine in his acceptance of this conclusion of natural theology, in part because it does not seem to him to matter whether one accepts it or not. When all the appropriate disclaimers are built in, it is, as he says, a merely verbal matter whether one stresses, with the atheist, that the analogy is remote or stresses, with the theist, that even a remote analogy is still an analogy. What does matter, however, is whether or not one goes on to use the acceptance of the analogy as a ground for adherence to some form of institutional religion, for which Philo has nothing but abhorrence. Cleanthes keeps on *saying* he does. But Philo (Hume) knows better. He sees that Cleanthes' sort of civilized rational theologian will attempt to preserve what he perceives as his rationality by drawing no practical consequences from his theism that could not equally well be established without it. To Philo (Hume) the very practical and doctrinal emptiness of natural religion, thus understood, is a reason not for rejecting it but for giving it a "plain, philosophical assent." The last speech of Philo is to be seen, I suggest, as in part at least a message to the atheist to recognize in Cleanthes' sort of theologian a social and practical ally in the battle against the Demeas of this world who think religious beliefs ought to have specific consequences that unbelievers cannot arrive at for themselves. Cleanthes, of course, cannot be expected to understand any of this: but the good, secularizing influence he exercises on his fellow believers is best fostered if he does not. With enemies like Cleanthes, unbelievers do not need friends.

Even if all this is plausible, it does not account for all the nuances of Part XII. In particular, we still need to do more to determine what Philo means by that famous final statement: "To be a philosophical sceptic is, in a man of letters, the first and most essential step towards being a sound, believing Christian."[25]

To some degree this is plain enough. One thing Philo means is that his arguments in Parts II to XI have undermined all Cleanthes' claims to deduce any doctrines from the design hypothesis except the vague deistic pronouncement that constitutes the very unreligious religion that he and Philo share. But this cannot be all. For even this common doctrine is

---

[25] Ibid., p. 228.

more than the Philo of Parts II to XI seems to accept. His final statement must mean more than just this.

We can find a clue, I think, in the comment of Cleanthes that immediately precedes Philo's suggestion that theists and atheists differ only verbally.[26] Cleanthes says that the analogy of the world to "a machine of human contrivance" must "immediately strike all unprejudiced apprehensions" and that a skeptical critic can do no more than "start doubts and difficulties" in order to make us suspend judgment; yet this suspense is impossible for us. Philo replies that indeed it is impossible and that since the analogy is undeniable, the causes of the world and of machines must be analogous also; the only dispute remaining will then be the "verbal" issue of whether the fact of the analogy is of more importance than its remoteness. Again we must note that the very suspense that *Philo* tells us here is impossible is nevertheless the logical outcome of his own negative arguments in Parts II to XI. Here he accepts that there *is* analogy between the cause or causes of order in the world and human intelligence. It is the subsequent implications of this acceptance that lead into the verbal disputes. This amounts to an admission that all he has done hitherto is to start the "doubts and difficulties" Cleanthes has referred to and that the perception of design in nature is not destroyed by them.

Now Hume surely thinks that Philo has succeeded in refuting all Cleanthes' *arguments* for the design hypothesis, as indeed he has. But if this is so, Philo's concession in Part XII can only represent an admission that the perception of design in nature is a prephilosophical interpretation of it—a natural belief that is not established by argument but that, for that very reason, is not eliminated when arguments in its favor are refuted. Hence all that Philo's doubts and difficulties can achieve is to prevent our drawing specific moral or religious consequences from it. This is of course of vital importance, but it is less than Philo's own arguments suggest. Hume seems to be committed to the existence of a vague universal deism that he does not think the arguments of mitigated skepticism can wholly eradicate, even though they can render it harmless in practice for the "man of letters." Once again he has felt obliged to concede the psychological impotence of his own skeptical arguments.

But the concession, though a major one, is one that Philo has meticulously circumscribed. It amounts to an admission that men are unable to

---

[26] Ibid., p. 216.

refrain from ascribing some degree of teleology to the cause or causes of nature, but it prevents any rational speculation about the specific character of that teleology. Such further speculation will be the handiwork of the "haughty dogmatist" who is "persuaded that he can erect a complete system of theology by the mere help of philosophy." Skeptical arguments may not produce total suspension of judgment, but they can inhibit us from following in his footsteps. Philo does not stop here, however; he goes on to say that, faced with the "obscurity" of natural theology, a "well-disposed mind" will "fly to revealed truth with the greatest avidity" in order to rescue itself from its ignorance. Skeptical humility about the powers of reason will lead such a mind to embrace the claims of revelation.

One has to be very gullible indeed to suppose that Hume himself has such a well-disposed mind. Philo's own recent comments about the evils of popular religion, and Hume's onslaughts upon it in the *Natural History of Religion*, block any such line of interpretation. But in spite of this it seems that Hume is concluding that those apologists who have seen skepticism as the ally of religion have shown a clearer understanding of who their natural allies are than those who have followed Locke and Cleanthes in urging the reasonableness of Christianity. For to such dogmatists revelation is, in Philo's phrase, an "adventitious instructor," which can in the long run be dispensed with. Although skepticism cannot *establish* the claims of revelation, it can make it crystal clear (to the well-disposed mind) that there is no philosophical substitute for what it offers. So Philo's last remark has, as its secondary meaning, the conclusion that Lockean theologians are looking for support in the wrong place.

In summary, I suggest that the calm and reflective Philo of Part XII concedes that his own negative arguments have not been enough to prevent our natural acceptance of some principle of design in nature, but he does consider them enough to prevent this acceptance from serving as the basis for practical inferences or moral speculations. A skeptic who recognizes the inevitability of a "plain philosophical assent" to this principle can reach a practical accommodation with the humane secularizing theologians who urge it upon him. He also sees that those who are prone to those pathological forces that he sees at work in popular religion can readily point to the skeptic's own arguments as a reason for succumbing to them, even though he does not believe that we are all in this psychological predicament.

VIII

How far does Philo's final position represent a modification of Hume's skepticism as we encounter it in his earlier writings? I think that in one important respect it involves a return from the position of the *Enquiry* to that of the *Treatise*. In the *Enquiry* Hume advises us to keep off theology and stay with the affairs of common life. Philo's arguments in Parts II to XI must no doubt be read as demonstrating the wisdom of that advice and as showing us the chronic inconclusiveness of theological speculation. But Philo's final position involves the concession that in spite of this we cannot be prevented from committing outselves to the first principle that natural theologians, with their bad arguments, are laboring to establish. All that mitigated skepticism can do is render it practically and psychologically harmless. So we cannot wholly keep away from natural theology; we should, instead, indulge it to the extent of giving its first principle a "plain, philosophical assent." Indeed, it would seem that Hume is even suggesting once more that if we attempt to remain in a state of intellectual suspense with regard to it, as a "careless" (or Pyrrhonian) skeptic would have us do, we open our minds to the very anxieties for which the dubious blandishments of revelation might seem to be the only cure. So the best solution is to say yes and then trust that the resources of common life (which the secularized theologian values as much as we do) can serve to protect us against indecision and false religion.

But although Philo's position does involve this degree of mitigation of mitigated skepticism, it does not involve its abandonment. There seems no reason to question that Philo does consider his arguments to block the way to "dogmatism," that is, to philosophical speculation that proceeds beyond the minimal natural theology he regards as unavoidable. Indeed, while he has extended the scope of natural belief beyond the affairs of common life, he has done nothing to encourage us to philosophize one inch past the point where natural belief peters out. That remains "haughty" dogmatism; and the prudential veto of the *Enquiry* has been not removed but, in Hume's view, strengthened, by the acceptance of the proposition into which "the whole of natural theology" resolves itself. This would seem to be Hume's final answer to Butler, with whom Mossner has plausibly identified Cleanthes.[27] Butler assumes that his readers will accept that the world is created by an intelligence, and he

---

[27] See E. C. Mossner, "The Enigma of Hume," *Mind* 45 (1936): 334-49.

argues in the *Analogy of Religion* that anyone who accepts this ought to accept as probable that this intelligence is moral, that it provides for our future survival, and that it guides the universe providentially as Christianity teaches us. Philo, on the contrary, ends the *Dialogues* by conceding the premise of Butler's argument and denying all its conclusions: to accept the being of God is to go nowhere in theology. For that very reason the inability of skeptical argument to shake us free from this acceptance need not alarm a man of letters in the least.

IX

If this is indeed Hume's final position, what are we to make of it? I will begin by assuming for the sake of argument that Hume is right when he says that negative arguments like Philo's cannot eliminate our acceptance of intelligent design. If this is true, it leaves two major difficulties. First, there is an obvious problem of consistency. Mitigated skepticism does not prohibit us from engaging in the reflections necessary to common life merely because these reflections are based on beliefs that cannot be philosophically justified. It is of the essence of mitigated skepticism that one accepts what one must and proceeds from there. If one now extends the list of unavoidable beliefs to include the belief in intelligent design, parity of reasoning ought surely to permit us to explore the whole of natural theology. The second, and more important, difficulty seems to me to be this. Hume has given no reason to think that, consistency aside, we *can* stop in our tracks where he recommends that we stop. If we cannot not think there is intelligent design, it might be hard for any of us, and impossible for some of us, not to wonder what sort of mind lies behind it. There might be some plausibility in recommending self-denial if we could refrain from postulating design in the first place; but the case is immeasurably weaker if one concedes that we cannot do even this. So Philo's concession, even if logically consistent with mitigated skepticism, is psychologically at odds with it.

But these criticisms assume that Hume needs to make the concession in the first place. I now wish to question this. Earlier I argued that Hume is wrong to suggest that the Pyrrhonist's doubts about the beliefs of common life cannot be sustained, and wrong to think that the Pyrrhonist's practical accommodations cannot be accompanied by an inner suspense of judgment. I would now like to apply this to the one proposition of natural theology. Hume seems to think that we cannot suspend judgment about that proposition, but that, to our good fortune, we can see it is harmless and reach a practical consensus with the unsuspecting theologian. But its harmlessness would depend on our being able to restrain our tendency to dogmatize beyond it; and why do we *have* to accept it at all? The sort of practical consensus that Hume desires is surely more likely if we are able to suspend judgment inwardly but accommodate ourselves outwardly, in the manner of Sextus. Hume is once again underestimating the capacity of the skeptic to sustain his own doubts in the face of the psychological pressures to believe. He is underestimating the psychological power of his own critical arguments. No doubt this is due in part to his dislike of the dogmatism of the atheists of his day, and also to his own sense of isolation in the face of the nearly universal orthodoxy that surrounded him. But in our day, when agnosticism is commonplace and practical agreement between believers and unbelievers about the affairs of common life very frequent, the matter looks different. Indeed, suspense of judgment about theological questions is no longer confined to men of letters. And Hume, in spite of his self-doubts, has had as much to do with this as any other single person.

No doubt some will say that these criticisms are criticisms of a position Hume does not hold, that he is as much an agnostic as those of our contemporaries who learn their atheology from him. I can only submit that this reading, tempting though it is, cannot supply an adequate account of the text. I think the text has to be read in the light of Hume's attempt to take the measure of the skeptical tradition, in particular its insistence on the inability of reason to establish truth and its recommendation to universal doubt. His acceptance of the one and his denial of the other lead him into difficulties that follow him to the very end of his career.

Philo Confounded

P. S. Wadia

> *Reasonable men may be allowed to differ, where no one can reasonably be positive.*
> Hume, *Dialogues*

I

TOWARD THE CLOSE OF PART III of Hume's *Dialogues concerning Natural Religion* something rather unusual happens. Most of this part is taken up with Cleanthes' attempt to rebut criticisms already made by Philo against the argument from design for God's existence that Cleanthes has put forward earlier. When Cleanthes is done, Pamphilus, the narrator of the *Dialogues*, takes a rare opportunity to break in in order to declare:

> I could observe . . . that PHILO was a little embarrassed and confounded: But while he hesistated in delivering an answer, luckily for him, DEMEA broke in upon the discourse, and saved his countenance.[1]

What are we to make of this description of a piece of behavior that is so out of tune with the character of the normally loquacious Philo? Should we accept it at face value, thus accepting that Hume *intended* Cleanthes' challenge to Philo in Part III to be taken seriously, or should we dismiss this challenge as an empty one, and so include the passage among those instances in the *Dialogues* in which Hume resorts to his famous irony to mask his real intentions?

How we answer these questions will, of course, depend on whether or not we believe there is anything particularly noteworthy about the objections raised by Cleanthes against Philo's criticisms that could explain why it is that the latter was unable to find a satisfactory reply to them. In his now classical study of the *Dialogues*, Kemp Smith, in line with the

---

I am grateful to my colleagues Professors Gail Belaief, Martha Bolton, and Peter Klein for their comments and suggestions on an earlier draft of this paper. My thanks also to the Rutgers Research Council for financial assistance toward the preparation of this paper for publication.

[1] Ed. Norman Kemp Smith (Indianapolis: Bobbs-Merrill, 1947), III, p. 155 (hereafter cited as *Dialogues*).

rather small opinion he holds of Cleanthes, suggested that Philo's reaction at this point represents a stylistic trick executed by Hume "to preserve Cleanthes' dignity and to cover over his failure to make any effective reply."[2] It is my considered view that Kemp Smith is mistaken at this point in his interpretation. After explaining the proper context in which Cleanthes' rebuttal should be understood, I will urge in Section II below that this rebuttal can be seen to contain a believable challenge to Philo's radical rejection of "experimental theism" in Part II. I will end by briefly discussing an issue in one of Hume's other writings that lends some unexpected support to my view as to why Cleanthes' challenge goes unanswered by Philo.

Two advantages incidental to my reading of Part III may be mentioned. Kemp Smith's account of the exclusively literary means used by Hume to soothe over Cleanthes' alleged utter lack of philosophical acuity, in order that "the reader's respect" for him may be maintained, has an unconvincing ring about it at many points. My interpretation has the advantage, first, of going some way toward rehabilitating Cleanthes' intellectual contribution and thus improving the *quality* of the confrontation between him and Philo.

Kemp Smith's chief contention in his commentaries is that it is Philo who "from start to finish, represents Hume" and that what has since come to be called "Philo's confession" in the last part of the *Dialogues* concedes precious little to Cleanthes' aim of establishing a full-blown "natural religion."[3] Now, in general, I agree with both barrels of Kemp Smith's contention. As a matter of fact I believe that my reading of Part III is altogether consistent with Kemp Smith's view of Philo's final position in Part XII, namely, that the design argument can at most support a blief in God of such a highly attenuated form as to be religiously insignificant. But the other advantage I would claim for my way of interpreting Part III is this. With scant regard for Hume's skills as a dialogist, Kemp Smith, along with most (if not all) other commentators on the *Dialogues*, is content to view the action in the last part as being, if not altogether discontinuous with what has gone before, then at least as being an abrupt and unexpected development. My interpretation would go some way toward remedying this situation. If I am right, then so far as the argued content of the *Dialogues* is concerned, the turning point in

---

[2] Ibid., p. 64.
[3] Ibid., pp. 68-75.

Philo's attitude toward the design argument comes earlier in Part III wherein his initial extreme skepticism with regard to the argument is checked for the first time. It thus becomes possible to see Philo's final position as a dialectically more plausible development growing out of a concession first exacted from him during an earlier stage in the discussion.[4]

II

In his opening remarks in the *Dialogues*, Philo comes very close to espousing an unremitting form of Pyrrhonism. He is properly berated for this view by Cleanthes, but it is not long before he agrees that it is impossible for any skeptic, his theoretical scruples to the contrary notwithstanding, to adopt with any degree of seriousness a suspensive attitude toward our common-sense ideas of truth and evidence.

Thus the issue between Philo and Cleanthes is joined. The issue is not Pyrrhonism, in either its extreme or moderate form, as some commentators have thought. It is rather this: granted that "in our reasonings concerning matter of fact, there are all imaginable degrees of assurance, from the highest certainty to the lowest species of moral evidence,"[5] are there any truths that can be derived from experience, with a reasonable degree of certitude, concerning the existence, and more particularly the nature, of God?

The monolithic weapon in Cleanthes' armory to prove the existence of God and certain of his attributes, without exceeding the bounds of experience and without recourse to revelation, is, of course, the design argument. This argument, in its various forms, had but recently come into favor among the more enlightened theologians of the age who took

---

[4] Nelson Pike is the only other commentator I know of who takes Cleanthes' challenge in Part III seriously and explicitly states that Philo really was confounded (see his recent edition of the *Dialogues* [Bobbs-Merrill, 1970, pp. 222-28]). But Pike's interpretation is altogether at odds with the one I adopt in this paper. He suggests that there are two versions of the design argument put forward by Cleanthes in the *Dialogues*: the obviously scientific version, put forward in Part II, and another version described as "irregular" that is briefly outlined in Part III and not brought up again till Part XII. Pike goes on to urge (though with some misgivings) that it is this "irregular" version of the design argument that Philo (as well as Hume) finally accepts in Part XII. No doubt there is *some* textual evidence for Pike's interpretation, but I believe that, all things considered, it is not a plausible reading. However, I have not the space here to deal with this issue.

[5] *An Enquiry concerning Human Understanding*, ed. L. A. Selby-Bigge, 2nd ed. (Oxford: Clarendon Press, 1902), X, I, p. 110 (hereafter cited as first *Enquiry*).

their cue from science, many of whom may have found both the "superstition" as well as the a priorism of an earlier age no less distasteful than did Hume himself. The argument is stated by Cleanthes in Part II and shortly thereafter recast by Philo for the benefit of Demea, who, understandably, is scandalized by *his* reading of the argument, according to which, since the argument is not a "demonstration," it cannot take us beyond "experience and probability." We have all been made excessively familiar with Cleanthes' version of the argument; I prefer to quote here a few lines from Philo's subsequent formulation of it, for it helps to focus attention on an issue that is of some importance to my discussion.

> According to this method of reasoning, DEMEA, it follows . . . that order, arrangement, or the adjustment of final causes is not, of itself, any proof of design. . . . For aught we can know *a priori*, matter may contain the source or spring of order originally, within itself, as well as mind does. . . . The equal possibility of both these suppositions is allowed. By experience we find . . . that there is a difference between them. Throw several pieces of steel together, without shape or form; they will never arrange themselves so as to compose a watch. . . . But the ideas in a human mind, we see, by an unknown, inexplicable economy, arrange themselves so as to form the plan of a watch or house. Experience, therefore, proves, that there is an original principle of order in mind, not in matter. From similar effects we infer similar causes. The adjustment of means to ends is alike in the universe, as in a machine of human contrivance. The causes, therefore, must be resembling.[6]

Cleanthes having allowed that Philo has "made a fair representation" of his argument, Philo proceeds at once to attack it. But before we turn to Philo's criticisms let us take a closer look at just what it is that the argument is supposed to establish and how it does so. If the argument were valid it would prove three distinct propositions to be true. (1) There exists somewhere a Source or Principle (for the moment, indeterminate) from which the observed order in the universe is derived. (In other words, all this does is to foreclose the possibility that the order in the universe is wholly a product of the fortuitous behavior of material forces, however conceived, without implying any claims as to the attributes possessed by such a Source.) (2) The Source or Principle of organization possesses intelligence, not unlike the human. (3) Finally, since the universe is said

---

[6] *Dialogues*, II, p. 146.

to be an artifact, this Source or Principle is not inherent in it but, on the contrary, is external to it.

Concerning the nature of the design argument, the most important thing to be noted is that implicit in it is an appeal to the notion of a *reasonable* man. In general, the reasonable man will wish, as Cleanthes states at one point, "to adhere to common sense and the plain instincts of nature; and to assent, wherever any reasons strike him with so full a force, that he cannot, without the greatest violence, prevent it."[7] So a reasonable man will accept without hesitation the testimony of his senses in normal everyday situations, notwithstanding the fact that they do sometimes deceive him. He will continue in the same vein where inductive or analogical inferences are concerned. He will accept the position that such inferences can, and frequently do, yield conclusions that are not merely probable, but certain. A priori, "every chimera of his fancy would be upon an equal footing," but after experience, particularly after repeated experience of a certain regular kind, he can come to discover (as Philo puts it) "the true cause of any phenomenon."[8] In short, Cleanthes' view is that there are perfectly unambiguous situations in which it would be simply pathological to deny that we have knowledge of the world around us that is both true and certain, in perfectly natural and correct senses of these words. And, in reformulating Cleanthes' argument, Philo is giving clear notice that he is prepared to meet Cleanthes on Cleanthes' own terms.

Now, Cleanthes' contention is that experience *proves* beyond a reasonable doubt that this world had an external intelligent Designer. And given the terms in which his argument for this contention is presented, the sole avenue of criticism left to one who feels his assurance in it to be misplaced is to show that such assurance is not warranted by the available evidence.

According to what we might label the "textbook interpretation," Philo's attack against the design argument results in his rejecting all three of its main conclusions stated a while back, thus leaving it open that the regulated course of nature might have come about by chance. Now I suggest that this is a perfectly proper way to interpret the damage inflicted by Philo's opening salvo on the design argument. But the fact is that *after* Part III Philo backs down from (or at least never again explicitly avows)

---

[7] Ibid., III, p. 154.
[8] Ibid., II, pp. 145–46.

his earlier agnosticism concerning the existence of a Source that would explain the order prevailing in the universe and seeks to demonstrate only that no definite claims can be made concerning the nature of such a Source (or sources). And if (following a practice quite widely prevalent in Hume's day)[9] we identify this ultimate Source ("the ultimate springs and principles" of Hume's *Treatise* and *Enquiries*) with the concept of God, Philo's attitude after Part III turns out to be in accord with the oft-repeated mandate of the *Dialogues*, which is to probe the question of the *nature* of God and not his *being*.

Let us now see how Philo is led to moderate his initial skepticism. In brief summary, we can say that Philo's assault against the design argument in Part II is carried out in three stages.[10] He argues in the first place that the similarity between the universe and things of human contrivance, such as houses and machines, is not so "exact" as to justify including the former in the class of things intelligently designed. But, secondly, intelligence "is no more than one of the springs and principles of the universe," and even were it the only principle we knew of from which order could proceed *within* nature, we would not be justified in so wide a step as would be involved in making it account for the origin of order in nature *as a whole*. But the most serious charge made against the design argument — one which, if valid, would cripple it altogether — is brought in at the third stage:

> How this argument can have place, where the objects, as in the present case, are single, individual, without parallel, or specific resemblance, may be difficult to explain. . . . To ascertain this reasoning, it were requisite, that we had experience of the origin of worlds; and it is not sufficient surely, that we have seen ships and cities arise from human art and contrivance. . . .[11]

---

[9] See Section III in Kemp Smith's commentaries, entitled "Hume's Reasons for Retaining the Terms 'God' and 'Religion' in Defining His Own Positions as Bearing on the Argument of the *Dialogues*" (ibid., pp. 25-44).

[10] Ibid., II, pp. 147-50. It is a fine point whether what we have here are three different arguments, one complex argument presented in three different stages, or one argument set forth in three different ways. I am inclined to favor either the second or the third alternative, but, admittedly, either of these would put a better face on my interpretation of Cleanthes' rebuttal than the first. For a recent discussion of the philosophical force of the argument, see J. C. A. Gaskin, "The Design Argument," *Religious Studies* 12 (1976): 331-45.

[11] *Dialogues*, II, pp. 149-50.

It is generally believed that what Cleanthes says in Part III makes no dent at all in this initial case made by Philo against the design argument. And Kemp Smith's interpretation of Cleanthes' remarks more than bears out this belief. Cleanthes himself opens Part III by asserting that "the similarity of the works of nature to those of art," which (as everyone knows) is at the core of his argument, "is self-evident and undeniable." Therefore, he continues, Philo's cavils and objections "ought to be refuted . . . by illustrations, examples, and instances, rather than by serious argument and philosophy."[12] According to Kemp Smith, Cleanthes is engaged here in an attempt to reinforce his earlier point about the legitimacy of the passage from certain observed particulars in our surroundings to a Designer of the universe, but the illustrations he now resorts to are "both irrelevant and misleading."[13] What is so bewildering about these latest moves of Cleanthes, however, is this: one expects him to confine his illustrations to familiar things in the world around him, such as the movement of planets in their orbits or the complementary anatomies of the male and female bodies. Instead, we find this stalwart defender of common sense—who disdains "inventions" and "too luxuriant a fertility" in a philosopher—resorting to two examples that are at once imaginary and bizarre in the extreme. One is that of a voice in the clouds heard at the same instant around the world, speaking "to each nation in its own language and dialect" and conveying "some instruction altogether worthy of a benevolent Being, superior to mankind." The other, of a curious vegetable library full of books "which perpetuate themselves . . . by descent and propagation." So the question is, What is the point behind these curious illustrations?

Cleanthes himself states explicitly on two occasions that his examples successfully get around the objections Philo has raised against the design argument in Part II. And certainly one obvious way of understanding his claim is the following. It will be recalled that Philo has insisted all along that "unless the cases be exactly similar, ["just reasoners"] repose no perfect confidence in applying their past observations to any particular phenomenon."[14] But now take, for instance, the illustration of the voice in the clouds. *If* such a voice were heard, a reasonable person (or so at least seems to be Cleanthes' claim) would have no hesitation in drawing the inference that it proceeded from an unseen, nonhuman, intelligent

---

[12] Ibid., III., p. 152.
[13] Ibid., p. 101.
[14] Ibid., II, p. 147.

source, beyond the clouds, as it were. And this notwithstanding the fact that "by its loudness and flexibility to all languages" it "bears so little analogy to any human voice. . . ." But Cleanthes' move, understood thus as an attempt *merely* to meet what in effect is the first stage of Philo's objection in Part II, seems only too obviously unsuccessful.[15] For, as Kemp Smith points out,

> the effect appealed to [i.e., the voice in the clouds] is an instance of a *species* familiar in experience, and as described maintains the degree of analogy required for concluding that it has the same *species* of previously experienced cause [i.e., an intelligent source]. Philo is not, therefore, concerned to challenge the force of the illustration as an illustration of what, under the supposed circumstances, would be a legitimate inference by analogy.[16]

I submit, however, that this interpretation of Cleanthes' move, and Kemp Smith's reply, falls short of appreciating the full force of Cleanthes' rejoinder. We must recall that Philo has not merely said that given the world as we find it, there *is* no evidence to justify an inference to a Designer, but, further, that there *could* be no such evidence. What Philo has maintained is that *no* inference by analogy to the existence of a Designer is possible unless "we had experience of the origin of worlds." And, since obviously no one can satisfy such a condition, this claim amounts to saying that it is impossible (not merely improbable) that the world should supply any empirical evidence whatsoever to force a man to believe in a Source for the order within it. I submit that the illustrations Cleanthes gives in Part III can be, and ought rightly to be, interpreted as supplying a rebuttal to this extreme position taken by Philo. What Cleanthes has done with his illustrations is to give descriptions of possible states of affairs that could obtain *within* our world that would *force* even a skeptic like Philo to posit an intelligent Source who controls (at least some of) the laws of nature. Confronted with such extraordinary events as those described in the illustrations, Cleanthes' question is what a reasonable person's reaction ought to be. Would it be reasonable, he asks rhetorically at one point about his versatile voice in the clouds, that such "a rational, wise, coherent speech proceeded, you knew not

---

[15] I say "seems" because to do proper justice to Cleanthes' illustrations, other complex and difficult issues would have to be raised in addition to the one I consider in what follows.
[16] *Dialogues*, p. 101.

whence, from some accidental whistling of the winds, not from any divine reason or intelligence?" No reasonable man could for a moment believe that an extraordinary conjunction of the laws of meteorology and sound could produce such a voice as this with its "flexibility to all languages" and climes. Of course it is logically possible that such an explanation could hold but, remember, that for a reasonable man the mere logical possibility is not enough to overthrow reasoning drawn from common life and experience. In a perfectly plain sense of the word "impossible," it is impossible that the sun will rise in the west tomorrow and impossible that such an extraordinary event as the voice described by Cleanthes result from anything but "design and intention."

In Part II Philo has chosen to take the very strong line that it is not even conceivable that we should ever have any empirical evidence in the world that would support a reasonable belief in the existence of a divine Source for the order and design found in it. Kemp Smith readily concedes that Cleanthes has been able to supply "an illustration of what, under the supposed circumstances, would be a legitimate inference by analogy." What Kemp Smith does not see is that this is all that Cleanthes requires to show Philo the error of his ways in rejecting the design argument out of hand on the basis of what earlier has been referred to as his (Philo's) "general unspecified scruples." And I contend that it is the fact that Cleanthes' rebuttal has this dimension to it that I have been describing that explains why Philo is so unceremoniously stopped in his tracks.

In a recent article John Bricke, after echoing what Kemp Smith says about Cleanthes' illustrations, makes the telling point that one must not make the mistake of assuming, simply "from the fact that one of his characters [in the *Dialogues*] fails to make a satisfactory reply to objections, that the author could make no reply."[17] On the other hand, if in a specific instance of this kind, one could produce evidence to show that Hume in fact did not have a satisfactory answer, then it would also at the same time be grounds for sticking to a literal reading of the passage in which the character in question is shown as failing to produce such a reply. I believe that, in the case of the instance we have been dealing with in this paper, there may be grounds for speculating on the availability of just this sort of evidence. It is to a discussion of this issue that I want finally to turn.

---

[17] "On The Interpretation of Hume's *Dialogues*," *Religious Studies* 11 (1975): 1-18.

III

It will readily be seen that if my reading of Cleanthes' move in Part III is correct, then what he has done in effect is to give a new twist to the discussion of the design argument by injecting into it an issue that is strongly reminiscent of the problem of the possibility of miracles. The illustration of the voice in the clouds is especially telling on this score: for such an event, if it were to take place, would be religiously significant, would preclude an explanation in scientific terms, and, at the same time, would be strongly analogous to events brought about intentionally by rational agents. But these are exactly the three features that, when they characterize an event, are said to justify us in calling such an event a miracle.[18] Thus it would not be too much to expect that if we turned to

---

[18] See, for example, R. F. Holland, "The Miraculous," *American Philosophical Quarterly* 2 (1965):1-18; also Richard Swinburne, *The Concept of Miracle* (London: Macmillan, 1970).

During the McGill Bicentennial Hume Congress, Antony Flew, who just the previous week had debated the question of the existence of God with Rev. Thomas Warren in Texas, related a delightful episode in which the voice from the clouds came again to "confound" a modern skeptic. Professor Flew was kind enough to write me a letter on this topic, part of which I reproduce below.

Having now both read and heard your paper "Philo Confounded" I thought I should put it on record for you that Life recently imitated Art in this respect. In "The Debate of the Century" at Denton, Texas last week my theist antagonist Thomas Warren developed as a challenge to me the supposition that a voice from the heavens might predict bizarre ongoings in North Texas, ongoings which forthwith occured. In my Philo-like role as Warren's Stratonician atheist antagonist I did indeed feel at least momentarily confounded. For this would be a falsifiable doctrine derivable from some sort of god hypothesis.

My actual response was to point out: first, that nothing of such a nature has ever actually occurred (nor, I believe is it going to occur); and, second, that this testable ongoing is going to occur is not a consequence which can be derived from the "God hypothesis" of classical theism in the Mosaic traditions.

What I conclude from all this, and from Penelhum's paper, is that Philo (Hume) still allowed that the order of nature does suggest an innocuous and toothless Design, because science in his day could offer no account of how species and organs adapted to their functions and environments could arise without design. Thus Hume has to take just a little literally his own and everyone else's talk of the Wisdom of Nature, even though, as a Stratonician, Philo/Hume would insist that this Design can be immanent not transcendent. The whole business illustrates the point that in such fundamental areas our conclusions must depend both on philosophical insights and upon estimates of what the contingent facts are: if the world were very different it would be reasonable to infer Design, even though that would still leave us a long way from Warren's single, omnipotent, fundamentalist, Christian God.

Hume's famous discussion of miracles,[19] some clue might be found in it that would explain why Philo reacted in the extraordinary manner he did when confronted by this issue.

It is well known that in this famous discussion Hume's attack against the belief in miracles is confined to giving philosophical and factual grounds for impugning the credibility of any historical testimony bearing on the occurrence of miraculous events. Critics have been quick to point out that this limitation is sufficient to vitiate the credibility of Hume's own attack. A recent critic puts the matter thus:

> Hume supposes that the conflict about what happens is a conflict between testimony and scientific knowledge. . . . But sometimes the evidence available to an inquirer consists not merely of testimony of others but of one's own apparently remembered observations. Some men have the evidence of their own eyes, not merely the testimony of others. What, one wonders, would Hume say, if he himself apparently saw a man walk on water?[20]

To bring that rhetorical question closer to home: What, one wonders, would Hume's reaction be if he himself were among the millions in the world who simultaneously heard the voice in the clouds of Cleanthes' illustration? In a recently published paper I have tried to argue that Hume fell into certain confusions in his discussion of miracles on account of his espousal of a mistaken theory of belief and that, once his discussion is freed of these confusions, the difficulty posed to it by the question asked here would not arise.[21] But given the fact that Hume's discussion of miracles does contain these confusions, it is more likely that the critics are correct in suggesting that he cannot make a satisfactory reply to Cleanthes' question. But if Hume cannot, then, by a kind of poetic necessity, neither can Philo.[22]

---

[19] First *Enquiry*, X.

[20] Swinburne, p. 35.

[21] P. S. Wadia, "Miracles and Common Understanding," *Philosophical Quarterly* 26 (1976): 69-81.

[22] In 1751 Hume dispatched some portions of his manuscript of the *Dialogues* to his friend Sir Gilbert Elliot, requesting assistance in strengthening Cleanthes' side of the argument (Hume to Elliot, 10 March 1751, in *The Letters of David Hume*, ed. J. Y. T. Greig, 2 vols. [Oxford: Clarendon Press, 1932], 1:153-57). In view of this letter, it has been suggested to me that my interpretation may be running the danger of making Cleanthes' case stronger than Hume himself apparently thought it to be. I do not agree. We have no way of knowing whether Hume made any changes in his manuscript after hearing from Elliot, even though (according to Kemp Smith) Hume's request for assistance proved "unavailing." (We are

told that Elliot's letter survives in the form of a draft, but, unfortunately, I have not had the opportunity of seeing it [*Dialogues*, p. 88].) However, as far as I can see, there is nothing in Hume's letter that ought to prevent anyone from arguing that Philo/Hume accepts the design argument in the very attenuated sense mentioned above. Apart from mentioning the difficulty of the analogy between "the Works of Nature" and "the usual Effects of Mind," the letter makes the significant point that "the propensity" to draw the inference of the design argument is not "as strong and universal as that to believe in our senses and experience." This is one more nail in the coffin of the view held by some that Hume thought of belief in God as "unavoidable" on the model of his doctrine of "natural belief." See the comment by J. C. A. Gaskin in his "God, Hume and Natural Belief," *Philosophy* 49 (1974):289. This paper contains an excellent defense of the view that such a "natural belief" interpretation of Hume will not wash, though Gaskin himself believes that Philo/Hume does accept the attenuated version of the design argument.

Hume, Induction, and Natural Selection

J. P. Monteiro

I

THE RELEVANCE OF HUME'S NEGATIVE ARGUMENT concerning the logical foundation of induction is recognized by many, including Ayer, Quine, Popper, and Flew.[1] Some assert that to this logical, negative argument he simply added a psychological theory of the process of inductive inference.[2] But is this all? Or is there another sort of explanation to be found in Hume's philosophy? Cannot we find in his writings something more than a logical refutation of induction, followed by a psychological description of the workings of that central principle, custom or habit? We cannot hope, of course, for a logical justification of induction, for this is precisely what Hume's negative argument proved to be impossible. But maybe we can hope for an explanation of the presence of habit among the principles of human nature, and even for an explanation of the success of inductive reasoning.

Hume would at first seem to refuse to take this step, resting contented with his psychological theory. He denies pretending to give the ultimate cause of the propensity to make inductive inferences: "We only point out a principle of human nature which is universally acknowledged, and which is well known by its effects. Perhaps we can push our enquiries no farther, or pretend to give the cause of this cause; but must rest contented with it as the ultimate principle, which we can assign, of all our conclusions from experience."[3]

Perhaps Hume did push his inquiries a little farther. This is what he seems to announce in Section V of his first *Enquiry*. Near the end of Part I he says that he could stop his researches there but that it is

---

[1] A. J. Ayer, *Language, Truth and Logic* (Harmondsworth, England: Penguin Books, 1972), pp. 96, 126–27, 198; idem, *The Problem of Knowledge* (Penguin Books, 1956), pp. 29–30, 72–75; W. V. O. Quine, "Epistemology Naturalized," in *Ontological Relativity and other Essays* (New York: Columbia University Press, 1971), p. 72; Karl Popper, *The Logic of Scientific Discovery* (London: Hutchinson, 1974), pp. 29, 369; idem, *Conjectures and Refutations* (London: Routledge & Kegan Paul, 1974), p. 42; idem, *Objective Knowledge* (Oxford: Clarendon Press, 1973), pp. 4, 6, 15, 38; Antony Flew, *Hume's Philosophy of Belief* (London: Routledge & Kegal Paul, 1961), p. 93.

[2] Popper, *Objective Knowledge*, pp. 4–6; Flew, pp. 211–12.

[3] *An Enquiry concerning Human Understanding*, ed. L. A. Selby-Bigge, 3rd ed. rev. P. H. Nidditch (Oxford: Clarendon Press, 1975), V, I, p. 43 (hereafter cited as first *Enquiry*).

"pardonable, perhaps commendable," to let curiosity "carry us on to still farther researches." Somewhat mysteriously, he adds that his "new explications and analogies" in Part II may give satisfaction "to such as love the abstract sciences, and can be entertained with speculations which, however accurate, may still retain a degree of doubt and uncertainty." Readers "of a different taste," he says, may neglect these new arguments.[4]

The most significant, and also the most "abstract" of these arguments are probably those in the two concluding paragraphs of Part II. Habit is defined as an instinct, implanted in us by "the wisdom of nature." As an instrument of survival, it is incomparably superior to "the fallacious deductions of our reason." Nature had to choose habit: "It is more conformable to the ordinary wisdom of nature to secure so necessary an act of the mind by some instinct or mechanical tendency, which may be infallible in its operations, may discover itself at the first appearance of life and thought, and may be independent of all the laboured deductions of the understanding."[5]

That the operation that produces belief is, like the mechanism of passion, a species of natural instinct, had already been told by Hume to readers of all "tastes." He had also stressed that custom is a necessary condition of human action.[6] Now he adds that this instinct, one of our instruments of survival, was given to us by something called the wisdom of nature. Nature herself offered us, with this instinct, the possibility of predicting her own regularities. But how should we understand the meaning of the word "wisdom"? What are those peculiar ways of nature, through which she is supposed to be able to give us an instinct that allows us to infer like effects from like causes,[7] to predict future events, and thus to survive in the world in which we live?

One of the consequences of habit, Hume tells us in the same paragraphs, is "a kind of pre-established harmony between the course of nature and the succession of our ideas."[8] This is not, of course, an adoption of Leibnizian metaphysics. In the first section of the first *Enquiry* Hume had claimed that "we must cultivate true metaphysics with

---

[4] Ibid., p. 47.
[5] Ibid., II, p. 55.
[6] Ibid., I, pp. 46-47, 45.
[7] Ibid., II, p. 55.
[8] Ibid., p. 54.

some care, in order to destroy the false and adulterate."⁹ Leibniz's theory of knowledge, with its doctrine of pre-established harmony and its explanation of the truth of human knowledge in terms of final causes,¹⁰ could only be, to Hume, an example of false metaphysics. In the same paragraph of Section V, he adds a clearly ironic reference to final causes. After presenting habit as a principle through which is effected the agreement between human knowledge and the course of nature, he adds: "Those who delight in the discovery and contemplation of *final causes*, have here ample subject to employ their wonder and admiration."¹¹ We must accept Flew's interpretation that this is an ironic remark.¹² In the *Treatise* Hume openly refuses the distinction between efficient and final causes, or of any other kind: "All causes are of the same kind."¹³ Final causes have no place in Hume's philosophy.

Leibniz's *harmonia praestabilita* is an explanation of the agreement between human knowledge and the natural world; and this harmony is in turn explained by God's design. God chose the best of possible universes, one in which there is an agreement and correspondence between all created things, each substance being "a perpetual mirror of the universe," and the order of perceptions in the soul truly representing the order of the universe.¹⁴ Hume could never accept such an explanation. But the seemingly paradoxical conclusion of Section V might point toward another explanation of the correspondence between our inferences and the order of nature. This might be an alternative to the Leibnizian explanation, a Humean explanation of the presence of habit among the principles of human nature, as well as of the success of induction.

Without habit, Hume argues, "we should never have been able to adjust means to ends." It is through this principle that we become adapted to the natural world, by an unconscious adaptation similar to the adjustment of our body to muscular motion: "As nature has taught us the use of our limbs without giving us the knowledge of the muscles and nerves by which they are actuated; so has she implanted in us an instinct, which

---

⁹ Ibid., I, p. 12.

¹⁰ Leibniz, *Principes de la Nature et de la Grâce*, secs. 3, 11, 13; *Principes de la Philosophie ou Monadologie*, secs. 53, 54, 56, 62, 78, 79.

¹¹ First *Enquiry*, V, II, p. 55.

¹² Flew, p. 105.

¹³ *A Treatise of Human Nature*, ed. L. A. Selby-Bigge (Oxford, 1888), I, III, XIV, p. 171 (hereafter cited as *Treatise*).

¹⁴ *Monadologie*, secs. 53-56, 59, 62, 63, 90.

carries forward the thought in a correspondent course to that which she has established among external objects; though we are ignorant of those powers and forces on which this regular course totally depends."[15] Or, as James Noxon puts it, "Man's adaptation to his environment is not an achievement of reason" but must be attributed to a natural instinct.[16]

A teleological explanation of habit and of the success of its operation, in terms of final causes, could only meet with Hume's contempt and irony. According to Flew, this becomes clear later in the first *Enquiry*: "Hume can afford the irony. For in Section XI he is going to uncover the fallacy of trying to argue from order and adjustment within the Universe to Design outside it." And Flew sees the last paragraphs of Section V, together with Section IX, "Of the Reason of Animals," as the expression of a central aspect in Hume's world outlook: "The vision of man as a part of nature."[17]

Design could never serve as a basis for a Humean explanation of any particular instance of natural adaptation. Flew shows how Section II, in spite of the multiple "veils of discretion" that obscure the point (probably due to problems with religious censorship),[18] refuses this kind of explanation, concluding that "the deity of philosophical theism could not conceivably serve as a term in any scientific explanation."[19] Hume's assault on the design argument, rejecting its anthropomorphism, forbids any interpretation of his "wisdom of nature" in theistic or teleological terms. What kind of an explanation, then, could Hume accept? Section II does not offer a clear answer; but it does hint at a completely different explanation: "The ordinary course of nature may convince us that almost everything is regulated by principles and maxims very different from ours."[20]

II

The hypothesis favored by the theist Cleanthes in the *Dialogues*, the "religious hypothesis" based on the design argument, is precisely the opposite. According to this theory, nature is regulated by principles and

---

[15] First *Enquiry*, V, II, p. 55.
[16] *Hume's Philosophical Development* (Oxford: Clarendon Press, 1973), p. 159.
[17] Flew, pp. 105, 167.
[18] Ibid., pp. 217-18, 230-33; and Noxon, pp. 173-74.
[19] Flew, p. 169.
[20] First *Enquiry*, XI, p. 146.

maxims very *similar* to ours: "The curious adapting of means to ends, throughout all nature, resembles exactly, though it much exceeds, the productions of human contrivance; of human design, thought, wisdom, and intelligence." Nature is full of examples of adaptation. All its "machines" are "adjusted to each other with an accuracy which ravishes into admiration all men who have every contemplated them." Cleanthes explains all these phenomena by the analogy between them and the usual effects of human design, an analogy that is extended to the causes of both kinds of effects. The wisdom of nature is to Cleanthes the wisdom of a divine author: "The order and arrangement of nature, the curious adjustment of final causes, the plain use and intention of every part and organ; all these bespeak in the clearest language an intelligent cause or Author."[21]

This is an equivalent of Aquinas's fifth way of proving the existence of God[22] and was an argument widely accepted by philosophers, and not only by theologians, in the seventeenth and eighteenth centuries. Among its most famous champions we must include Berkeley, Butler, Leibniz, Voltaire, Locke, and Newton.[23] Cleanthes' position in the *Dialogues* represents a very powerful philosophical tradition.

Philo, the "skeptic" of the *Dialogues*, opposes this venerable tradition, but not merely by a refutation of the religious hypothesis. He proposes an alternative conjecture as an explanation for order and adaptation in the natural world. In Part VI he excludes any explanation in terms of transcendent principles or causes external to nature. The most plausible system, he argues, will be "that which ascribes an eternal, inherent principle of order to the world." This is, he admits, a very general solution, perhaps "not entirely complete and satisfactory"; be that as it may, it "at once solves all difficulties" and is a theory "that we must, sooner or later, have recourse to, whatever system we embrace." And he insists on the necessity of such an immanent principle as an explanation for the order, adjustment, and adaptation we contemplate in nature: "How

---

[21] *Dialogues concerning Natural Religion*, ed. Norman Kemp Smith, 2nd ed. (Indianapolis: Bobbs-Merrill, 1947), II, p. 143; IV, p. 163 (hereafter cited as *Dialogues*).

[22] Aquinas, *Summa theologiae*, I, Q. 2, A. 3.

[23] Berkeley, *A Treatise concerning the Principles of Human Nature*, secs. 60, 62, 63; *Siris*, sec. 154; Butler, *The Analogy of Religion*, 2 vols. (London, 1855); 1:187, 2:320; Leibniz, *De la Nature en elle-même*, in *Opuscules Philosophiques Choisis*, ed. P. Schrecker (Paris: Hatier-Boivin, 1954), pp. 94, 98; Voltaire, *Traité de Métaphysique*, in *Philosophie* (Paris: La Renaissance du Livre, n.d.), p. 140; Locke, *An Essay concerning Human Understanding*, III, vi, 12; Newton, *Opticks* (New York: Dover Publications, 1952), pp. 402-3.

could things have been as they are, were there not an original, inherent principle of order somewhere, in thought or in matter?"[24] As G. J. Nathan puts it, "Philo proves that a principle internal to the universe is the required explanation of the order because it alone is a necessary and sufficient condition of order."[25] The alternative "thought or matter" is going to be decided in Part VIII, where this inherent principle is defined as an entirely material one. Quite consistently: thought could not be an acceptable alternative, for this would involve, at least in part, surrendering to Cleanthes' anthropomorphism. And already in Part II Philo had warned us against such a solution: "What peculiar privilege has this little agitation of the brain which we call thought, that we must thus make it the model of the whole universe?"[26]

Philo's conjecture in Part VIII proposes a material principle of order as an explanation for adjustment and adaptation in nature. Before this, he evokes the cosmogony of Epicurus, with a slight alteration: the original number of particles in the universe is supposed finite instead of infinite. But Philo immediately abandons the Epicurean theory to substitute for it what he calls "a new hypothesis of cosmogony."[27] This new conjecture is different from the first, and not simply its continuation, as Kemp Smith, for instance, seems to believe.[28]

The new conjecture is not a corpuscular or atomistic theory, although it can be explicated in these terms, as is done by Nelson Pike.[29] It simply supposes original, unorganized matter in motion, that is, in continual agitation and change. This "principle of continual change" is strongly established in a reply to Demea, the third character in the *Dialogues*: "Whatever the causes are, the fact is certain, that matter is, and always has been in continual agitation, as far as human experience or tradition reaches. There is not probably, at present, in the whole universe, one particle of matter at absolute rest."[30] The theory that follows, without any further reference to particles, is Philo's alternative for design.

We see in nature, Philo argues, that while that perpetual agitation goes

---

[24] *Dialogues*, VI, p. 174.
[25] "Hume's Immanent God," in *Hume*, ed. V. C. Chappell (London: Macmillan, 1970), pp. 422-23.
[26] *Dialogues*, II, p. 148.
[27] Ibid., VIII, pp. 182, 183.
[28] Ibid., p. 113.
[29] *Dialogues concerning Natural Religion*, ed. Nelson Pike (Indianapolis: Bobbs-Merrill, 1970), p. 178.
[30] *Dialogues*, VIII, p. 183.

on a certain constancy in natural forms is preserved: "Is there a system, an order, an economy of things, by which matter can preserve that perpetual agitation, which seems essential to it, and yet maintain a constancy in the forms, which it produces? There certainly is such an economy: For this is actually the case with the present world." Philo explains how such a constancy is preserved:

> All the parts of each form must have a relation to each other, and to the whole: And the whole itself must have a relation to the other parts of the universe; to the element, in which the form subsists; to the materials, with which it repairs its waste and decay; and to every other form, which is hostile or friendly. A defect in any of these particulars destroys the form; and the matter, of which it is composed, is again set loose, and is thrown into irregular motions and fermentations, till it unite itself to some other regular form.[31]

It is clear that Philo believes his conjecture to be reason enough to discard any teleological explanation: "Wherever matter is so poised, arranged, and adjusted, as to continue in perpetual motion, and yet preserve a constancy in the forms, its situation must, of necessity, have all the same appearance of art and contrivance which we observe at present."[32] Art and contrivance, design and wisdom in nature are but appearance and illusion, an illusion created by the fact that natural events and forces *simulate* a project and an intention as the origin of order and adaptation.[33] Here Philo is very firm: "It is in vain, therefore, to insist upon the uses of the parts in animals or vegetables, and their curious adjustment to each other. I would fain know how an animal could subsist, unless its parts were so adjusted?"[34] He could have added that any being that is not adapted to its environment could never survive, so that it is senseless to insist upon its admirable adaptation as a proof of the existence of a transcendent author of this adaptation. It would be in vain to do so, of course, to the theistic, religious philosopher. To the "skeptic," those instances of adaptation are precisely the empirical basis of his conjecture.

---

[31] Ibid.
[32] Ibid.
[33] Cf. Spinoza's *Ethics*, I, App., in *Oeuvres Complètes* (Paris: Gallimard, 1962), pp. 348ff. (this edition used in subsequent citations).
[34] *Dialogues*, VIII, p. 185.

III

Thus Philo maintains that order and adaptation are sufficiently explained by natural principles and ought not to be taken as evidence of a designer. Teleological explanation is replaced by another kind of explanation, which admits only of inherent natural principles. The observable facts of order and adaptation are, of course, compatible with the theistic theory, but this is not enough. If those facts are also explained by natural forces that are supposed to eliminate all forms unfit for survival and to preserve only those that are fit, then to call observable instances of adaptation "admirable," and to take them as evidence of an anthropomorphic author of the natural world, whose intentions would explain those instances, is going against the most elementary rules of scientific method. Newton's first rule, his version of Ockham's Razor, forbids us to multiply causes beyond what is sufficient to explain the phenomena.[35] If a "principle of elimination of the unfit" is enough to explain the observable adaptation of living beings and the mutual adjustment of their parts, then any recourse to a divine cause is the same as an unnecessary multiplication of causes. The religious hypothesis is plainly anti-Newtonian, and God is an entity that can easily be dispensed with in any explanation of natural order—not only for Philo, but also for a Newtonian philosopher such as Hume who wants to be consistent.

Philo's elimination of the unfit is clearly a natural-selection principle—an example of pre-Darwinian natural selection. Conway Zirkle says that Hume makes use of the theory of natural selection to explain adaptation, in the passage quoted above, concerning the adjustment of the parts of living beings.[36] And Pike gives the same name—natural selection—to Philo's inherent principle of order. Commenting on his own illustration of Philo's theory, in terms of particles (hooked atoms) like the ancient cosmogonies, Pike says that this is not a pure "chance explanation" and that the situation of atoms meeting by chance, but staying together because they have formed "hooked clusters," is a situation that "has all the ingredients to explain the datum in terms of a principle of *natural selection*," which must be considered "a genuine explanatory principle." Thus is explained the fact that in the universe we find that "curious

---

[35] Newton, *Principia*, trans. A. Motte, ed. F. Cajori, 2 vols. (Berkeley: University of California Press, 1962), 2:398.
[36] "Natural Selection before the 'Origin of the Species'," *Proceedings of the American Philosophical Society* 84 (1941):95-96.

adaptation of means to ends," which is also the starting point for the teleological explanation of the theists.[37]

Zirkle and Pike are quite correct in giving to Philo's explanatory principle the name of natural selection. Philo's conjecture is, of course, a pre-Darwinian theory, but this would be no reason to reject the use of that name to describe this theory or its central principle. Commenting on "Natural Selection, Darwinian and Pre-Darwinian," Theodosius Dobzhansky includes Maupertuis and Buffon, Hume's near contemporaries, among those who developed the idea of natural selection before Darwin.[38] Bentley Glass has pointed out the similarity between Maupertuis's view of nature and Part VIII of Hume's *Dialogues*, as well as the rejection, by both philosophers, of any teleological explanation in the biological realm.[39] This rejection they both share with Charles Darwin, whose most fundamental conviction, according to Arthur Lovejoy, was that "teleological explanations are to be excluded from natural history."[40] And according to Francis Haber, Erasmus Darwin (Charles's grandfather) took the part of Philo against Cleanthes in his view of the origin of life, the two main influences on his cosmogony being an empirical discovery (that of fossils) and the philosophy of Hume.[41] In Erasmus Darwin's *Zoonomia*, the *Dialogues* are directly evoked, and Philo's hypothesis is taken quite seriously: "The late Mr. David Hume, in his posthumous works, places the powers of generation much above those of our boasted reason; and . . . he concludes that the world itself might have been generated, rather than created; that is, it might have been gradually produced from very small beginnings, increasing by the activity of its inherent principles, rather than by a sudden evolution of the whole by the Almighty fiat."[42]

Philo's theory, although it proposes a natural selection explanation, is not exactly an evolutionary theory. Nowhere does Hume employ such an evolutionary language as that of his contemporary La Mettrie: "What an infinity of arrangements matter had to go through, before arriving at the

---

[37] Pike, pp. 178-81.
[38] *Mankind Evolving* (New Haven: Yale University Press, 1975), p. 130.
[39] "Maupertuis, Pioneer of Genetics and Evolution," in *Forerunners of Darwin: 1745-1859*, ed. Bentley Glass, Owsei Temkin, and W. L. Straus, Jr. (Baltimore: Johns Hopkins Press, 1959), p. 58 (hereafter cited as *Forerunners*).
[40] "Herder: Progressionism without Transformism," *Forerunners*, p. 221.
[41] "Fossils and the Idea of a Process of Time in Natural History," *Forerunners*, pp. 250-51.
[42] Quoted in Haber, p. 251.

only one that could produce a perfect animal! How many others, before the generations had attained the level of perfection they have today!"[43] Nowhere does Hume make such definitely evolutionary suggestions as those of his friend Diderot, who asks himself whether metals, plants, and animals have always been and will always be what they are today,[44] and who says that some day today's worms will be enormous animals, and maybe the large animals we know are on their way to becoming worms in the distant future.[45] There is no such transformism in Hume, who never suggests the possibility that the existing species originated in other species now extinct. In Part XI of the *Dialogues* he says that "as far as history and tradition reaches, there appears not to be any single species which has yet been extinguished in the universe."[46] In the *Dialogues* we have pre-Darwinian natural selection, but not pre-Darwinian evolution. Philo's hypothesis is that our ordered world, full of adapted beings as it is, was gradually formed from original disorder through selection of the fit — but not that these already adapted beings have suffered any kind of further transformation of their natures.

The nonevolutionary character of Philo's conjecture is no difficulty for Zirkle's or Pike's interpretation. For natural selection is not necessarily an evolutionary concept, although it can have meaning only in an "ecological" framework, that is, in an approach that tries to explain phenomena in terms of environmental factors. Before Darwin, Edward Blyth proposed an antievolutionary theory of natural selection, this principle being there conceived as an agent that keeps species *constant* (which is also one of its functions in post-Darwinian evolutionary theory).[47] Philo's natural selection explanation has its place in an ecological approach to the problems of order and adaptation in nature as an alternative for design explanations, even though this is not proposed from a fully evolutionary standpoint.

Pike sees in Philo's argument against design "one of the most sophisticated and effective critiques of a theological argument one is likely to find in Western philosophical literature." But I do not think he went far enough in his analysis of that argument. He argues, for instance, that

---

[43] La Mettrie, *Abrégé des Systèmes*, in *Textes Choisis* (Paris: Éditions Sociales, 1954), p. 139.
[44] *Pensées sur l' Interprétation de la Nature* (London, 1754), p. 90.
[45] *Entretien entre D'Alembert et Diderot* (Paris: Bossard, 1921), p. 44.
[46] *Dialogues*, XI, p. 207.
[47] Dobzhansky, p. 131.

"Philo makes no comment that would suggest whether he regards his alternative to the hypothesis of design as more or less probable than its competitors"; whereas I believe that Philo's explanation of natural adaptation is the only one that stands on its feet, as a net result of the whole argument, and the only one that is compatible with Hume's own rejection of final causes. (And, as I will show in Section IV, it is also the only one that can give a meaning to Hume's "skeptical solution" to the problem of inductive reasoning.) The relevance of Philo's explanation, in its connection with Darwinian science, is clearly mentioned by Pike, but in a rather noncommittal way: "We know that Charles Darwin . . . abandoned his religious convictions partly because he came to believe that an explanation of adaptation utilizing the principle of natural selection is preferable to theistic explanation. Darwin apparently decided that the hypothesis of design could not be rationally maintained in the face of the challenge from the partisans of Natural Selection. I will leave it to the reader to determine whether Darwin was right about this." As to Philo's conclusion, it would be, according to Pike, that we should reject all hypotheses concerning the origin of adaptation, an attitude he identifies as "skepticism."[48]

Robert Hurlbutt also mentions natural selection in his discussion of Hume's critique of the design argument, but in the following terms: "Hume, insofar as I know, used neither the notion of natural selection nor of evolution in general." Now Philo certainly does not use *Darwinian* natural selection, nor is his approach evolutionary. But he does use pre-Darwinian natural selection, in an ecological approach. This is much more than simply making "some interesting remarks" in his logical comments upon the design argument, or simply suggesting a theoretical possibility as an alternative for design, thus setting "the logical stage for the profound effect that the doctrine of evolution had upon the traditionally accepted design argument." Darwinian theory, of course, does fill in the "evidential gaps" suggested by Hume's arguments.[49] But Philo's theory goes, I think, beyond this. Both Hurlbutt and Pike seem to accept the traditional interpretation of Philo's role as exclusively destructive and negative, the role of a "Pyrrhonian skeptic," although Pike sees a principle of natural selection where Hurlbutt sees none. I

---

[48] Pike, pp. 181–82.
[49] Robert Hurlbutt, *Hume, Newton, and the Design Argument* (Lincoln, Nebr.: University of Nebraska Press, 1965), p. 180.

think that this principle is the core of Philo's positive theory of natural adaptation and also that this theory lies behind Hume's general conception of the world, including human nature.

In Part XI Philo gives a description of present, observable nature that is not only entirely compatible with but almost a necessary outcome of the origin of natural order proposed in Part VIII. The "official" subject is the origin of evil. But all of Philo's examples tend to draw a general picture of the natural world such that it would be contradictory to ascribe it to design. The world is regulated by general laws: were it administered by the particular volitions of a perfect being, the result would be more perfect, for uncertainty would be eliminated. Besides, the springs and principles of nature show an "inaccurate workmanship." Winds and rains, as well as human passions, all have their utility; but sometimes they become pernicious. Nature has not guarded, "with the requisite accuracy, against all disorder and confusion."[50] Also, in animal creation, pains, and not only pleasures, "are employed to excite all creatures to action, and make them vigilant in the great work of self-preservation." It would have been better to employ only pleasure, and its occasional diminution, to attain the same end.[51] All this tends to refute the hypothesis of design, in favor of an explanation in terms of blind, natural forces of selection.

Another of Philo's examples is "the great frugality with which all powers and faculties are distributed to every particular being," including the human species. These powers are only those strictly sufficient to secure survival: "Every animal has the requisite endowments; but these endowments are bestowed with so scrupulous an economy, that any considerable diminution must entirely destroy the creature." Nature is a "rigid master": she formed "an exact calculation of the necessities of her creatures." Were she an "indulgent parent," she would have given to her creatures more than the strict minimum, in order to guarantee them against accidents and misfortunes.[52] In other words, were the world created according to the design and intention of a benevolent god, creatures would have that surplus of powers and faculties they so obviously lack. Of course, if the natural order is viewed as a result of natural selection forces, such as those suggested in Part VIII, everything becomes much more intelligible.

---

[50] Cf. Spinoza's *Ethics*, I, App., pp. 348, 353.
[51] *Dialogues*, XI, pp. 206-7, 209-10, 205-6.
[52] Ibid., pp. 207, 208.

IV

To return to Hume's theory of induction, everything would be much *less* intelligible in it if habit were simply the name of an occult faculty or quality of human nature; that is, if the words "the wisdom of nature," which explain the existence of that quality, were words without a meaning. Any recourse to faculties or occult qualities, in place of legitimate explanations, always receives Hume's most extreme disdain. Philo says to his friend,

> It was usual with the PERIPATETICS, you know, CLEANTHES, when the cause of any phenomenon was demanded, to have recourse to their *faculties* or *occult qualities*, and to say, for instance, that bread nourished by its nutritive faculty, and senna purged by its purgative: But it has been discovered, that this subterfuge was nothing but the disguise of ignorance; and that these philosophers, though less ingenuous, really said the same thing with the sceptics or the vulgar, who fairly confessed, that they knew not the cause of these phenomena.[53]

Hume asserts the same in the *Treatise*, when he ironically presents the invention of the words "faculty" and "occult quality" as a consolation for philosophers, who can have, thanks to them, the illusion of discovery: "They need only say, that any phenomenon, which puzzles them, arises from a faculty or an occult quality, and there is an end of all dispute and enquiry upon the matter."[54] But one reason why habit is not, in Hume's theory, the name of an occult quality of human nature—some mysterious "inductive" that would be the cause of our capacity for induction—is that this quality is in turn the object of an explanation.

Hume's explanation of our inductive powers involves a close relationship between his conception of human nature and his world outlook, in the terms proposed by Flew—conceiving man as a part of nature. To this I would add: conceiving man as a product of natural selection. This is the conception we find in the *Dialogues*. The human species is one among the productions of nature. It distinguishes itself, according to Philo, by its intellectual powers; but nature in her "rigidity" has made it "the most necessitous, and the most deficient in bodily advantages"—an argument also employed by Hume in the *Treatise*, in his explanation of the origin of

---

[53] Ibid., IV, pp. 162-63.
[54] *Treatise*, I, IV, IV, p. 224.

society as a compensation for those biological deficiencies.[55] Human nature thus appears as produced by the same natural selection principles that are responsible for the particular qualities of every other creature. Human nature is a consequence of "the ordinary wisdom of nature"; but this is only the metaphorical "wisdom" of the blind and mechanical forces of selection active in nature.

Hume saw one of the most important principles of human nature, custom or habit, as a production of the wisdom of nature. If this wisdom is sufficiently understood, if the ways of nature become the object of a plausible theory, as they do in the *Dialogues*, the existence of that principle of human nature and the success of its results will be, in turn, the object of at least a partial explanation. Cleanthes' explanation of adaptation by design, by the intention and project of an intelligent creator of natural beings, is incompatible with Hume's philosophy: his anthropomorphic principle is precisely the "particular providence" that Section XI of the *Enquiry* so effectively, if somewhat obscurely, strives to refute. But Philo's conjecture offers something better than this.

Not only can Philo and Hume reach an agreement that is impossible in the case of Cleanthes, but also Philo's conception of the wisdom of nature is capable of explaining why habit, as an instinct of induction, is part of human nature, as well as why induction succeeds as it does. The explanation of the success of induction and that of the existence of habit are one and the same: for the human species to be counted among the survivors from Philo's "destruction principle" it had to be endowed with a generally successful capacity to predict the natural events on which its survival so often depends. Philo's argument concerning the parts of animals and vegetables could be applied here: we have no reason to be "full of admiration" for the success of our inductions, because it is unimaginable that we could subsist without a "harmony" between our inductive capacity and the course of nature. Maybe Hume would have agreed with Quine, that "in induction nothing succeeds like success." And maybe he would have found Quine's explanation of induction, based on innate, naturally selected similarity standards, curiously akin to his own philosophy.[56] I think he would also be deeply interested in the contemporary trend known as evolutionary epistemology, possibly recognizing some of its representatives as his true successors.[57] In any case,

---

[55] *Dialogues*, XI, pp. 207-8; *Treatise*, III, II, II, pp. 484-85.

[56] Quine, "Natural Kinds," in *Ontological Relativity*, pp. 125-29.

[57] See D. T. Campbell, "Evolutionary Epistemology," in *The Philosophy of Karl Popper*, ed. P. A. Schilpp, 2 vols (La Salle, Ill.: Open Court, 1974), 1:413-63.

it remains that in this plausible, "Philo-Hume thesis," the apparent wisdom of nature, which explains habit and induction as well as other instances of adaptation, is a result of the natural process of selection whereby only beings that are adapted to their environment have survived.

It is because habit, "the great guide of human life,"[58] is an inseparable part of his nature that man is adapted to his environment, the natural world. The same adaptation is found in animals, an adaptation made possible by the same kind of principle, which is the root of their "reason."[59] Habit is one of the most powerful instruments of survival. Hume repeatedly asserts that the capacity to predict natural regularities offered by this instinct is "essential to the subsistence of all human creatures," and "necessary to the subsistence of our species." Also, in the case of animals, habit is said to be an instinct "of immense consequences in life."[60] Quine says the same about the capacity of induction in general: "Creatures inveterately wrong in their inductions have a pathetic but praiseworthy tendency to die before reproducing their kind."[61] In Hume's theory habit is not, of course, a "guaranty" of survival; it is not a sufficient condition, but only a necessary condition of survival. Hume's thesis is simply that without this natural mechanism animals and men would not be completely adapted to their general environment, and as a consequence their survival would be impossible. Had he believed that human cognitive capacity was a production of Divine Design, maybe Hume could have shared the Cartesian dream of a "guaranty of truth." But in Hume's case, to understand that capacity as a result of natural selection is also to understand its limitations—and to be prepared to accept them as part of our natural inheritance.

Hume's harmony between knowledge and nature is indeed "pre-established," but not in a Leibnizian sense. It is pre-established only in the sense that the forms and beings that have survived the original "destruction principle"[62] are those that are adapted, and the instinct called habit was a viable instrument of adaptation to the environment we share with animals. Animals and men can survive only if they are able to predict natural regularities; this is why they have in their natures a principle that makes possible those predictions. The same explanation applies to the

---

[58] First *Enquiry*, V, I, p. 44.
[59] Ibid., IX, pp. 105–6; see also *Treatise*, I, III, XVI, pp. 177–78.
[60] First *Enquiry*, V, II, p. 55; I, pp. 44–45; IX, p. 106.
[61] Quine, p. 126.
[62] Pike, p. 179.

other animal instincts, such as incubation (Hume's example in Section IX of the first *Enquiry*).[63]

It would be untenable to interpret Hume's "wisdom of nature" in the light of Cleanthes' theistic and teleological explanations. On the other hand, as was noted by Noxon, no one ever suggested that Hume could be identified with the other protagonist in the *Dialogues*, Demea the "orthodox" theologian. Should our conclusion be that the *Dialogues* have a merely negative, or skeptical import, as Pike, Hurlbutt, and so many others seem to think — a temptation to which Noxon has also succumbed, saying that Hume wrote the *Dialogues* only to reveal the futility of theological argument?[64] What, then, is the *positive* significance of the theories presented by Philo? These theories, especially those in parts VIII and IX, give an intelligible meaning to Hume's wisdom of nature. This wisdom, as a metaphor for the blind but efficient process of selection active in nature, which Hume himself presents as the general cause of such an essential cognitive mechanism as that of habit, is the central concept in the Humean explanation of the origin of this mechanism, and of the agreement between its operation and the regularities that occur in nature. The wisdom of nature is the cause of custom. If this wisdom is an example of pre-Darwinian natural selection, then natural selection is the cause of custom, and the central element of the success of its operation. The words "wisdom of nature" must have some meaning — in a book written by David Hume — and this meaning is not intelligible without recourse to Philo's conjectures, the only ones that allow us to understand Hume's explanation of induction.

If the final lesson in the *Dialogues* was a Pyrrhonian lesson, the "total suspense of judgment" Philo seems to recommend at the end of Part VIII,[65] Hume could never have consistently asserted that habit is an instinct produced by the wisdom of nature. In this theory, as in the *Dialogues*, Hume the "moral philosopher" is of course making room for a different Hume, a philosopher who thinks that inquiries about natural or biological origins are of the utmost importance, as Nicholas Capaldi has

---

[63] First *Enquiry*, IX, p. 108; *Treatise* I, III, XVI, p. 177. See Noam Chomsky, *Problems of Knowledge and Freedom* (New York: Random House, 1971), pp. 4-5; and idem, *Reflections on Language* (New York: Random House, 1975), p. 225. I am in deep agreement with Chomsky's view of Hume, especially in the latter work, pp. 12-13, 72, 166, 224-26.

[64] Noxon, pp. 173-74, and idem, "Hume's Agnosticism," in *Hume*, ed. Chappell, pp. 364, 378-79.

[65] *Dialogues*, VIII, p. 186.

recently shown.⁶⁶ Was not this other kind of philosophy what Hume was announcing when he defined Part II of Section V as an example of a more "abstract" science, of a speculation that, "however accurate, may still retain a degree of doubt and uncertainty?" And is this not precisely an example, perhaps an extreme one, of that profound, more abstract and accurate philosophy that the first section of the first *Enquiry* calls *metaphysics*, a "different species" of philosophy that Hume by no means rejects in favor of the "easy" kind? According to Capaldi, "Hume did not reject metaphysics as the positivists claim they do, but specifically school and divinity-school metaphysics."⁶⁷ If Hume had rejected it, it would have been pointless for him to say, as he did, that in spite of the fact that the profound philosophy had until then been dominated by "superstition," philosophers ought not to leave her "in possession of her retreat"; they ought to perceive "the necessity of carrying the war into the most secret recesses of the enemy," opposing "true metaphysics" to the adulterate kind cultivated by the "religious philosophers." Human understanding is, of course, said to be unfit for "remote and abstruse subjects."⁶⁸ But Hume nowhere gives us any reason to believe that the natural origin of the understanding itself, or the explanation of order and adaptation, must be counted among those inaccessible subjects. The "nature of the Gods," or the precise origin of worlds, yes, these have to be considered too remote to be accessible to philosophy; but not those causes of natural phenomena concerning which philosophy is able to invent plausible explanatory conjectures.

Nowhere does Hume define such requirements of "testability" as would justify the exclusion of Philo's natural selection theory from the realm of true philosophy, or the denial of its significance for the explanation of induction. Hume's position concerning hypotheses of any kind, including the hypotheses in his own science of human nature, is that in all cases we should choose, always in a tentative and provisory way (to be a Humean, says John Passmore, is to accept no theory as final or ultimate),⁶⁹ the conjecture that offers the most plausible explanation—a point I have tried to prove elsewhere.⁷⁰ I believe this to be the true nature

---

⁶⁶ *David Hume: The Newtonian Philosopher* (Boston: Twayne, 1975), pp. 48, 134, 210.
⁶⁷ Ibid., p. 214.
⁶⁸ First *Enquiry*, I, pp. 6, 9, 11, 12.
⁶⁹ *Hume's Intentions* (London: Duckworth, 1968), p. 159.
⁷⁰ "Indução e Hipótese na Filosofia de Hume," forthcoming in *Manuscrito*; and "Hume's Conception of Science," a paper presented to the Sixth Hume Conference, University of Virginia, 1977.

of Hume's skepticism, or at least the most plausible conjecture concerning his philosophy. This conjecture might receive some authority from passages such as the following: "According to all rules of just reasoning, every fact must pass for undisputed, when it is supported by all the arguments which its nature admits of, even though these arguments be not, in themselves, very numerous or forcible." It is Philo who speaks like this, in the final part of the *Dialogues*.[71] I think we should accept this as a truly Humean proposition—unless we want to accept the legend of Hume's "positivism."

Hume may, of course, have considered his explanation of habit by the wisdom of nature as being of a less certain kind than some of his other theories. Does he not announce, for that part of the first *Enquiry*, speculations that "may still retain a degree of doubt and uncertainty?" But he also says that these speculations are *accurate*, thus forbidding us to believe that he thought them to be "airy speculations" or some kind of "sophistry and illusion." In the first *Enquiry* he also says that in our reasonings "there are all imaginable degrees of assurance, from the highest certainty to the lowest species of moral evidence."[72] If this applies to Hume's belief or assurance concerning his own theories, his position cannot be equivalent to a rejection of his own less certain conjectures. It must be an acceptance proportioned to the weight of each argument, taking into account, in every case, "the nature of the subject." It is in this light that we may believe that he himself was convinced of the acceptability of his own explanation of induction.[73]

---

[71] *Dialogues*, XII, p. 216.
[72] First *Enquiry*, X, I, p. 110.
[73] I am grateful to the editors of this volume, and to Bernard Rollin, for helpful comments on earlier versions of this paper.

Hume and His Scottish Critics

David Fate Norton

IT IS WELL KNOWN THAT DAVID HUME'S PHILOSOPHICAL VIEWS were actively criticized by a number of his Scottish contemporaries: first by Henry Home, Lord Kames, and later by Thomas Reid, James Beattie, and others—all generally known as Scottish common-sense philosophers, or as Scottish realists. It is perhaps equally well known that Hume is said to have made no reply to these criticisms. This alleged failure of effort has been puzzling and has seemed to require explanation.[1] However, each of the explanations fails, in my opinion, for the simple reason that Hume did reply to his Scottish critics, as can be seen if one looks more closely at one of the central and essential tenets of eighteenth-century Scottish realism and then reviews Hume's explicitly stated view of this tenet.

I

I know of three answers to the question, Why did Hume not reply to his Scottish critics? The earliest, I suspect, is that given by James Boswell and at least implied by the Scottish philosophers themselves: Hume did not answer because he could not answer, because he himself had been answered and silenced. In Boswell's account, Henry Home (later Lord Kames), to whom Hume had submitted the *Treatise* for criticism, finally, one spring morning when there was nothing more important to do, read the book and made observations on it. When next the two kinsmen met, Home greeted Hume, saying, "Well, David, I'll tell you News. I understand your book quite well." And then, according to Boswell, he "shewed him his Objections, and David, who was not very ready to yield, acknowledged he was right in every one of them."[2] If all of Hume's Scottish critics were as astute as Kames is alleged to have been, then it

---

[1] See, e.g., Ernest Mossner, *The Life of David Hume* (Edinburgh: Thomas Nelson and Sons, 1954), pp. 297-99; Norman Kemp Smith, *The Philosophy of Hume* (London: Macmillan, 1941), pp. 3-8.

[2] James Boswell, *Private Papers . . . from Malahide Castle*, ed. G. Scott and F. A. Pottle, 18 vols. (New York: [privately printed], 1928-34), 15:273-74. For an account of Kames's relations with Hume see Mossner, passim, and Ian S. Ross, *Lord Kames and the Scotland of his Day* (Oxford: Oxford University Press, 1972), pp. 75ff. Kames's copy of Hume's *Treatise of Human Nature* is located in the Hoose Library of Philosophy,

seems likely that Hume did not reply because he had nothing to say — nothing, that is, except that difficult-to-make acknowledgement of error. But in that case we should have to wonder why Hume went on writing and publishing essentially the same errors. For it was after this conversation with Kames that he published (and revised and republished many times) his *Enquiries*, a number of essays, and both the *Natural History of Religion* and the posthumous *Dialogues on Natural Religion*. Thus we can scarcely take Boswell's suggestion as a satisfactory answer to the question posed.

Another answer, nearly as old and of even greater authority, is that of Hume himself. Very early in life, he tells us in his brief autobiography, he vowed never to enter into any dispute, and much that we know of Hume's life confirms that he was in fact of a nondisputatious character. Two points must be noticed, however: Hume's vow, as with so many resolutions, was not always kept, as his recently discovered *Letter from a Gentleman* makes abundantly clear. And even if he did not want to enter into a public dispute, Hume was willing to discuss philosophical issues with his friends and did so regularly in the large body of his correspondence that has been preserved. Hume may on principle have refused to write a reply to Kames, Reid, or Beattie, but that would not preclude his having and expressing disagreement with them. Privately, in fact, Hume did express his contempt for Beattie and is reported to have angrily denounced the *Essay on Truth* as "a horrible large lie in octavo."[3] Despite his anger, he kept his resolve in this case never to answer opponents directly. The most he would do was to compose a brief "Advertisement," which was thereafter to be included in all editions of his *Essays and Treatises* and in which he disowns the *Treatise* as the unsatisfactory product of his immature thought. This advertisement, wrote Hume to Strahan, his printer, "is a compleat Answer to Dr Reid and to that bigotted silly Fellow, Beattie." In some sense Hume may be correct; the advertisement may be the "complete answer" he took it to be. Nevertheless, his account of his silence is scarcely more satisfying than is Boswell's.[4] Neither account touches philosophical issues or adds to our

---

University of Southern California. For a list of Hume's corrections found in this copy see Wallace Nethery, "Hume's Manuscript Corrections in a Copy of *A Treatise of Human Nature*," *Papers of the Bibliographic Society of America* 57 (1963): 446–47.

[3] Mossner, p. 581.

[4] Hume to William Strahan, 26 October 1775, in *The Letters of David Hume*, ed. J. Y. T. Greig, 2 vols. (Oxford: Clarendon Press, 1932), 2: 299–302 (hereafter cited as *Letters*). The

understanding of the philosophical differences between Hume and his Scottish critics, assuming that there were such differences.

A third account of Hume's silence, also with roots in the eighteenth century, is of some philosophical interest, for it asserts that there were, in effect, no such differences. In part, this answer is the converse of Boswell's; that is, Hume was silent not because he was proved wrong but because he was in essential agreement with his Scottish critics, and thus there was nothing he needed to say. The Scottish philosophers, Kant remarked, were forever missing Hume's point, and forever proving what he never doubted. In that case, there would be little point in replying to them, and nothing substantive to reply. Kant adds a philosophical dimension to his account when he suggests that Hume did not reply to the Scottish philosophers because their views, as far as they went, were not unlike his own. "I should think," said Kant, "that Hume might fairly have laid as much claim to common sense as Beattie and, in addition, to a critical reason (such as the latter did not possess). . . ."[5] In the twentieth century this suggestion by Kant has been taken very seriously and has become, in fact, the leading philosophical explanation for Hume's alleged failure to reply. Thus Norman Kemp Smith has argued that Hume had no reason to reply to Reid or even to Beattie, for Hume could see from his perusal of their work that there were no essential differences between him and them. With the common-sense beliefs maintained by Reid and Beattie, says Smith, Hume

> had no quarrel; he was no less ready than Reid or Beattie to agree that a philosophy stands self-condemned if it forbids us to indulge in them. Any attempt to displace them either by other beliefs or by a sheerly sceptical refusal to entertain any beliefs whatsoever is, Hume has insisted, bound to be self-defeating. If the choice be only between them and a philosophy which denies them, it is common sense that must be held to.[6]

Our foremost historian of skepticism, Richard H. Popkin, has accepted this view and enshrined its orthodoxy in the *Encyclopedia of Philosophy*, where we are told that

---

advertisement first appeared in 1777. Mossner says of it that "complete answer, certainly, it is not. As a matter of fact, it is no answer at all, but the petulant retort of an aging man, tired of controversy and sick in body" (p. 582).

[5] *Prolegomena to Any Future Metaphysics*, Carus-Beck trans. (Indianapolis: Bobbs-Merrill, 1950), Intro., p. 7.

[6] Kemp Smith, p. 8.

Hume was unimpressed by Reid's argument. Reid, he believed, had seen the problem but actually had only offered Hume's own solution, that nature does not allow us to live as if all were in doubt, even though we are unable to resolve all doubt theoretically. The Scottish common-sense school of Oswald, Beattie, Stewart, Brown and others kept reiterating its claim to having refuted Hume's skepticism by appealing to natural belief, while at the same time conceding that Hume's fundamental arguments could not be answered. Thomas Brown, an early nineteenth-century disciple of Reid, admitted that Reid and Hume differed more in words than in opinions. . . .[7]

But this account, though philosophically interesting, is not satisfactory either, for the simple reason that it is mistaken. Hume's philosophy is essentially different from that of Kames, Reid, and Beattie; his opinions — not just his words — vary from theirs. If we look again at their philosophy, we will see that this is so, and how it is that Hume has replied to them.

II

The Scottish common-sense philosophers were centrally concerned to refute skepticism. This is not to say that there is nothing in their philosophy that can be appreciated independently of this concern, but it does seem clear that they were to a great extent motivated by a common desire to refute the influential and allegedly dangerous views of the skeptics. In this, as in much else, the common-sense philosophers follow closely the lead of the earlier moral-sense philosophers; Shaftesbury, Hutcheson, and Turnbull had been alarmed by the moral skepticism of Hobbes and Mandeville and had sought to counter that skepticism by establishing the reality of virtue and the veracity of our moral faculties. For example, Turnbull, who quite openly acknowledges his debt to Shaftesbury and Hutcheson, and who was Reid's teacher at Aberdeen, professes a concern over "scepticism about internal experience" or about those "scepticks" who "shock all common sense" by ascribing all our social behavior to "art, custom, and superadded habit" and who otherwise zealously

---

[7] *The Encyclopedia of Philosophy*, ed. Paul Edwards, 8 vols. (New York: Macmillan and Free Press, 1967), s.v. "Skepticism." Brown's comment may contain an important element of truth, but as will be shown, it glosses over important differences between Hume and Reid.

propagate "doctrines tending to discourage virtue" and "throw a most gloomy damp upon all truly noble and generous ambition."[8]

Kames, Reid, Beattie, and the other common-sense philosophers were equally alarmed by the epistemological and metaphysical skepticism they thought implicit in Locke, partially explicit in Berkeley, and fully explicit — and openly celebrated — in Hume. This skepticism was thought equally dangerous, and equally in need of refutation. Thus we find Kames expressing the fear that the "metaphysical paradoxes" of Berkeley and Hume will have an adverse influence, leading others to the same kind of perversions of nature.[9] And Reid goes into considerable detail on this topic. Skeptics are dangerous, he says, because their views are contrary not only to the Christian faith but also to both natural and moral philosophy and the prudence and virtue of the ordinary man. If skepticism reigned, he insists, all "piety, patriotism, friendship, parental affection, and private virtue, would appear as ridiculous as knight-errantry."[10] It is true, of course, that much of what the skeptics claim is patently absurd; but they strike at the very heart of truth and virtue by denigrating human capacity until man not only appears a mere Yahoo but feels debased as well. The skeptical philosopher, he says,

> sees human nature in an odd, unamiable, and mortifying light. He considers himself, and the rest of his species, as born under a necessity of believing ten thousand absurdities and contradictions, and endowed with such a pittance of reason, as is just sufficient to make this happy discovery: and this is all the fruit of his profound speculations. Such notions of human nature tend to slacken every nerve of the soul, to put every noble purpose and sentiment out of countenance, and spread a melancholy gloom over the whole face of things.[11]

Beattie, who was not to be outdone in this regard, remarks that

---

[8] George Turnbull, *Principles of Moral Philosophy*, 2 vols. (London, 1739-40), 1:12-13 (hereafter cited as *Principles*). The views of Turnbull discussed here are treated more fully in my "George Turnbull and the Furniture of the Mind." *Journal of the History of Ideas* 36 (Oct.-Dec., 1975): 701-16.

[9] Henry Home, Lord Kames, *Essays on the Principles of Morality and Natural Religion* (Edinburgh, 1751), pp. 234-35, 239-40, 284. This edition was published anonymously, but the preface to the third edition is signed by Kames.

[10] *The Works of Thomas Reid*, ed. Sir William Hamilton, 7th ed., 2 vols. (Edinburgh, 1872), 1:95 (hereafter cited as *Works*).

[11] Ibid., pp. 102, 107.

every doctrine is dangerous that tends to discredit the evidence of our senses, external or internal, and to subvert the original instinctive principles of human belief. In this respect the most unnatural and incomprehensible absurdities, such as the doctrine of the non-existence of matter, and of perceptions without a percipient, are far from being harmless; as they seem to lead, and actually have led, to universal scepticism; and set an example of a method of reasoning sufficient to overturn all truth, and pervert every human faculty. . . . When a sceptic attacks one principle of common sense, he doth in effect attack all; for if we are made distrustful of the veracity of instinctive conviction in one instance, we must, or at least may, become equally distrustful in every other. A little scepticism introduced into science will soon assimilate the whole to its own nature; the fatal fermentation, once begun, spreads wider and wider every moment, till all the mass be transformed into rottenness and poison.[12]

Skepticism, it was thus agreed, is a lively and dangerous influence and must be countered. Just how is one to do this? The first matter to consider is the nature of philosophy itself and the manner in which it ought to be pursued. It is Reid, I would say, who speaks most systematically on this point. Philosophers must, he insists, follow the directions given them by Bacon, and the example set by Newton. True philosophy is said to be like a good tree, in that it bears good fruit, whereas "false and counterfeit philosophy," which includes skepticism, bears no fruit or evil fruit. In general, such false philosophy is said to be the result of a tendency to substitute hypothesis and speculation for factual inquiry. A more particular form of this misguided speculative tendency, Reid discloses, is analogical reasoning, or a tendency to explain one part of the world in terms drawn from the explanation of other aspects of the world. The view, for example, that we perceive external objects not directly but through the medium of ideas—the view Reid calls the "hypothesis of ideas" and in which he finds the source of Hume's skeptical conclusions—this view he takes to be the result of such a speculative, analogical tendency. Modern philosophers, he says, have "taken over what transpires in the movement of bodies, and too rashly applied it to the thought of the soul." The more judicious philosopher, one who prizes accuracy, refuses altogether to hypothesize concerning that which he does not know, and when faced with

---

[12] James Beattie, *An Essay on the Nature and Immutability of Truth, in Opposition to Sophistry and Scepticism* (London, 1770), pp. 496-98 (hereafter cited as *Essay*). Elsewhere (p. 12), Beattie says that Hume's philosophy "hath done great harm." See also pp. 7-11.

phenomena that are dark and difficult he will admit ignorance rather than allow himself to be drawn into distinctions and subtleties of speculation.[13]

The true philosopher, however, need not be anti-intellectual. Speculation is rejected, but we can nonetheless follow the inductive, observational method recommended by Bacon and proved beyond all doubt by Newton. We must, Reid says, put hypotheses aside and seek knowledge of principles "from observation and experience alone." The true philosopher will not speculate, will not construct theories; the true philosopher will, following Bacon's advice, observe the particulars of experience, and, if he is able, derive from these the general and descriptive laws to which they conform. From the particulars that "are first known in the nature of things, by means of the senses, experience, testimony and other modes" it is "the task and work of the philosopher . . . to ascend legitimately to laws of nature and general axioms. . . ."[14] Or, as Reid puts it on another occasion, to "trace out the laws of nature, is all that true philosophy aims at, and all it can ever reach."[15]

When the Scottish philosophers put aside speculation and devoted themselves in what they were satisfied was a factual, scientific fashion to the subject that most concerned them—human nature or the human mind—they made, so it seemed, surprising progress. Not only did they discover much about man and his mind, but they also found themselves remarkably in accord with one another. What they found, in the most general terms, was that the human mind has a specifiable constitution, or nature, that it has innately a set of faculties, powers, or instincts that enable us to know the world around us. Turnbull, for example, undertook to "consider a little the faculties and dispositions with which we are provided and furnished for making progress in knowledge," and as a result he concludes that man is impressively well adapted for knowledge of the world. Man has elements of prerational knowledge "which it is necessary for us to have in our infant state"; other things that must be known for survival and general well-being—natural connections, perspective, language—are learned very easily. In addition, pain or "uneasy

---

[13] Thomas Reid, *The Philosophical Orations . . . Delivered at the Graduation Ceremonies in King's College, Aberdeen, 1753, 1756, 1759, 1762*, ed. W. R. Humphries (Aberdeen: Aberdeen University Press, 1937), pp. 20-21, 36.
[14] Ibid., pp. 16, 39.
[15] *Works*, 1:157.

sensation" serve to warn and guide man, and he has also a disposition to be satisified with the kind of probable evidence on which he must rely, despite the fact that the connections of nature "lie open to our view." Finally, Turnbull finds that man has a set of "natural furniture for knowledge"—a natural appetite for knowledge, which delights him, a natural curiosity for the new that is properly balanced by a natural tendency to form habits, as well as "several faculties and powers by which we are fitted for knowledge."[16]

Kames, Reid, and Beattie say much the same thing. According to Kames, we are so constituted by nature that we cannot in fact doubt what the senses tell us: their authority cannot be questioned. "There is nothing," he says, "to which all mankind are more necessarily determined, than to put confidence in their senses. We entertain no doubt in their authority, because we are so constituted that it is not in our power to doubt." These authoritative senses, functioning naturally, tell us that there is an external world, and hence we know that there is such a world. We have, he adds, "a thorough conviction of the reality of external objects; it rises to the highest certainty of belief; and we act, in consequence of it, with the greatest security of not being deceived. Nor are we in fact deceived. When we put the matter to a trial, every experiment answers to our perceptions, and confirms us more and more in our belief." And, he argues, we have similar senses, internal and external, that give us unimpeachable knowledge of our own identity or of necessary connection.[17] Reid, for his part, was so impressed with the design of the human mind that he began his *Inquiry into the Human Mind on the Principles of Common Sense* by announcing that "the fabric of the human mind is as curious and wonderful as that of the human body. The faculties of the mind are with no less wisdom adapted to their several ends than are the organs of the other."[18] It is no surprise, then, that Reid is unable to accept Locke's view that the mind merely passively receives the imprint of the world. On the contrary, Reid describes the mind in terms that remind one of a well-equipped factory: he speaks of the "natural furniture," of the "tools and engines," of the "powers" of the mind, for

---

[16] *Principles*, 1:38-52. Turnbull mentions further instincts, or furniture, of this sort from time to time. As he says, the "human mind is a very complicated structure . . . composed not of one, but of many principles. . ." (*Discourse upon the Nature and Origin of Moral and Civil Laws* [London, 1740], p. 293).
[17] Kames, pp. 227, 239, 268-69.
[18] Reid, 1:97.

example, and specifically defines "faculties" as those "powers of the mind which are innate and natural, and which also make a part of the constitution of the mind."[19] When taken together, Reid's "discoveries," like those of Turnbull and Kames, lead to the conclusion that we know and understand the world in which we live, for our faculties and powers give us reliable information about the world.

Taking what has so far been said of later Scottish Realism in its most general sense, it is possible to see how it might be thought that the views of Reid and company are not essentially different from those of Hume. The *Treatise of Human Nature*, after all, is "an attempt to introduce the experimental method into the moral sciences," and in the introduction Hume argues that it is time to dispense with speculation in favor of the methods lately developed and proven in natural philosophy. Furthermore, the propensities and instincts discovered by Hume are not necessarily unlike those made so much of by the common-sense philosophers. Hume, too, finds that the mind is made up of certain natural powers, and these function to make our belief in certain important matters—the existence of the external world or necessary connection, for example—more or less automatic and unavoidable. However, if we look beyond superficial similarities, a difference of great significance can be seen.

A crucial difference between Hume and his Scottish critics has already been suggested. However often Hume may say that we have certain natural propensities to believe this or that, he does not (in his epistemology or metaphysics)[20] go so far as to say that what we must naturally

___

[19] Ibid., pp. 208, 218, 221. Beattie, though never much given to understatement, seems no more extreme on this point than his predecessors. Speaking of the "internal senses" and the "moral feelings" they produce, he says, "I cannot prove . . . that they are conformable to any extrinsic and external relations of things; but I know that my constitution necessarily determines me to believe . . . that I myself exist, and that things are as my external senses represent them. . . . We cannot disbelieve the evidence of internal sense, without offering violence to our nature." He illustrates his position by the following: "'I ought to be grateful for a favor received. Why? Because my conscience tells me so. How do you know that you ought to do that of which your conscience enjoins the performance? I can give no further reason for it; but I *feel* that such is my duty'. Here the investigation must stop; or if carried a little further, it must return to this point:—'I know that I ought to do what my conscience enjoins, because God is the author of my constitution; and I obey His will when I act according to the principles of my constitution. Why do you obey the will of God? Because it is my duty. How know you that? Because my conscience tells me so', &c." (*Essay*, pp. 70-74). Very similar remarks are made about the external senses (see ibid., pp. 60-90).

[20] Hume's moral theory presents a different view, as I have outlined in "Hume's Common Sense Morality," *Canadian Journal of Philosophy* 5 (December, 1975): 523-43.

believe must naturally be *true*. Or, as one could say, Hume does not confuse *psychological* certainty with *epistemological* certainty or in any way suggest that the latter necessarily follows from the former. Yet his Scottish critics seem repeatedly—and characteristically—to conflate these two kinds of certainty, to insist that what we cannot avoid *believing* must be reliable, or *true*. The determinations of our nature, says Turnbull, are by no means deceitful; *all* of them are "right guides, or guides which do not deceive, or lead astray," and hence what we *must* believe can be taken as necessarily true.[21] We cannot doubt our senses, says Kames, but must necessarily repose our confidence in them. If we can trust our natural faculties, says Reid—and he is sure we can—then there can be no question about the objective existence of matter. "We are," says Beattie, "convinced, [for example] by a proof, because our constitution is such, that we must be convinced by it." Whether our belief in such cases is consistent with the real nature of things is, he adds, "a question which no person of a sound mind can have any scruple to answer, with the fullest assurance, in the affirmative."[22]

When we go on to ask why the realists are so doubly certain, we can easily see their crucial differences from Hume. Hume tells us that our natural propensities lead us to specifiable beliefs, but he remains diffident about those beliefs; he does not insist upon their truth or reliability, though he grants that they may be the best we have and more effective than the productions of philosophy. The common-sense philosophers, on the other hand, insist that what we naturally believe is true must be accepted as true. Why this difference? The answer, though little remarked, is not difficult to come by: our natural faculties, say the realists, are God-given, are a part of the overall design of a *providential* nature, and can be trusted implicitly. What we *naturally* believe is in fact *supernaturally* guaranteed.

Even leaving aside general cultural reasons (Reid was a Presbyterian clergyman, for example) it is not difficult to see why the realists' thought took this religious turn. Dangerous skepticism was loose in the land, and any foothold it might gain would in time poison the whole of society. For them, it was not enough to say, as Hume had, that there are natural faculties and consequent natural beliefs, for the nature of the enemy required that one know, not merely believe. But how are we to guarantee

---

[21] *Principles*, 2:164-65.
[22] One of Kames's remarks to this effect is cited above. In addition, see Reid, *Works*, 1:289; and Beattie, *Essay*, p. 59.

that we know that which the skeptic doubts? By looking to the source of those faculties that lead us to believe. Our perception of external objects, Reid tells us, is the result of the operation of one of the "original and simple powers of the mind and part of its constitution," and hence it is "by my nature" that I am led to believe in external objects. So, replies the skeptic, it may very well be that man's natural faculties lead him universally to a belief in an external material world, but it remains to be asked whether this belief is accurate. How does the fact that I am led naturally to this belief help to prove anything at all about the world? The answer returned, in its simplest form, is that our natural faculties are the "gift of heaven." Our natural faculties tell us that those things we distinctly perceive by our senses really do exist and are what we perceive them to be: and the reliability of these faculties themselves is guaranteed by the Creator. The Supreme Being has given us the powers that he saw would be necessary for our survival and progress, and he has implanted in us those faculties that lead us to think and act in a way suited to the rest of his creation. It is because the laws of our nature are established by the will of the Supreme Being that we can trust them implicitly. Because it is God himself who has made us believe in the external world, it is clear that we know as surely as man could ever know that there is an external world, and that it is as we believe it to be.[23] Beattie summarizes the position aptly:

> Certain it is, that our constitution is so framed, that we must believe that to be true, and conformable to universal nature, which is intimated to us by the original suggestions of our own understanding. If these suggestions are fallacious, it is the Deity who makes them so; and therefore we can never rectify, or even detect, the fallacy. But we cannot even suppose them fallacious, without violating our nature; nor, if we acknowledge a God, without the most absurd and audacious impiety; for in this supposition it is implied, that we suppose

---

[23] Reid, *Works*, 1:425, 445. See also, e.g., 1:152, 167, 198, 438, 468. Reid is careful to point out that he does not consider God a guarantor of beliefs in the same way that Descartes does. "The existence of a material world, and of what we perceive by our senses, is not self-evident, according to [modern] philosophy. Des Cartes founded it upon this argument, that God, who hath given us our senses, is no deceiver, and therefore they are not fallacious. I endeavoured to shew that, if it be not admitted as a first principle, that our faculties are not fallacious, nothing else can be admitted; and that it is impossible to prove this by argument, unless God should give new faculties to sit in judgment upon the old" (ibid., p. 464). For a comparison of Reid and Descartes on this point, see L. Marcil-Lacoste, "Dieu, garant de véracité ou Reid critique de Descartes," *Dialogue* 14 (December, 1975): 5–17.

the Deity a deceiver. Nor can we, consistently with such a supposition, acknowledge any distinction between truth and falsehood, or believe that one inch is less than ten thousand miles, or even that we ourselves exist.[24]

Interestingly, Kames's views seem significantly different from those of his fellow realists, for he readily admits not only that our senses deceive us but that they do so systematically. Nevertheless, this exception merely underscores the realists' trust in God's providential design of the mind. Our senses, Kames says, may be deceitful for one of two reasons: either because of some temporary adversity—distance, disturbance of the sense organ, irregularity in the sensory medium—or because there is a deception established by the laws of nature, as in the case of secondary qualities.[25] He still insists, however, that we both should and do retain full confidence in the evidence and authority of the senses. Any random fallacious perceptions give us warning of their fallaciousness (by being confused or obscure, for example), and hence these erroneous perceptions in "noway invalidate" the senses. Nor do the systematic deceptions present any great problem. The senses deceive us; but we not only find that Nature provides us with the means to correct these false appearances, we also discover that the so-called deceptions are by no means the result of any imperfection of design. On the contrary, they are "wisely contrived to give us such notice of things, as may best suit the purposes of life." Experience of secondary qualities, for example, greatly enhances and facilitates our existence; and all such systematic deceptions have a similar effect and are therefore further proof that man's nature is perfectly suited to his environment. We are in some ways regularly deceived, but these deceptions work to our overall good, which in itself proves that our faculties, although not absolutely truthful, are totally reliable and trustworthy.[26] In short, Kames's religious commitment enables him to turn some of the best evidence in favor of skepticism into, so he thinks, very strong evidence against skepticism; his religious perspective leads him to think that apparently unreliable faculties are nothing of the sort, and not the least ground for skepticism.

---

[24] *Essay*, pp. 59–60.
[25] *Essays*, pp. 237–38.
[26] Ibid., pp. 238ff.

III

That there was in fact a real and substantial difference between Hume and his Scottish critics is now, I trust, fully apparent. Hume agrees, of course, that the human mind includes instincts and propensities. He does not, however, accept the view that our natural beliefs are the appropriate standard by which *metaphysical* claims are to be judged, and he will not, he makes more than clear, try to put an end to "true metaphysics," notwithstanding the patent absurdities that have resulted from false metaphysics. A philosopher's reasonings, he admits, may indeed be "abstract and of difficult comprehension," but this "affords no presumption of their falsehood." Hence to insist that all abstract philosophy must be replaced by natural beliefs, to "throw up at once all pretensions" to metaphysical reasoning, would be more rash and dogmatical than the boldest affirmative speculations.[27]

Secondly, Hume is obviously not willing to rest his philosophical hopes or conclusions on the Deity or Providential Design, or on any appeals thereto. In his early correspondence with Hutcheson, for example, Hume is critical of the older moralist on precisely this point:

---

[27] *An Enquiry concerning Human Understanding*, ed. L. A. Selby-Bigge, 2nd ed. (Oxford, 1902), I, pp. 15-16 (hereafter cited as first *Enquiry*). On a number of occasions Hume insists that the useful and valid range of our natural beliefs is limited. In the introduction to the *Treatise*, for example, he notes that the science of man is hindered by the fact that it cannot fabricate experiments, because such "reflection and premeditation would so disturb the operation of my natural principles, as must render it impossible to form any just conclusion" from the phenomena under consideration. This same point is made even more forcefully later in the *Treatise*, where he says that an argument, "which wou'd have been esteem'd convincing in a reasoning concerning history or politics, has little or no influence in these abstruser subjects, even tho' it be perfectly comprehended; and that because there is requir'd a study and an effort of thought, in order to its being comprehended: And this effort of thought disturbs the operation of our sentiments, on which the belief depends" (*A Treatise of Human Nature*, ed. L. A. Selby-Bigge [Oxford, 1888], I, IV, I, p. 185).

That Hume intends to maintain this distinction between what is naturally believed and what is metaphysically correct is made clear in his correspondence with Gilbert Elliot, who asked Hume if he thought that we have instinctive *metaphysical* feelings (natural beliefs) that could be relied upon to settle metaphysical questions. Hume's response was clearly negative: "Your Notion of [the] correcting Subtility of Sentiment is certainly very just with regard to Morals, which depend upon Sentiment; & in Politics & natural Philosophy, whatever Conclusion is contrary to certain Matter of Fact must certainly be wrong. . . . But in Metaphysics or Theology, I cannot see how either of these plain & obvious Standards of Truth can have place. Nothing there can correct bad Reasoning but good Reasoning: and Sophistry must be oppos'd by Syllogism" (18 February 1751, *Letters*, 1:150-51).

> I cannot agree to your Sense of *Natural*. Tis founded on final Causes; which is a Consideration, that appears to me pretty uncertain & unphilosophical. For pray, what is the End of Man? Is he created for Happiness or for Virtue? For this Life or for the next? For himself or for his Maker? Your Definition of *Natural* depends upon solving these Questions, which are endless, & quite wide of my Purpose.[28]

Similarly, in the *Enquiry concerning Human Understanding*, Hume flatly rejects the occasionalist account of causal relations, scornfully terming it *quasi deus ex machina*. The occasionalists explain all creatures and creaturely activities by reference to God's agency, but for Hume the entire account is quite unconvincing, for it rests on claims not only beyond our experience, but apparently beyond the very reach of our faculties — which is to say that sound philosophy, for Hume, is not based on religious appeals.[29]

Thirdly, Hume specifically rejects any attempt to give a divine guarantee to our faculties. Men are, he grants, led by "a blind and powerful instinct of nature" to "repose faith" in their senses, and to believe that external objects correspond to their perceptions. However, this "universal primary opinion of all men is soon destroyed by the slightest philosophy," for this teaches us otherwise. Philosophy makes us doubt that objects are entirely — or even partially — like our perceptions of them, and thus we are "necessitated by reasoning" to depart from our natural beliefs. Then, however, complication following complication, the teachings of philosophy come in for scrutiny, and we find ourselves unable by any chain of reasoning to prove, as our philosophical system teaches, that perceptions are caused by resembling objects. At this point we can "no longer plead the infallible and irresistible instinct of nature," for philosophical reasoning has shown instinct to be deficient; nor can we have recourse to the Supreme Being as the guarantor of our beliefs, for that appeal is both inconsistent and question-begging:

> To have recourse to the veracity of the supreme Being, in order to prove the veracity of our senses, is surely making a very unexpected circuit. If his veracity were at all concerned in this matter, our senses would be entirely infallible; because it is not possible that he can ever

---

[28] Hume to Hutcheson, 17 September 1739, *Letters*, 1:33.
[29] First *Enquiry*, VII, I, p. 69. The phrase *quasi deus ex machina* occurs in the first and second editions of this work; in subsequent editions Hume substituted Θεὸς ἀπὸ μηχανής.

deceive. Not to mention, that, if the external world be once called in question, we shall be at a loss to find arguments, by which we may prove the existence of that Being or any of his attributes.[30]

Finally, and perhaps most obviously, Hume's philosophy contained from the very beginning the basis for the critical treatment of the argument from design that the posthumous *Dialogues concerning Natural Religion* was intended to reinforce. That is to say, the *Treatise*, written in the mid-1730s, pronounces clearly Hume's view that our knowledge of causes and effects is dependent on experience, as is, indeed, our belief in causal connections. It is these conclusions about causal relations that enable Hume so effectively to undercut the argument from design. On the other hand, the religious foundation of the Scottish realists' position itself depends on acceptance of precisely this argument, and indeed, one variation of the argument is obvious in their work. The mind, they find, is well designed; therefore, they add, it must be the work of a wise and benevolent creator. Furthermore, since it is a work of such providential design, the mind and its various faculties must be reliable, which means that our faculties do not deceive us. Or, in briefest form: design of mind discovers Providence, Providence vouches for mind.

One need not rehearse Hume's strictures on the argument from design to realize that he could not accept this microcosmic version of it. There are no better grounds for arguing that there is a wise and benevolent providence who is responsible for and who guarantees the "design" of the microcosm than there are for arguing that there is a wise and benevolent providence responsible for the "designs" of the macrocosm. Given Hume's remarks to Hutcheson and his other comments about our chances of discovering the ultimate springs and principles of the mind, it is difficult to believe that Hume had not realized this, and easy to suppose that he thought his objections to this mode of thought were as clear as they needed to be. In conclusion, then, I suggest that Hume did answer his Scottish critics, and that he did so by striking at the one feature of

---

[30] First *Enquiry*, XII, I, p. 153. Hume does speak of "a kind of pre-established harmony between the course of nature and the succession of our ideas" (ibid., V, II, p. 54), and not, I think, entirely ironically. But nothing he says suggests that he agrees with the theistically oriented teleology of his Scottish contemporaries, or of Leibniz, for that matter. What he may mean is very helpfully discussed in J.-P. Monteiro's contribution to this volume, "Hume, Induction, and Natural Selection."

their philosophy most unlike anything in his own and essential to their criticisms of his skeptical conclusions. That is, he struck at what he believed to be, and ably tried to show to be, the unphilosophical, religious foundation upon which their conclusions rested. The irony is, of course—and this no doubt explains why Hume has been thought to be silent before his Scottish critics—that he provided the central features of his answer before the criticisms were made public.

Hume and the American Revolution:
The Dying Thoughts of a North Briton

J. G. A. Pocock

THIS ESSAY BEGINS BY EXPLORING the second part of its title and then enlarges upon some wider implications of the first. That is to say, I want in the first instance to consider Hume's perception of the crises in English and American politics that marked the last decade and a half of his life and were at a crescendo when he died; and I want to consider what doing so may tell us about his perception of the historical world he was about to leave. I have emphasized the words "English" and "American" in order to hint, by exclusion, at something already implied by the title: that Hume's view of the British world in disruption was very much a view from Edinburgh; and my concern will be with Hume as publicist, historian, and political theorist, prior to Hume as philosopher. From Hume's perception of the American Revolution, I shall turn in conclusion to say something about his role in the ideological history of that great event, one as replete with paradox as even Duncan Forbes[1] could desire.

The thrust of this paper is historicist, in the sense that it emphasizes Hume's consciousness of history and of the moment in history that his individual life had occupied and was about to leave. Neither his historiography nor his philosophy is historicist in any of the principal senses that word was later created to express. But Hume was a historian as well as a philosopher and, in the former role as well as the latter, one of the greatest of his century. Edward Gibbon, who thought Tacitus the greatest historian of all time, once called Hume "le Tacite de l'Ecosse,"[2] and he did not mean the compliment to be an empty one. Discussions of Hume are predominantly discussions of his philosophy in the strict sense, which may perhaps appear as much a contemporary as a historical phenomenon. But it seems desirable to draw attention to Hume as a historian, as a historical figure, and as a figure in history as he himself perceived it. The second related point that needs to be made is that, as well as a philosopher, Hume was a *philosophe*, a leader in the great eighteenth-century secularization of the intelligible universe, when secular

---

[1] *Hume's Philosophical Politics* (Cambridge: Cambridge University Press, 1975).

[2] *The Letters of Edward Gibbon*, ed. J. E. Norton, 3 vols. (London: Cassell, 1956), 2:107.

man, ceasing to be the subject of a miraculous redemption, became instead an actor in civil history. The earthly city with its ideals of political virtue and cultivated taste replaced the heavenly; and the political city, or commonwealth, together with the opportunity for virtue it afforded, had since the Florentine Renaissance been seen as involved in increasingly complex historical contingencies. These—the processes that built up or broke down commonwealths—had come, from about a century before Hume's lifetime, to be discerned more and more in terms of political economy, or of the interactions between polity and economy. Like his bicentennial peers Gibbon, Smith, and Jefferson, Hume was deeply involved in patterns of thought that had descended from Machiavelli, Harrington, and Montesquieu. He employed these as historian, essayist, moralist, and commentator on his own times; and in employing them, he took part in their profound and important modification. We therefore have a Hume who was an analyst of his own moment in history and in the same act a maker and changer of intellectual history. It is this historical Hume I mean to discuss. The aim will be to consider his handling of the historical and political vocabularies of his age, without making very much attempt to connect this with his analyses of natural and moral philosophy.

A superficial reader of Mossner's still unsurpassed *Life* might gain the impression that, following the disastrous imbroglio with Rousseau and his final stint as an amateur diplomat, Hume retired to Edinburgh in the late 1760s and did little more than potter amiably about the New Town until the onset of his fatal illness. Hume's letters, however, leave a different impression; there is much about them in these concluding years that is not particularly cozy. Hume wrote many letters to his London publisher, William Strahan, that are outstandingly but not abnormally cantankerous in their kind,[3] though he was always distressed when he discovered he had distressed his correspondent. Poor Strahan indeed lived to be denounced by David Hume as an English Whig, and by Benjamin Franklin as a British Tory, a fate perhaps unduly severe even for a London Scot with ambitions in eighteenth-century politics. Hume, for instance, affected to hold Strahan blameable for the City of London's 1770

---

[3] For letters in this tone on business as opposed to political matters, see *The Letters of David Hume*, ed. J. Y. T. Greig, 2 vols. (Oxford: Clarendon Press, 1932), 2:212, 218f., 223f., 225, 227f., 236, 277f., 279f., 359-61 (hereafter cited as *Letters*).

petition for a dissolution of Parliament and the removal of evil ministers.[4] This letter comes close to one addressed to Gilbert Elliot, in which Hume declares from Edinburgh: "Our Government has become a Chimera; and is too perfect in point of Liberty, for so vile a Beast as an Englishman, who is a Man, a bad Animal too, corrupted by above a Century of Licentiousness. The Misfortune is, that this Liberty can scarcely be retrench'd without Danger of being entirely lost. . . . I may wish that the Catastrophe shou'd rather fall on our Posterity; but it hastens on with such large Strides, as leaves little Room for this hope."[5] There is little reason to think that the philosopher's feelings were more moderate in the last months of his life.

Hume tells Elliot that he is revising the text of his *History*, with sentiments like the above in mind, and is bent upon purging it of the last taint of Whig prejudices. He is blowing off steam, no doubt, but there is too much of this kind of thing to be neglected. The vigor with which he denounced the excesses of liberty have led some readers to suppose that he swung to a reactionary and even a Tory political attitude in his last years, though Giuseppe Giarrizzo's attempt to relate this to changes in his philosophy has been vigorously opposed by Duncan Forbes.[6] I shall not try to consider whether Hume's philosophy, in the technical and academic sense, can be said to have changed in ways that can be politically explained, but it will further my theme if I offer some consideration of why both the word "reactionary" and the word "Tory" fail to do justice to the ambivalence of contemporary political thought in general, and of Hume's political thought in which it is many times redoubled. Giarrizzo's study was an admirable contribution to the study of this ambivalence, which Forbes has carried into further degrees of elaboration.

Ambivalence indeed is our keynote; we have to understand how it was that the fierce enemy of popular liberty also wrote, "I am an American in my Principles, and wish we would let them alone to govern or misgovern themselves as they think proper," adding in the same letter that "to punish those insolent Rascals in London and Middlesex" was a far worthier object of government in October 1775.[7] The entirely typical

---

[4] Ibid., pp. 217–18.

[5] Ibid., p. 216.

[6] Giuseppe Giarrizzo, *Hume politico e storico* (Turin: Einaudi, 1962); review by Forbes, *The Historical Journal* 6 (1963): 280–95.

[7] *Letters*, 2:303.

letter of 1770, from which I first quoted, can help us reach this goal if we analyze two of its components: first, its Anglophobia, which in Hume's case is never to be forgotten; second, the thinking it reveals on the relations of authority and liberty, which the English constitution had carried to greater heights of fruitful complexity than had been attained elsewhere. If Hume thought the English a bad lot, he considered their constitution a marvellous creation in its way — ambivalence again, which can be explained in terms of national identity.

Hume may be termed a North Briton, a term signifying a Scotsman who in the eighteenth century believed that the Union of 1707 had established either a common nationality or an equality between two nationalities. But the insecurity of referring to Scotland as North Britain is underlined when we consider the unsuccessful experiment (which was also made) of referring to England as South Britain. Eighteenth-century Scotsmen had no reason to believe that they had been admitted to an equal partnership, nor did the English attempt to persuade them that they had. Not the least revealing fact uncovered by Mossner is the circumstance that Hume all his life conversed in broad Scots and yet gave anxious care to the complete Anglicization of his and his friends' written and spoken language. He advised William Robertson on the elimination of Scotticisms from the latter's histories; and he was active in the importation of an Irish elocutionist to Edinburgh to teach a perfectly English manner of speech,[8] the reason being that any trace of a Scots accent was considered a bar to professional or political advancement in London, supposed to be the British capital. Hume's generation, in short, confronted a problem in bilingualism, but once it was considered a matter of the relation between the metropolitan and a provincial version of the same culture, the Scots had no alternative to outplaying the English at their own games. That is what lies behind Hume's pronouncement that this was the historical age and this the historical nation.[9] There was no political nationalism in Scotland because no Scot had any belief in his country's ancient constitution or any desire to hear the auld sang sung again. But from David Hume to John Millar, the Scottish historical intellect developed enormously in the attempt to understand the English constitution better than the English did themselves. It was the abrasive

---

[8] E. C. Mossner, *The Life of David Hume* (Austin, Texas: University of Texas Press, 1954), pp. 370-75.

[9] *Letters*, 2:230.

Hume who wrote a *History of England*, the far smoother Robertson who wrote a *History of Scotland*, and there is no question to which of the two the English paid attention.

A North Briton, then, was a Scotsman committed to a restatement of English culture in such terms that it would become British and that Scotsmen would make their own way in it. The vehement Anglophobia that Hume at times allowed himself to express may be attributed to insuperable doubts about whether this enterprise was succeeding. The place of men of letters in eighteenth-century society was always of profound concern to him: as a young adult he diagnosed his own psychosomatic disorder as entirely occasioned by this problem,[10] and as a classical humanist of his age he saw it as very largely a question of political order. It is desirable to stress how many of the *Essays Moral, Political and Literary* are essays about the politics of culture. This concern persisted to the end of his life, as when in March 1776 he wrote to congratulate Gibbon on the first volume of the *Decline and Fall* and expressed surprise that it was possible for an Englishman to write history in a society given over to faction for more than a generation.[11] Perhaps we should not make too much of Hume's disappointment, some thirty-five years before, over the failure of his *Treatise* to attract public attention; but when in 1741-42 he set about reestablishing his reputation with the *Essays*, he addressed himself to the great paper war among Walpole, Bolingbroke, and the wits of England, kept alive as an issue by Walpole's recent fall from power. He warned both parties against factionalism, in language showing that his sympathies were already leaning toward Walpole's side of the constitutional issue. But the 1742 volume contained a "Character of Sir Robert Walpole," in which we find the judgment that under this minister "trade has flourished, liberty declined, and learning gone to ruin."[12] Hume suppressed this verdict in later years, but in 1742 it clearly if mildly echoed the hatred that Pope, Gay, and Swift felt for Walpole as for one whose corruption of politics was destroying the arts. Hume's judgment of Walpole is ambivalent, and the *Essays* are in large part a reconsideration of the relations of the three elements he had named: trade, liberty and learning. Here is as good a point as any at

---

[10] Mossner, pp. 66-88.

[11] *Letters*, 2:309-11.

[12] For the bibliographical history of this passage see Mossner, pp. 142-44. See also Bertrand A. Goldgar, *Walpole and the Wits: The Relation of Politics to Literature, 1722-1742* (Lincoln, Nebr.: University of Nebraska Press, 1976).

which to begin our journey over that "terrible campaign country" that Forbes has described Hume as presenting to the reader,[13] in the hope of arriving at some understanding of that hatred of English faction so evident in the letters of Hume's last years.

The political ideology—Commonwealth and Country, Old Whig and Tory in restless but stable combination—which had united Bolingbroke and the English poets in the denunciation of Walpole,[14] supposed that the constitution was founded upon a principle of balance between independent parts. To abandon balance or to compromise independence was to corrupt both constitution and virtue, since the political balance offered the only conditions under which the individual could flourish as a moral and civic being. To think of the poet, scholar, or man of letters as engaged in the practice of public virtue was to affirm that he, too, was corrupted and frustrated by the rule of a corrupt minister; hence the great polemics of the so-called Tory satirists. Walpole was supposed to be wielding two great instruments of corruption, of which the first was parliamentary patronage and the second public credit. The latter, which produced rule by a class of investors mutually dependent with the executive, had much to do with the expansion of trade, though the two were logically separable. The Commonwealth ideology, which appealed to urban and suburban Old Whigs, was also a Country ideology with appeal to Tory gentry, because the ideal of independence within balance suggested that ultimately the civic individual should be a proprietor of land—real property conferring independence, mobile property tending to corruption and dependence. But at this point there arose a contradiction within the politics of culture. The financial politics of Walpole might be said to corrupt the arts: but were not the arts themselves a source of corruption? It was widely held that at the end of the agrarian Middle Ages the revival of trade and the revival of learning had tempted the warrior freeholders to pay others to defend and govern them, sacrificing liberty and virtue the better to enjoy commerce and culture. The arts might therefore be the cause of their own decline, and trade, liberty, and learning might be at odds rather than in harmony.

---

[13] *Hume's Philosophical Politics*, p. viii.

[14] Isaac F. Kramnick, *Bolingbroke and his Circle: The Politics of Nostalgia in the Age of Walpole* (Cambridge, Mass.: Harvard University Press, 1968); Maynard Mack, *The Garden and the City: Retirement and Politics in the Later Poetry of Pope, 1731-1743* (Toronto: University of Toronto Press, 1969); Caroline Robbins, *The Eighteenth-Century Commonwealthman* (Cambridge, Mass.: Harvard University Press, 1959); J. G. A. Pocock, *The Machiavellian Moment* (Princeton: Princeton University Press, 1975).

Scots were less liable than Englishmen to the temptations of agrarian primitivism. It was all too easy to remind them that if they wanted to know what a society of warrior peasants was really like, they had only to look north of the Highland Line, and that the journey to Darien or Hudson Bay was well worth making in order to overcome such barbarism. The Scotland of 1707-45, in which Hume grew up and began to write, was one deeply committed to the pursuit of trade and taste, commerce and culture; and Hume's own commitment to the life of a man of letters must hold him back from any kind of primitivist romanticism. This was why he was never happy with his friend Adam Ferguson's *Essay on the History of Civil Society*,[15] and why his emotions discharged themselves on the evident fraud of Macpherson's *Ossian* with something like relief.[16] And yet, his deep fascination with the personality of Rousseau shows that he was anything but insensitive to the underlying dualities of his age; on the contrary, he was like every other philosopher of the time seeking to work them out in his own terms. He could not join with the Bolingbroke circle in the desperation of their assaults on Walpole and preferred to suggest that both parties were overstressing the importance of a single minister's impact on the health of the constitution.[17] To say this was to undermine the ideology of virtue and corruption at its source, and if it was Tory to assail Walpole and Whig to affect a pose of moderation, then Hume's argument at this point is Whig in a somewhat Addisonian sense. But he could not deny that Walpole had been the enemy of letters; for it was an evident fact that English letters at their most polite—and Hume held that the first author of polite English prose had been Swift[18]—considered Walpole their enemy. To grasp the next stage in the analysis of paradox, it is necessary to understand that the ideology of the anti-Walpolean polemic was quite as much republican as it was Tory. Bolingbroke's nominally Tory circle had embraced the ideology of constitutional balance to the point of representing the principles of English government as those of a commonwealth based on a landed interest. To defend monarchy in the teeth of such an assault was to defend the commercial oligarchy of the Hanoverian Whigs, of which the Anglo-Scottish Union was one of the props.

---

[15] *Letters*, 1:304, 308; 2:120, 125-26, 131-32, 133, 136.

[16] Ibid., 2:310-11.

[17] See the latter part of Hume's essay "That politics may be reduced to a Science," in *The Philosophical Works*, ed. T. H. Green and T. H. Grose, 4 vols. (London, 1886), 3:98-108 (hereafter cited as *Works*).

[18] "Of Civil Liberty," *Works*, 3:159 and note.

We may consequently abridge[19] the Hume of the *Essays* as, first, adopting the position—from which he was never altogether to retreat—that a virtuous and frugal republic is in theory the ideal form of human government; and second, as arguing that it is under republican government that commerce and culture initially flourish. Because republics are ruled by public law, property and expression are guaranteed their safety, and prosperity and politeness can develop. The foundations of the republic are therefore not in agrarian austerity, and we find in the *Essays* the beginnings of the suggestion, to be carried further by Montesquieu, that where ancient republics were violent and harsh in their politics or their manners, it was precisely because commerce and politeness were lacking. It is therefore not certain that the growth of civilization necessitates the continuance of the ancient republican form; there are ways in which polite letters and manners can be seen to develop best under monarchy, and it is possible for monarchies to learn from republics the discipline of public law.[20] Hume can be seen at this point sharing with Montesquieu and Gibbon the widespread eighteenth-century conviction that Bourbon France is the most friendly, gracious, and polite to men of letters of all societies the world has seen.[21] In republican and partly republican societies, on the other hand—and England is one of these—liberty and equality beget a necessary ungraciousness,[22] a social style unfriendly to the man of letters (especially, we may surmise, if he is a provincial or a foreigner). It may be observed, first, that virtue is still political and has found no other supportive environment than the free republic; second, that the gap between liberty on the one hand and culture on the other has in no sense been bridged. It seems of importance to the interpretation of Hume to put forward the suggestion that it never was to be.

Hume was no ideologue and could not for obvious reasons carry out the schematic logic of suggesting that Walpole's commercial society was more friendly to politeness than were its adversaries. But he did not join with the poetic counterculture of Pope and Gay (one wonders if he knew how bitterly its members despised Scotsmen who were not as Anglicized

---

[19] "Of Civil Liberty," "Of Eloquence," and "Of the Rise and Progress of the Arts and Sciences" contain most of what is summarized here.

[20] "Of Civil Liberty," *Works*, 3:157–59; "Arts and Sciences," *Works*, 3:176–81, 184–87.

[21] "Of Civil Liberty," *Works*, 3:159.

[22] "Arts and Sciences," *Works* 3:187–88.

as Arbuthnot). By the end of his life he was to decide that both government and opposition in England were altogether incapable of politeness in any form, but one suspects that this was a discovery of the 1760s. Meanwhile, the *Essays* contain two important adjustments to the anti-Walpolean polemic: Hume accepts one and rejects the other of the great devices of corruption attributed to Walpole, but he does both in a manner that implies rejection of the pure country-commonwealth tradition. He accepts the premise that government in a society such as that of eighteenth-century England requires a plentiful supply of parliamentary patronage, in the form of offices the executive may distribute to aspiring politicians.[23] This was to reject the opposition thesis that government must be a pure balance, and to concede that the executive must have a dominant role; and it was to reject the republican ideal that government must rest on a foundation of virtue, and to concede that passion and interest must be recognized and even harnessed. But the ideal is rejected only as incapable of realization, not as an ideal in itself, for Hume is conceding that a measure of corruption is necessary and beneficial in a world of commerce—and we already know that commerce is a prerequisite to the development of culture. Virtue and politeness therefore remain nonidentical, and the latter has taken an important step away from the republican matrix in which it developed.

The second great device of Walpolean government was supposed to be public credit, which brought the executive and its creditors into dependence one upon another. Here Hume is unqualified in his condemnation, though he characteristically remarks that it is republics rather than monarchies that tend to contract increasing public debts: a despot can declare himself bankrupt with impunity, but in commonwealths, where the public authority rests upon the public faith, the machinery of public credit becomes irreversible.[24] Hume never receded from this position. Duncan Forbes, who sometimes yields to the temptation to torpedo a conclusion before we know exactly what it might have been, emphasizes the circumstance that Hume invested in the public funds and wrote a letter about selling part of his holdings at a profit.[25] But the philosopher's awareness of the gulf between ideal and practice is surely enough to make

---

[23] "Of the First Principles of Government," *Works*, 3:112-13; "Of the Independency of Parliament," *Works*, 3:120-21; "Whether the British Government inclines more to Absolute Monarchy, or to a Republic," *Works*, 3:123-26.

[24] "Of Civil Liberty," *Works*, 3:162-63.

[25] *Hume's Philosophical Politics*, pp. 126-27.

it clear that he knew what he meant when he wrote such sentences as "Either the nation must destroy public credit, or public credit will destroy the nation."[26] Hume was on friendly terms with Isaac Pinto, the only political economist of the age to argue that national debt was a thoroughly healthy phenomenon,[27] but he retained a vivid image of a society destroying itself by heaping up the public indebtedness to the point where trade and agriculture were both brought to ruin. We shall see that this was an important feature of contemporary interpretations of the American Revolution.

But if virtue and culture are ultimately unreconciled, and if the commerce the republic begets leads to a condition of public debt that destroys both liberty and prosperity, we are left with an account of the forces at work in history that is based upon a fundamental and acknowledged contradiction. The civilized monarchy Hume has begun to show signs of preferring is no more than a temporary compromise with these warring forces. To summarize the contradiction in a single sentence is to express it in more dramatic and dialectical a form than was congenial to the mind of Hume, yet his essay "Whether the British Government inclines more to Absolute Monarchy, or to a Republic" clearly indicates that it must incline one way or another, and must end sooner or later in an easy death or a violent one.[28] Hume's temperament, his politics, and his philosophy were such that he chose to express the historicist contradiction of his age in terms not of the dramatic juxtaposition of opposites but of the inexhaustibly subtle ambivalence that provides Forbes with his "terrible campaign country." There is no statement that does not contain its own ambiguity or is not offset by another statement somewhere else. But there is Hume's fascination with the personality of Rousseau, inviting the explanation that he recognized him as one who sensed as many and as complex contradictions as he did and who dramatized every one of them in his own personality. Rousseau was the undramatic Hume's antiself; the tragic farce of the encounter arose from the circumstance that Rousseau was by this time so paranoid that he was antiself to everybody he met. If we follow Forbes through the debatable marches and borderlands

---

[26] This sentence was added in 1764 to "Of Public Credit" (Forbes, *Hume's Philosophical Politics*, pp. 174-75; *Works*, 3:370).

[27] See Richard H. Popkin, "Hume and de Pinto," *Texas Studies in Literature* 12 (1970) 417-30; idem, "Hume and Isaac de Pinto: Five Unpublished Letters," in William B. Todd, ed., *Hume and the Enlightenment: Essays Presented to Ernest Campbell Mossner* (Edinburgh: University of Edinburgh Press; Austin, Texas: University of Texas Press, 1974).

[28] *Works*, 3:125-26. The same antithesis occurs in "Of Public Credit," *Works*, 3: 372-74.

of the Hume country, it is to study one who converted his awareness of the ambivalent forces at work in history and personality into polite letters, skeptical philosophy, and magisterial history. We may try to pursue some of these themes down to Hume's farewell to existence in 1776.

A historicist explanation of Hume's philosophy—that is, one that related it to his historical awareness—would be a bold attempt if pursued in detail and would certainly encounter far more phenomena than it could hope to explain. But if we see him as one aware, like so many others in his age, that virtue must give way, for good and ill, to the commerce and refinement it generates in the course of history, we can add that trade and letters were perceived by the age as resting upon imagination and the passions, and as necessitating forms of government unlike those that rested upon republican austerity. A Marxist explanation of Hume would certainly stress that the eighteenth century was caught between an intensely realistic conception of the rationality of real property and an equally intense awareness of the mobile character of the property that was coming to replace it (and eighteenth-century thinking is sufficiently proto-Marxist to convince non-Marxists such as myself that it often invented Marxist explanations of itself). In this sense there is a relationship between the shift from real to mobile property and Hume's thought on the connection between reason and the passions.[29]

In Hume's social history of ideas the independence and self-knowledge of the virtuous citizen helped bring into being a commerce and culture bound to transform his nature because they rested upon passion and imagination rather than on reason. An empire of reason had raised up one of passion to succeed it. But it followed that reason was incomplete without the passion it partly generated, especially once it was decided that the virtuous citizen was less rational, because less polite, than the inhabitant of a commercial society. History would here reinforce any epistemology that might otherwise suggest that reason required the imagination to feed on, but a history that started from the ancient citizen would retain the precommercial republic as a paradigm of virtue. The world of imagination would continue to require the discipline of classical criticism; the civilized monarchy—the form of government best suited to a polished and commercial nation—would continue to require the discipline of republican freedom. But if this suggested that liberty was linked with freedom and government with the passions, it would be equally convincing to equate liberty with the empire of the passions, government

---

[29] Cf. *The Machiavellian Moment*, chaps. 13-14.

with the insecure supremacy of reason. Hume held that authority and liberty could never be reconciled and that neither could replace the other.[30] Following Sir William Temple, he reworded Harrington to suggest that property and force were on the side of the governed and that it was opinion and interest that operated in favor of the government,[31] and he held a very similar view of the unstable relations of reason and passion. His historicism was therefore in a double relationship with his skepticism: he held that reason always gave way to passion and therefore had never really preceded it; but his image of the role that reason might enjoy was classical as well as modern.

Consequently, Hume saw history as the work of passional forces converted into rationality by a variety of agencies of which government was the chief. Commerce and culture were important but could not do its work for it and contained their own tendencies toward unreason. The Commonwealth and Country ideology, to which Hume was attracted, but which he could never accept, professed an eighteenth-century version of Ancient Constitution thinking, according to which the principles of balance were original to a constitutional system that must be prevented from moving away from them. But Hume had no belief in original rationality; he saw governmental forms as disciplining the original dynamism of passion, whose primacy was so complete that only experience and custom, rather than rational prudence or legislative wisdom, could bring government into being and maintain it. He therefore preferred to see government as modern and to look back in time toward periods when it had been less coherent than it was now. This modernism, however, did not originate with Hume or with his philosophy. It had been the position of Walpole's apologists about 1730, and half a century earlier of the High Tory historians around Robert Brady, who had defended the monarchy of the 1680s by arguing that feudal history made it impossible that there should ever have been an Ancient Constitution. Writers of the eighteenth century, both English and American, did not fail to notice the curious way in which Tory arguments in one age had become Court Whig arguments in another, and Hume's cautious sympathy for the Walpolean position laid him open to the charge of being a seventeenth-century Tory at a time when eighteenth-century Tories were using Commonwealth arguments. He was not without sympathy for the latter position, for it contained elements no eighteenth-century mind could altogether reject. But

---

[30] "Of the Origin of Government," *Works*, 3:116.
[31] "Of the First Principles of Government," *Works*, 3:109-12.

it may be true—at least we have his word for it—that as he grew older he eliminated from his *History* more and more elements he had come to regard as Whig, at a time when he considered English Whiggism increasingly factious.[32] The ambiguity of the word "Tory" in England, however, coupled with its relative inapplicability in Scotland, should warn us against considering that Hume became a Tory in any eighteenth-century sense as his interpretation of the past became more Tory in a seventeenth-century one.

The changes in the *History of England*, it has been thought, tend to shift the emphasis from the view that the pre–Civil War constitution was ambiguous and incoherent toward the view that, given its ambiguity and incoherence, the case for the prerogatives of the crown was much stronger than Whig historiography would admit. Hume saw political history as a tug-of-war between authority and liberty, and it appears as if his sympathy for the element of authority increased as his disgust with faction— which is the excess of liberty—grew. The opinion that the English constitution allows too much to liberty, which we find in the letters about 1770, is echoed nearly thirty years before, in such essays as "Whether the British Government inclines more to Absolute Monarchy, or to a Republic." We read here that the balance between authority and liberty is inherently unstable—as philosophically it must be. Property and the passion for liberty are all on one side, and the government has only its command of patronage and the power to corrupt leaders of opposition with which to counter the impulses of the governed. However, patronage is on the way to becoming so dominant a species of property that an absolute monarchy having the whole kingdom in its grip is perhaps the likeliest outcome, and very arguably we should prefer this "easiest death" or "euthanasia" to the violent death of faction and republicanism. This essay, however, could easily be read as a pessimistic version of a Country tract; and when we find the only self-evident truth mentioned in Tom Paine's *Common Sense* to be that the King of Great Britain exercises despotic authority because he has come to monopolize parliamentary patronage,[33] we must recognize that Paine is saying (consciously or otherwise) that Hume's prophecy has been already if violently fulfilled. By the year of his own decease, on the other hand, Hume saw British government as threatened by the violent death of faction if not by that of bankruptcy as well. To understand his attitude to the American crisis we must consider how this came about.

---

[32] "My Own Life," *Works*, 3:5.
[33] *Common Sense*, chap. 1.

Hume saw liberty and authority as in unstable relation, and liberty as always liable to break down in faction, because he saw both philosophy and history as necessarily—he was no pessimist—the partial discipline of passion by reason. He thought in this way because he was a historian of enlightenment as well as of civil society; and the *philosophe* historian had to explain the persistence of religion, just as the historian of taste had to explain the persistence of the barbaric. To account for the persistence of irrational elements in culture and politics he had to resort to the combination of passion with habit. The undisciplined imagination generated absurd ideas in the mind; the personality then folded itself around them; and the undisciplined sociability of mankind led to the rise of combative sects, in taste and philosophy[34] as well as in religion and politics,[35] that pitted one irrationally retained habit of mind against another. Hume knew far too much about the role of imagination in creating liberty, commerce, culture, and knowledge itself to take a merely negative and repressive view of the need for rational and political discipline. The great originality of his history of the Puritan Revolution is his insistence that the fanaticism of the Puritan sects was both an excessive threat to rational freedom and a necessary step toward its establishment. But like other observers of the first three decades of George III's reign, Hume was troubled by the revival of quasi-revolutionary slogans in the confused politics of the time. Here we may link him directly with the tradition of Bolingbroke; for he concurred with that analyst[36] in thinking of parties and factions as irrational survivals of seventeenth-century principles in an age when they had lost their meaning, and also in thinking that the equilibrium of eighteenth-century society was threatened by corruption from above as by faction from below, so much so that it might have to choose the manner of its death. But where Country and Commonwealth thinkers united in considering corruption the enemy, it is part of Hume's skeptical Whiggism (rather than his conservatism) that he saw faction as the principal danger.

It is safe to suppose that part of Hume's detestation of the London radicals, in whom he saw English liberty as mere licentiousness, originated from the savage anti-Scotticism of Wilkes and Churchill and of Number 45 of *The North Briton*. Hume had always been careful not to carry his *History* into the era between 1688 and his own time, or to give

---

[34] "Of the Dignity or Meanness of Human Nature," *Works*, 3:150-51.
[35] "Of Parties in General," *Works*, 3:129-33.
[36] See Bolingbroke's *Dissertation upon Parties, passim*.

his analysis of recent and contemporary British politics. But his acquaintance Tobias Smollett, the London Scot, had not hesitated to publish an avowed continuation of Hume's *History*,[37] in which he analyzed post-Revolution Britain in terms more Tory, Country, and anticommercial than Hume would have permitted himself. This had left him in the role of professional apologist for Lord Bute and the young George III; and faced with the anti-Scottish frenzies of *The North Briton*, Smollett had been destroyed. His health and his position in journalism were wrecked, and he retired to Italy to complete *Humphry Clinker* — a novel of the interactions of Scotland and Wales with a highly corrupt England — and to die soon after. Hume was not especially close to Smollett or to Bute, and his political outlook was very different from theirs, but the incident is very likely to have been connected with Hume's conviction that political faction was making the life of the man of letters impossible in England.

We may think of the leaders of the London radicals at this juncture as a breakaway movement originating among the followers of William Pitt, who throve on patriot and Old Whig rhetoric until he destroyed his position by accepting a peerage. But if Pitt was a lost leader to the Londoners and Americans, in Hume's eyes he was the evil genius — "that wicked Madman, Pitt"[38] — who had done most to precipitate the crisis of the sixties and seventies. If we anatomize the sins and lunacies of Pitt as Hume saw them, we shall find three elements. In the first place, he had encouraged the growth of populist, factious, and fanatical rhetoric and had quite obviously done so for his own ends, in the manner of the classical demagogue. In the second place, however, he had been responsible for a vast and unneeded expansion of empire; for it was clear to Hume that a mixed form of government, in which authority and liberty, reason and passion, stood in a precarious relationship, ought not to expand,[39] because — as Polybius had accurately prophesied in the case of Rome — to do so placed too great a strain on the relationship among its components. When empire was a popular cause it meant the expansion of liberty and faction at the expense of reason and authority. Hume wanted to see the Americans independent not because he thought the London radicals right but because he thought them foolish and wicked, like their evil angel Pitt, and wanted to see them deprived of their rallying cry. There

---

[37] Tobias Smollett, *A History of England* (1757).
[38] Hume to Wm. Strahan, 26 October 1775, *Letters*, 2:301.
[39] Ibid., pp. 300-301, and the following two letters, pp. 303-5.

are some remarkably splenetic passages in the letters, in which Hume hopes to see America in revolt, London depopulated, and authority restored to the nobility and gentry of both kingdoms.[40] Empire breeds faction, and faction fanaticism.

Like Adam Smith in Scotland and Josiah Tucker in England, Hume desired American independence for the strictly Tory reason—Tory, at least, as that word would be used in the generation following his own—that empire had come to be a radical burden on the structure of British politics. The Whig regime had been among other things a balance between the forces of landed oligarchy, making for stability, and London commerce, making for empire. Faced with a choice between the two, the conservative mind would sacrifice empire to stability without hesitation—especially if it meant jettisoning Pitt's and Wilkes's radical Londoners along the way. Hume's increasing Anglophobia—his conviction that English factions were the enemy of Scottish intellect—makes him prophesy the violent, not the easy, death of the constitution; but it would probably be a mistake to impute to him any nationalist desire to see the Union undone, even if he was disposed to think the Anglo-Scottish experiment a failure. We make him a man of theory rather than practice, however, when we stress his inability to visualize any *via media* between the violent and the easy death; he did not foresee the Britain of the younger Pitt, and he did not live to see it.

Hume had striven all his life to adhere to the mainstream of Court Whig thinking, accepting the rise of commerce and politeness in full awareness of the moral and political price they exacted. But the repudiation of empire, even in the form of a repudiation of faction, was bound to aggravate the anti-Whig and anti-commercial strain in his opinions. The third of his reasons for calling the elder Pitt a wicked madman turns out to have been that the great war for empire that Pitt had waged had increased the national debt to near the point at which Hume thought it must prove ruinous to society.[41] Like Adam Smith on the one hand and the English radicals on the other, Hume may have thought the American crisis had originated in an attempt to make the colonies contribute revenue toward the debt's reduction. Smith thought this demand not in itself unreasonable. If the colonists would not contribute to the costs of

---

[40] Hume to Gilbert Elliot, 22 July 1768, *Letters*, 2:184; Hume to Strahan, 25 October 1769, *Letters*, 2:210; Hume to Adam Smith, 8 February 1776, *Letters*, 2:308.

[41] Hume to Strahan, 11 March 1771, *Letters*, 2:237; Hume to Strahan, 22 July 1771, *Letters*, 2:248.

imperial partnership, they should cease to form part of it. Not being an Englishman, Smith did not feel it imperative to maintain Parliament's authority as a necessary shibboleth.[42] But no less vehemently than Smith, Hume contended that empire was not worth having at the price of expanded debt and ought to be repudiated as the main cause of debt's expansion. Hume here seems to step right back into the tradition of Swift and Bolingbroke, denouncing Pitt, as they had once denounced Marlborough, as the author of war, debt, and corruption; but there are important dissimilarities, as well as similarities, between the positions.

Hume's conviction that national debt could reach the point of subverting the whole fabric of society may be thought of as a blockage in his economic thinking, one that not even Smith could quite overcome or Pinto persuade him to abandon. But there is evidence that it had a wider meaning. As far back as Anne's reign, we find signs that the overinvested society was perceived as one in which the value of everything was reducible to the fluctuating loan rate or the daily price of government stock and was no more than an index to the state of confidence in society's ability to meet its obligations in an unforeseeable future. Such a society could be governed only by imaginary hopes and fears; it was the economic equivalent of religious superstition. Many analysts, and Hume among them, had argued that speculation, like other modes of the empire of passion, could be disciplined and rendered creative by subjection to the checks of political control by the owners of land; but if the empire of debt expanded to include the value of land, all might still be lost. We can now see why Hume might feel that the expansion of debt in the war for empire was, if not a cause, at least a linked phenomenon with faction in politics, barbarism in taste, and fanaticism in religion. The demagogues of London—like those of Boston, if he ever thought about them—were part of the state of things they affected to denounce, and it was a marvel that Gibbon should have produced a great work of letters in so insane a society.[43] The seventeenth- and eighteenth-century strands of Toryism in Hume are beginning to come together, in a pattern not altogether unlike that of Swift's rhetoric under Marlborough or Pope's under Walpole.

"Among many other marks of Decline," wrote Hume to Gibbon that March, "the Prevalence of Superstition in England, prognosticates the

---

[42] *The Wealth of Nations*, concluding chapter, "Of Public Debts," and the closing sentence of the entire work.

[43] Hume to Gibbon, 18 March 1776, *Letters*, 2:309-10; Hume to Adam Smith, 1 April 1776, *Letters*, 2:312.

Fall of Philosophy and Decay of Taste."[44] The language suggests that of Pope at the close of the *Dunciad*, but what is more curious is that the fear of a revival of Puritan fanaticism had not yet reached the heights it was to attain. Had Hume lived to hear about the Gordon Riots, he would have had a new item to add to his jeremiad. It is therefore the more piquant to discover, as a warm admirer of Hume's diagnosis of the American crisis, none other than Dr. Richard Price—dissenting minister, radical Whig, torchbearer of the natural rights of Americans, Englishmen, and Frenchmen, Unitarian millennialist, and future object of the passionate denunciations of Edmund Burke. And what Price most applauded in Hume was the support he could give to the reduction of the whole crisis to the single issue of the National Debt.[45] Needless to say, Price believed that the growth of debt had corrupted the executive and set it conspiring to take away the liberties of Americans first and Englishmen after; whereas Hume's point was that debt had encouraged faction and fanaticism—the very characteristics that, though he liked Price personally, he might well have joined Tucker and later Burke in seeing him as embodying—while leaving the euthanasia of executive corruption as the only if preferable alternative. Hume and Price are the two sides of the Tory-radical medal; and the question with which we are left in conclusion is that of how far Hume's irony, ambivalence, and skepticism were contained within tensions that, in the year of his death, he saw as having passed out of control. He died peacefully, without patriotic lamentations for the fate of his country. But that may mean simply that he found it easier to surrender existence than to trouble about solving the riddles of history. Gibbon, whether as an Englishman or as an expatriate, probably knew in his heart that what was happening to Britain was not a Decline and Fall. Hume seems to have built himself the scenario of an almost insuperable contradiction. That his philosophy enabled him to quit the scene with equanimity we know; whether his history permitted him to prognosticate the next act is a question we may leave open.

Hume was a name to conjure with among the American founders, and I will revive the theme of ambivalence by adding a few words about that in coda. The late Douglass Adair showed[46] how he might be considered a

---

[44] Hume to Gibbon, *Letters*, 2:310.

[45] Price, *Two Tracts on Civil Liberty, the War with America, and the Debts and Finances of the Kingdom* (London, 1778); "Additional Observations," pp. xiii-xiv, 25, 38-39, 47, 51-52, 153n.

[46] *Fame and the Founding Fathers* (Williamsburg and New York: Institute for Early American History and Culture, 1974), pp. 93-123.

contributor to Madison's Tenth *Federalist Paper*, in which the conversion of passions and interests into a multiplicity of groups checking and balancing one another becomes a solution to the problem of the republic of great size, at payment of the usual cost of compromising the ideal of classical virtue. In Gerald Stourzh's masterly study of Alexander Hamilton, we see how the reading of Hume helped the greatest of Federalists accept the view that the United States must be a commercial empire, with a strong system of executive patronage and public credit finance.[47] But though Hume could live with a politics of patronage, the combination of empire and public credit sat ill with him. These were the very points at which Madison broke with Hamilton and moved into his alliance with Jefferson. To that purest of Commonwealth and Country thinkers, Hume was the posthumous ideologist of a conspiracy of British exporters, American merchants, and Federalist politicians to fasten the horrors of a Walpolean constitution upon the infant republic. Jefferson was at pains to exclude him from the reading of students at Charlottesville, and he encouraged the publication of a revised version of the *History of England* by an obscure London democrat, with all the facts left in and all the conclusions corrected.[48] After death, as in life, Hume was a master of the ambiguities of eighteenth-century historiography. It may be doubted that he expected to escape them.

---

[47] *Alexander Hamilton and the Idea of Republican Government* (Stanford: Stanford University Press, 1970).
[48] Craig Walton, "Hume and Jefferson on the Uses of History," in D. Livingstone and J. King, eds., *Hume: A Re-evaluation* (DeKalb, Ill.: Northern Ilinois University Press, 1976). It would be appropriate, if iconoclastic, to apply to Jefferson Hume's observation that William Tytler "confesses to me & all the World that I am . . . right in my Facts, and am only wrong in my Inferences" (Hume to [Lord Elibank?], [late 1759 or early 1760], *Letters*, 1:321).

Citation Index

Additional, more general references to the *Dialogues*, first *Enquiry*, and *Treatise* and to other works by Hume are to be found in the General Index under the entry for Hume, David.

Dialogues concerning Natural Religion
"Pamphilus to Hermippus:" 243, 246-47; Pt. I: 234, 248, 253, 271; Pt. II: 215, 242-43, 281-285, 294; Pt. III: 244, 279, 281-82, 284-85; Pt. IV: 222, 234, 302; Pt. V: 243; Pt. VI: 244, 295-96; Pt. VII: 223; Pt. VIII: 296-97, 306; Pt. X: 224; Pt. XI: 155, 224, 302, 304; Pt. XII: 153-54, 242, 244, 250, 272, 281, 308

Enquiry concerning Human Understanding
Sec. I: 6, 53, 178, 236, 239, 307, 321; Sec. IV: 69, 213-14, 216-18, 225, 233; Sec. V: 219, 291, 293-94, 305, 323; Sec. VII: 18, 66, 225, 323; Sec. VIII: 18, 71, 224; Sec. IX: 23, 103, 166, 305-6; Sec. X: 3, 137, 224, 237, 281, 289, 308; Sec. XI: 3, 153, 185, 199, 201, 247, 294; Sec. XII: 108, 147, 177-78, 233-35, 242-43, 247-48, 253, 259, 263, 265, 323

A Treatise of Human Nature
Introduction: 24, 131
Bk. I, Pt. I, Sec. I: 94, 136, 139, 186; Bk. I, Pt. I, Sec. II: 14, 186, 190; Bk. I, Pt. I, Sec. IV: 15, 84, 113, 138-40, 225; Bk. I, Pt. I, Sec. VI: 138; Bk. I, Pt. I, Sec. VII: 113, 138, 225
Bk. I, Pt. II, Sec. II: 183; Bk. I, Pt. II, Sec. III: 106, 145, 225; Bk. I, Pt. II, Sec. IV: 62, 69; Bk. I, Pt. II, Sec. V: 136, 225, 230; Bk. I, Pt. II, Sec. VI: 77, 139
Bk. I, Pt. III, Sec. I: 128; Bk. I, Pt. III, Sec. II: 71, 75, 105, 142; Bk. I, Pt. III, Sec. III: 38, 65, 71, 109, 128, 213; Bk. I, Pt. III, Sec. V: 186; Bk. I, Pt. III, Sec. VI: 126, 128, 130-33, 138, 141, 229; Bk. I, Pt. III, Sec. VII: 118, 130, 134, 136, 225; Bk. I, Pt. III, Sec. VIII: 76, 128, 130, 136-37, 142, 225; Bk. I, Pt. III, Sec. IX: 77, 108, 117, 138, 230, 233, 237; Bk. I, Pt. III, Sec. X: 77, 109, 136, 138; Bk. I, Pt. III, Sec. XII: 106, 109, 111, 130, 220; Bk. I, Pt. III, Sec. XIII: 73, 109, 111, 113, 116, 138, 230-31, 233; Bk. I, Pt. III, Sec. XIV: 71, 83, 94, 104-6, 112-13, 115-16, 119, 123, 128, 130, 140, 142-45, 293; Bk. I, Pt. III, Sec. XV: 40, 109, 111, 117, 126, 136; Bk. I, Pt. III, Sec. XVI: 23, 128, 136, 138, 166, 305-6
Bk. I, Pt. IV, Sec. I: 138, 227, 229-30, 232-34, 253, 257, 321; Bk. I, Pt. IV, Sec. II: 72, 74, 77, 89, 91, 130, 138, 182, 225, 230, 232, 264; Bk. I, Pt. IV, Sec. III: 138, 230; Bk. I, Pt. IV, Sec. IV: 136, 139, 141, 230, 233, 236, 302; Bk. I, Pt. IV, Sec. V: 77, 138, 230; Bk. I, Pt. IV, Sec. VI: 79, 85, 91-93, 96, 99, 138, 233; Bk. I, Pt. IV, Sec. VII: 73, 138, 230-31, 233, 236, 252-53, 259, 262

Bk. II, Pt. I, Sec. I: 114; Bk. II, Pt. I, Sec. III: 136; Bk. II, Pt. I, Sec. IV: 138-39; Bk. II, Pt. I, Sec. V: 139; Bk. II, Pt. I, Sec. VI: 73, 136, 138; Bk. II, Pt. I, Sec. VIII: 136; Bk. II, Pt. I, Sec. IX: 38; Bk. II, Pt. I, Sec. X: 38, 114; Bk. II, Pt. I, Sec. XI: 109, 138; Bk. II, Pt. I, Sec. XII: 23, 136, 138
Bk. II, Pt. II, Sec. II: 39; Bk. II, Pt. II, Sec. IV: 93; Bk. II, Pt. II, Sec. V: 39, 40, 84, 138; Bk. II, Pt. II, Sec. VII: 138; Bk. II, Pt. II, Sec. X: 115, 136; Bk. II, Pt. II, Sec. XII: 23, 114, 136
Bk. II, Pt. III, Sec. I: 115, 128, 170; Bk. II, Pt. III, Sec. II: 38, 116-17; Bk. II, Pt. III, Sec. VII: 191-93; Bk. II, Pt. III, Sec. VIII: 190, 193; Bk. II, Pt. III, Sec. IX: 73, 114, 249; Bk. II, Pt. III, Sec. X: 118
Bk. III, Pt. I, Sec. I: 221
Bk. III, Pt. II, Sec. II: 24, 49-51, 138, 198, 304; Bk. III, Pt. II, Sec. III: 37, 38, 40; Bk. III, Pt. II, Sec. VI: 49, 136; Bk. III, Pt. II, Sec. X: 195-96
Bk. III, Pt. III, Sec. I: 40, 52, 107, 128, 136, 174; Bk. III, Pt. III, Sec. II: 39; Bk. III, Pt. III, Sec. IV: 118, 120; Bk. III, Pt. III, Sec. VI: 118
Appendix: 15, 16, 73, 80, 97, 138

General Index

For references to works by Hume, see the entries under his name or the preceding Citation Index.

Aberdeen, 312
absolute idealists, 187
abstract philosophy, 246; reasoning, 233n
Academic skepticism, 227-29, 231, 233, 236
acatalepsy, 256, 258
accidental regularity, 106
action, 163
active powers of the mind, 101
activity, 15
act of will, 114
Adair, Douglass, 342
Adam, 216
adaptation, 297, 301-2, 305; natural, 302, 307; organic, 223
Addison, Joseph, 161n, 331
aestheticism, 43-44, 46
aesthetics, 61, 107
Aesthetic, Transcendental, 67
affection, natural, 30, 39
affinity, theory of, 64n
agency interpretation of reasoning, 8-9
agnosticism, 278, 284
Allison, Henry E., 64n
Alston, William, 227n
American politics, 325; Revolution, 325, 334
Americans, 339-40, 342
analogical reasoning, 314
Analogies, 73n
analogy, 273-74; argument by, 20
Analogy of Religion, 277
analysis, 12, 21; conceptual, 124; formal, 5-7; historical, 7; philosophical, 266
analytic judgment, 65, 69
Ancient Constitution, 336
Anderson, George, 251
Anglophobia, 327-28, 340
Anglo-Saxon jurisprudence, 20; Scottish Union, 331, 328, 340
animals, 23, 37n
Anne's reign, 341
anti-Cartesian, 59; -dogmatism, 12; -Newtonian, 298; -Wolffians, 66
antinomy, 69n
apartheid, 159
apatheia, 256

Apologie de Raimond Sebond, 16
apologists, Christian, 217
a posteriori propositions, 66, 75, 78
appearance of unity, 96-97
appetites, bodily, 114
a priori arguments, 18; propositions, 20, 65, 67-68, 70, 73, 75-76, 78
Aquinas, 149, 295
Arbuthnot, John, 333
Archimedes, 60
Árdal, Páll S., 4, 107n, 109n
Arendt, Hannah, 23n, 37n
argument, a priori, 18; by analogy, 20; demonstrative, 211, 213-14; from design, 16-17, 239, 242; probable, 211; transcendental, 10, 13
Aristotelian explanation, 102-3; philosophy, 48
Aristotle, 102-4, 115, 120, 166-67, 200, 207, 215, 239
Armstrong, D. M., 85
Arnauld, Antoine, 124, 127n
art, 179
arts and sciences, 161
arts of luxury, 163
Ashley, Lawrence, 79n, 89n
assessments, non-deductive, 206
association, 26, 39-40; laws of, 101; narrative, 190, 194, 199; principles of, 84
associationism, 112-13, 116, 118-19
association of ideas, 15, 72-75, 77, 83-84, 137-38, 140-41, 144
ataraxia, 256, 258
atheism, 45, 147, 151, 155, 249, 250, 273-74, 278
atomistic reductionism, 43-44
Atticus, 243
authority, 10, 31
Ayer, A. J., 108n, 128n, 131-32, 187, 291

Bacon, Francis, 16, 68, 69n, 70, 76, 78, 126, 129n, 134-35, 137, 139, 215, 218, 314-15
Baconian empiricists, 210, 212, 215-16; tradition, 56-57
Bacon's bell, 215-16, 220
balanced judgments, 169

[347]

Balbus, 244n
barbarians, 34
Battersby, Christine, 3, 6, 17
Bayle, Pierre, 56, 148n, 157n, 166n, 176n
Beattie, James, 17, 121n, 132n, 238, 253, 309-14, 316-19
Beauchamp, Tom L., 4, 110n
beauty of virtue, 46, 50
Beck, Lewis White, 5, 17-18
Belaief, Gail, 279
belief, 13, 72, 74, 134; causal, 73; natural, 112, 141, 261-62, 276, 312, 318, 321-22; noncausal influences on, 237
benevolence, 30-31, 38, 49, 156
Bennett, Jonathan, 124n, 143n
Bentham, Jeremy, 183
Bergmann, Gustav, 103n, 113, 115
Berkeley, George, 43-50, 52, 54, 56-62, 295, 313
Berlin enlighteners, 66
Berman, David, 47n, 147n
"Bible-Christianity," 216
bilingualism, 328
Blanshard, Brand, 101-2, 107, 119
Blyth, Edward, 300
bodily appetites, 114
body, 59
Bolingbroke, Henry St. John, 161n, 329-31, 338, 341
Bolton, Martha, 279
Bongie, Laurence, 54n
Boring, E. G., 103n, 112, 117-18
Bosanquet, Bernard, 187
Boston, 341
Boswell, James, 309-10
Brady, Robert, 336
brain, 9, 15
Breazeale, Daniel, 228n
Brentano, Franz, 145
Brett, Nathan, 89n, 227n, 253
Bricke, John, 248, 287
Britain, North, 328-29; South, 328
Brown, Thomas, 61, 312
Buchdahl, Gerd, 123n, 128n, 133n, 136n, 141n
Buffon, Georges, 299
Bundle of Contradiction Theory, 122n
Burke, Edmund, 198, 342
Bute, Lord, 339
Butler, Joseph, 24, 29, 31, 114n, 117-18, 276-77, 295

Campbell, D. T., 304n
Capaldi, Nicholas, 4, 121n, 135n, 138n, 233n, 306-7
Carmichael, Gershom, 48, 57

Carnap, Rudolf, 206, 214-15, 219n
Cartesianism, 44, 53, 59, 126, 181-85, 195-96, 210, 213, 305
Cassirer, Ernst, 27
categories, 19
causality, 37n, 38, 104
causation, 17-18, 40, 64, 72, 74-75, 78-79, 86, 90-91, 93-96, 101, 120, 128
causal beliefs, 73, 118; connections, 66, 78; explanation, 72; inferences, 66, 101-2, 104, 108n, 113-15, 117, 120, 123, 130-31, 132-34, 137, 141-43; judgments, 65-66, 69-70, 98-99, 107-8, 230, 237; laws, 213; necessity, 115; operations of the mind, 233; principles, 65, 67, 69-70; reasoning, 18, 230n, 232, 237; regularity, 106; relations, 19, 322-23
cause, 230; defined, 104-5, 112; final, 31n, 293, 295, 301, 322; first, 13; necessary, 69; secret, 9, 12; ultimate, 12
cause and effect, 91, 213, 323
Celtic Sea, 56
certain knowledge, 228, 233
certainty, 249, 318
Chambers, Robert, 127n
Chambers's *Cyclopaedia*, 127-28n
Charlottesville, 343
chemistry, 76n
Chisholm, R. M., 107n
Chomsky, Noam, 306
Christian apologists, 271; faith, 313; theists, 208, 210
Christianity, 244n, 275, 277
Churchill, Charles, 338
Cicero, 36; influence of, 6; influence of, on the *Dialogues*, 239-44, 248, 250-51; moderation in 166-67, 171, 177n; skepticism in, 176
civilization, 51, 53, 55
civilized monarchies, 28
civil law, 36-37; liberty, 54-55, 57; obligation, 250; society, 338
Clarke, John, Dean of Salisbury, 135n
Clarke, Samuel, 213
Cleanthes, 17, 153, 222, 242-45, 247, 251, 270-76, 279-83, 285-89, 294, 296, 303-4
Code de la Nature, 183
coherence of experience, 73, 75
Coleridge, Samuel, 101-2, 107, 119
collections of perceptions, 79, 85-88
College of Edinburgh, 36
Collingwood, R. G., 125n
Collins, Anthony, 147
Colwell, Gary, 264
common sense, 10, 43-45, 48, 52, 56, 59-60, 62

GENERAL INDEX   349

common-sense philosophers, 238, 254, 317–18; Scottish, 312
commonwealth, 171, 326, 330–31, 333, 336, 343
comparative assessments of conclusiveness, 204–6
complex ideas, 84, 190
Comte, Auguste, 197
conative impulse, 114–15, 117
concept, 187–88; formation, 190; entailing the past, 188
conception of rationality, 5
conceptual analysis, 124; development, 5–6
conclusiveness, comparative assessments of, 204–6
conditionals, subjunctive, 106
Condorcet, Marquis de, 197
conjunction, constant, *see* constant conjunction
connexion, causal, 66, 78; necessary, 37, 71, 73n, 81–83, 96, 98–99, 108n, 116; real, 15, 80–81, 95
Connon, Robert, 4–5, 15, 18
conscience, 31
constant conjunction, 11, 23, 39–40, 74, 82, 95–96, 108–10, 118
Constitution, Ancient, 336
construction theory of history, 187
contiguity, 39–40, 72, 93, 95, 112–13, 231
contradiction, 19, 58, 104
conventions, 40
conversation, 245–46
conversible subjects, 246
Copernican Revolution, Kant's, 63; turn, 18
copy principle, 186
cosmogony, 296–99
Cotta, 244n
credulity, 108
critical deists, 151
critics, Scottish, 10, 13, 17, 21, 309, 311, 317–18, 321, 323–24
Crusius, Christian August, 65, 68, 76n
culture, 329, 334–36, 338
Cummins, Phillip D., 235
custom, 72, 82–84, 87, 133, 142, 264

Danto, Arthur, 188n
Darien, 331
Darwin, Erasmus, 299
Darwin, Charles, 299, 301
Dauer, F. W., 63n
Davie, George,, 6, 121n, 145
Dean of Salisbury, John Clarke, 135n
Decline and Fall, 329
Debate of the Century, 288n

Debt, National, 333–34, 340–42
deducibility, judgment of, 204–5
deduction, 130
Deduction, Metaphysical, 68; Transcendental, 68, 73n
deductive reasoning, 228
definitions of cause, 104–5, 112
deism, 151, 274
deists, 45; critical, 151
Deleule, Didier, 125n
Deleuze, Gilles, 143n
Demé, Nelly G., 135n, 145n
Demea, 223, 244, 270–71, 273, 279, 282, 296, 306
demonstration, 69n, 131, 282
demonstrative arguments, 211, 213–14
Descartes, René, 8, 18, 25, 56, 127n, 129n, 181–83, 185, 253, 319n
design, 277; alternative to, 296; argument from, 16–17, 212, 221, 239, 242, 280–84, 287–89, 294, 323; belief in, 13; hypothesis of, 273–74, 301–2; immanent, 288n; transcendent, 288n
Designer, intelligent, 283
determination of the mind, 94, 137, 143
determinism, 11–12, 18, 224
development, free, 52
de Vleeschauwer, H. J., 68n
Devlin, Lord, 159
Dialectic, 67
Diderot, Denis, 239, 300
directly accessible propositions, 216
Discourse on Method, 181–82
dispositions, 18, 95, 102, 113–16
distinct existences, 80
Divine, the, 55–58
division of labor, 49
Dobzhansky, Theodosius, 299
doctrine of double existence, 74, 182–83
dogma, 54
dogmatic slumber, 69
dogmatism, 11, 17, 227, 229, 242, 258, 271, 275–76, 278
Dostoevski, Feodor, 148
double existence, doctrine of, 74, 182–83
doubt, 177, 265–66, 277
Dublin, 44, 46, 48, 57
Dublin Post-boy, 58
Dubos, Abbé, 161, 162n, 163n, 165n
Ducasse, C. J., 118

easy philosophy, 246
economics, 44, 54, 61
economism, 46
economy, 326
ecological framework, 300–301

education, 108n, 117
Edinburgh, 56, 326-28; College of, 36
Edmonds, C. E., 166n
egoistic utilitarianism, 43-44
Elliot, Sir Gilbert, 243, 247, 289n, 321n, 327
eloquence, 51n, 54
emotions, 23
emotivism, 107-8
empirical generalization, 77; law, 76n; representations, 19; science, 128
empiricism, 43, 46, 57, 59, 94-95, 132n, 186-88, 210, 212, 215-16
Encyclopedia of Philosophy, 311
England, 55, 328, 337, 339-40
English, the, 54, 56
English politics, 325
enlightenment, 52, 338
Enlightenment, Irish, 43-44
Epicureanism, 176, 255
Epicurus, cosmogony of, 296
epistemological certainty, 318; skepticism, 313
epistemology, 7, 21, 251, 335; evolutionary, 304
equality before the law, 49, 54
Erdmann, Benno, 68n, 70n
ethical theories, 107
ethics, 43-44, 51, 55, 237; theological, 47
Euclid, 60
evidence, probable, 316
evil, 302; natural, 223, 256
evolution, 299-300
evolutionary epistemology, 304
Ewing, A. C., 104
exchange economy, 49
experimental method, 317; philosophy, 58, 117; reasoning, 23-26, 35-36, 103-4; sciences, 55; theism, 280
explanation, causal, 72; Humean, 102-3
external goods, 38; objects, 39, 90, 314, 316, 319, 322; world, 58-59, 232, 234-35, 261, 269, 316-17, 319, 323
extrinsic relations, 317n

Fable of the Bees, 30, 48, 57
faculties, 67, 115
faith, Christian, 313
fallacies, 207-8
fallibilism, inductive, 218-19
fancy, 37, 72, 139, 230-36
Farrington, Benjamin, 129n
fear of future state, 150, 152-53
Federalist Papers, Tenth, 343
Federalists, 343
feeling of determination, 137, 143
Ferguson, Adam, 331

Ferrier, James, 48, 61-62
Fielder, John, 227n
final causes, 31n, 36, 293, 295, 301, 322
First Analogy, 73n, 77
Flew, Antony, 3, 142n, 228n, 288n, 291n
Florentine Renaissance, 326
Fogelin, Robert, 3-4
formal analysis, 5-7
formalism, 19
Forbes, Duncan, 25, 121n, 327, 330, 333-34
Forrester, James, 32-33
foundation of morality, 148
Fourier, Charles, 197-99
Fowler, T., 218n, 219
France, 28, 33-34, 54; Bourbon, 332
Franklin, Benjamin, 326
free development, 52
freedom, 11-12, 14, 18, 224
free thinkers, 43, 45-46, 55, 58
Frege, Gottlob, 6n

Galileo, 16
Gardner, Martin, 16n
Garve, Christian, 70n
Gaskin, J. C. A., 3, 6, 17, 20, 272n, 284n, 290n
Gay, John, 329, 332
Gay, Peter, 239n
generality, 109-10
general properties, 231, 234
genocide, 159
geometry, 69n
George III, 338-39
Germany, 66, 159
Giarrizzo, Giuseppe, 327
Gibbon, Edward, 239, 325-26, 329, 332, 341-42
Glanvill, Joseph, 137n
Glasgow, 44, 48, 57, 59
Glass, Bentley, 299
God, 12, 16, 20, 26, 247, 249, 277, 322; attributes of, 92, 241-42, 246; Berkeley's view of, 45-47; existence of, 13, 132n, 241-42, 272, 281; nature of, 281, 284; gives mankind reliable natural faculties, 318-20
Goldgar, Bertrand A., 329
good regard, 156
Gordon Riots, 342
government, republican, 28
gravitation, 84, 137-38
Great Britain, 28; King of, 337
Greece, 28, 53
Greek method in mathematics, 59-60; models, 166
Green, T. H., 121n, 253
Groos, Karl, 68n

Grossmann, Reinhardt, 115n

Haber, Francis, 299
habits, 14, 82, 264, 291-92, 297, 303-5, 316
Hamann, J. G., 63
Hamilton, Alexander, 343
Hamilton, Sir William, 61
Hampshire, Stuart, 6
happiness, 163, 322
harmony, pre-established, 65, 292-93, 305, 323n
Harrington, James, 326, 336
Harrison, Jonathan, 102, 105n
hate, 23
Hausman, Alan, 94, 106n, 108n
Hearn, Thomas K., Jr., 236n
Hebrew-Christian tradition, 197
hedonism, 45
Hegel, 189
Hendel, Charles, W., 127n
Herder, Johann, 63
Herz, Marcus, 68
historical conception of reason, 186; institutions, 194; testimony, 289
historicist, 325, 335
historiography, 343
history, 15, 337; construction theory of, 187
Hobbes, 12, 23, 25, 129n, 134, 137, 139n, 150, 154-55, 213, 249n, 312
Holland, 54
Holland, R. F., 288n
Home, Henry, *see* Kames, Henry Home, Lord
Homer, 164
honor, 29-30
Howell, Wilbur Samuel, 127n
Howells, Edmund, 239n
Hudson Bay, 301
humanity, 164
human nature, 6, 24, 26-30, 34, 36
HUME, DAVID, WORKS: *Abstract of a Treatise of Human Nature*, 24, 124-25, 127-28, 137-40, 143, 145, 176, 211, 229; "Character of Sir Robert Walpole," 329; "A Dialogue," 196, 247; *Dialogues concerning Natural Religion*, 3, 13, 16-17, 20, 92, 152-53, 176, 221-24, 239-52, 253-78, 279-90, 294-96, 299, 300, 304, 306, 308, 310, 322; "Dissertation on the Passions," 38, 180; "Early Memoranda," 35-36, 157, 161; *Enquiry concerning Human Understanding*, 3, 6, 13, 55, 58, 142, 174, 177-79, 185, 198-99, 211, 221, 224, 227-38, 242, 253, 259, 263, 271, 276, 284, 291, 294, 304, 306-8, 310, 322; *Enquiry con-

HUME, DAVID, WORKS (*continued*)
cerning the Principles of Morals, 20, 136, 151, 153, 155-56, 158, 166-67, 174-75, 284, 310; *Essays and Treatises*, Advertisement to, 238, 311-12; Hume's index to, 136, 142; *Essays, Moral and Political*, Preface to original edition, 161; *Essays, Moral, Political, and Literary*, 41, 243, 245, 329, 332-33; "Historical Essay on Chivalry and Modern Honour," 34, 167; *History of England*, 41, 55, 153-54, 249, 327, 329, 337-39, 343; "Idea of a Perfect Commonwealth," 171-72; *Letter from a Gentleman*, 253, 263n, 264, 310; *Letters of David Hume*, 31, 33, 34, 35, 50, 52, 56, 69n, 71n, 166, 174, 243, 247, 289, 310, 321-22, 326-29, 331, 339-41, 343; "My Own Life," 36, 337; *Natural History of Religion*, 55, 56, 154, 170, 240, 248-50, 262, 275, 310; "Of Civil Liberty," 51, 169, 331-32; "Of Commerce," 163; "Of Delicacy of Taste and Passion," 168; "Of Eloquence," 51, 332; "Of Essay Writing," 34, 53, 172, 178, 246; "Of Interest," 168; "Of Money," 168; "Of National Characters," 162, 169, 249; "Of Parties in General," 171, 184, 338; "Of Public Credit," 334; "Of Refinement in the Arts," 51, 163-64; "Of Simplicity and Refinement in Writing," 167; "Of Suicide," 236; "Of Superstition and Enthusiasm," 171, 249; "Of the Balance of Power," 168, 172; "Of the Balance of Trade," 172, 180; "Of the Coalition of Parties," 169, 171-72, 178; "Of the Dignity or Meanness of Human Nature," 23, 27, 166-67, 338; "Of the First Principles of Government," 172, 333, 336; "Of the Immortality of the Soul," 171, 234; "Of the Origin of Government," 162, 165, 336; "Of the Original Contract," 169-72, 175, 178, 186; "Of the Parties of Great Britain," 169; "Of the Populousness of Ancient Nations," 168, 170; "Of the Protestant Succession," 170, 172; "Of the Rise and Progress of the Arts and Sciences," 28, 51, 165-66, 176, 241, 243, 332; "Of the Standard of Taste," 107, 170, 174, 178; "Of the Study of History," 179; "Of Tragedy," 168; "On the Independency of Parliament," 168, 171-72, 178; *Political Discourses*, 35, 41; "That Politics may be reduced to a Science," 171, 331; "The Epicurean," 172, 245; "The Platonist," 245; "The Sceptic," 168, 170, 173-178, 245, 253; "The Stoic," 170, 173,

HUME, DAVID, WORKS (*continued*)
245; *Treatise of Human Nature*, 3, 4, 10, 13-16, 21, 23, 24, 31, 36, 50, 61, 64, 68-70, 79, 81, 83, 88, 121, 135-36, 138, 140-42, 145, 161, 170, 176, 184, 198, 211, 221, 227-38, 249, 253, 258-59, 263, 284, 303, 308, 310, 317, 322, 329; "Whether the British Government inclines more to Absolute Monarchy or to a Republic," 333-34, 337
Hume's Bell, 220; Italian madness, 252
Humeneutics, 253
humility, 23
Humphrey Clinker, 339
Humprey, G., 103n
Hurlburt, Robert, 301, 306
Husserl, Edmund, 47, 132n, 143n, 144n, 145
Hutcheson, Francis, 24, 29-32, 38, 43-44, 46-52, 54-62, 84, 166, 312, 321-23
hypothesis of ideas, 314

idea of nature, 31
idealist, 48, 187-88
identity, as dependent upon various standards, 89-91, 98; in plants and animals, 93; in the appendix, 4; of the self, 14-15, 61, 68n, 79-88, 89-93, 96-99, 232, 234, 253, 261, 264, 316
ideology, political, 330
imagination, 21, 74, 108-9, 118, 335, 338; constituted by general principles, 73, 230-31, 234-37; constituted by trivial principles, 230-36; disguised Kantian understanding, 63; influenced by repetition, 34; regulated by judgment, 21; related to passions, 249, 251; related to society, 34-40
immanent design, 288n
immateriality of the soul, 234n
Immerwahr, John, 4, 13, 16
immortality, 147, 263
impartiality, 168
impression, 77; internal, 94; of reflection, 86, 94, 114-16; of sensation, 139n
impulse, conative, 114-15, 117
incompatibilism, 224
inconsistency, 79
indifference, judgments of, 205, 222
individualism, 49, 52
individuation, 97-98
indoctrination, 271
indolence, 163
induction, 65, 71-72, 74-75, 117, 122, 126, 130, 133-34, 141n, 206, 211-12, 253-54, 269, 291, 303-4, 308, 315

inductive fallibilism, 218-19; infallibilism, 213; reasoning, 228, 230
industry, 163
infallibilism, inductive, 213
inferences, analogical, 283, 286-87; causal, 66, 101-2, 104, 108n, 113-15, 117, 123, 128, 130-31, 132-34, 137, 141-43; inductive, 283; scientific, 125
infinite regress, 232n
informal reasoning, 10; rules, 10-21
influences on belief, 237
initial probabilities, 214
innate ideas, 26
inquiry, scientific, 271
instinct, 23, 26-27, 292, 316n, 317, 321
intelligible objects, 69n; voice, 244
intelligent Designer, 283, 285-86
intersensorial speculation, 48, 52, 57-58, 61
Intuition, 69n
intuitionism, 43-44, 58
Ireland, 56
Irish Enlightenment, 43-44
irrelevance, judgments of, 204, 206
Italian madness, Hume's, 252

Jefferson, Thomas, 326, 343
judgments, 134n, 233; analytic, 65, 69; balanced, 169; causal, 65-66, 69-70, 98-99, 107-8, 230, 237; moral, 107-8; noncausal, 230; suspended, 256, 263; synthetic, 65, 70; of deducibility, 204-5; of indifference, 205, 222; of irrelevance, 204, 216; of nondeducibility, 204-5; of preference, 205, 223; of probability, 228; of reiterated probability, 229, 234; of relevance, 204
Jones, Peter, 4, 7, 21, 127n
Jupiter, 93
jurisprudence, 20
justice, 32, 37, 40, 49-50, 54
justification, objective, 105, 108; rational, 254, 260-61; subjective, 110, 117-18, 120
Justinian, 36

Kames, Henry Home, Lord, 32, 309-10, 312-13, 316-18, 320
Kant, Immanuel, 12, 311; a priori principles, 75; Copernican turn, 18, 63; on progressive history, 197; on the real world, 8; on skepticism, 266; relations to Hume, 5, 11, 17, 64, 76-78, 113, 116; role of activity, 101, 103-4; treatment of causation, 64-70
Kemp Smith interpretation, 254, 257
Keynes, John Maynard, 204-5
Klein, Peter, 279
knowledge, 6, 19, 56, 164, 283, 315; certain, 228, 233; probable, 227; scientific, 289;

knowledge (*continued*)
   synthetic, 67; *see* Theory of, Sociology of, and Objects of
Kramnick, Isaac F., 330
Kuypers, Mary Shaw, 125n

labor theory of property, 37n
labor, division of, 49
La Flèche, 34
Laing, B. M., 227n, 247n
Laird, John, 24n, 166n, 227n
Lambert, J. H., 68
La Mettrie, Julien Offray de, 299-300
language, visible, 46, 57-58
Lauener, Henri, 64n
Law, John, 56
law, civil, 36-37; civilizing influence of, 51-52, 165; equality before the, 49; natural, 26, 36, 185; public, 332; rational form of, 20; Roman, 36
laws, 76n; of learning, 116; of mechanics, 11; of nature, 18, 315
lawyers, natural, 25, 36
laziness of the mind, 232
learned subjects, 246
Leibniz, Gottfried Wilhelm, 18, 47, 124, 295, 323n; metaphysics, 292-93, 305
Lenz, John, 108n
Lewis, C. I., 187
Lewis, Douglas, 234n
liberty, 30; declining in England, 327, 329; related to authority, 328, 334-39; required for politeness and culture, 28, 332; *see* Civil liberty
Light of Reason, 127
literature, 54
Livingston, Donald, 5, 7, 21
Locke, John, 8, 18, 24, 43, 56, 124, 207, 213; acceptance of Aquinas's Fifth Way, 295; association of ideas, 138; implicit skepticism, 121n, 128, 141, 313; political theory, 37-38; reasonableness of Christianity, 275; social philosophy, 25-28; theory of passive mind, 316; view of coexistence, 74; view of God's punishment of sinners, 150; view of religion as the foundation of morality, 148; view of skeptics as atheists and/or irrational, 147, 271; Way of Ideas, 45, 253
logic, 127; Scholastic or schools, 126, 129, 176
logical empiricism, 186-87; necessity, 65, 131; probability, 214
London, 326-28, 338-41
love, 23
Lovejoy, A. O., 76

Lucretius, 225

Mably, Abbé de, 183
Macauley, Catherine, 181, 198
McCloskey, H. J., 225n
McGilvary, E. B., 133n
McGuire, J. E., 125-26
Machiavelli, Niccolò, 326
McIntyre, Jane, 4, 14-15
Mack, Maynard, 330n
Mackie, J. L., 225n
Mackintosh, Sir James, 44, 62
Maclaurin, Colin, 60
MacNabb, D. G. C., 88
MacPherson, C. B., 331
MacRae, Robert, 127n
Madison, James, 343
madness, Hume's Italian, 252
Malebranche, 25, 47, 56, 68, 124, 126, 127n, 166n
Mall, R. A., 63n
man, hunter, 162; social animal, 171, 173, 177
Mandeville, Bernard de, 24-25, 28-30, 32, 39-40, 43, 45-46, 48-52, 56, 312
Mappes, T. A., 110n
Marcuse, Herbert, 196-97, 199
Marlborough, John Churchill, Lord, 341
Marxist interpretation of Hume, 335
Marx, Karl, 37n, 157, 183, 197
material objects, 68n, 101, 268; principles of order, 296; world, 61
mathematical foundations, 59
mathematics, 59-61, 68n, 127
Mathur, G. B., 63n
matter, 314, 318
matters of fact, 129, 131, 135, 139, 281
Maupertuis, Pierre Louis Moreau de, 66, 299
mechanical hypothesis, 15; -physiological explanation, 9; science, 12
mechanics, laws of, 11
mechanism of sympathy, 156
Meiland, Jack, 187
memory, 85, 93, 103
Mendelssohn, Moses, 66n
mental associations, 101; motion, 144; substance, 14
Meslier, Jean, 182-83
metaphysical claims, 234; feelings, 321n; necessity, 71; rebellion, 182; skepticism, 313
Metaphysical Deduction, 68
metaphysics, 32, 67, 184, 235, 260-62, 271, 292-93, 305, 307, 321
methodology of science, 8, 136
Middlesex, 327

Mill, John Stuart, 71, 183n, 218
Millar, John, 328
mind, 9, 12, 15, 47, 80, 97, 101, 116, 127, 232-33
mind-body problem, 8-9, 11-12
minima sensibilia, 60
miracles, 237, 288-89
mistaken doubts, 266
Mitchell, Basil, 159
mitigated skepticism, *see* Skepticism, mitigated or moderate
models of human nature in society, Hume's, 34, 36; Locke's, 26, 28; Mandeville's, 28-29; Shaftesbury's, 26-28
moderate skepticism, *see* Skepticism, mitigated or moderate
moderation, 166-72, 263
modern science, 125
modus, 170-71
monarchy, 28, 165, 331, 334-37
Montaigne, Michel de, 16
Monteiro, João-Paulo, 4-5, 7, 15, 18, 323n
Montesquieu, Charles de Secondat, Baron de, 239, 326, 332
Monthly Review, The, 152
Moore, James, 6, 21
Moore, G. E., 110n, 132-33, 261n, 265-66
moral absolutism, 20; atheism, 155; authority, 10; consequences of religion, 153-54; evidence, 281; philosophy, 26, 31, 35; relativism, 19; science, 317; sense, 30-31, 50; skepticism, 312; subjects, 235-38; theory, 317n; world, 191, 194
morality, 11, 17-18, 32, 148, 155-57
morals, 3, 47
Morelly, 183
Morrisroe, Michael Jr., 241-42, 245n
Mossner, E. C., 3, 36, 235n, 237, 252n, 276, 309n, 310n, 326, 328
motivation, 119
mystics, 35

narrative association, 189, 194, 199; character, 189
Nathan, G. J., 296
Nathanson, Stephen, 82
National Debt, 333-34, 340-42
natural, meaning of, 29; adaptation, 302, 307; affection, 30, 39; assent, 265; belief, 122, 141, 261-62, 274, 276, 289n, 312, 318, 321-22; belief in body, 58-59; evil, 223; instinct, 292; law, 36, 185; lawyers, 25, 36; philosophy, 35-36, 37n; powers, 316-17; relations, 39, 93-97; religion, 35, 239, 273, 280; right, 37, 342; sciences, 36, 235-37; selection, 9, 15, 17, 298-303, 306;

natural (*continued*)
sociability, 26, 29; temper, 27; theologians, 276-77; theology, 271-73, 275
naturalism, 3, 7, 17-18, 25, 63, 122, 253-55, 257
nature, idea of, 31
Nature of the Gods, 239, 243-45
Nazi Germany, 159
necessary connection, 37, 71, 73n, 81-83, 96, 98-99, 108n, 116, 316-17; truths, 214
necessity, 13, 18-19, 65, 69, 71, 76n, 115, 131, 144
Nelson, John O., 235n, 238n
neopositivist interpretation, 9
Newton, Isaac, 8, 11, 15, 26, 84, 125-27, 132n, 135n, 136, 138-39, 141n, 144, 168, 179, 210, 271, 295, 314-15; *see* Rules of reasoning
Newtonian mechanical hypothesis, 15, 135n; method of reasoning, 35, 135n; program, 21; theorists, 24, 35
Newton of history, 197
New York Times, 5
New Philosophy, 126-27
Nethery, Wallace, 310n
Nichomachean Ethics, 167
Niemeyer, Gerhardt, 183n
Nietzsche, Friedrich, 157
noncausal influences on belief, 237; judgments, 230; operations of the mind, 233; reasoning, 232
normative past, 194-96
North Britain, 328-29
North Briton, 338
Norton, David Fate, 4, 13, 21, 27n, 32n
noumenal world, 67
Nova dilucidatio, 65
Noxon, James, 89n, 228n, 245n, 250, 251n, 294, 306

Oakeshott, Michael, 187
objective, meaning of, 95; events, 78; justification, 105, 108; necessity, 65; validity, 19
objectivism, 108
object of knowledge, 129; of sight, 46-48, 57-58; of touch, 46-48, 57-58
obligation, civil, 194-95, 250; "interested," 155-57; transcendental, 149
occasionalist account, 322
Ockham's Razor, 298
Ohmori, Shozo, 139n
oligarchy, 340
ontology, 10
operations of the understanding, 95, 97, 127
optimism, social, 54-55

General Index

original imitation, 240
origin of the world, 263, 270
Ossian, 331
Oswald, James, 78, 312
other minds, 46
Outlines of Pyrrhonism, 255
Oxford view of the *Treatise*, 121-24, 128, 130-31, 140-41

Paine, Tom, 337
Pamphilus, 240-41, 243-47, 279
parliamentary patronage, 330, 333, 337
parties, 184-85
passions, 6, 14, 23, 27, 194, 249, 254, 256, 335-36, 338-39, 341, 343
passive obedience, 31
passivity, 102, 118
Passmore, John, 88, 123, 136n, 307
past-entailing concepts, 188; existences, 191; principle, 186
past, normative, 194-96
patronage, parliamentary, *see* Parliamentary patronage
Pears, David, 6n
Peirce, C. S., 137n
Penelhum, Terence, 3-4, 13, 16, 82, 90, 122n, 123n, 288n
perception, 48, 95, 97, 232, 253, 264; collections of, 79, 85-88
Peripatetics, 166
personal identity, 14-15, 61, 79-84, 86, 89-93, 95-97, 99, 232, 234, 264
personality, 119
persuasion, 168
phenomenalism, 77, 121, 145, 186-87
phenomenal world, 67
Philo, 16-17, 153, 222-23, 240-41, 243-45, 247-48, 250-51, 270-75, 277, 279-87, 288n, 289, 295-96, 299-300, 302, 307
philosophical analysis, 266; probability, 232n; relations, 93-96; skepticism, 270
philosophy, 174-75, 178; Aristotelian, 48; Scottish, 43-44, 48, 54, 58, 61; of pure reason, 129; of science, 57
physical world, 76n
physiology, 15
Pike, Nelson, 272, 281n, 286, 288-301, 306
Pinto, Isaac de, 334, 341
Pitt, William, 339-40
Plantinga, Alvin, 225n
Plato, 8, 68, 244n, 271
Platonism, 176, 244n
pleasure, 163, 179
Pocock, J. G. A., 6, 21
poetry, 36, 51n, 53, 164
politeness, 27-29, 32-34, 39, 332-33, 340

polite society, 28
political authority, 10; economy, 326, 334; history, 337; ideology, 330
politics, 7, 35, 41, 53, 181-85, 195-96, 321n, 325, 341; of culture, 329-30
Polybius, 339
polytheism, 249-50
Pope, Alexander, 329, 332, 341-42
Popkin, Richard H., 123n, 137n, 228n, 255, 257-59, 262, 311-12, 334n
Popper, Sir Karl, 211, 220, 291n
Port Royal, 127
post-Renaissance, 61
power, 38; natural, 316-17
powers of the mind, 101
practical atheism, 147
pragmatism, 63, 186-87
pre-Darwinian natural selection, 298, 306
predictions, 106
pre-established harmony, 65, 292-93, 305, 323n
Presbyterian belt, 56
preference, judgments of, 205, 223
presuming, act of, 132, 141-42
Price, H. H., 63, 73n, 121n, 124n, 132n
Price, J. V., 245n
Price, Richard, 184, 342
pride, 23, 29, 39
principles, associative, 84; causal, 65, 67, 69-70; copy, 186; empiricist, 94-95; of contradiction, 65; of the imagination, 230-37; of sufficient reason, 65; ordering, 296; past-entailing, 186; regulative, 76; ultimate, 323; uniformity-producing, 132
Pritchard, H. A., 3, 108n, 115
probable arguments, 211; evidence, 316; knowledge, 227; reasoning, 122n, 125, 127-28, 135-36, 141, 143
probabilities, 124-25, 211, 232n; initial, 214
probability, judgments of, 228-29, 234; logical, 214; philosophical, 232n; unphilosophical, 109, 111, 232n
propensities, 63, 66, 94-95, 99, 113, 115-16, 191-92, 317-18, 321
property, 32, 36-38, 40, 330, 332, 335-37; general, 231, 234; labor theory of, 37n
propositional attitude, 105; content, 105-6
propositions, compatible, 224; directly accessible, 216
Protestant "Bible-Christianity," 216
Proudhon, Pierre Joseph, 183, 195n
Providence, 323
providential narrative associations, 199; theory of social order, 181, 196-201
Prussian Hume, 63

psychological act of presuming, 132, 137; certainty, 318; considerations, 255; mechanism of sympathy, 156; necessity, 13; theory, 119
psychology, 5, 9-10, 13, 15, 121
psychology of cognition and thought, 119; of probable reasoning, 127
Ptolemaic-Copernican controversy, 16
Pufendorf, Samuel, 57, 166n
pure physics, 76n; reason, 18, 67, 129
Puritan Revolution, 338
Puritans, 35
Pyrrho, 255-57
Pyrrhonian arguments, 258-59, 265; doubts, 266-68, 277; skeptic, 264-65, 276, 301
Pyrrhonism, 177, 227-29, 231, 233-34, 238, 251, 255, 257, 259-60, 263, 270-71, 281

qualitative identity, 85
Quine, W. V. O., 291n, 304-5

Ramism, 127
Ramsay, Michael, 32-33
Ramus, Petrus, 127n
rational faculties, 67; justification, 16, 254, 261, 280; theory of social order, 181-96
rationalism, 43
rational metaphysicians, 235; philosophers, 8, 13, 59
rationality, conception of, 5; in law, 20
real connexion, 15, 80-81, 95
Realism, Scottish, 309, 317, 323
reason, 23, 25; eighteenth-century use, 130; historical conception of, 186-96
Reason, Light of, 127
reasonable man, 283, 286-87
reasoning, 134n; abstract, 233n; agency interpretation of, 8-9; analogical, 314; causal, 18, 230n, 232, 237; experimental, 23-26, 103-4; inductive, 228, 230; Newtonian Rules of, 125-26, 136n, 141, 298; noncausal, 232; probable, 122n, 125, 127-28, 141
reductionism, 57; atomistic, 43-44
reflection, impression of, 86, 114-16
regard, 156
regulative principle, 76
Reid, Thomas, 48, 61, 65, 78, 121n, 132n, 238, 253, 265, 309-19
Reid-Beattie interpretation, 254
reidentification, 86
Reinhold, K. L., 65n
religion, 3, 7, 16, 55-56, 117, 148-49, 153-54, 235, 237, 239, 261, 338, 341; natural, 35, 280

religious hypothesis, 10, 13-14, 16, 298; liberty, 55
Renaissance, 53, 166
representations, empirical, 19
republican government, 28
republics, 165, 332-34, 343
resemblance, 20, 39-40, 93, 96-97, 231-32
de Retz, Cardinal, 111
revelation, 275, 281
review of *Dialogues*, 152
Rheims, 34
rhetoric, 127n
Richards, Thomas J., 104n
right, natural, 37
Robbins, Caroline, 330n
Robertson, J. M., 328-29
Robinson, J. A., 94n, 95n, 104
Robinson, L., 69n
Robison, Wade, 4, 15, 63n, 82, 253n
Rollin, Bernard, 308
Roman empire, 34; law, 36; state, 164
Rome, 28, 53, 166, 339
Ross, Ian S., 309n
Ross, J. M., 244n
Rousseau, Jean-Jacques, 183, 239, 326, 331, 334
Royal Society, 215
Rules of Reasoning, Newton's First, 298; Second, 141; Third, 125-26, 136n, 141; Fourth, 136n
Russell, Bertrand, 128n

savage state of man, 162
science, 3, 5, 8, 24, 36, 51, 53, 73, 76n, 165, 314; empirical, 10, 128; exact, 51; experimental, 55; mechanical, 12; modern, 125; moral, 317; natural, 235-37
scientific inferences, 125; inquiry, 271; knowledge, 289; reasoning, 230
Scotland, 55n, 56, 328, 331, 337, 339-40
Scott, W. R., 46
Scotticisms, 328
Scottish common-sense school, 312; critics, 10, 13, 17, 21, 309, 311, 317-18, 321, 323-24; enlightenment, 32; philosophy, 43-44, 48, 54, 58, 61; Realism, 309, 317, 323
Scottish Kant, 63, 75
Second Analogy, 73n, 75, 77-78
secret causes, 9, 12; springs and principles, 32, 323
self, 7, 11, 14, 80, 82, 88, 93; -identity, 68n, 253, 261, 316; -interest, 156; -liking, 29; -love, 45, 118
sensation, impressions of, 139n
sensible faculties, 67
sentiment, 25

separability thesis, 225
Sextus Empiricus, 227n, 255-58, 269, 278
Shaftesbury, Anthony Ashley Cooper, Lord, 24-30, 32, 38, 43-47, 148, 150, 157n, 159, 166-67, 171, 312
sight, object of, 46-48, 57-58
similarity, 79, 86
Simpson, Robert, 48
Skeptic School, 243, 244n, 255-56
skeptical assessments of conclusiveness, 208-9, 212
skepticism, 3-5, 7, 9-14, 16-17, 19-20, 56, 61, 90, 122-23, 143, 176, 203, 210, 227, 240, 248, 253, 259, 269, 271, 281, 284, 286, 301, 308, 311-14, 318-20, 324, 335-36; Academic, 227-29, 231, 233, 236; epistemological, 7-8, 19, 140, 313; mitigated or moderate, 21, 177, 233, 236-38, 247, 251, 259-63, 271, 274, 276-77; metaphysical, 313; moral, 312; ontological, 7-8, 10; philosophical, 270; religious, 239
Smith, Adam, 48, 61, 149
Smith, Norman Kemp, 4, 16, 26n, 58, 81, 84, 104n, 121-22, 128n, 133-34, 144-45, 157n, 240, 244n, 247n, 250, 253, 254, 257, 270-72, 279-80, 284n, 285-87, 289n, 309n, 311, 326, 340-41
Smollet, Tobias, 339
sociability, natural, 26, 29
social animal, 21; authority, 10; -contract theory, 185-86; democrat, 158; optimism, 54-55; order, rationalist and providential theories of, 181-201; passions, 27; philosophy, 7, 21, 56-57, 59; scientist, 21
society, 7, 23-30, 32-41, 304, 338; polite, 28
sociology, 5, 15; of knowledge, 51, 53-54
sophistry, 321n
soul, 93, 234n, 263
South Africa, 159
space, 67
Spectator, The, 130n
speculative atheism, 147
Spinoza, Benedict, 297, 302
Stack, Michael, 79n, 89n
standard of identity, 89-91, 98
Stephen, Sir Leslie, 151
Sterne, Laurence, 142n
Stewart, John, 61, 69n, 312
stimulus-response, 112-14
Stoicism, 31, 176, 240,, 244n, 255-56, 270
story-laden Humean ideas, 189
Stourzh, Gerald, 343
Stove, D. C., 3-4, 123n, 227, 234n, 253n
Strahan, William, 310, 326-27
Stratonician, 288n
subjective justification, 110, 117-18, 120;

subjective justification (*continued*)
necessity, 19, 65; sequences, 78
subjunctive conditionals, 106
substance, 93; material, 81-82; mental, 14
succession, 94-95
Sulzer, J. G., 65
superstition, 73, 235-38, 281, 341
survival, 292, 297, 304-5
Swedenborg, Emanuel, 66
Swift, Jonathan, 329, 331, 341
syllogism, 321n
sympathy, 11, 21, 23, 39-40, 50, 52-53, 59, 141, 156, 194
synthetic judgment, 65, 70; knowledge, 67

Tacitus, 325
tautologies, 214
Taylor, A. E., 3
teleological explanation, 297, 299; idea of nature, 31, 275; social philosophies, 21; theology, 55, 323n
Temple, Sir William, 336
temporal passions, 194
tensed moral world, 191, 194; theories of meaning, 187, 190-91
Tetens, J. H., 68n
theism, 149, 221, 270, 273-74, 280
theological ethic, 47
theologians, 35, 260-61, 276-77
theology, 61, 235, 237, 276
theory of affinity, 64n; of double existence, 74; of knowledge, 61, 63; of vision, 47
time, 67, 181, 191
tolerance, 12
Tonelli, Giorgio, 66n
Tory, 326-27, 330-31, 336, 339-40
touch, object of, 46-48, 57-58
Transcendental Aesthetic, 67
transcendental arguments, 10, 13, 266; design, 288n; framework, 19
Transcendental Deduction, 68, 73n
transcendentalism, 18, 63
transcendent obligations, 149; world, 140
transduction, 125
Tristram Shandy, 142n
truth, 5
Tucker, Josiah, 340, 342
Turgot, A. R. J., 197
Turnbull, George, 312-13, 315-18
Tyler, A. F., 31n
Tytler, William, 343n

ultimate causes, 12; *see* Secret springs and principles
uniformity of nature, 130
uniformity principle, 132

Union of 1707, 328, 331, 340
United States, 343
unity of the self, 80; see Self and Collection of perceptions
unphilosophical probability, 109, 111, 232n
utilitarianism, 43-44
utility, 20, 37, 194

Vaihinger, Hans, 64n, 68n
Vanterpool, P. V., 73n
vegetable library, 285
Velleius, 244n
verbal matters, 91-92
Vinnius, Arnoldus, 36
Virgil, 36
virtue, 30, 33, 46, 50, 312, 331; the end of man, 322; necessary for government, 333; corrupted by culture and commerce, 330, 334-35
visible language, 46, 57-58
vision, theory of, 47
Voet, Johannes, 36
voice, intelligible in the clouds, 244, 285-88
Voltaire, François Marie Arouet, 66, 239, 295
de Vries, Gérard, 57

Wadia, Pheroze S., 3, 16-17

Walpole, Robert, 329-33, 336, 341
Walsh, W. H., 63
Walton, Craig, 343n
Warren, Rev. Thomas, 288n
Way of Ideas, 253
Weinbrot, Howard J., 240n
Whig, 326, 330, 339, 342; influences of, purged from *History*, 327, 337
Wilbanks, Jan, 227n, 228n
Wilkes, John, 338, 340
will, act of, 114
Willey, Basil, 101-2, 119
Wilson, Fred, 4-5
wisdom of nature, produces habit or custom, 292, 304; is nonteleological or theistic, 294-95, 306
Wittgenstein, Ludwig, 134, 266
Wolff, Christiann 65, 67
Wolff, Robert Paul, 65, 68n, 84, 101, 103, 108n, 112n, 113, 115-17
Wollaston, William, 147

Yahoo, 313

Zabeeh, Farhang, 228n
Zirkle, Conway, 298-300
Zoonomia, 299

DAVIDSON COLLEGE